JOHN CONSTANTINE, HELLBLAZER: THE GIFT

JOHN CONSTANTINE, HELLBLAZER:
THE GIFT

Mike Carey
Writer

"Down in the Ground
Where the Dead Men Go"
"R.S.V.P."
Leonardo Manco
Artist

"The Gift"
Frazer Irving
Artist

Lee Loughridge
Colorist

Jared K. Fletcher
Letterer

Tim Bradstreet
Original Series Covers

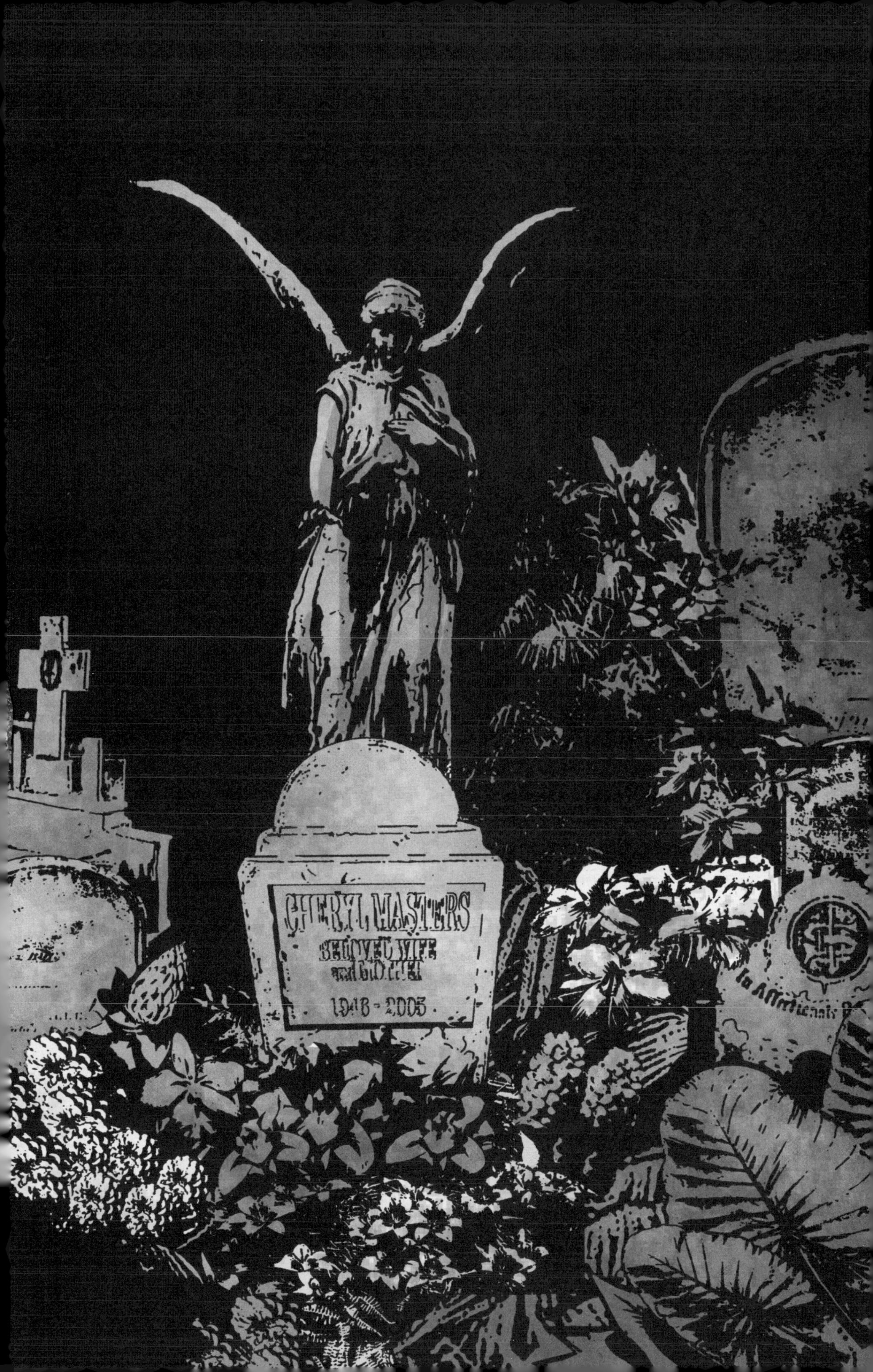
CHERYL MASTERS
BELOVED WIFE
1948 - 2005

Cover illustration by Tim Bradstreet.
Logo design by Nessim Higson

JOHN CONSTANTINE, HELLBLAZER: THE GIFT

Published by DC Comics. Cover and compilation copyright © 2007 DC Comics. All Rights Reserved.

Originally published in single magazine form as HELLBLAZER 207-215. Copyright © 2005, 2006 DC Comics. All Rights Reserved. VERTIGO and all characters, their distinctive likenesses and related elements featured in this publication are trademarks of DC Comics. The stories, characters and incidents featured in this publication are entirely fictional. DC Comics does not read or accept unsolicited submissions of ideas, stories or artwork.

DC Comics, 1700 Broadway, New York, NY 10019
A Warner Bros. Entertainment Company
Printed in Canada. Second Printing.

ISBN: 978-1-4012-1453-1

Down in the Ground Where the Dead Men Go CHAPTER ONE

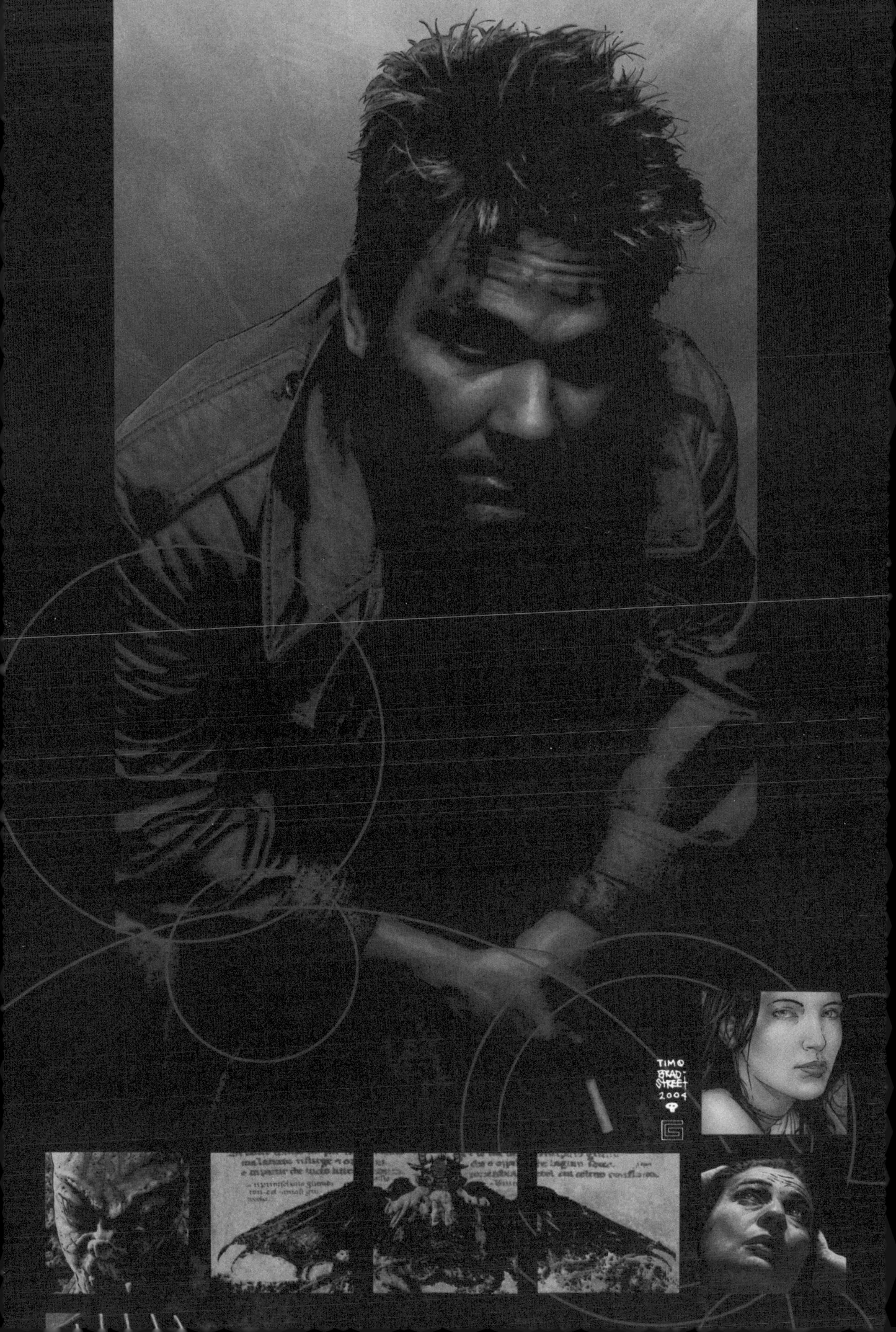
TIM© BRAD-STREET 2004

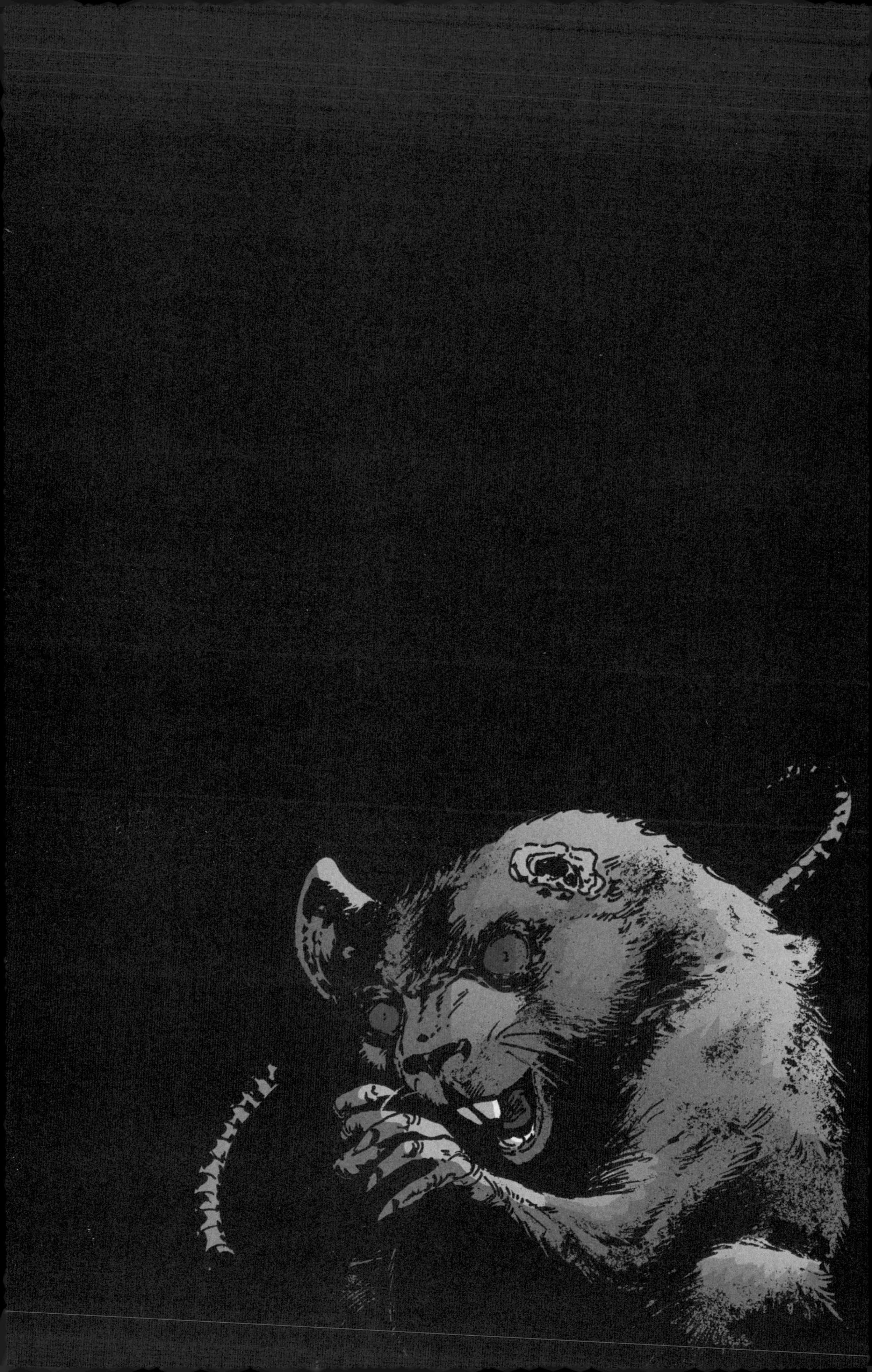

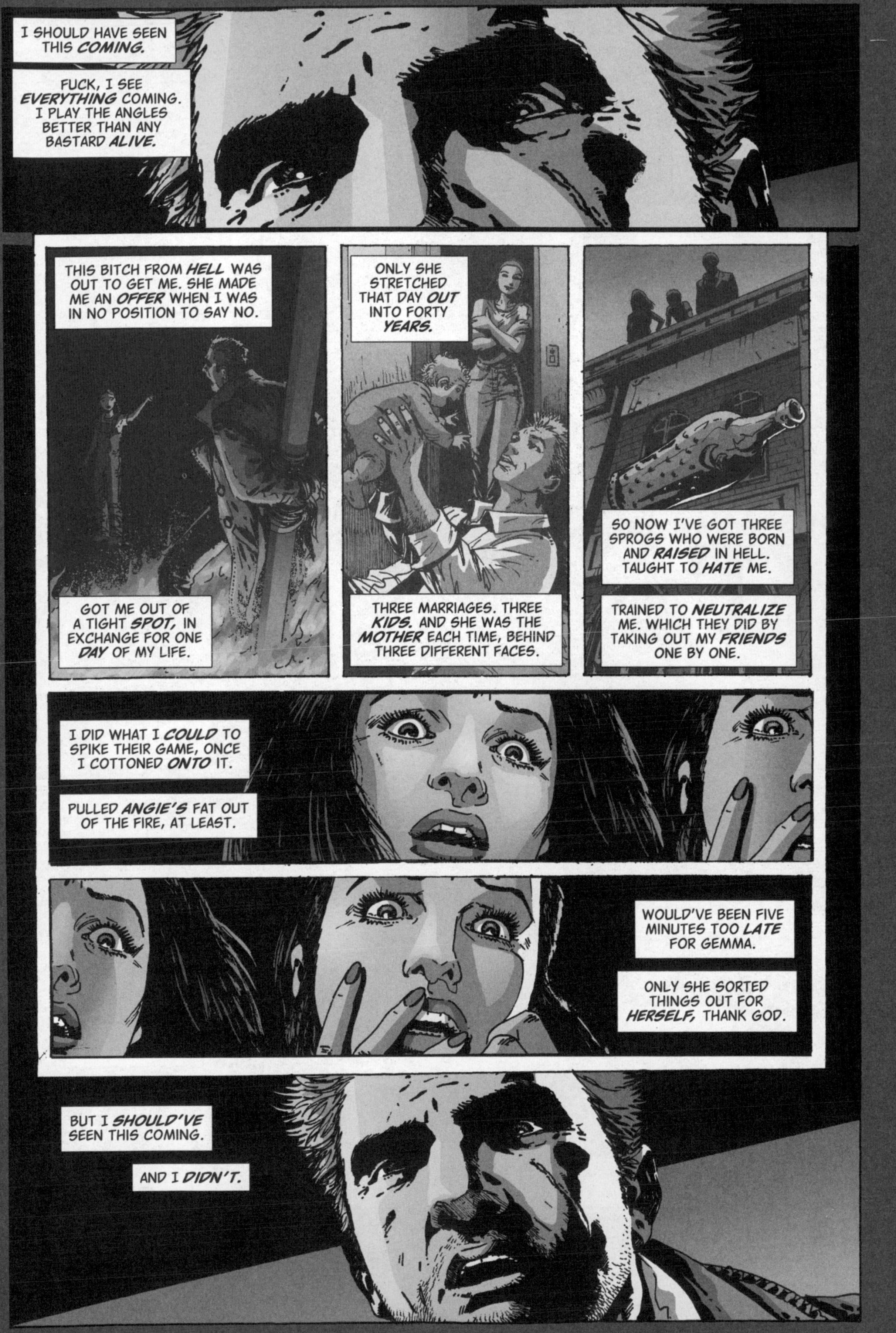
I SHOULD HAVE SEEN THIS COMING.
FUCK, I SEE EVERYTHING COMING. I PLAY THE ANGLES BETTER THAN ANY BASTARD ALIVE.
THIS BITCH FROM HELL WAS OUT TO GET ME. SHE MADE ME AN OFFER WHEN I WAS IN NO POSITION TO SAY NO.
GOT ME OUT OF A TIGHT SPOT, IN EXCHANGE FOR ONE DAY OF MY LIFE.
ONLY SHE STRETCHED THAT DAY OUT INTO FORTY YEARS.
THREE MARRIAGES. THREE KIDS. AND SHE WAS THE MOTHER EACH TIME, BEHIND THREE DIFFERENT FACES.
SO NOW I'VE GOT THREE SPROGS WHO WERE BORN AND RAISED IN HELL. TAUGHT TO HATE ME.
TRAINED TO NEUTRALIZE ME. WHICH THEY DID BY TAKING OUT MY FRIENDS ONE BY ONE.
I DID WHAT I COULD TO SPIKE THEIR GAME, ONCE I COTTONED ONTO IT.
PULLED ANGIE'S FAT OUT OF THE FIRE, AT LEAST.
WOULD'VE BEEN FIVE MINUTES TOO LATE FOR GEMMA.
ONLY SHE SORTED THINGS OUT FOR HERSELF, THANK GOD.
BUT I SHOULD'VE SEEN THIS COMING.
AND I DIDN'T.

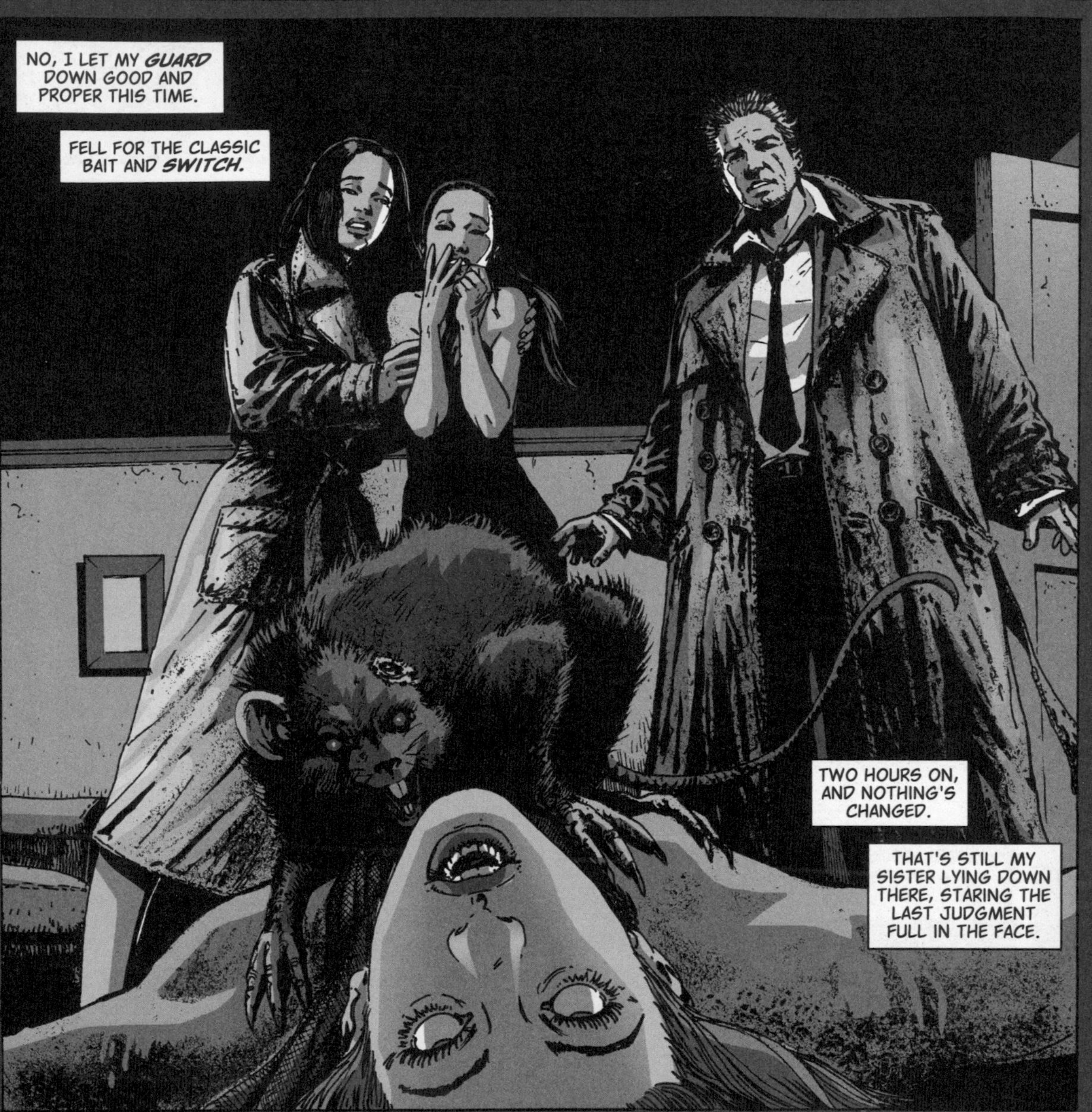
NO, I LET MY GUARD DOWN GOOD AND PROPER THIS TIME.
FELL FOR THE CLASSIC BAIT AND SWITCH.
TWO HOURS ON, AND NOTHING'S CHANGED.
THAT'S STILL MY SISTER LYING DOWN THERE, STARING THE LAST JUDGMENT FULL IN THE FACE.
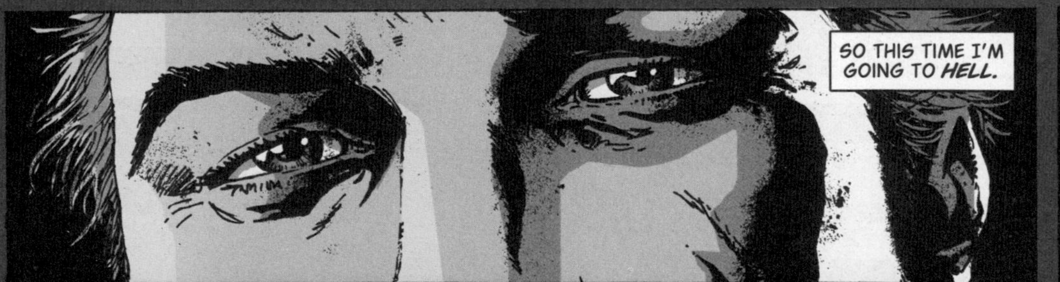
SO THIS TIME I'M GOING TO HELL.

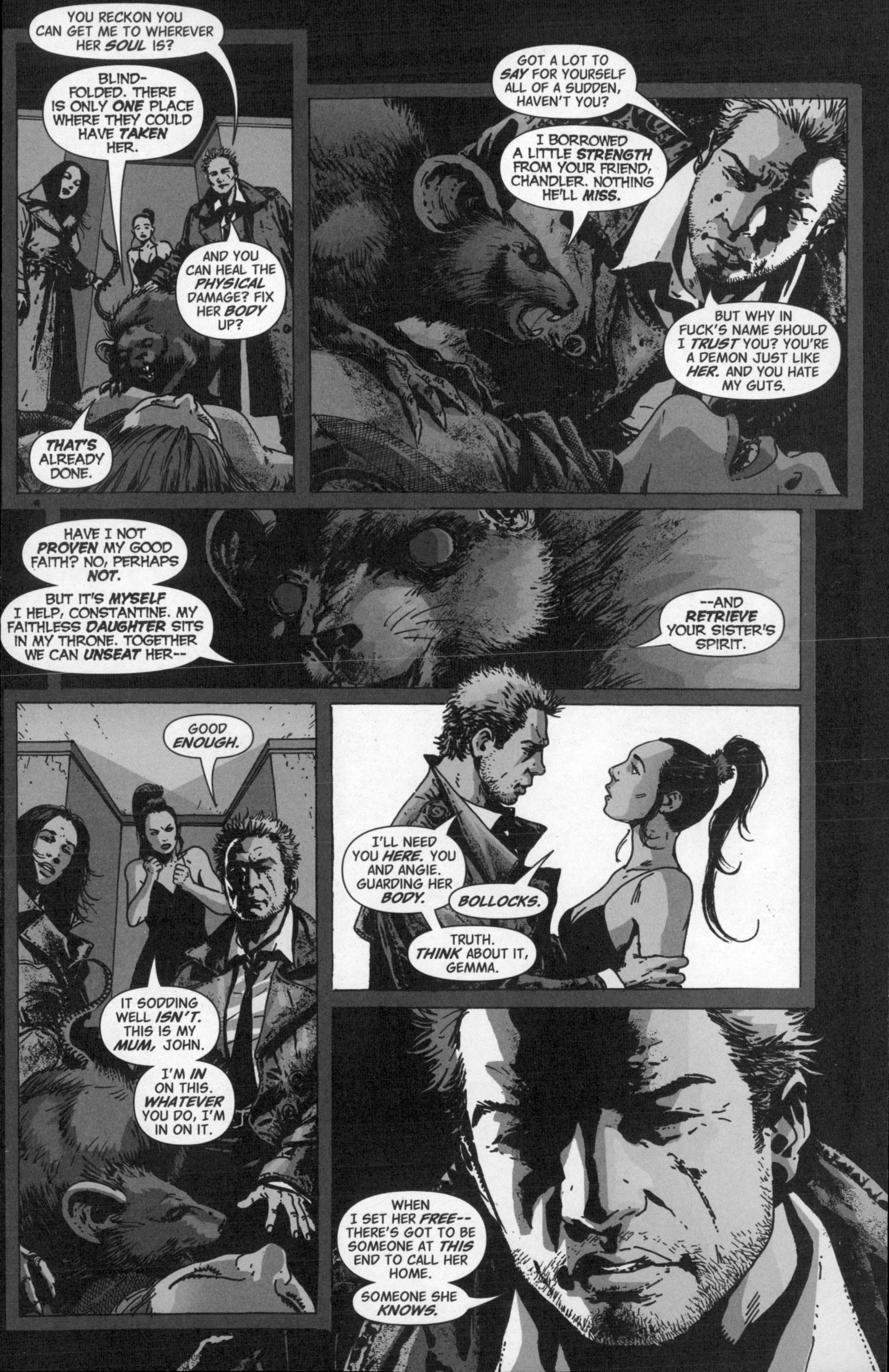
YOU RECKON YOU CAN GET ME TO WHEREVER HER SOUL IS?
BLIND-FOLDED. THERE IS ONLY ONE PLACE WHERE THEY COULD HAVE TAKEN HER.
AND YOU CAN HEAL THE PHYSICAL DAMAGE? FIX HER BODY UP?
THAT'S ALREADY DONE.
GOT A LOT TO SAY FOR YOURSELF ALL OF A SUDDEN, HAVEN'T YOU?
I BORROWED A LITTLE STRENGTH FROM YOUR FRIEND, CHANDLER. NOTHING HE'LL MISS.
BUT WHY IN FUCK'S NAME SHOULD I TRUST YOU? YOU'RE A DEMON JUST LIKE HER. AND YOU HATE MY GUTS.
HAVE I NOT PROVEN MY GOOD FAITH? NO, PERHAPS NOT.
BUT IT'S MYSELF I HELP, CONSTANTINE. MY FAITHLESS DAUGHTER SITS IN MY THRONE. TOGETHER WE CAN UNSEAT HER--
--AND RETRIEVE YOUR SISTER'S SPIRIT.
GOOD ENOUGH.
IT SODDING WELL ISN'T. THIS IS MY MUM, JOHN.
I'M IN ON THIS. WHATEVER YOU DO, I'M IN ON IT.
I'LL NEED YOU HERE. YOU AND ANGIE. GUARDING HER BODY.
BOLLOCKS.
TRUTH. THINK ABOUT IT, GEMMA.
WHEN I SET HER FREE-- THERE'S GOT TO BE SOMEONE AT THIS END TO CALL HER HOME.
SOMEONE SHE KNOWS.

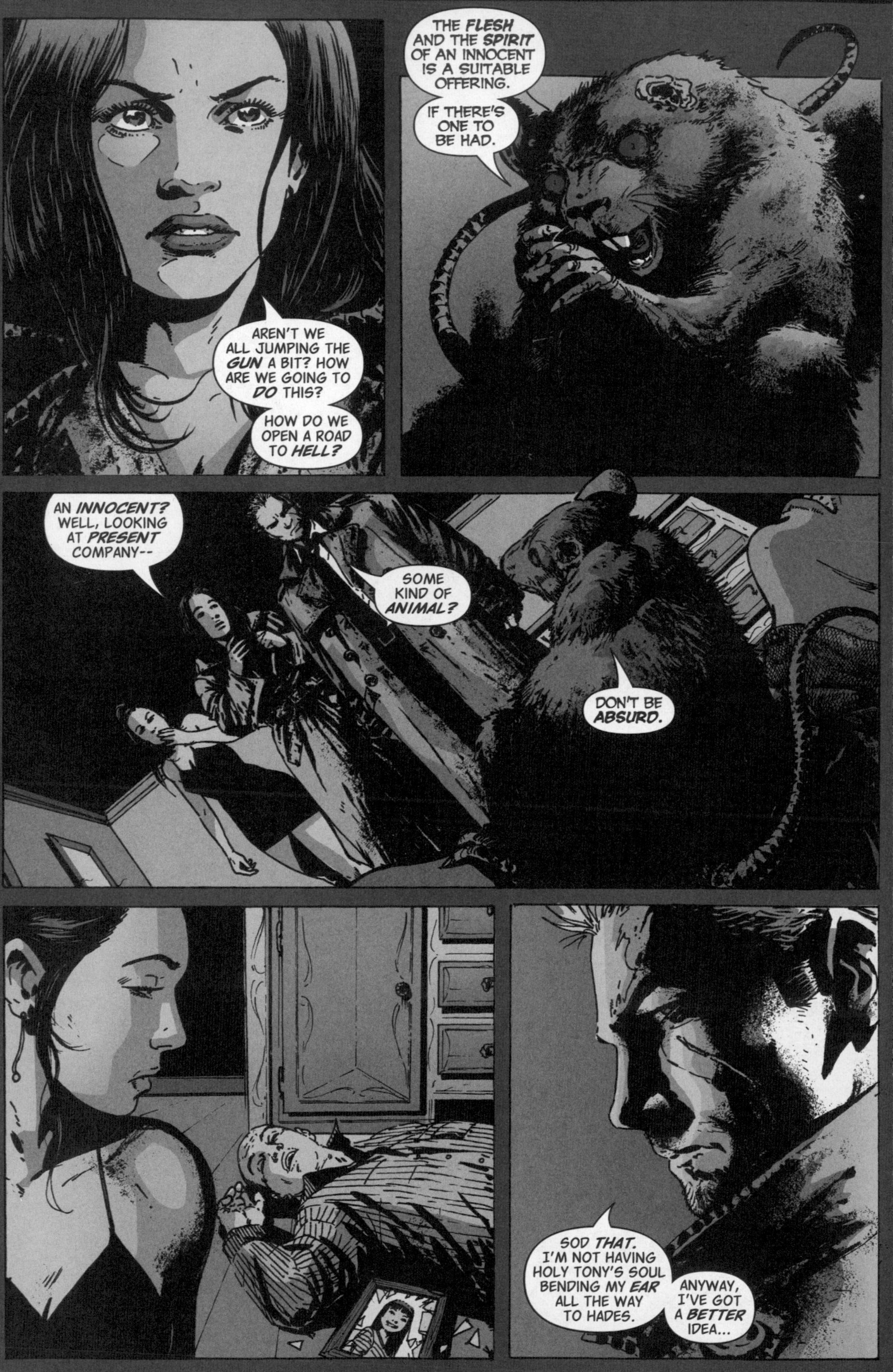
AREN'T WE ALL JUMPING THE GUN A BIT? HOW ARE WE GOING TO DO THIS?
HOW DO WE OPEN A ROAD TO HELL?
THE FLESH AND THE SPIRIT OF AN INNOCENT IS A SUITABLE OFFERING.
IF THERE'S ONE TO BE HAD.
AN INNOCENT? WELL, LOOKING AT PRESENT COMPANY--
SOME KIND OF ANIMAL?
DON'T BE ABSURD.
SOD THAT. I'M NOT HAVING HOLY TONY'S SOUL BENDING MY EAR ALL THE WAY TO HADES.
ANYWAY, I'VE GOT A BETTER IDEA...

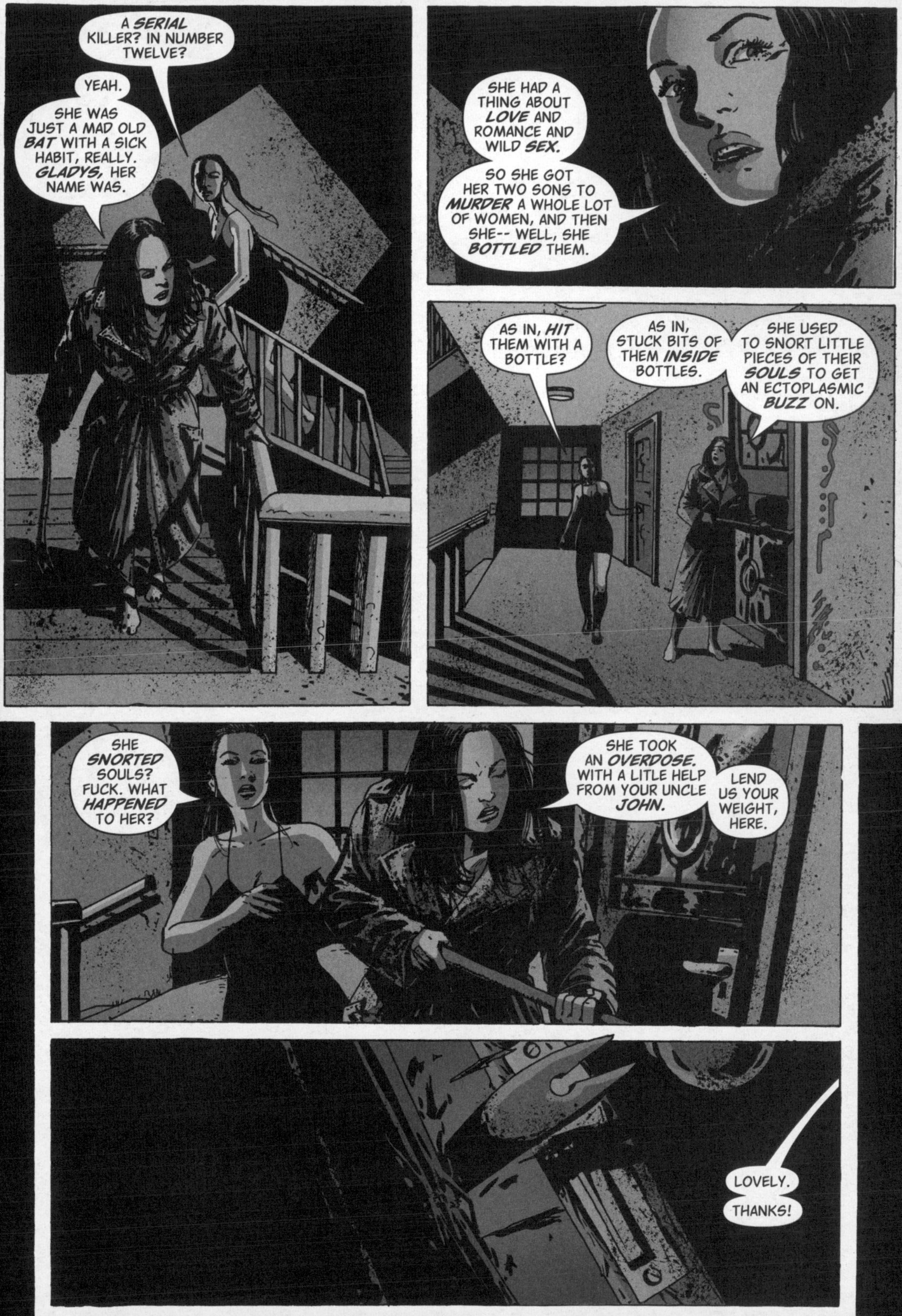
A SERIAL KILLER? IN NUMBER TWELVE?
YEAH.
SHE WAS JUST A MAD OLD BAT WITH A SICK HABIT, REALLY. GLADYS, HER NAME WAS.
SHE HAD A THING ABOUT LOVE AND ROMANCE AND WILD SEX.
SO SHE GOT HER TWO SONS TO MURDER A WHOLE LOT OF WOMEN, AND THEN SHE-- WELL, SHE BOTTLED THEM.
AS IN, HIT THEM WITH A BOTTLE?
AS IN, STUCK BITS OF THEM INSIDE BOTTLES.
SHE USED TO SNORT LITTLE PIECES OF THEIR SOULS TO GET AN ECTOPLASMIC BUZZ ON.
SHE SNORTED SOULS? FUCK. WHAT HAPPENED TO HER?
SHE TOOK AN OVERDOSE. WITH A LITLE HELP FROM YOUR UNCLE JOHN.
LEND US YOUR WEIGHT, HERE.
LOVELY.
THANKS!

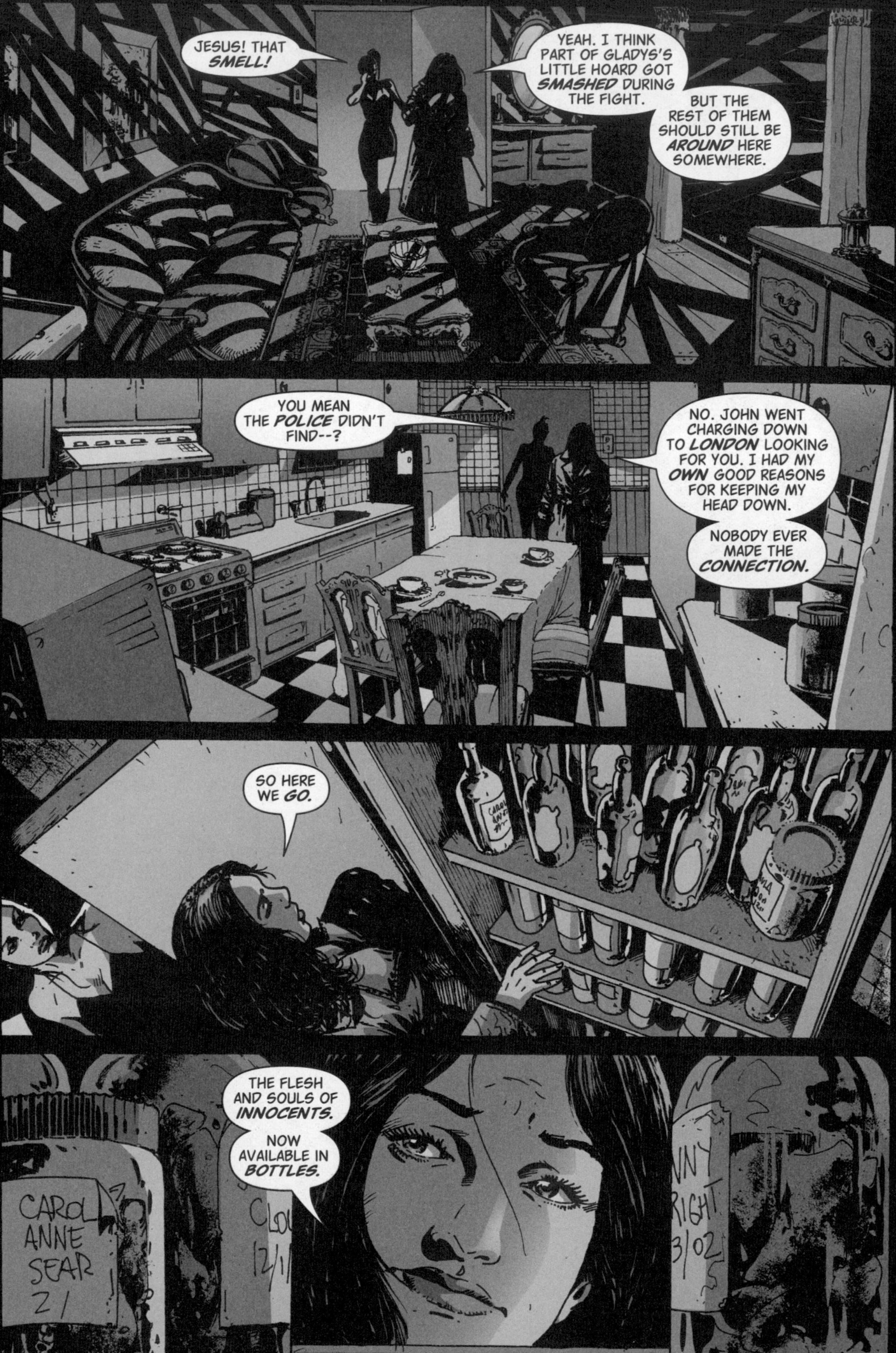
JESUS! THAT SMELL!
YEAH. I THINK PART OF GLADYS'S LITTLE HOARD GOT SMASHED DURING THE FIGHT.
BUT THE REST OF THEM SHOULD STILL BE AROUND HERE SOMEWHERE.
YOU MEAN THE POLICE DIDN'T FIND--?
NO. JOHN WENT CHARGING DOWN TO LONDON LOOKING FOR YOU. I HAD MY OWN GOOD REASONS FOR KEEPING MY HEAD DOWN.
NOBODY EVER MADE THE CONNECTION.
SO HERE WE GO.
THE FLESH AND SOULS OF INNOCENTS.
NOW AVAILABLE IN BOTTLES.
CAROL ANNE SEAR

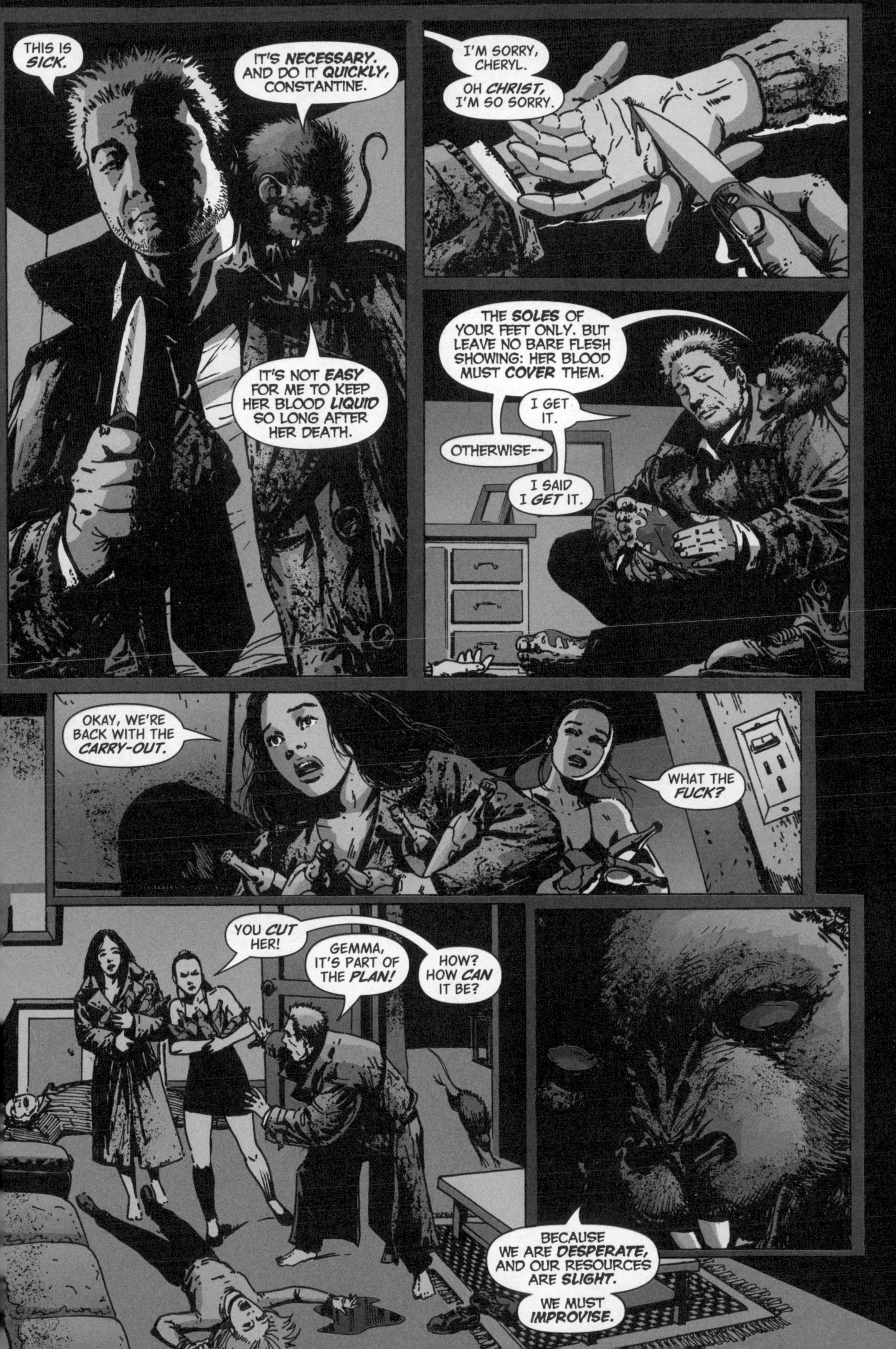
THIS IS *SICK.*
IT'S *NECESSARY.* AND DO IT *QUICKLY,* CONSTANTINE.
IT'S NOT *EASY* FOR ME TO KEEP HER BLOOD *LIQUID* SO LONG AFTER HER DEATH.
I'M SORRY, CHERYL.
OH *CHRIST,* I'M SO SORRY.
THE *SOLES* OF YOUR FEET ONLY. BUT LEAVE NO BARE FLESH SHOWING: HER BLOOD MUST *COVER* THEM.
I GET IT.
OTHERWISE--
I SAID I *GET* IT.
OKAY, WE'RE BACK WITH THE *CARRY-OUT.*
WHAT THE *FUCK?*
YOU *CUT* HER!
GEMMA, IT'S PART OF THE *PLAN!*
HOW? HOW *CAN* IT BE?
BECAUSE WE ARE *DESPERATE,* AND OUR RESOURCES ARE *SLIGHT.*
WE MUST *IMPROVISE.*

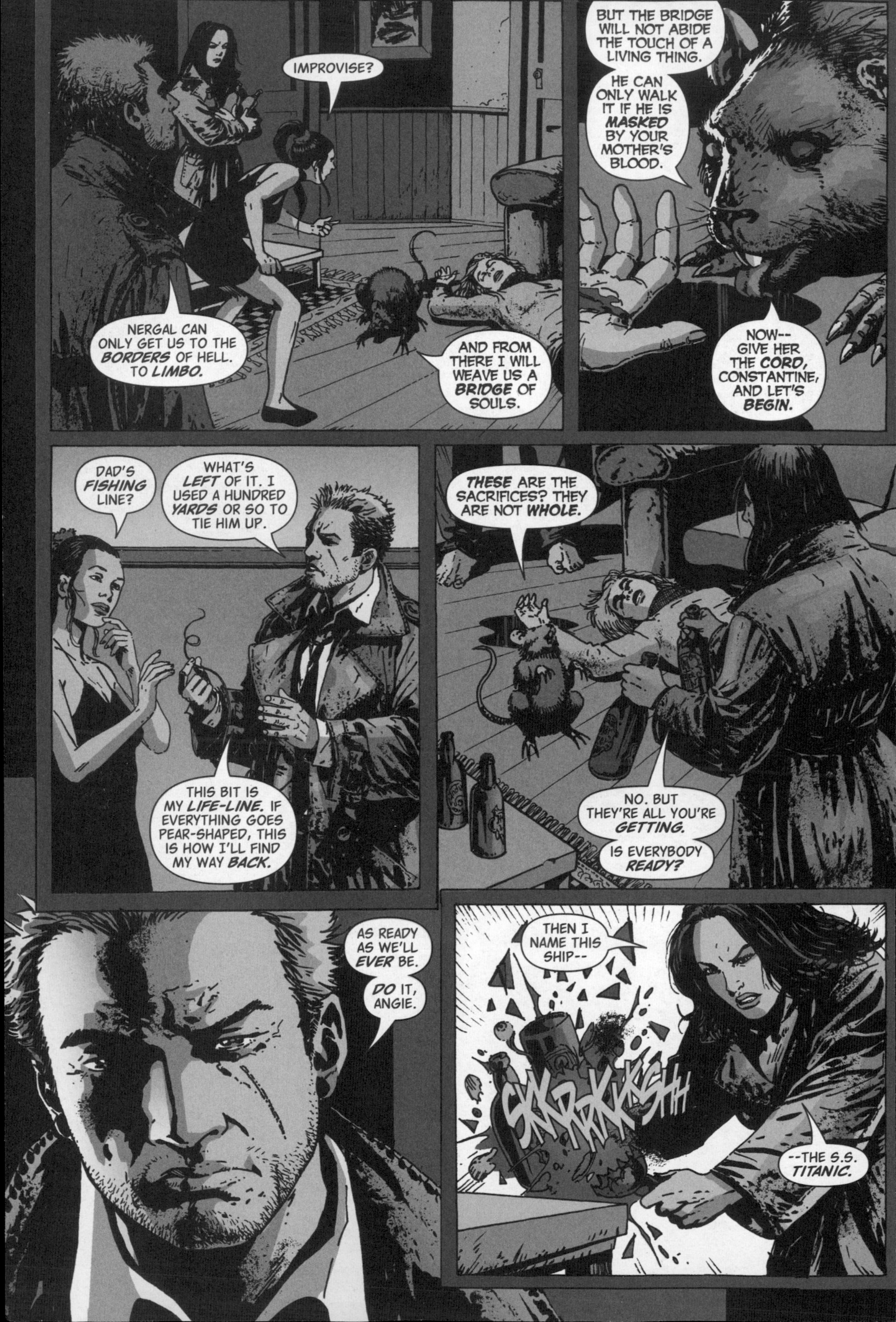
IMPROVISE?
NERGAL CAN ONLY GET US TO THE BORDERS OF HELL. TO LIMBO.
AND FROM THERE I WILL WEAVE US A BRIDGE OF SOULS.
BUT THE BRIDGE WILL NOT ABIDE THE TOUCH OF A LIVING THING.
HE CAN ONLY WALK IT IF HE IS MASKED BY YOUR MOTHER'S BLOOD.
NOW-- GIVE HER THE CORD, CONSTANTINE, AND LET'S BEGIN.
DAD'S FISHING LINE?
WHAT'S LEFT OF IT. I USED A HUNDRED YARDS OR SO TO TIE HIM UP.
THIS BIT IS MY LIFE-LINE. IF EVERYTHING GOES PEAR-SHAPED, THIS IS HOW I'LL FIND MY WAY BACK.
THESE ARE THE SACRIFICES? THEY ARE NOT WHOLE.
NO. BUT THEY'RE ALL YOU'RE GETTING.
IS EVERYBODY READY?
AS READY AS WE'LL EVER BE.
DO IT, ANGIE.
THEN I NAME THIS SHIP--
--THE S.S. TITANIC.

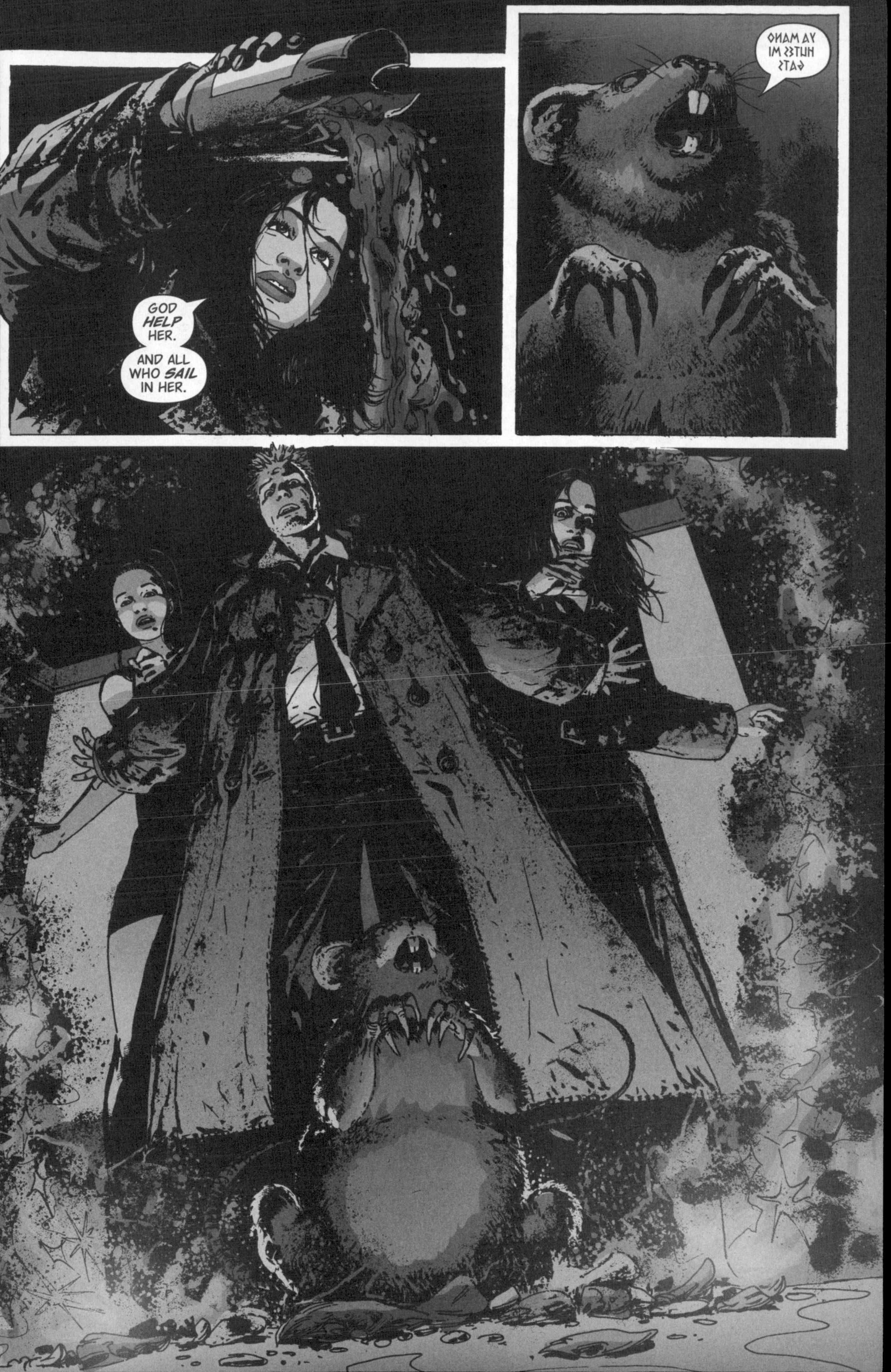
GOD HELP HER.
AND ALL WHO SAIL IN HER.
YA MANO HUTSS MI GATS

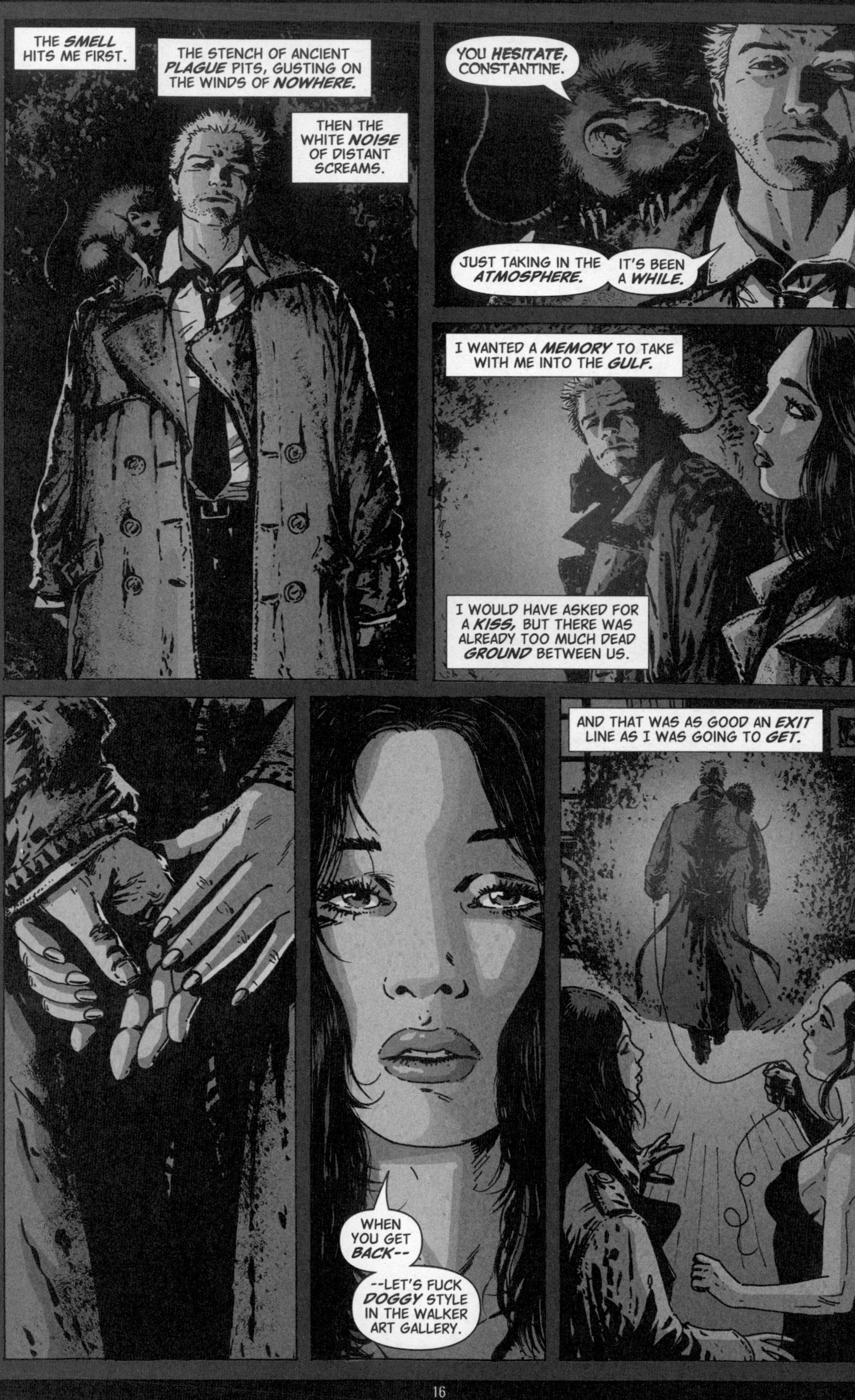
THE SMELL HITS ME FIRST.
THE STENCH OF ANCIENT PLAGUE PITS, GUSTING ON THE WINDS OF NOWHERE.
THEN THE WHITE NOISE OF DISTANT SCREAMS.
YOU HESITATE, CONSTANTINE.
JUST TAKING IN THE ATMOSPHERE.
IT'S BEEN A WHILE.
I WANTED A MEMORY TO TAKE WITH ME INTO THE GULF.
I WOULD HAVE ASKED FOR A KISS, BUT THERE WAS ALREADY TOO MUCH DEAD GROUND BETWEEN US.
WHEN YOU GET BACK--
--LET'S FUCK DOGGY STYLE IN THE WALKER ART GALLERY.
AND THAT WAS AS GOOD AN EXIT LINE AS I WAS GOING TO GET.

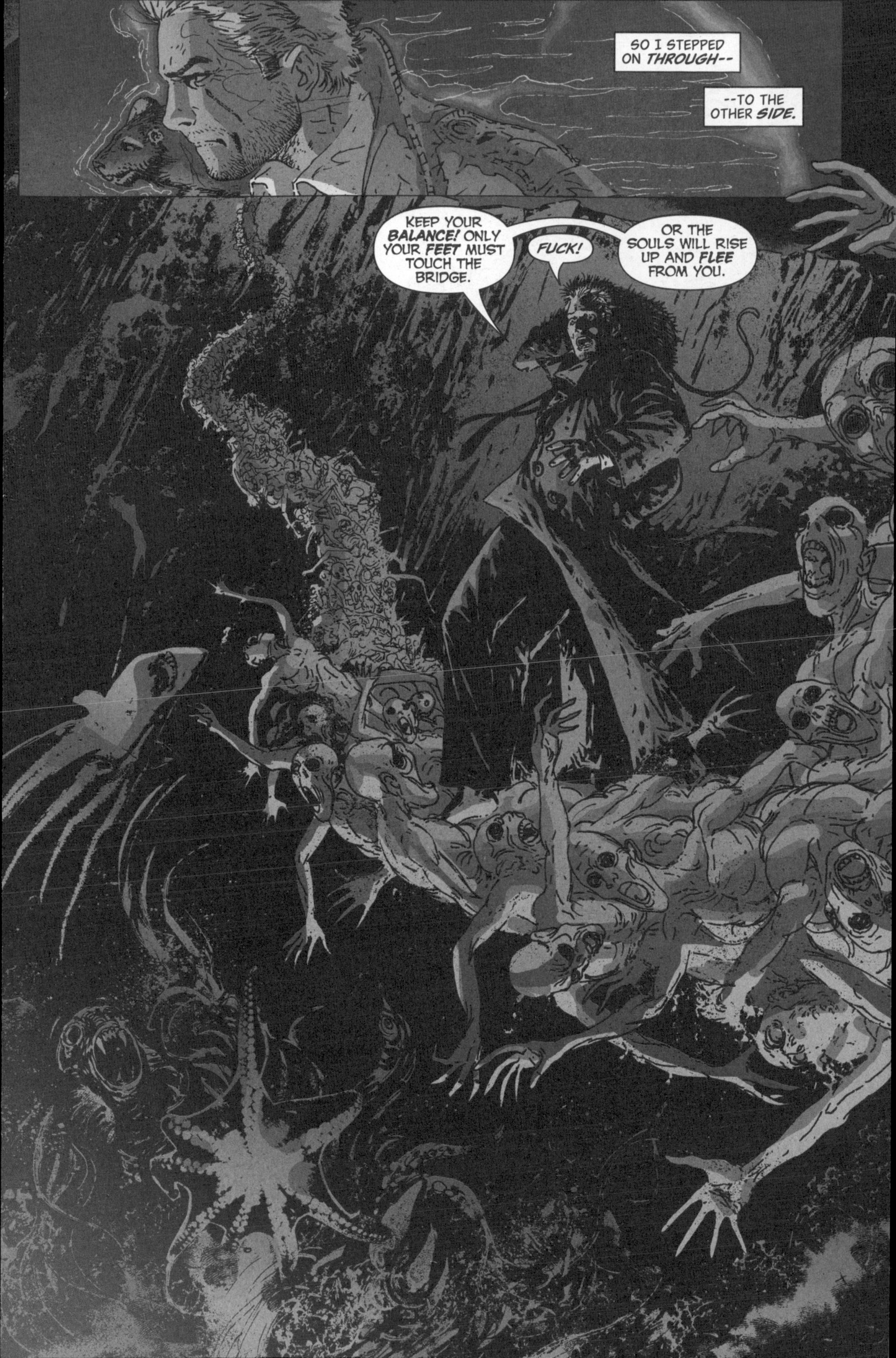
SO I STEPPED ON THROUGH--
--TO THE OTHER SIDE.
KEEP YOUR BALANCE! ONLY YOUR FEET MUST TOUCH THE BRIDGE.
FUCK!
OR THE SOULS WILL RISE UP AND FLEE FROM YOU.

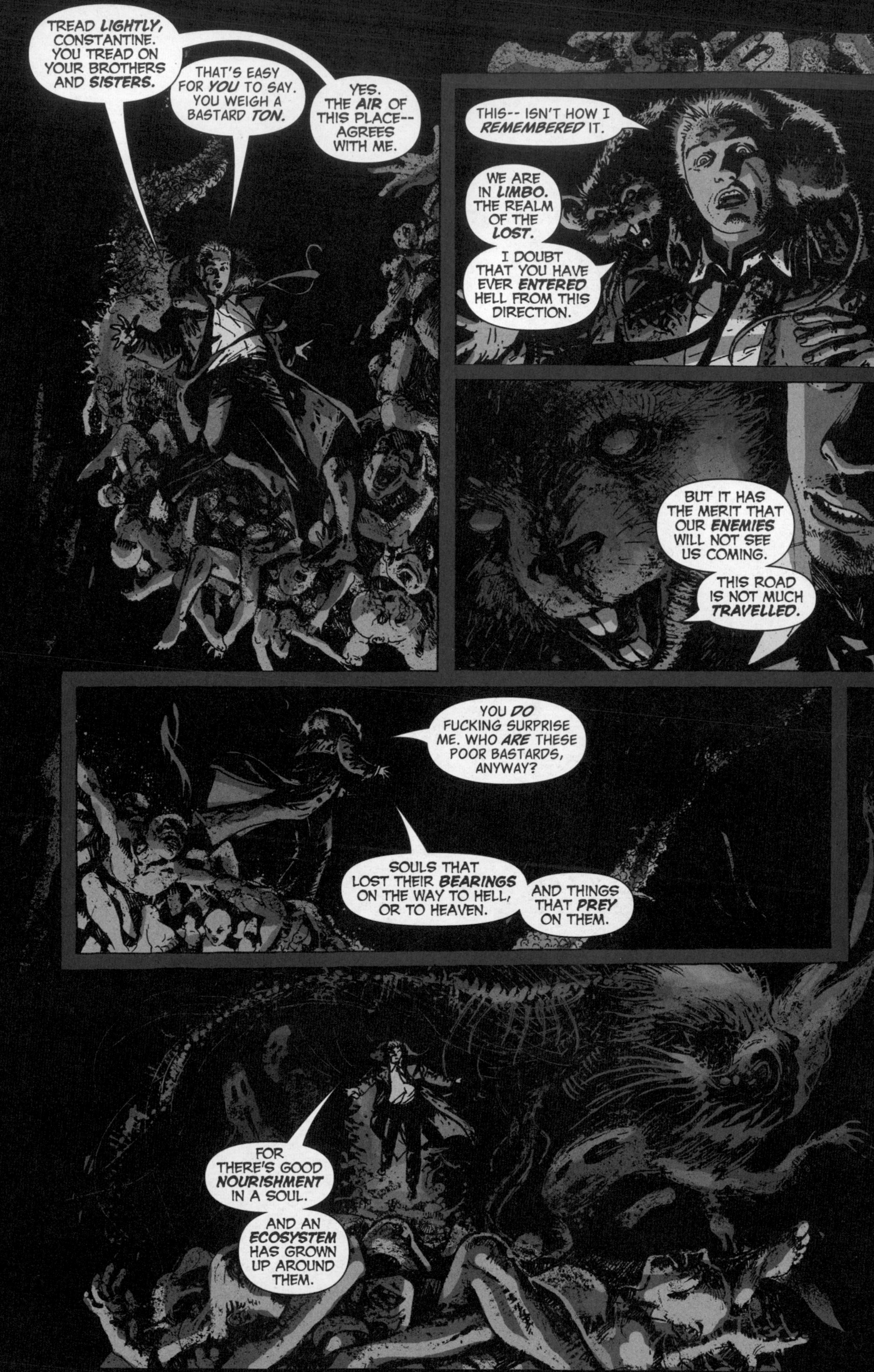
TREAD LIGHTLY, CONSTANTINE. YOU TREAD ON YOUR BROTHERS AND SISTERS.
THAT'S EASY FOR YOU TO SAY. YOU WEIGH A BASTARD TON.
YES. THE AIR OF THIS PLACE-- AGREES WITH ME.
THIS-- ISN'T HOW I REMEMBERED IT.
WE ARE IN LIMBO. THE REALM OF THE LOST.
I DOUBT THAT YOU HAVE EVER ENTERED HELL FROM THIS DIRECTION.
BUT IT HAS THE MERIT THAT OUR ENEMIES WILL NOT SEE US COMING.
THIS ROAD IS NOT MUCH TRAVELLED.
YOU DO FUCKING SURPRISE ME. WHO ARE THESE POOR BASTARDS, ANYWAY?
SOULS THAT LOST THEIR BEARINGS ON THE WAY TO HELL, OR TO HEAVEN.
AND THINGS THAT PREY ON THEM.
FOR THERE'S GOOD NOURISHMENT IN A SOUL.
AND AN ECOSYSTEM HAS GROWN UP AROUND THEM.

AND THAT THING?
THAT I HAVE NOT ENCOUNTERED BEFORE.
MOVE FORWARD SLOWLY. AND DO NOTHING UNTIL I TELL YOU TO.
GOOD MORROW TO YOU, TRAVELLER. I MUST QUESTION YOU AS TO YOUR BUSINESS IN HELL'S HINTERLANDS.
AND IF YOUR ANSWERS SATISFY ME, I WILL LET YOU PASS.
FIRST, WHO IS YOUR SPONSOR AND PROTECTOR HERE?
TO WHICH HOUSE OF HELL DO YOU CLAIM ALLEGIANCE?

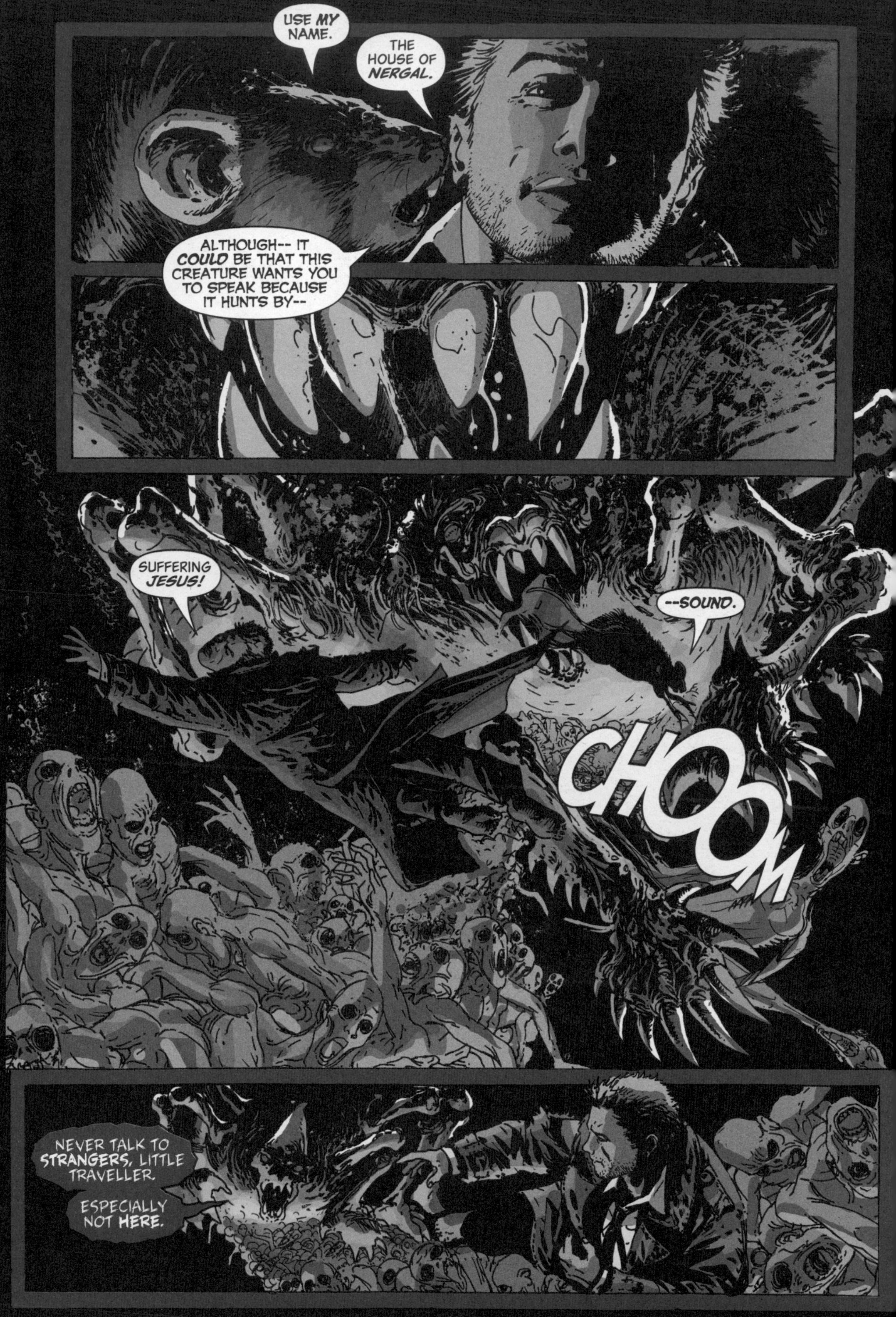
USE MY NAME.
THE HOUSE OF NERGAL.
ALTHOUGH-- IT COULD BE THAT THIS CREATURE WANTS YOU TO SPEAK BECAUSE IT HUNTS BY--
SUFFERING JESUS!
--SOUND.
CHOOOM
NEVER TALK TO STRANGERS, LITTLE TRAVELLER.
ESPECIALLY NOT HERE.

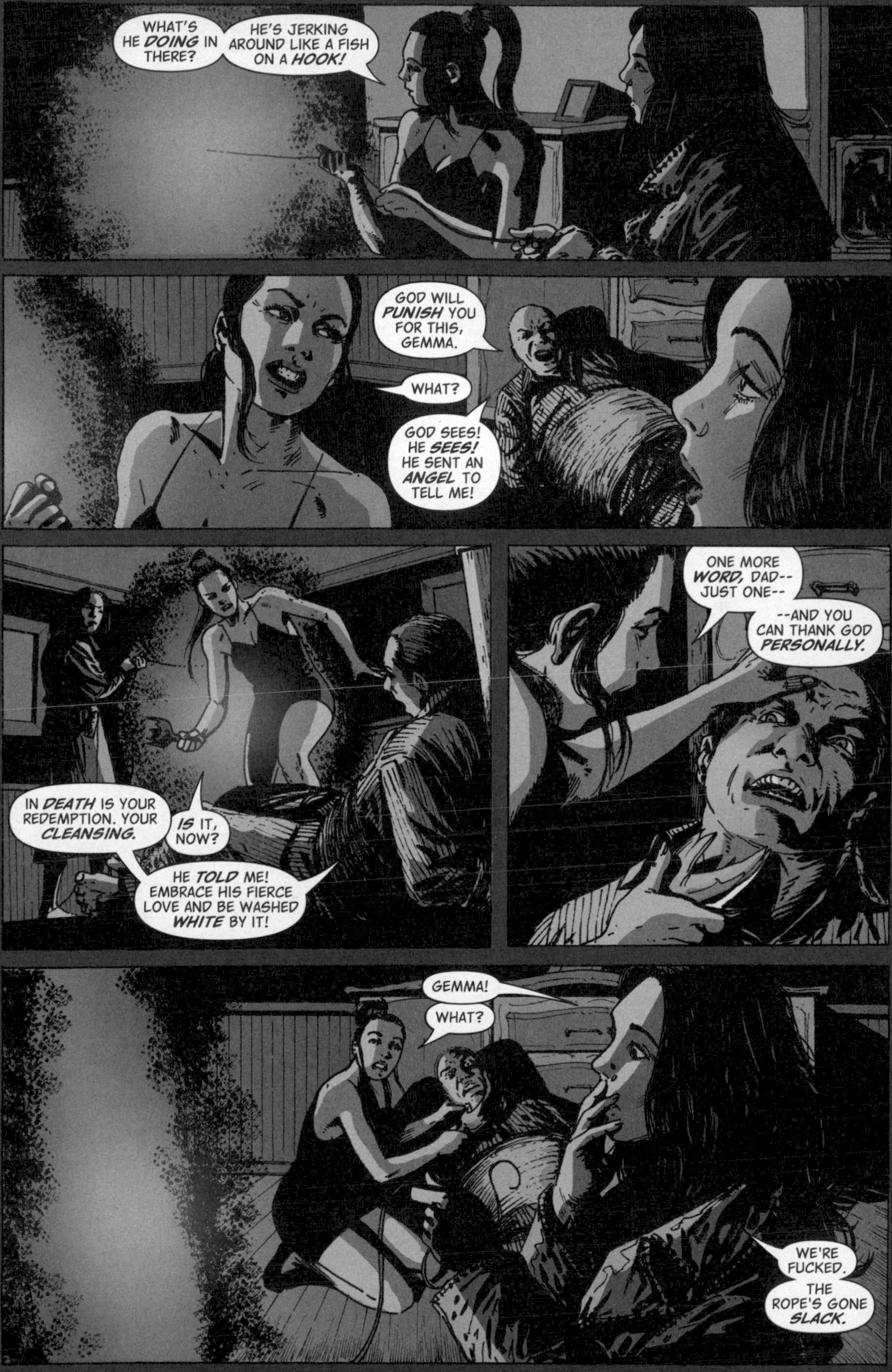
WHAT'S HE DOING IN THERE?
HE'S JERKING AROUND LIKE A FISH ON A HOOK!
GOD WILL PUNISH YOU FOR THIS, GEMMA.
WHAT?
GOD SEES! HE SEES! HE SENT AN ANGEL TO TELL ME!
IN DEATH IS YOUR REDEMPTION. YOUR CLEANSING.
IS IT, NOW?
HE TOLD ME! EMBRACE HIS FIERCE LOVE AND BE WASHED WHITE BY IT!
ONE MORE WORD, DAD-- JUST ONE--
--AND YOU CAN THANK GOD PERSONALLY.
GEMMA!
WHAT?
WE'RE FUCKED.
THE ROPE'S GONE SLACK.

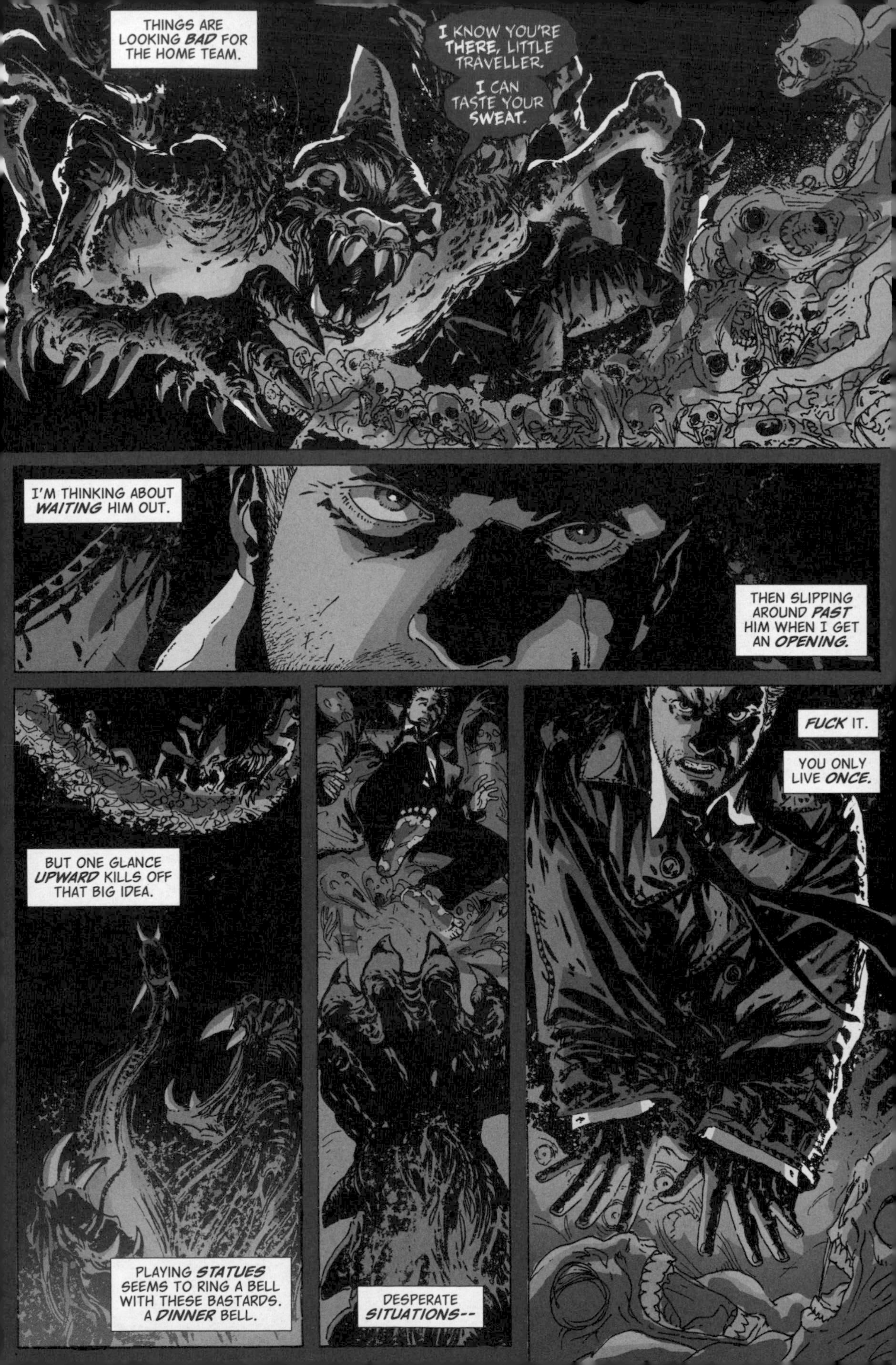
THINGS ARE LOOKING BAD FOR THE HOME TEAM.
I KNOW YOU'RE THERE, LITTLE TRAVELLER.
I CAN TASTE YOUR SWEAT.
I'M THINKING ABOUT WAITING HIM OUT.
THEN SLIPPING AROUND PAST HIM WHEN I GET AN OPENING.
BUT ONE GLANCE UPWARD KILLS OFF THAT BIG IDEA.
PLAYING STATUES SEEMS TO RING A BELL WITH THESE BASTARDS. A DINNER BELL.
DESPERATE SITUATIONS--
FUCK IT.
YOU ONLY LIVE ONCE.

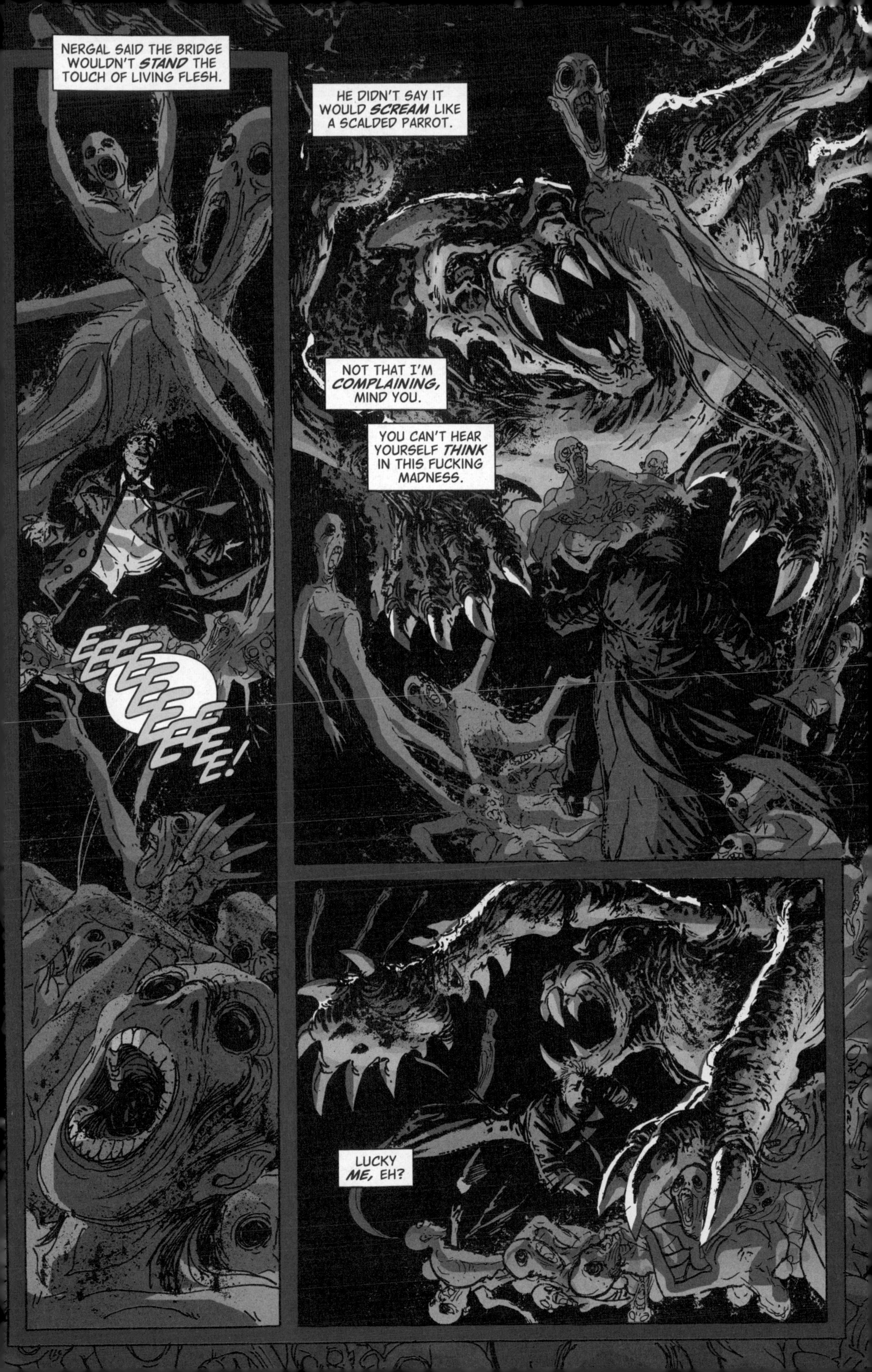
NERGAL SAID THE BRIDGE WOULDN'T STAND THE TOUCH OF LIVING FLESH.
EEEEEEEEEEEEE!
HE DIDN'T SAY IT WOULD SCREAM LIKE A SCALDED PARROT.
NOT THAT I'M COMPLAINING, MIND YOU.
YOU CAN'T HEAR YOURSELF THINK IN THIS FUCKING MADNESS.
LUCKY ME, EH?

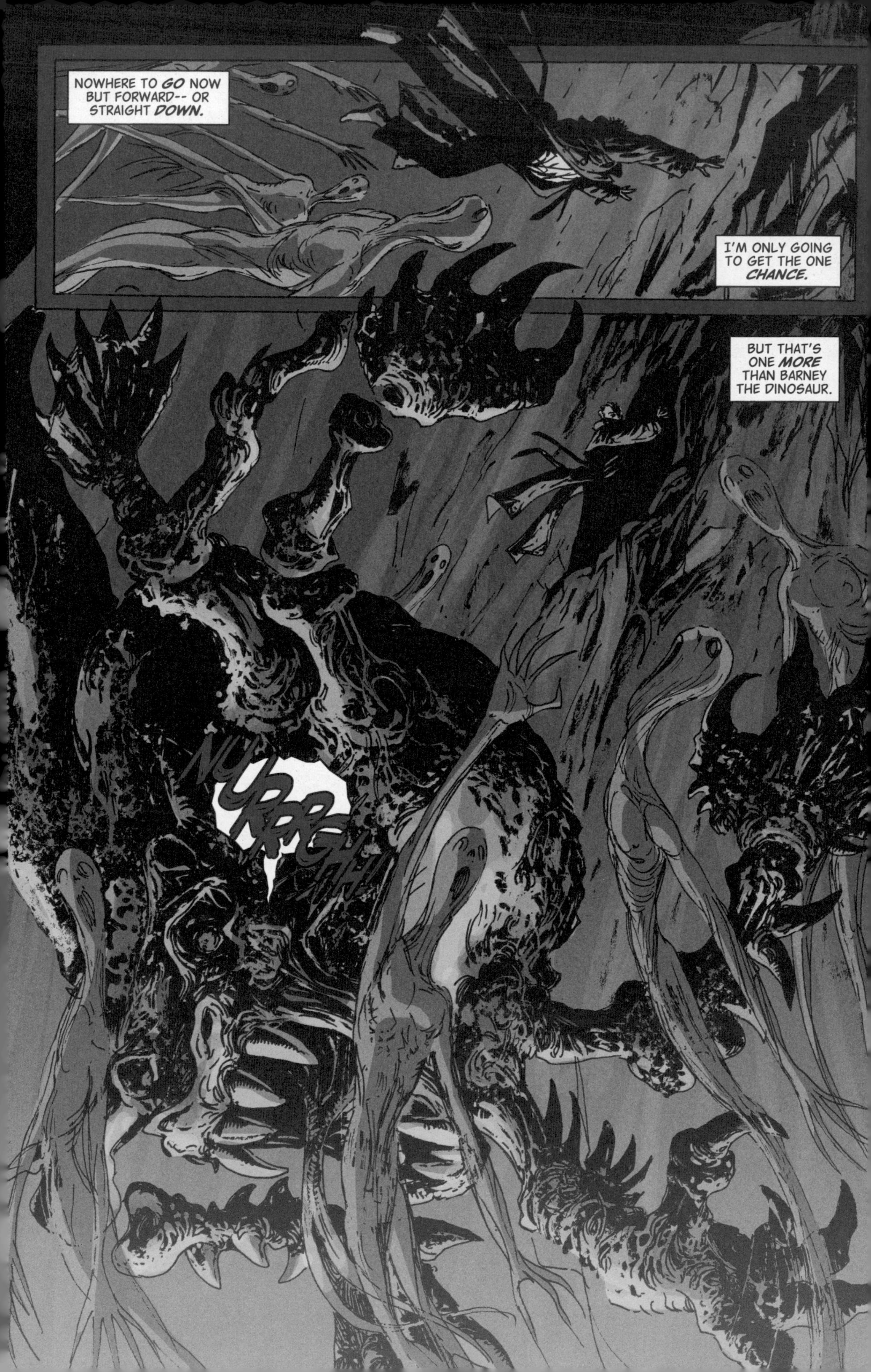
NOWHERE TO *GO* NOW BUT FORWARD-- OR STRAIGHT *DOWN.*
I'M ONLY GOING TO GET THE ONE *CHANCE.*
BUT THAT'S ONE *MORE* THAN BARNEY THE DINOSAUR.
NUURRRGHH!!

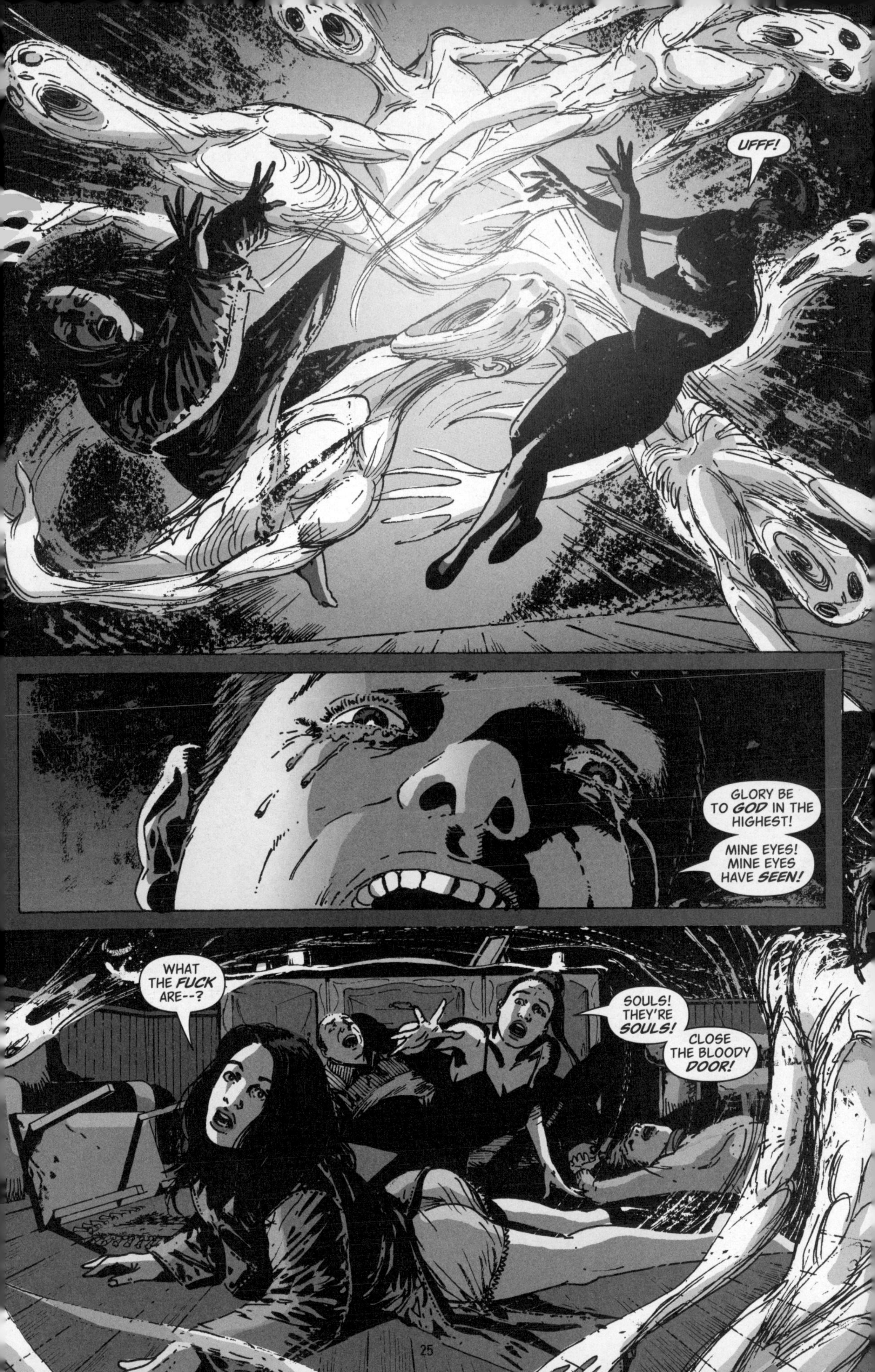
UFFF!
GLORY BE TO GOD IN THE HIGHEST!
MINE EYES! MINE EYES HAVE SEEN!
WHAT THE FUCK ARE--?
SOULS! THEY'RE SOULS!
CLOSE THE BLOODY DOOR!

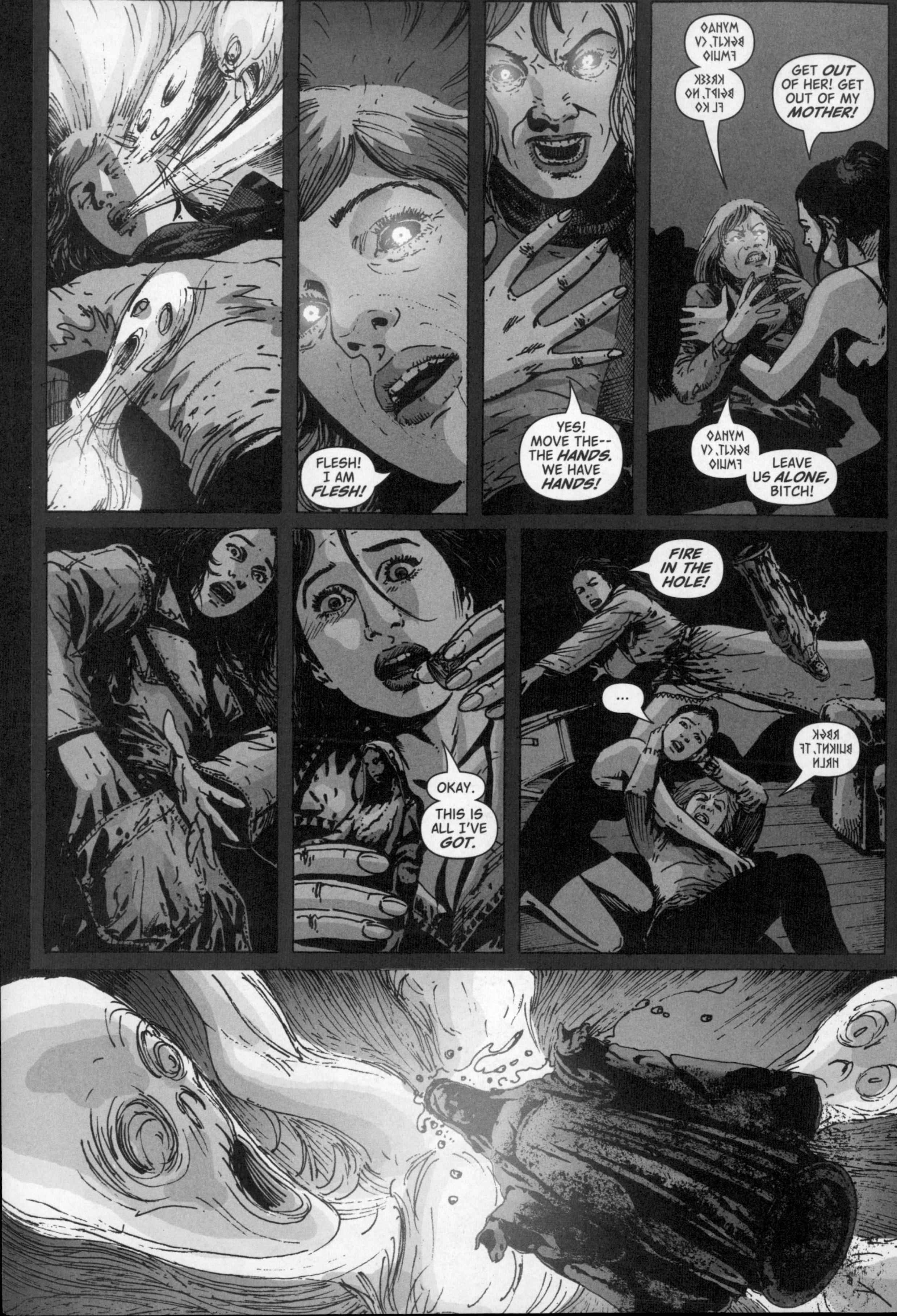
FLESH! I AM FLESH!
YES! MOVE THE-- THE HANDS. WE HAVE HANDS!
GET OUT OF HER! GET OUT OF MY MOTHER!
LEAVE US ALONE, BITCH!
OKAY. THIS IS ALL I'VE GOT.
FIRE IN THE HOLE!
...

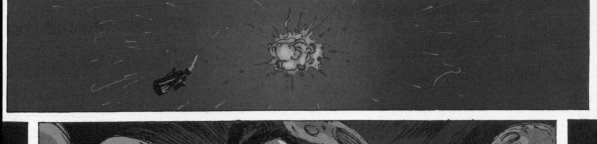

WHAT WAS *THAT?*

HOLY *WATER* IN A PLASTIC VIRGIN MARY.

A SOUVENIR FROM *LOURDES.*

SORRY ABOUT YOUR *DAD,* GEMMA.

MINE EYES-- A HA HA-- MINE EYES HAVE SEEN.

THEY'VE *SEEN.*

YEAH.

TO BE *HONEST--*

--I'M *MORE* WORRIED ABOUT UNCLE JOHN.

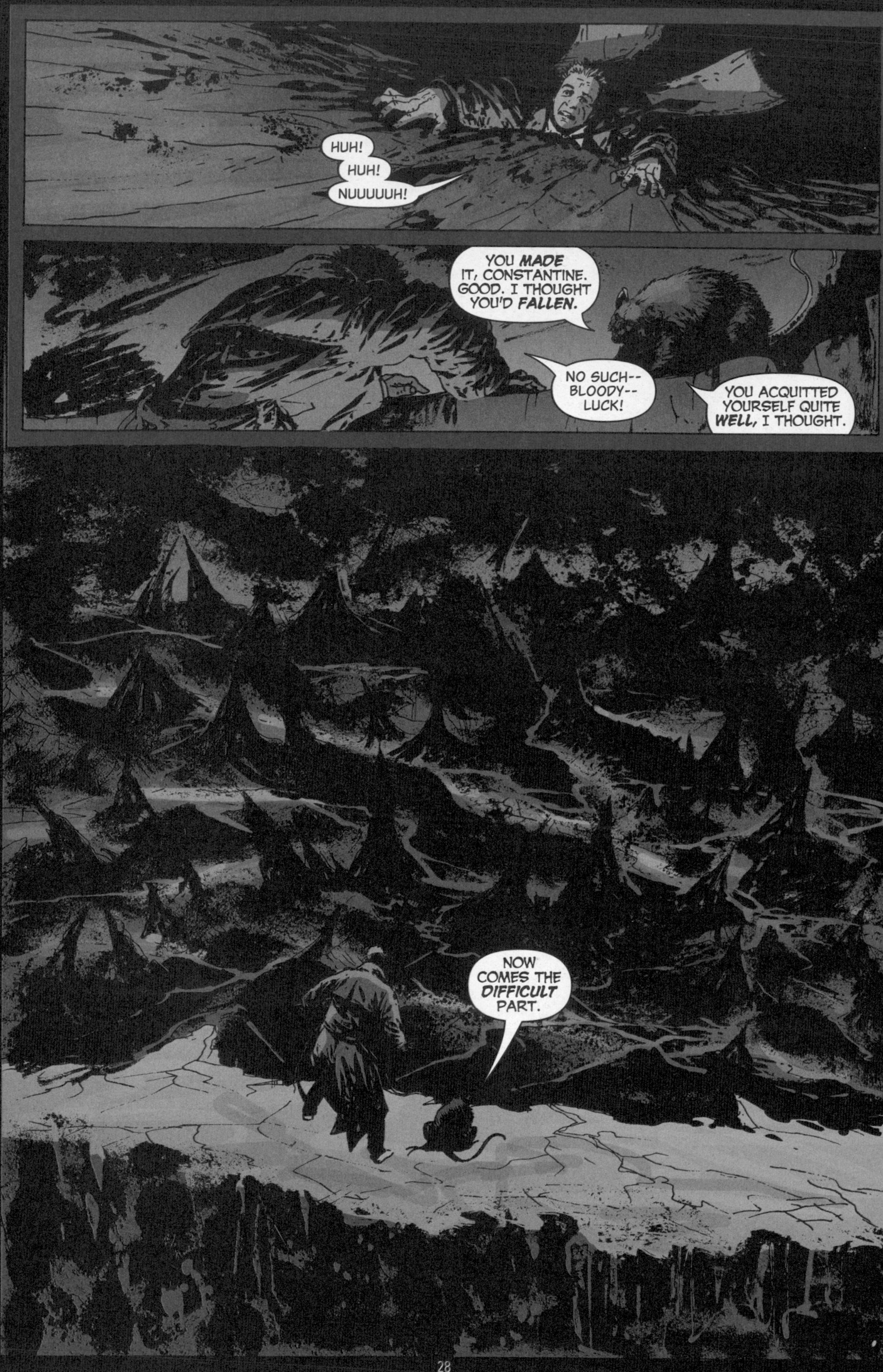
HUH!
HUH!
NUUUUUH!
YOU **MADE** IT, CONSTANTINE. GOOD. I THOUGHT YOU'D **FALLEN.**
NO SUCH-- BLOODY-- LUCK!
YOU ACQUITTED YOURSELF QUITE **WELL,** I THOUGHT.
NOW COMES THE **DIFFICULT** PART.

Down in the Ground Where the Dead Men Go CHAPTER TWO

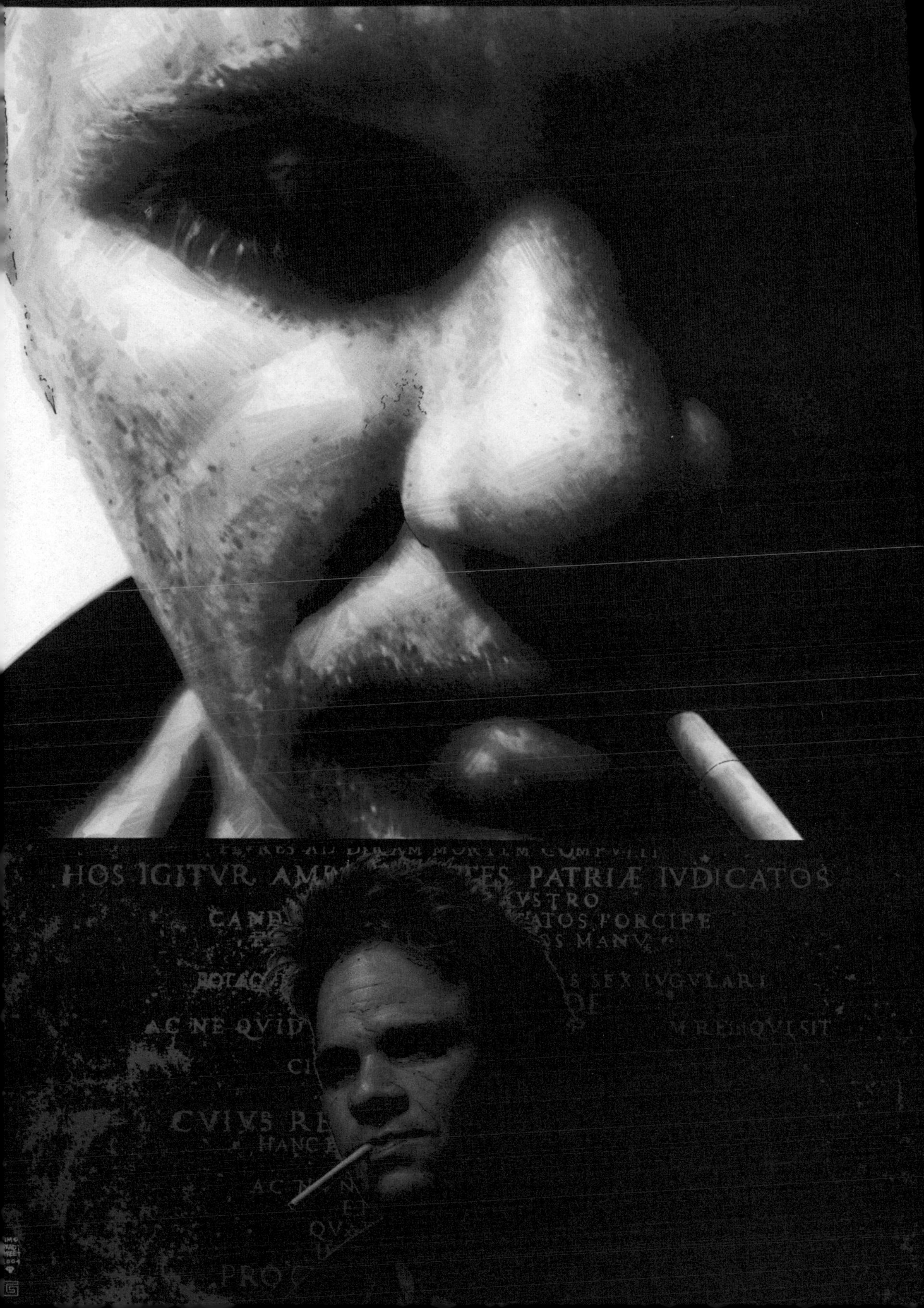

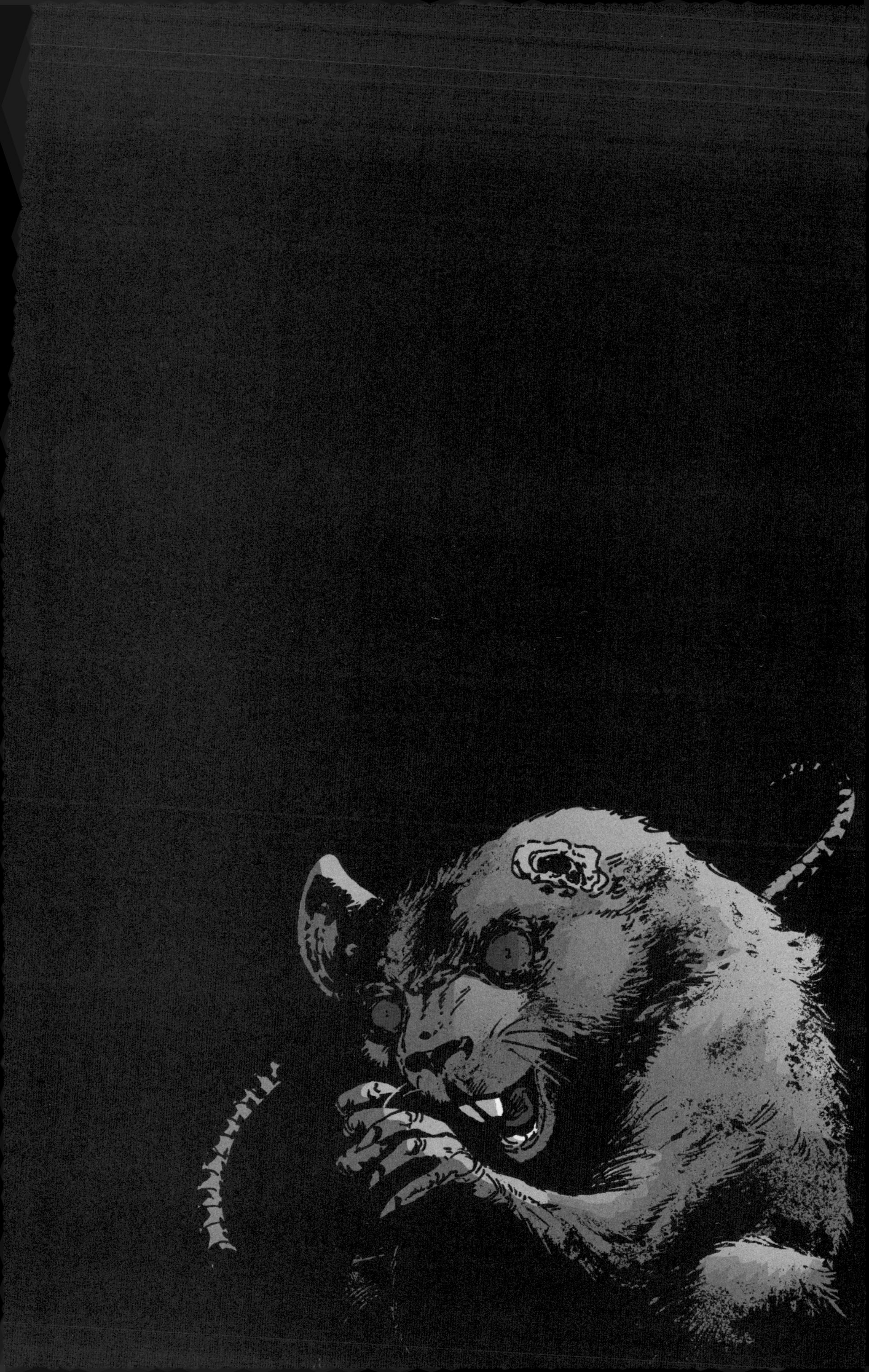

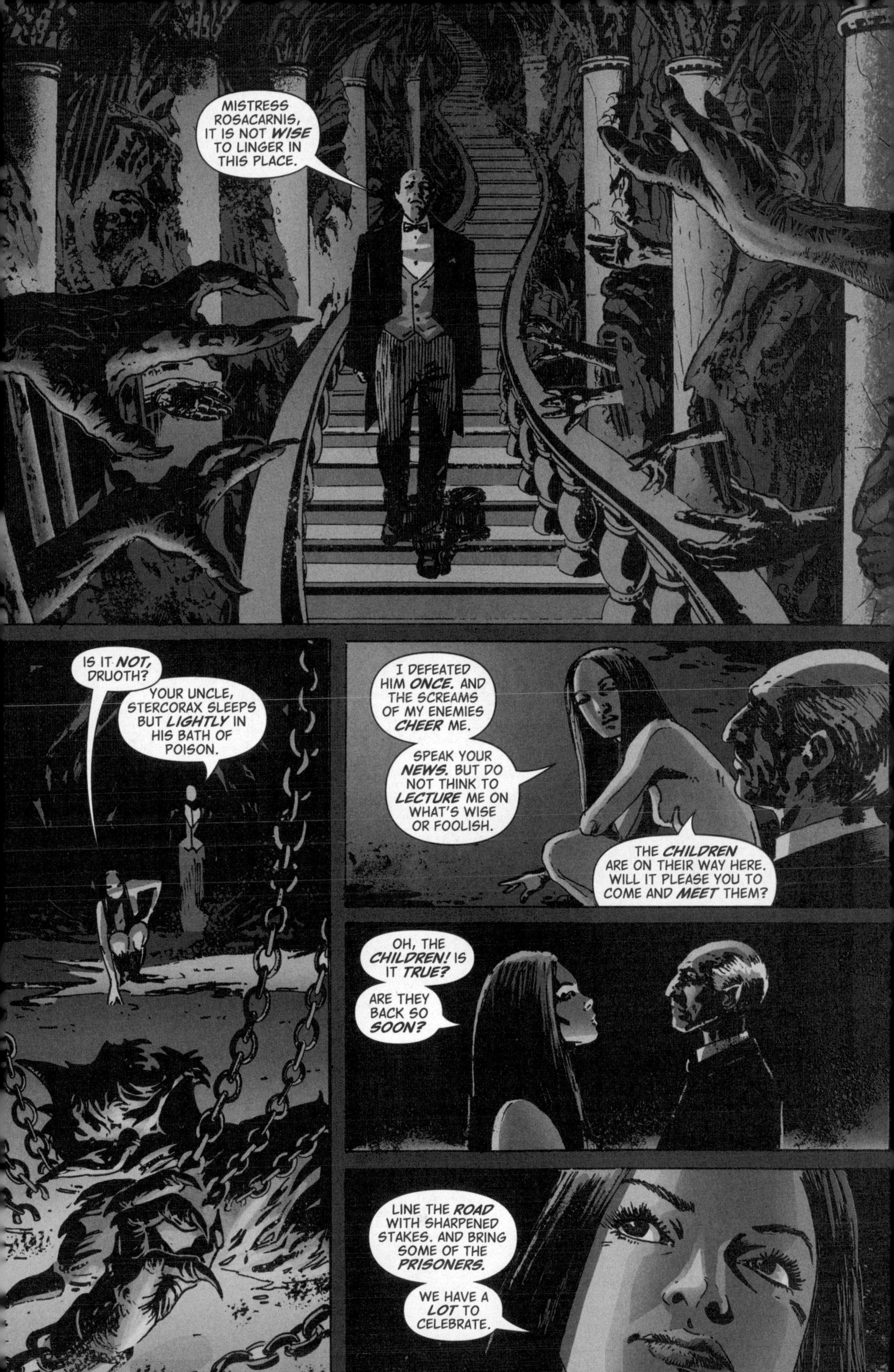
MISTRESS ROSACARNIS, IT IS NOT WISE TO LINGER IN THIS PLACE.
IS IT NOT, DRUOTH?
YOUR UNCLE, STERCORAX SLEEPS BUT LIGHTLY IN HIS BATH OF POISON.
I DEFEATED HIM ONCE. AND THE SCREAMS OF MY ENEMIES CHEER ME.
SPEAK YOUR NEWS. BUT DO NOT THINK TO LECTURE ME ON WHAT'S WISE OR FOOLISH.
THE CHILDREN ARE ON THEIR WAY HERE. WILL IT PLEASE YOU TO COME AND MEET THEM?
OH, THE CHILDREN! IS IT TRUE?
ARE THEY BACK SO SOON?
LINE THE ROAD WITH SHARPENED STAKES. AND BRING SOME OF THE PRISONERS.
WE HAVE A LOT TO CELEBRATE.

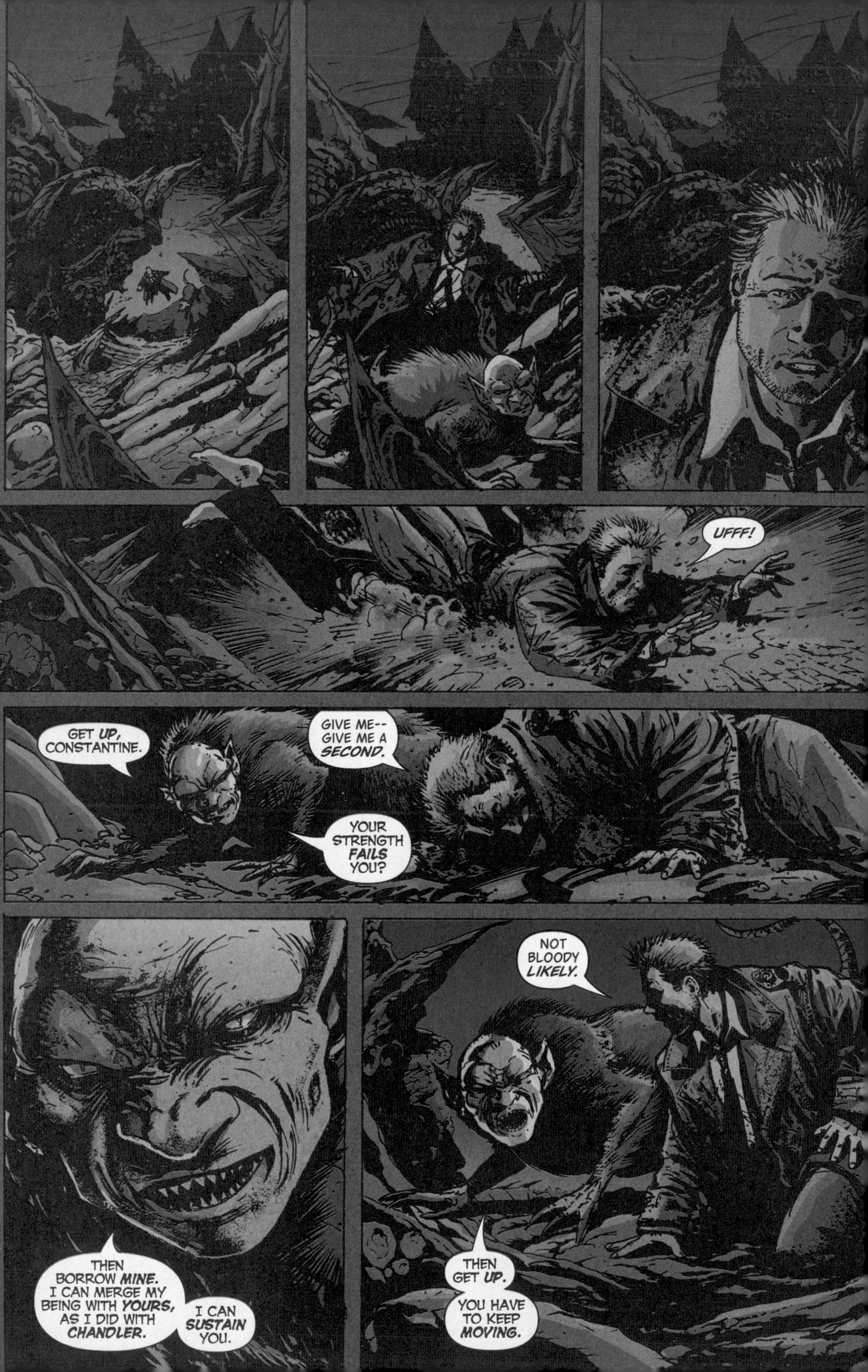
UFFF!
GET UP, CONSTANTINE.
GIVE ME-- GIVE ME A SECOND.
YOUR STRENGTH FAILS YOU?
THEN BORROW MINE. I CAN MERGE MY BEING WITH YOURS, AS I DID WITH CHANDLER.
I CAN SUSTAIN YOU.
NOT BLOODY LIKELY.
THEN GET UP.
YOU HAVE TO KEEP MOVING.

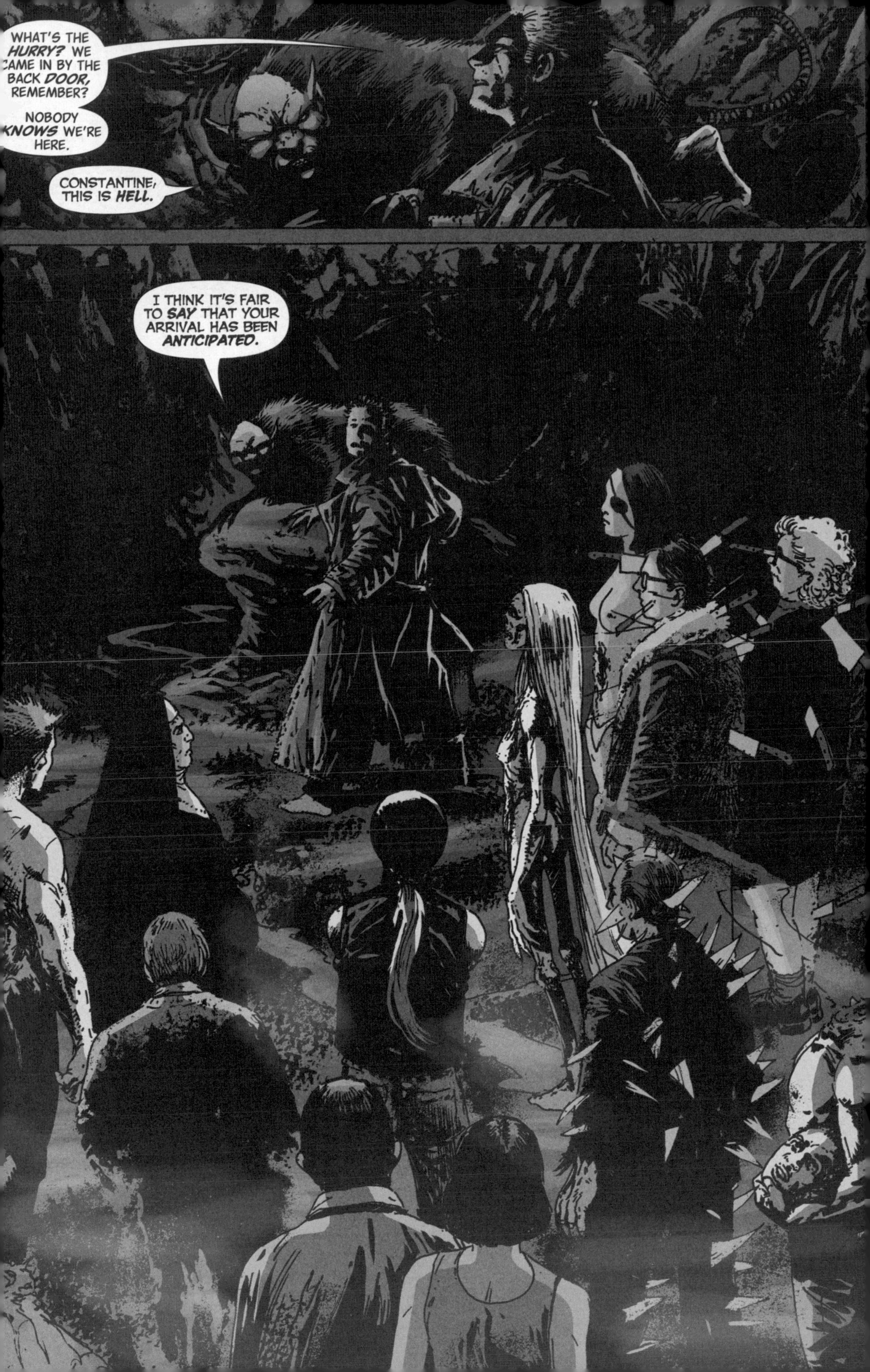
WHAT'S THE HURRY? WE CAME IN BY THE BACK DOOR, REMEMBER?
NOBODY KNOWS WE'RE HERE.
CONSTANTINE, THIS IS HELL.
I THINK IT'S FAIR TO SAY THAT YOUR ARRIVAL HAS BEEN ANTICIPATED.

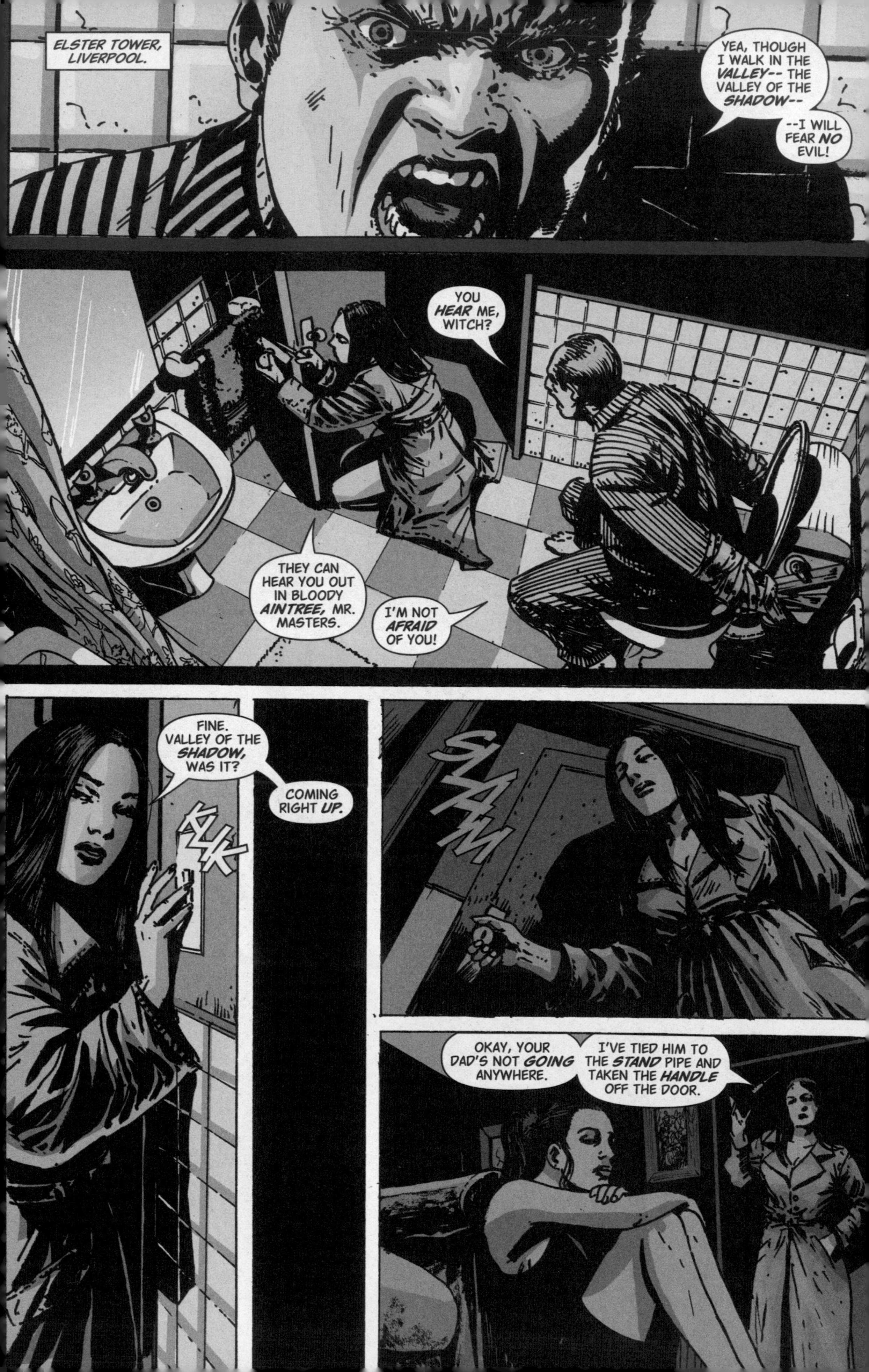
ELSTER TOWER, LIVERPOOL.
YEA, THOUGH I WALK IN THE VALLEY-- THE VALLEY OF THE SHADOW--
--I WILL FEAR NO EVIL!
YOU HEAR ME, WITCH?
THEY CAN HEAR YOU OUT IN BLOODY AINTREE, MR. MASTERS.
I'M NOT AFRAID OF YOU!
FINE. VALLEY OF THE SHADOW, WAS IT?
COMING RIGHT UP.
KLIK
SLAM
OKAY, YOUR DAD'S NOT GOING ANYWHERE.
I'VE TIED HIM TO THE STAND PIPE AND TAKEN THE HANDLE OFF THE DOOR.

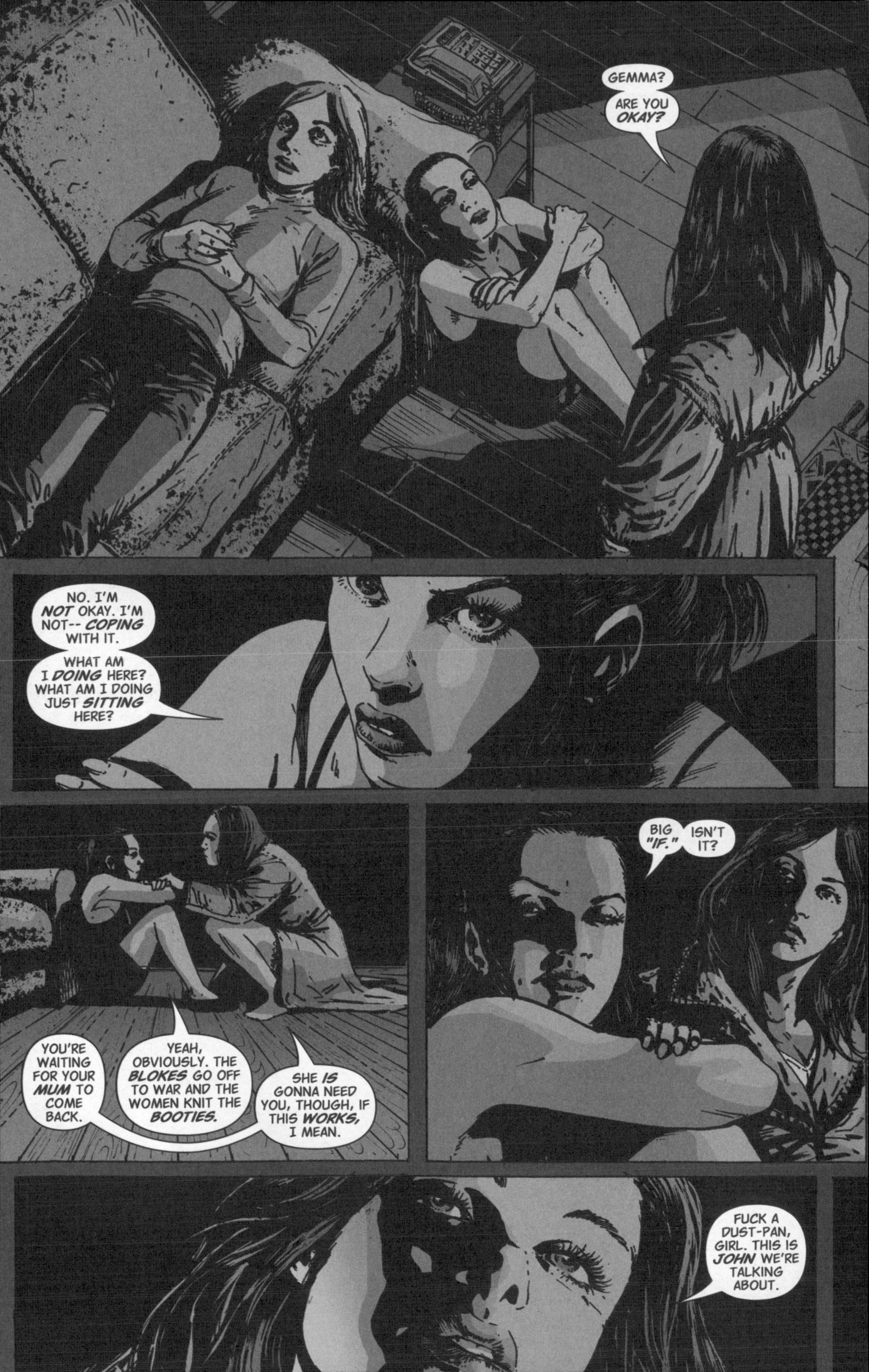
GEMMA?
ARE YOU OKAY?
NO. I'M NOT OKAY. I'M NOT-- COPING WITH IT.
WHAT AM I DOING HERE? WHAT AM I DOING JUST SITTING HERE?
YOU'RE WAITING FOR YOUR MUM TO COME BACK.
YEAH, OBVIOUSLY. THE BLOKES GO OFF TO WAR AND THE WOMEN KNIT THE BOOTIES.
SHE IS GONNA NEED YOU, THOUGH, IF THIS WORKS, I MEAN.
BIG "IF."
ISN'T IT?
FUCK A DUST-PAN, GIRL. THIS IS JOHN WE'RE TALKING ABOUT.

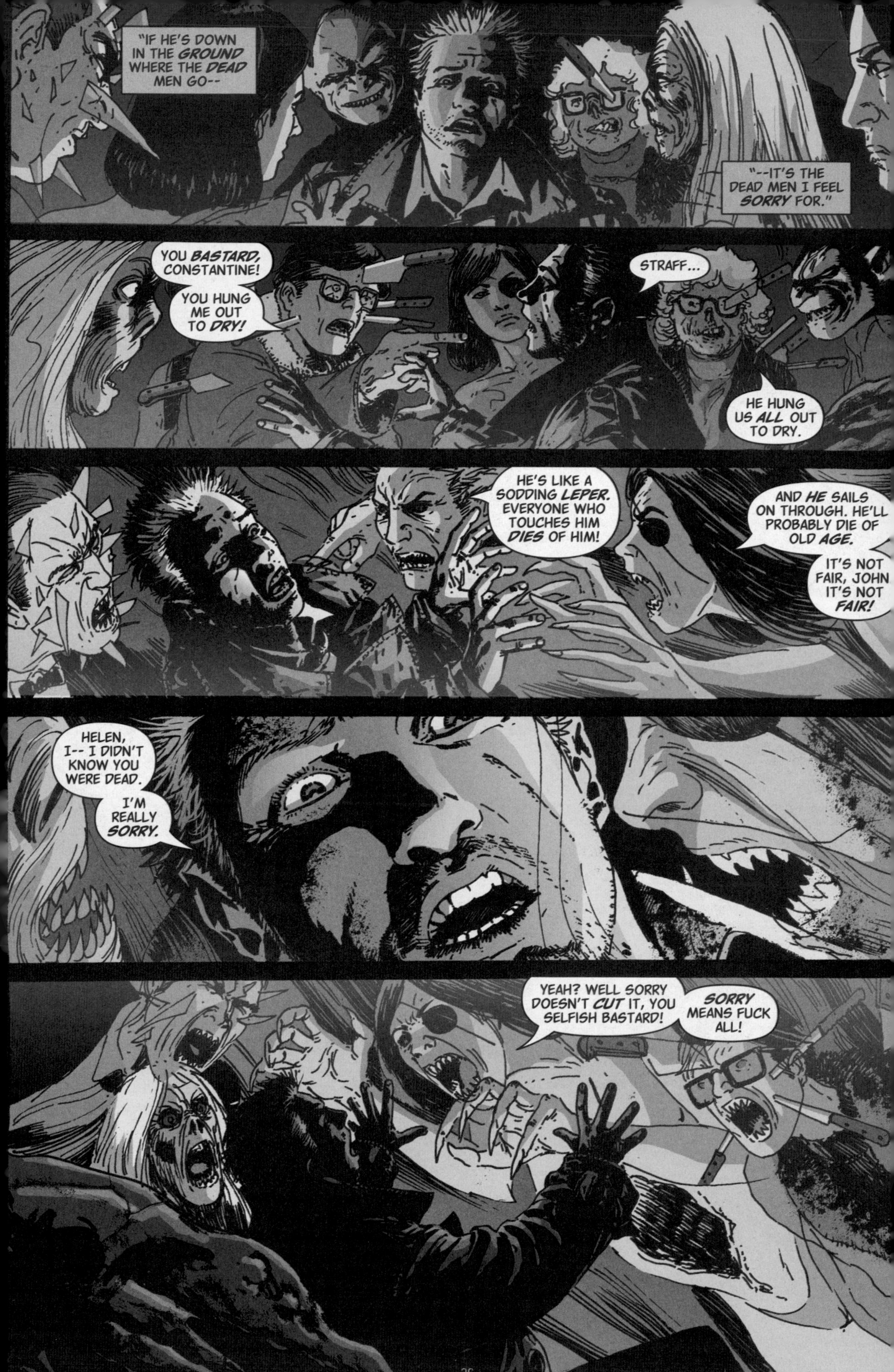
"IF HE'S DOWN IN THE GROUND WHERE THE DEAD MEN GO--
"--IT'S THE DEAD MEN I FEEL SORRY FOR."
YOU BASTARD, CONSTANTINE!
YOU HUNG ME OUT TO DRY!
STRAFF...
HE HUNG US ALL OUT TO DRY.
HE'S LIKE A SODDING LEPER. EVERYONE WHO TOUCHES HIM DIES OF HIM!
AND HE SAILS ON THROUGH. HE'LL PROBABLY DIE OF OLD AGE.
IT'S NOT FAIR, JOHN IT'S NOT FAIR!
HELEN, I-- I DIDN'T KNOW YOU WERE DEAD.
I'M REALLY SORRY.
YEAH? WELL SORRY DOESN'T CUT IT, YOU SELFISH BASTARD!
SORRY MEANS FUCK ALL!

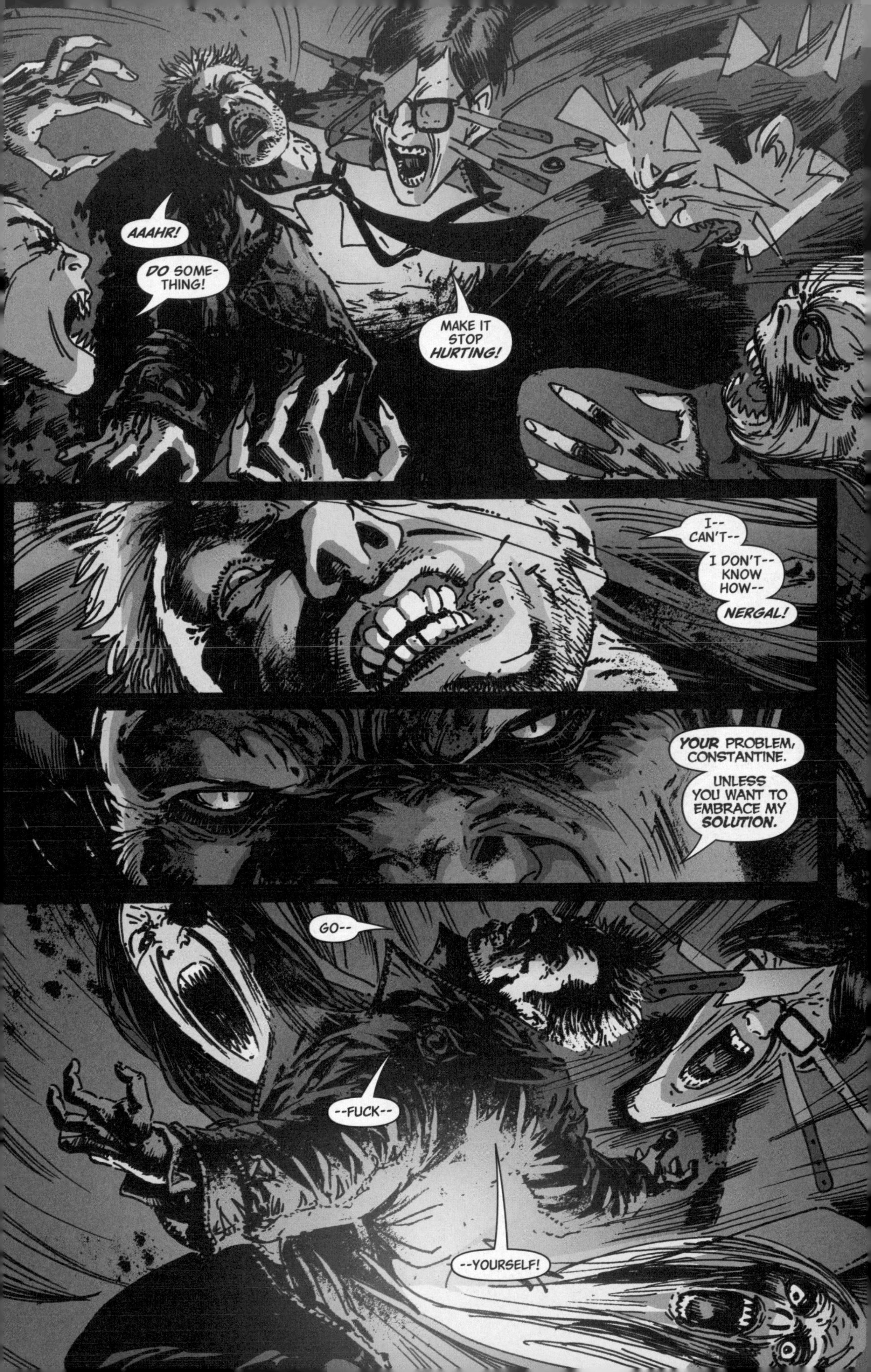
AAAHR!
DO SOME-THING!
MAKE IT STOP HURTING!
I-- CAN'T--
I DON'T-- KNOW HOW--
NERGAL!
YOUR PROBLEM, CONSTANTINE.
UNLESS YOU WANT TO EMBRACE MY SOLUTION.
GO--
--FUCK--
--YOURSELF!

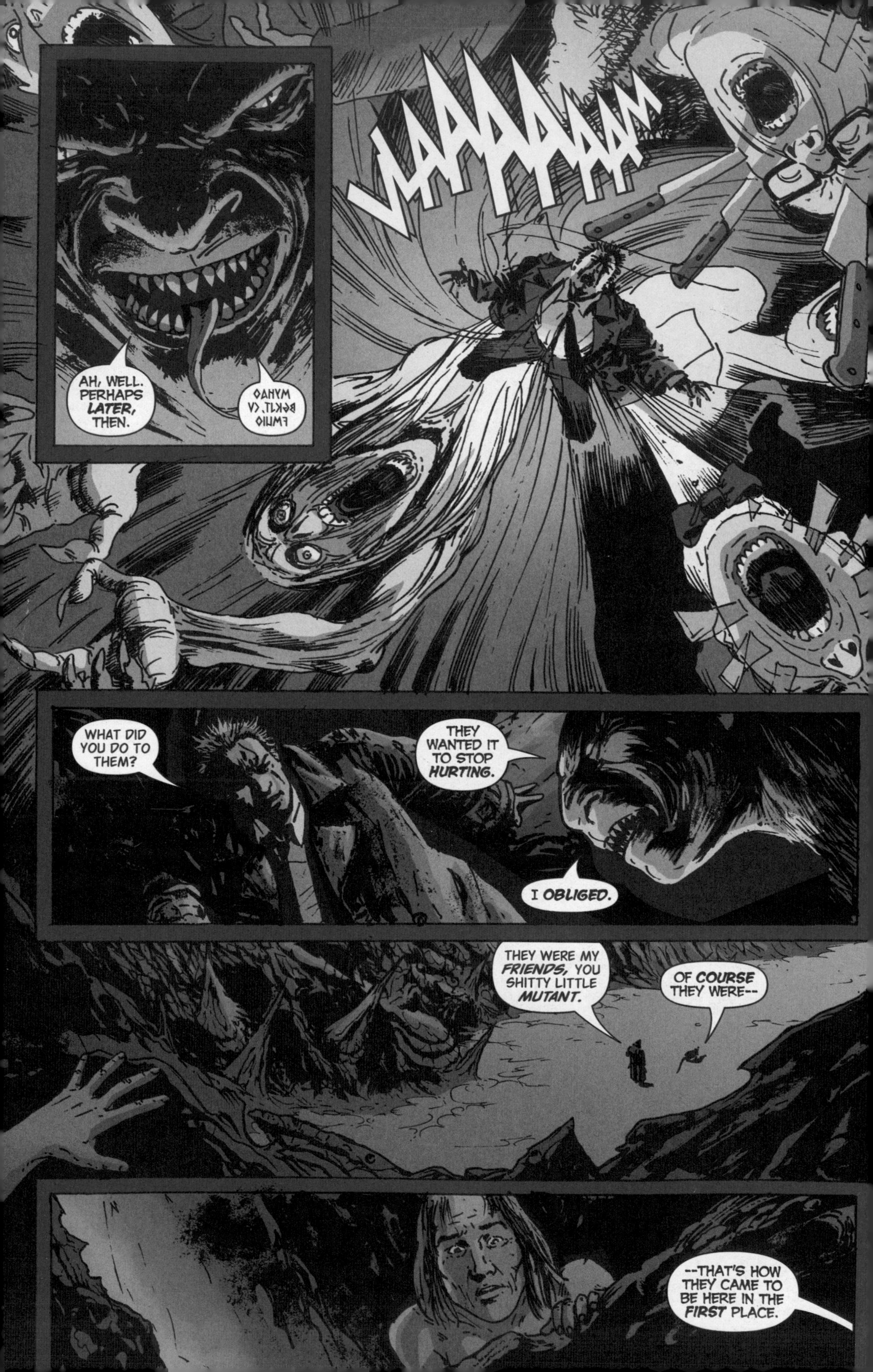
AH, WELL. PERHAPS LATER, THEN.
WHAT DID YOU DO TO THEM?
THEY WANTED IT TO STOP HURTING.
I OBLIGED.
THEY WERE MY FRIENDS, YOU SHITTY LITTLE MUTANT.
OF COURSE THEY WERE--
--THAT'S HOW THEY CAME TO BE HERE IN THE FIRST PLACE.

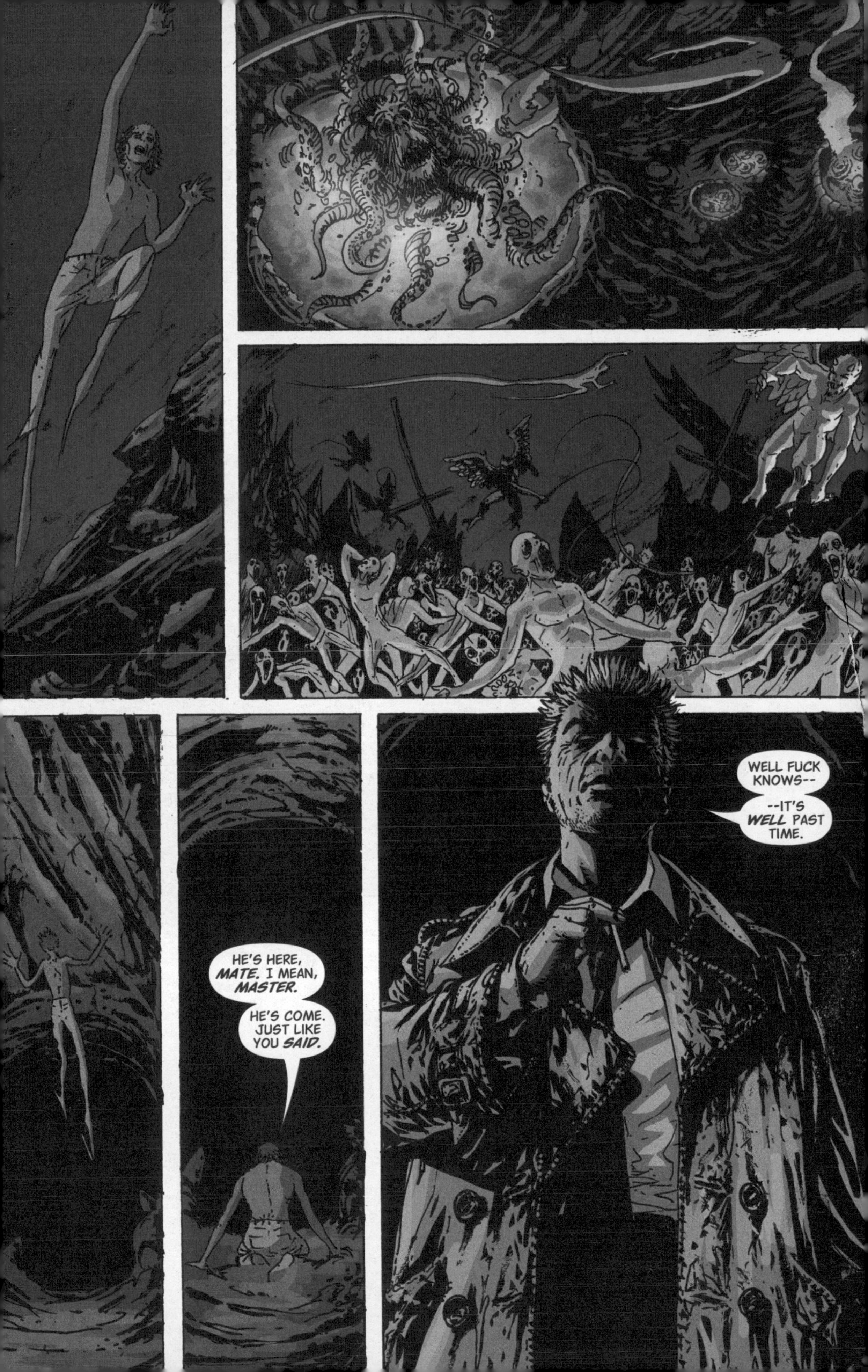

HE'S HERE, MATE. I MEAN, MASTER.
HE'S COME. JUST LIKE YOU SAID.
WELL FUCK KNOWS--
--IT'S WELL PAST TIME.

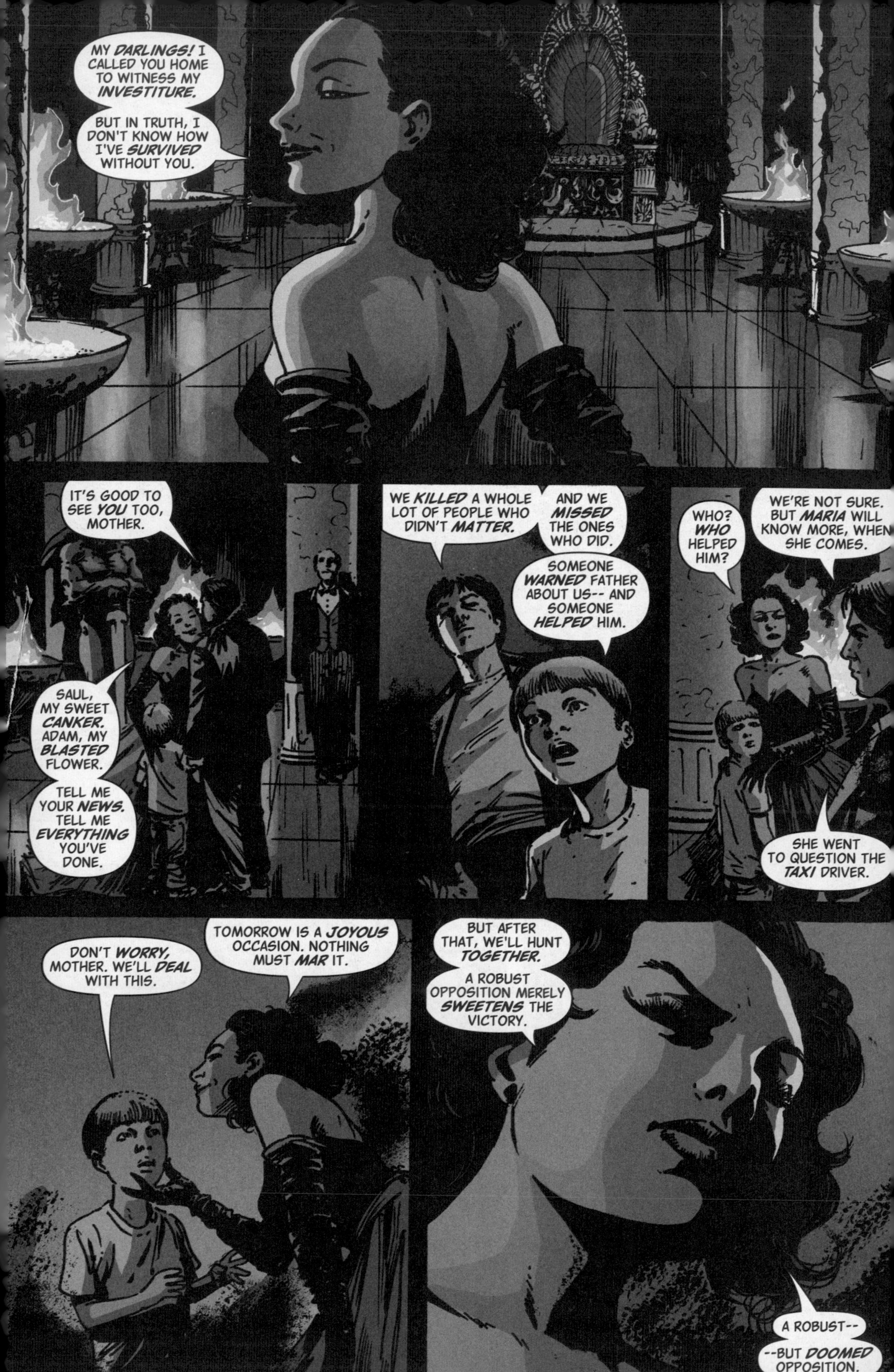
MY DARLINGS! I CALLED YOU HOME TO WITNESS MY INVESTITURE.
BUT IN TRUTH, I DON'T KNOW HOW I'VE SURVIVED WITHOUT YOU.
IT'S GOOD TO SEE YOU TOO, MOTHER.
SAUL, MY SWEET CANKER. ADAM, MY BLASTED FLOWER.
TELL ME YOUR NEWS. TELL ME EVERYTHING YOU'VE DONE.
WE KILLED A WHOLE LOT OF PEOPLE WHO DIDN'T MATTER.
AND WE MISSED THE ONES WHO DID.
SOMEONE WARNED FATHER ABOUT US-- AND SOMEONE HELPED HIM.
WHO? WHO HELPED HIM?
WE'RE NOT SURE. BUT MARIA WILL KNOW MORE, WHEN SHE COMES.
SHE WENT TO QUESTION THE TAXI DRIVER.
DON'T WORRY, MOTHER. WE'LL DEAL WITH THIS.
TOMORROW IS A JOYOUS OCCASION. NOTHING MUST MAR IT.
BUT AFTER THAT, WE'LL HUNT TOGETHER.
A ROBUST OPPOSITION MERELY SWEETENS THE VICTORY.
A ROBUST--
--BUT DOOMED OPPOSITION.

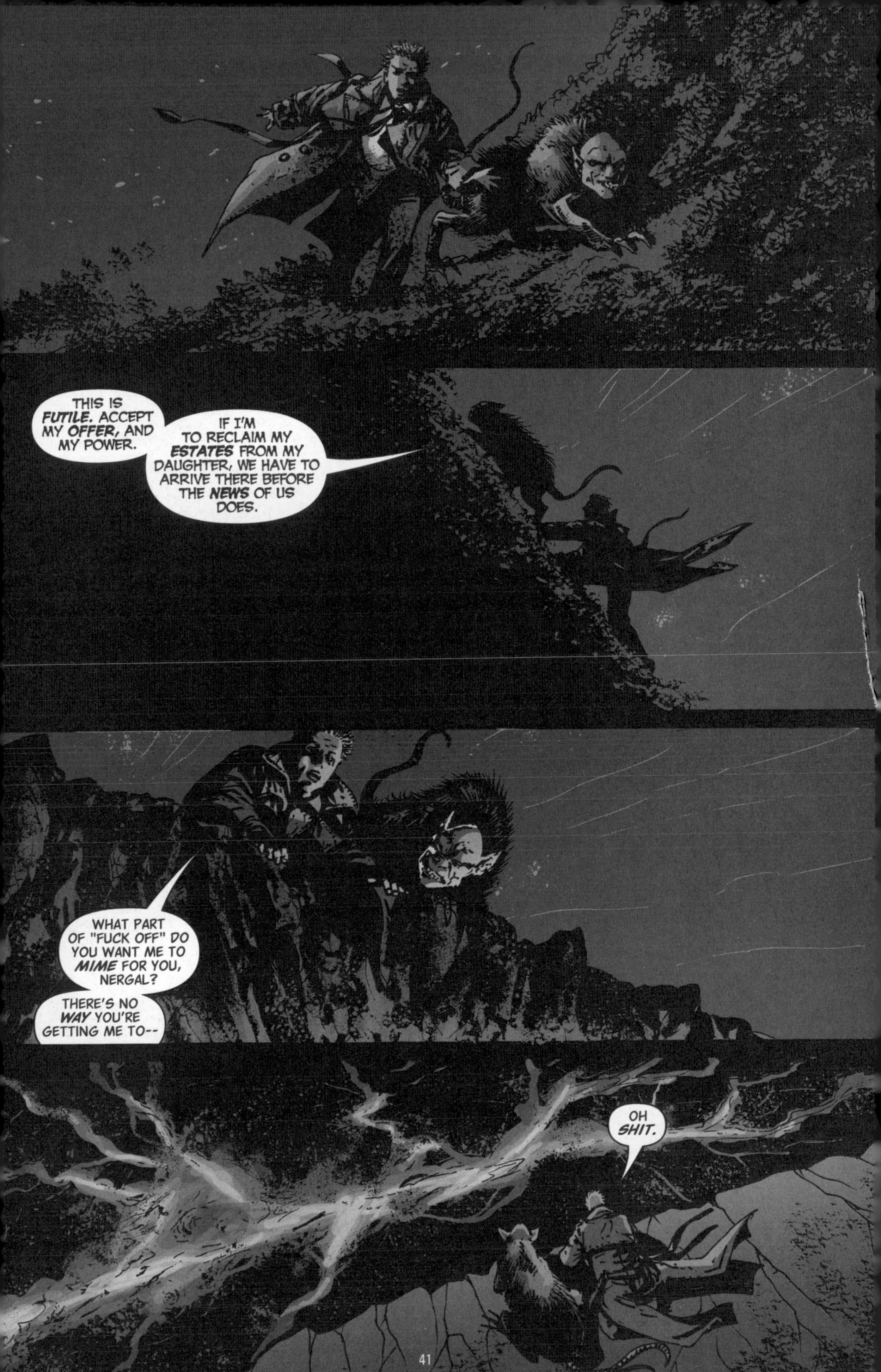
THIS IS FUTILE. ACCEPT MY OFFER, AND MY POWER.
IF I'M TO RECLAIM MY ESTATES FROM MY DAUGHTER, WE HAVE TO ARRIVE THERE BEFORE THE NEWS OF US DOES.
WHAT PART OF "FUCK OFF" DO YOU WANT ME TO MIME FOR YOU, NERGAL?
THERE'S NO WAY YOU'RE GETTING ME TO--
OH SHIT.

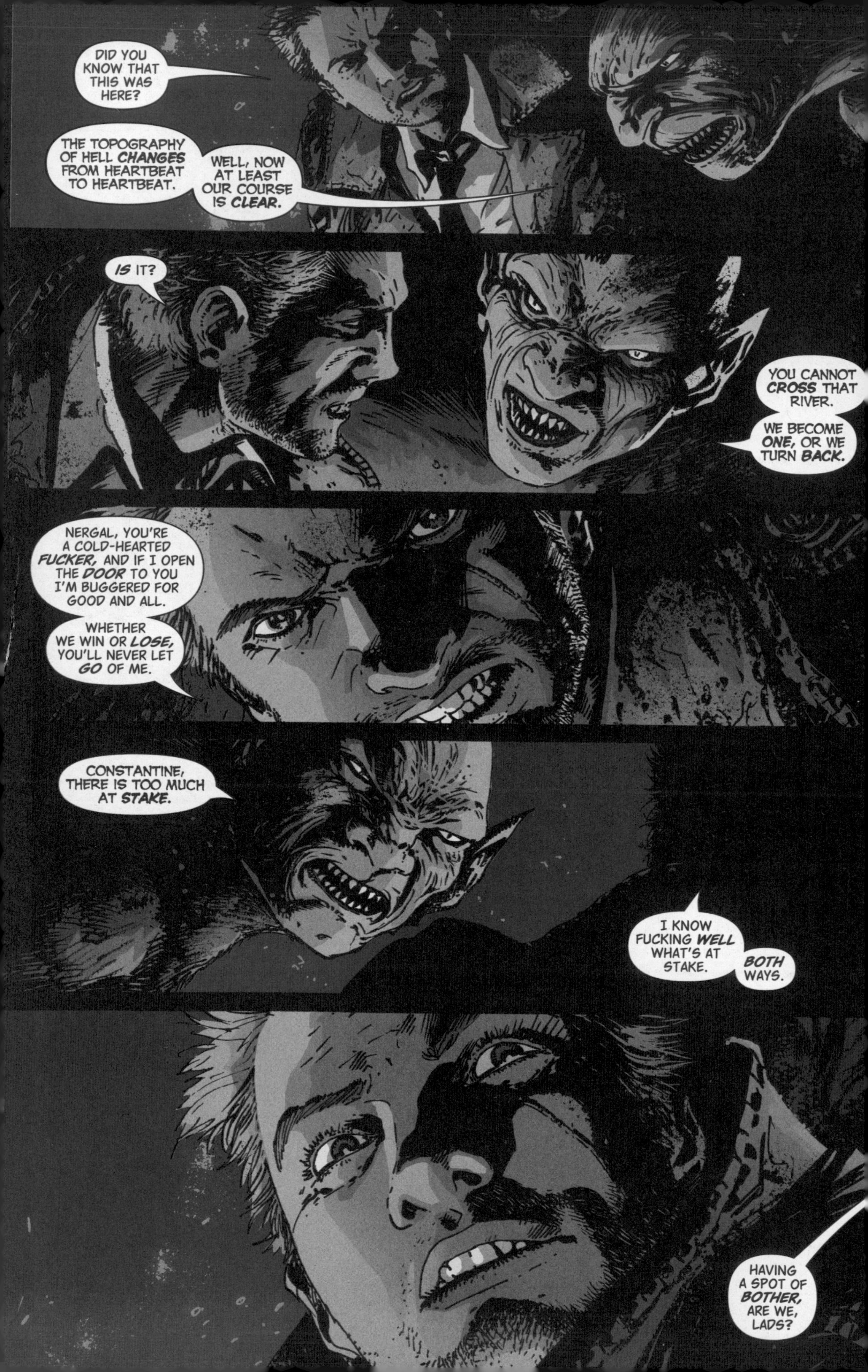
DID YOU KNOW THAT THIS WAS HERE?
THE TOPOGRAPHY OF HELL CHANGES FROM HEARTBEAT TO HEARTBEAT.
WELL, NOW AT LEAST OUR COURSE IS CLEAR.
IS IT?
YOU CANNOT CROSS THAT RIVER.
WE BECOME ONE, OR WE TURN BACK.
NERGAL, YOU'RE A COLD-HEARTED FUCKER, AND IF I OPEN THE DOOR TO YOU I'M BUGGERED FOR GOOD AND ALL.
WHETHER WE WIN OR LOSE, YOU'LL NEVER LET GO OF ME.
CONSTANTINE, THERE IS TOO MUCH AT STAKE.
I KNOW FUCKING WELL WHAT'S AT STAKE.
BOTH WAYS.
HAVING A SPOT OF BOTHER, ARE WE, LADS?

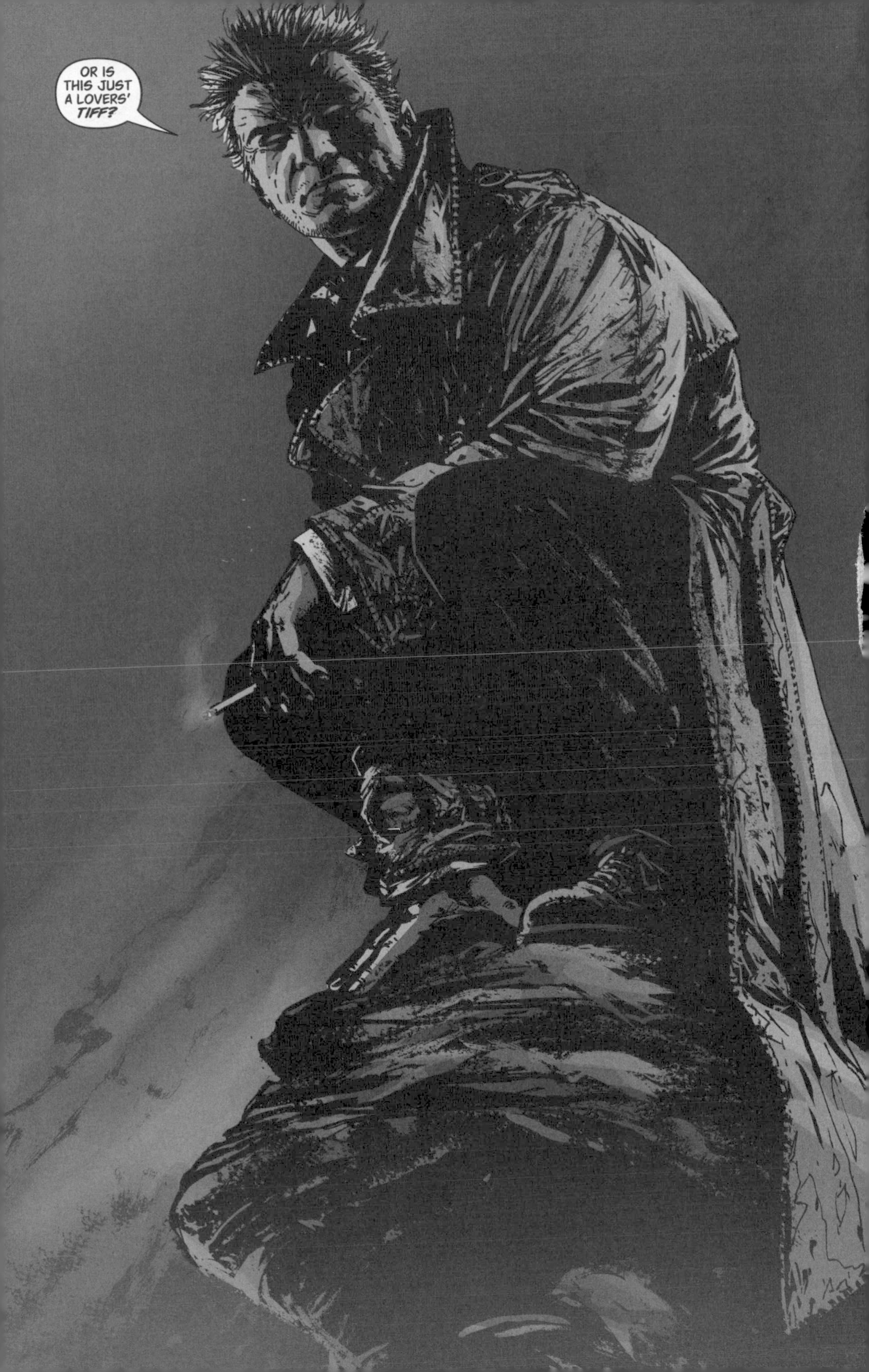
OR IS THIS JUST A LOVERS' *TIFF?*

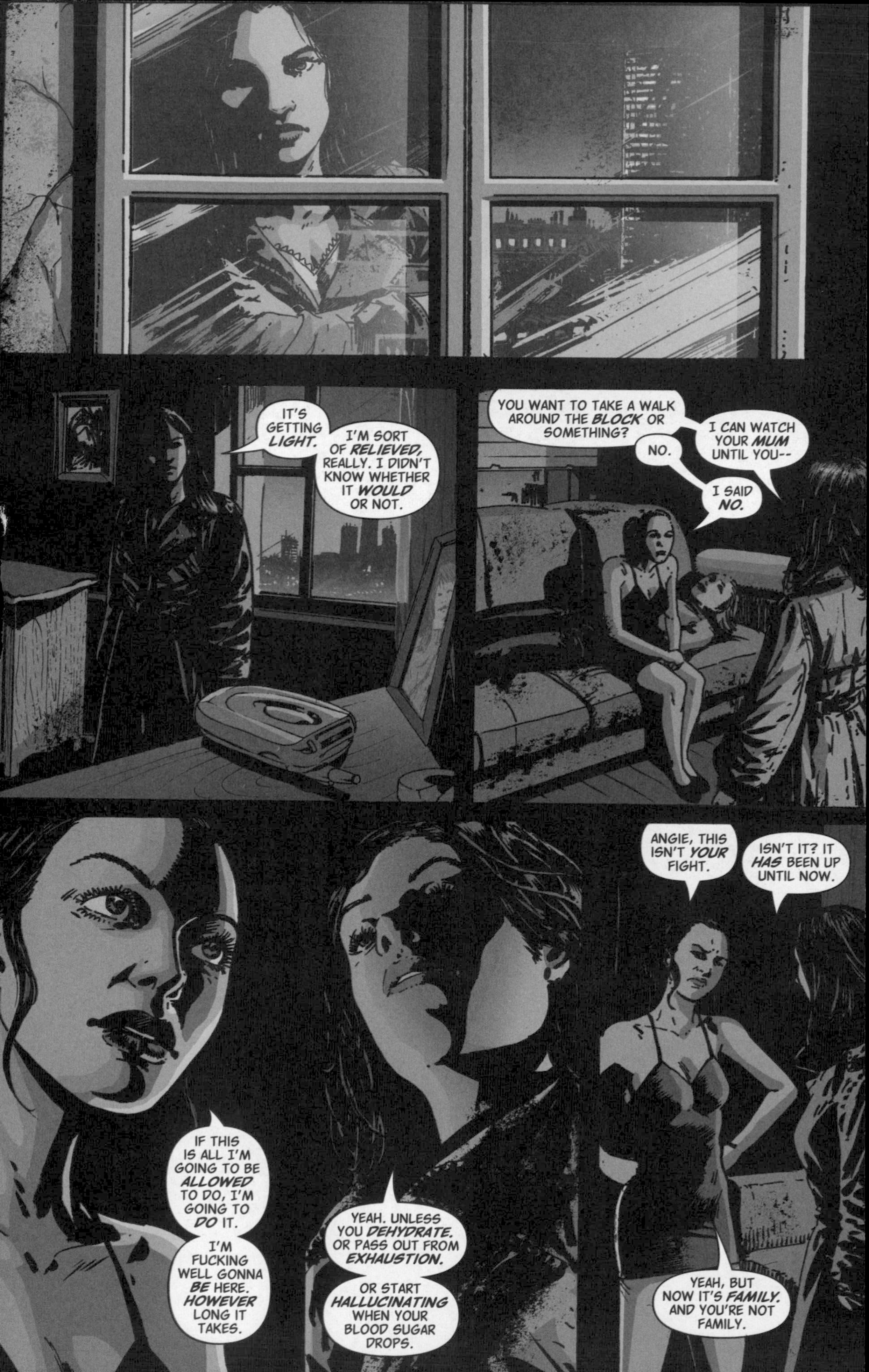

IT'S GETTING LIGHT.
I'M SORT OF RELIEVED, REALLY. I DIDN'T KNOW WHETHER IT WOULD OR NOT.
YOU WANT TO TAKE A WALK AROUND THE BLOCK OR SOMETHING?
NO.
I CAN WATCH YOUR MUM UNTIL YOU--
I SAID NO.
IF THIS IS ALL I'M GOING TO BE ALLOWED TO DO, I'M GOING TO DO IT.
I'M FUCKING WELL GONNA BE HERE. HOWEVER LONG IT TAKES.
YEAH. UNLESS YOU DEHYDRATE, OR PASS OUT FROM EXHAUSTION.
OR START HALLUCINATING WHEN YOUR BLOOD SUGAR DROPS.
ANGIE, THIS ISN'T YOUR FIGHT.
ISN'T IT? IT HAS BEEN UP UNTIL NOW.
YEAH, BUT NOW IT'S FAMILY. AND YOU'RE NOT FAMILY.

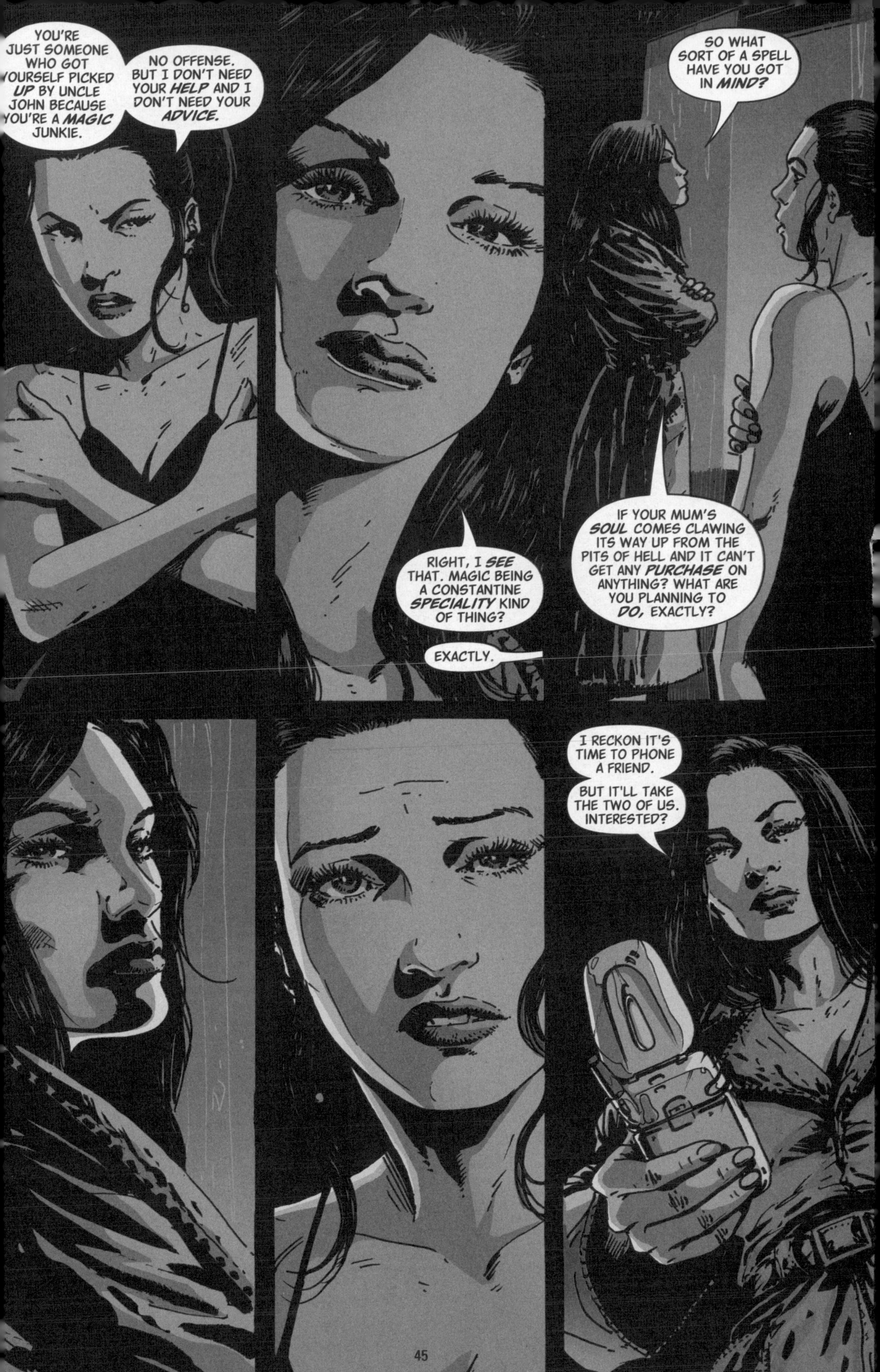
YOU'RE JUST SOMEONE WHO GOT YOURSELF PICKED UP BY UNCLE JOHN BECAUSE YOU'RE A MAGIC JUNKIE.
NO OFFENSE. BUT I DON'T NEED YOUR HELP AND I DON'T NEED YOUR ADVICE.
RIGHT, I SEE THAT. MAGIC BEING A CONSTANTINE SPECIALITY KIND OF THING?
EXACTLY.
SO WHAT SORT OF A SPELL HAVE YOU GOT IN MIND?
IF YOUR MUM'S SOUL COMES CLAWING ITS WAY UP FROM THE PITS OF HELL AND IT CAN'T GET ANY PURCHASE ON ANYTHING? WHAT ARE YOU PLANNING TO DO, EXACTLY?
I RECKON IT'S TIME TO PHONE A FRIEND.
BUT IT'LL TAKE THE TWO OF US. INTERESTED?

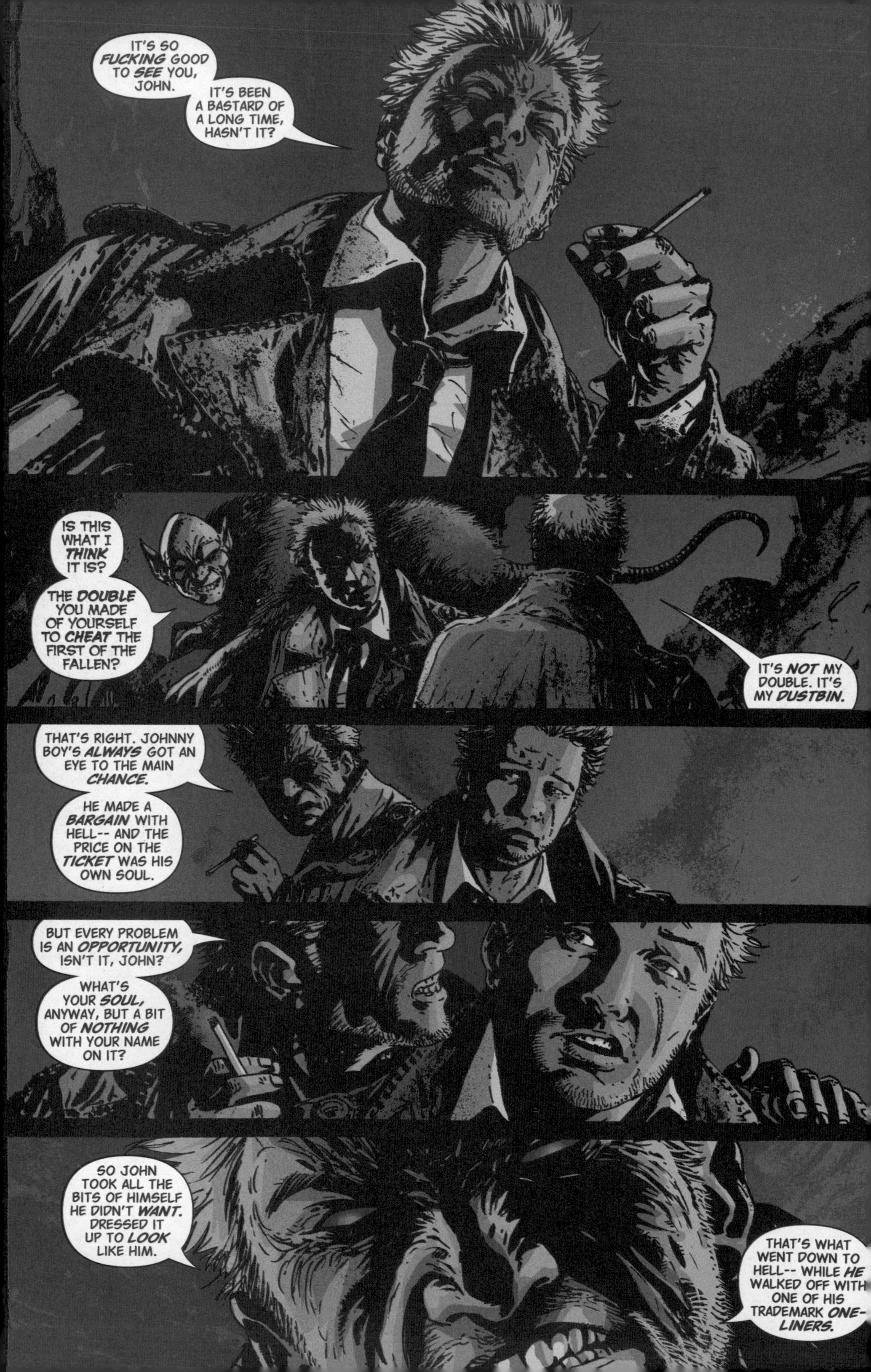
IT'S SO FUCKING GOOD TO SEE YOU, JOHN.
IT'S BEEN A BASTARD OF A LONG TIME, HASN'T IT?
IS THIS WHAT I THINK IT IS?
THE DOUBLE YOU MADE OF YOURSELF TO CHEAT THE FIRST OF THE FALLEN?
IT'S NOT MY DOUBLE. IT'S MY DUSTBIN.
THAT'S RIGHT. JOHNNY BOY'S ALWAYS GOT AN EYE TO THE MAIN CHANCE.
HE MADE A BARGAIN WITH HELL-- AND THE PRICE ON THE TICKET WAS HIS OWN SOUL.
BUT EVERY PROBLEM IS AN OPPORTUNITY, ISN'T IT, JOHN?
WHAT'S YOUR SOUL, ANYWAY, BUT A BIT OF NOTHING WITH YOUR NAME ON IT?
SO JOHN TOOK ALL THE BITS OF HIMSELF HE DIDN'T WANT. DRESSED IT UP TO LOOK LIKE HIM.
THAT'S WHAT WENT DOWN TO HELL-- WHILE HE WALKED OFF WITH ONE OF HIS TRADEMARK ONE-LINERS.

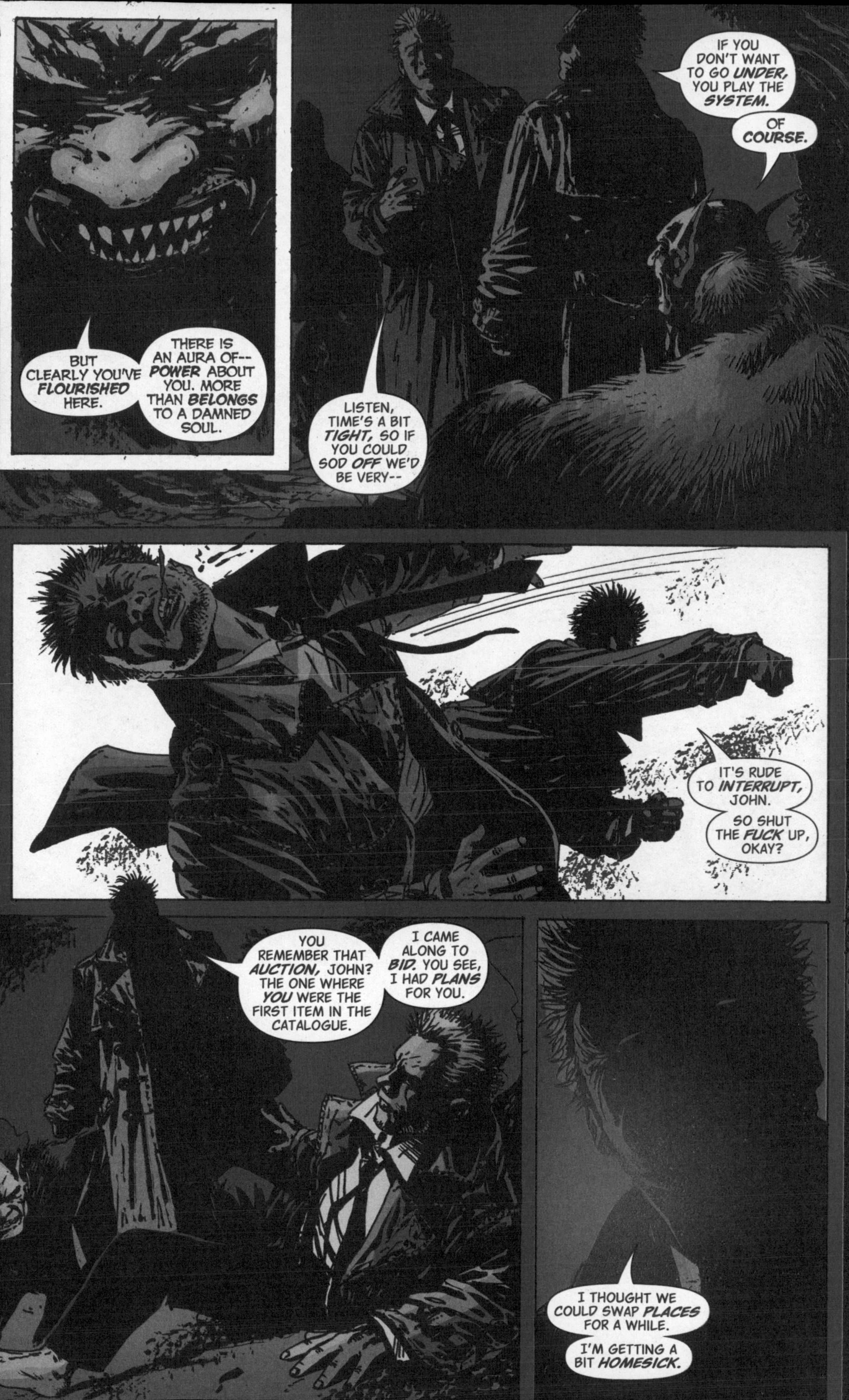
BUT CLEARLY YOU'VE FLOURISHED HERE.
THERE IS AN AURA OF-- POWER ABOUT YOU. MORE THAN BELONGS TO A DAMNED SOUL.
IF YOU DON'T WANT TO GO UNDER, YOU PLAY THE SYSTEM.
OF COURSE.
LISTEN, TIME'S A BIT TIGHT, SO IF YOU COULD SOD OFF WE'D BE VERY--
IT'S RUDE TO INTERRUPT, JOHN.
SO SHUT THE FUCK UP, OKAY?
YOU REMEMBER THAT AUCTION, JOHN? THE ONE WHERE YOU WERE THE FIRST ITEM IN THE CATALOGUE.
I CAME ALONG TO BID. YOU SEE, I HAD PLANS FOR YOU.
I THOUGHT WE COULD SWAP PLACES FOR A WHILE.
I'M GETTING A BIT HOMESICK.

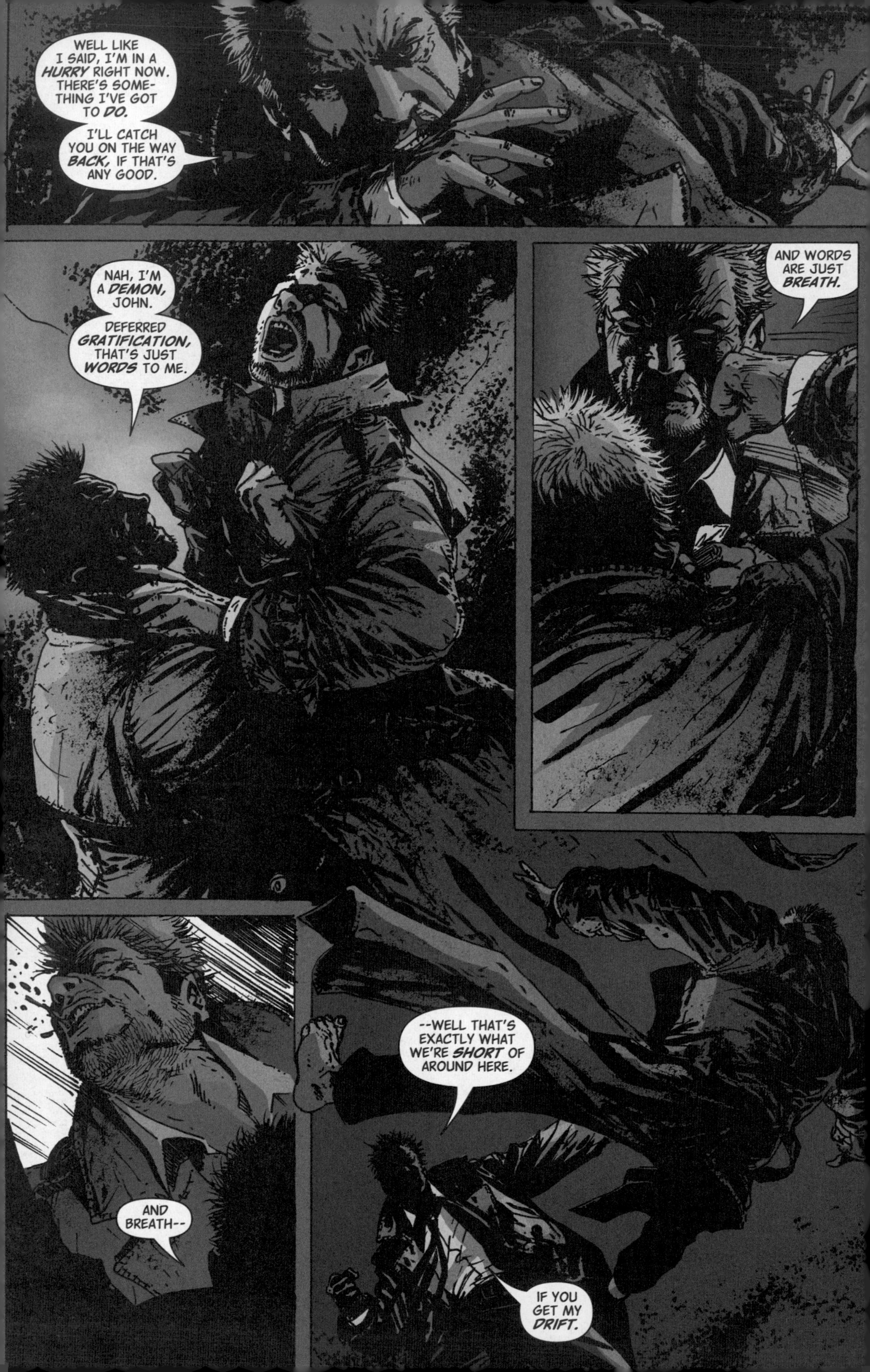
WELL LIKE I SAID, I'M IN A HURRY RIGHT NOW. THERE'S SOME-THING I'VE GOT TO DO.
I'LL CATCH YOU ON THE WAY BACK, IF THAT'S ANY GOOD.
NAH, I'M A DEMON, JOHN.
DEFERRED GRATIFICATION, THAT'S JUST WORDS TO ME.
AND WORDS ARE JUST BREATH.
AND BREATH--
--WELL THAT'S EXACTLY WHAT WE'RE SHORT OF AROUND HERE.
IF YOU GET MY DRIFT.

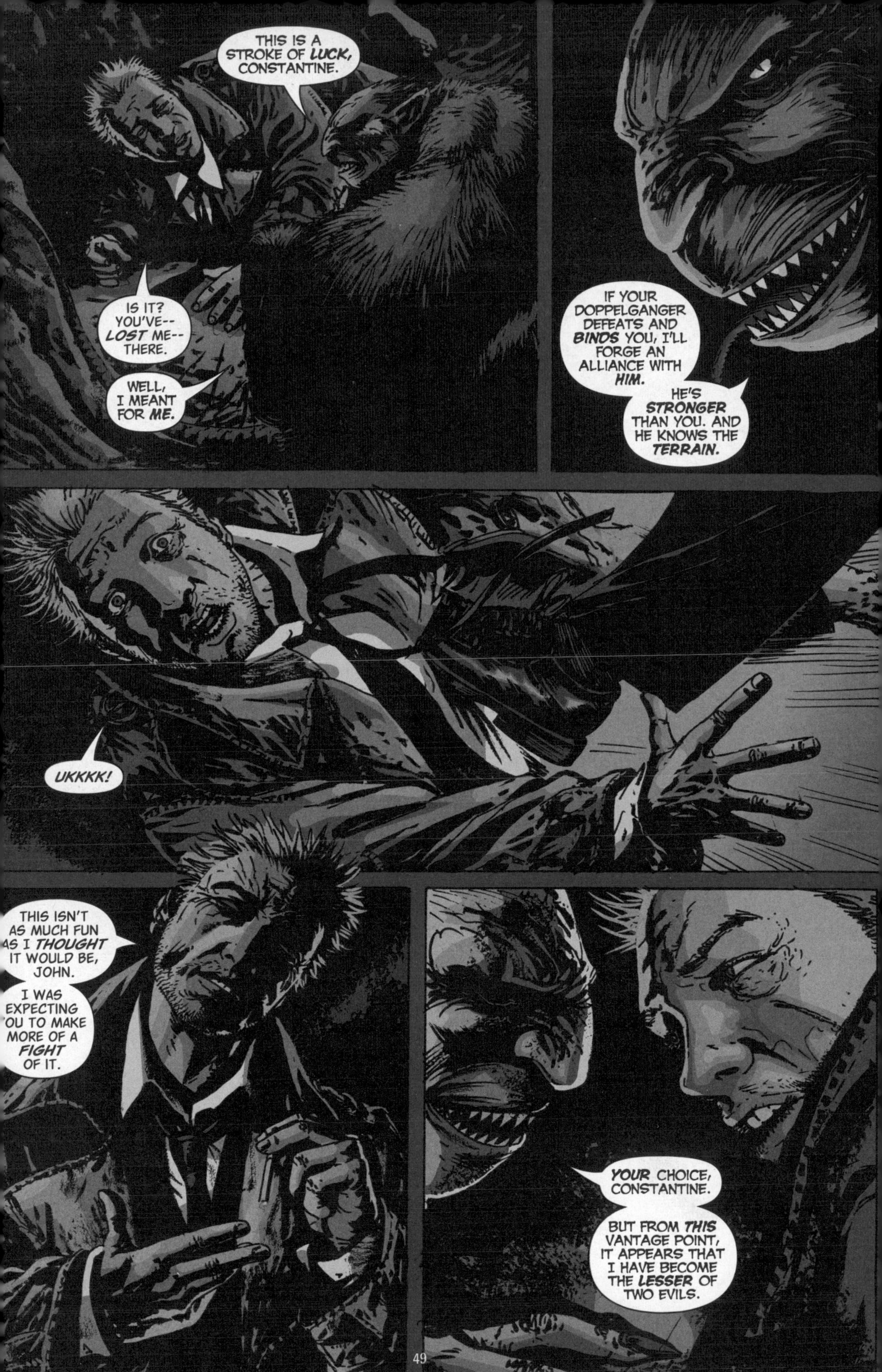
THIS IS A STROKE OF LUCK, CONSTANTINE.
IS IT? YOU'VE-- LOST ME-- THERE.
WELL, I MEANT FOR ME.
IF YOUR DOPPELGANGER DEFEATS AND BINDS YOU, I'LL FORGE AN ALLIANCE WITH HIM.
HE'S STRONGER THAN YOU. AND HE KNOWS THE TERRAIN.
UKKKK!
THIS ISN'T AS MUCH FUN AS I THOUGHT IT WOULD BE, JOHN.
I WAS EXPECTING YOU TO MAKE MORE OF A FIGHT OF IT.
YOUR CHOICE, CONSTANTINE.
BUT FROM THIS VANTAGE POINT, IT APPEARS THAT I HAVE BECOME THE LESSER OF TWO EVILS.

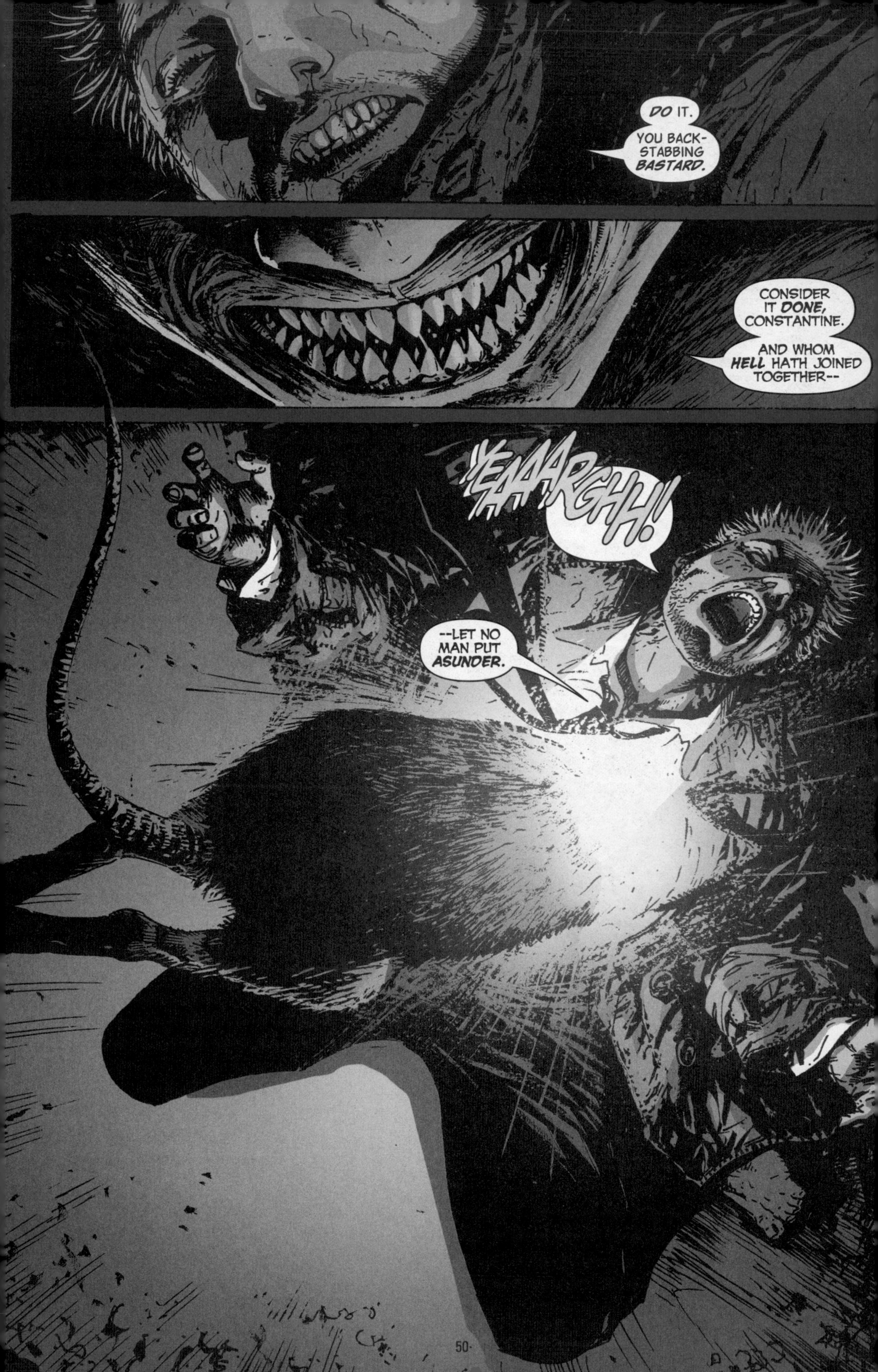
DO IT.
YOU BACK-STABBING BASTARD.
CONSIDER IT DONE, CONSTANTINE.
AND WHOM HELL HATH JOINED TOGETHER--
YEAAARGHH!
--LET NO MAN PUT ASUNDER.

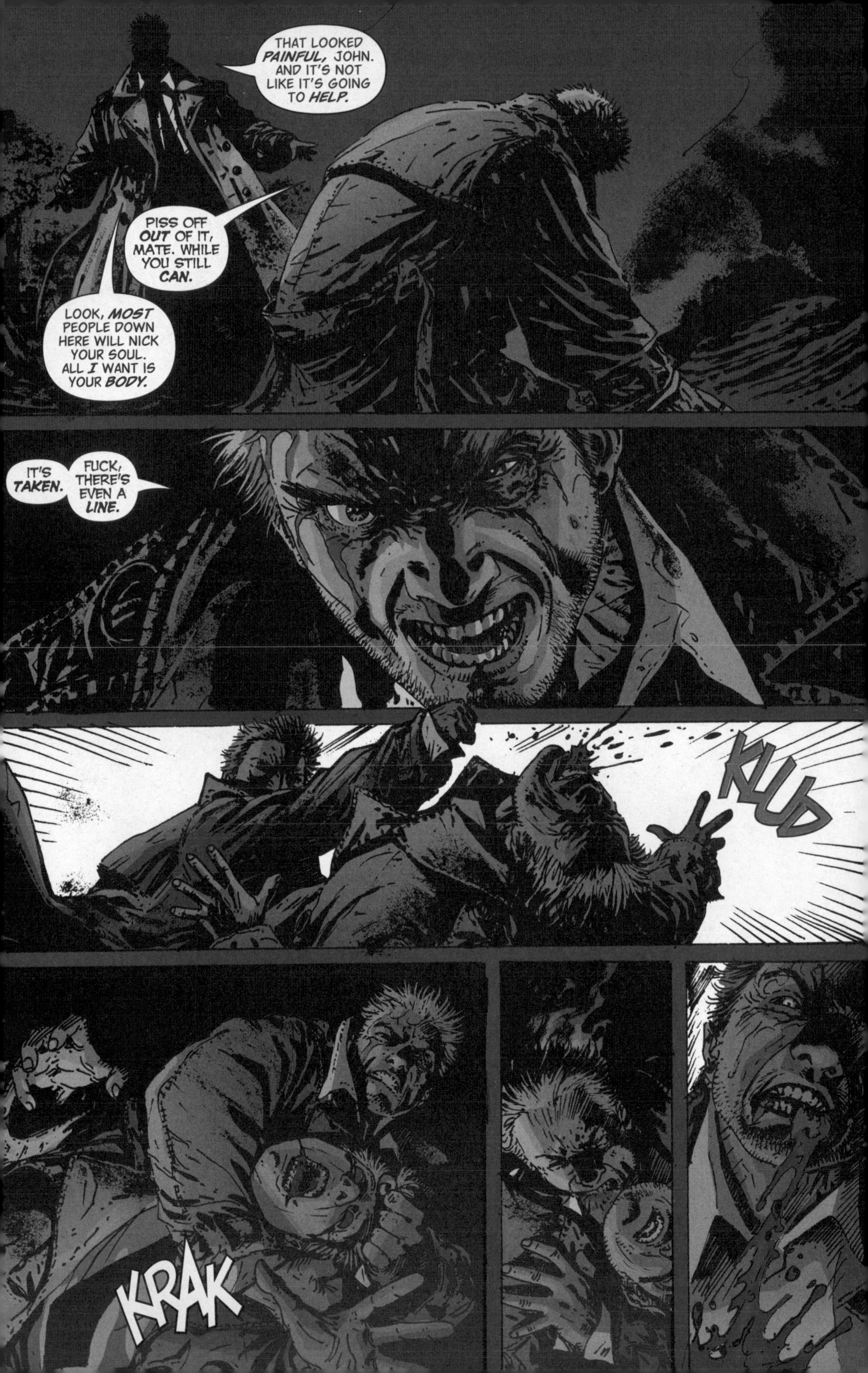
THAT LOOKED PAINFUL, JOHN. AND IT'S NOT LIKE IT'S GOING TO HELP.
PISS OFF OUT OF IT, MATE. WHILE YOU STILL CAN.
LOOK, MOST PEOPLE DOWN HERE WILL NICK YOUR SOUL. ALL I WANT IS YOUR BODY.
IT'S TAKEN.
FUCK, THERE'S EVEN A LINE.
KLUD
KRAK

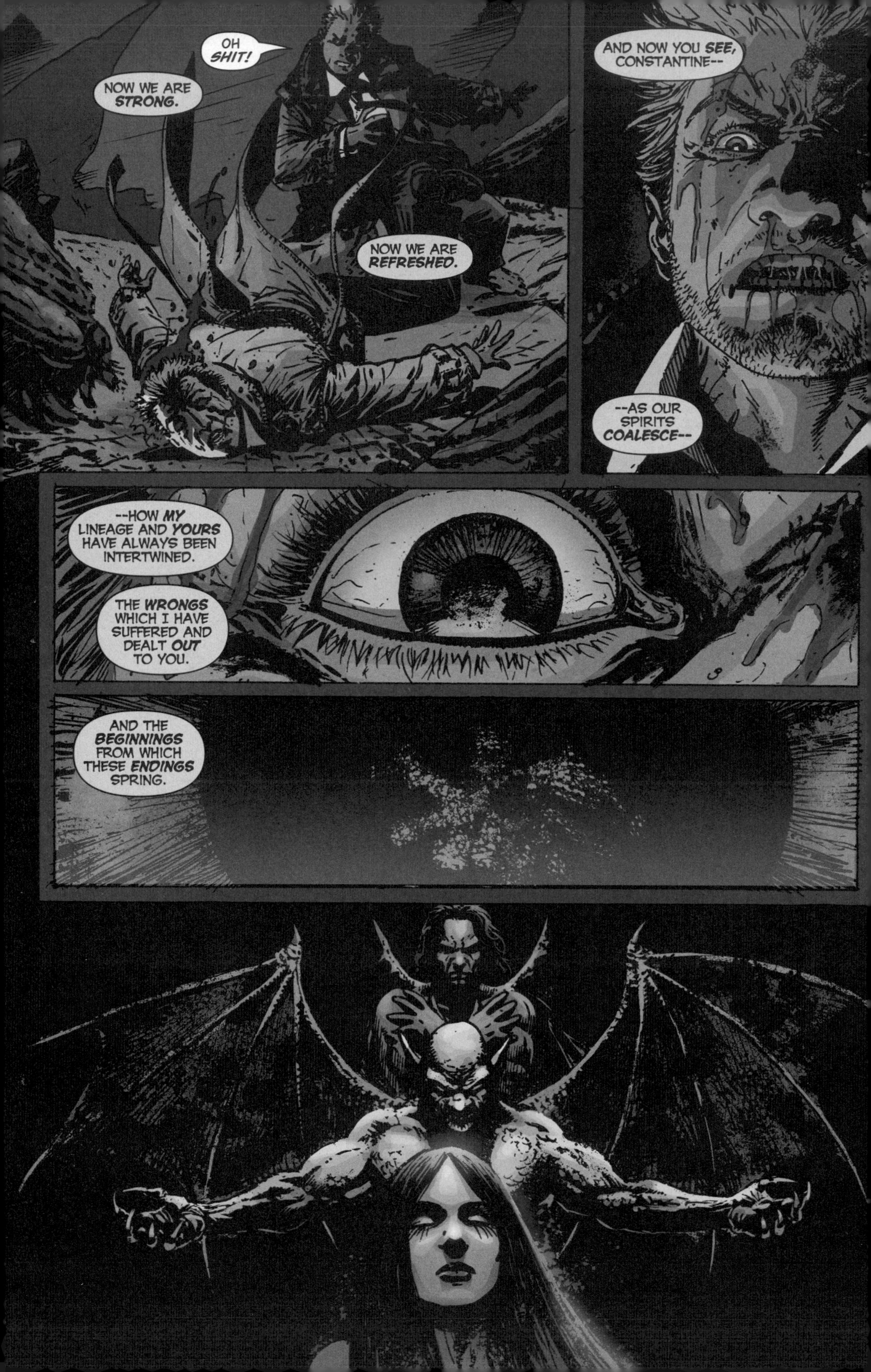
OH SHIT!
NOW WE ARE STRONG.
NOW WE ARE REFRESHED.
AND NOW YOU SEE, CONSTANTINE--
--AS OUR SPIRITS COALESCE--
--HOW MY LINEAGE AND YOURS HAVE ALWAYS BEEN INTERTWINED.
THE WRONGS WHICH I HAVE SUFFERED AND DEALT OUT TO YOU.
AND THE BEGINNINGS FROM WHICH THESE ENDINGS SPRING.

Down in the Ground Where the Dead Men Go CHAPTER THREE

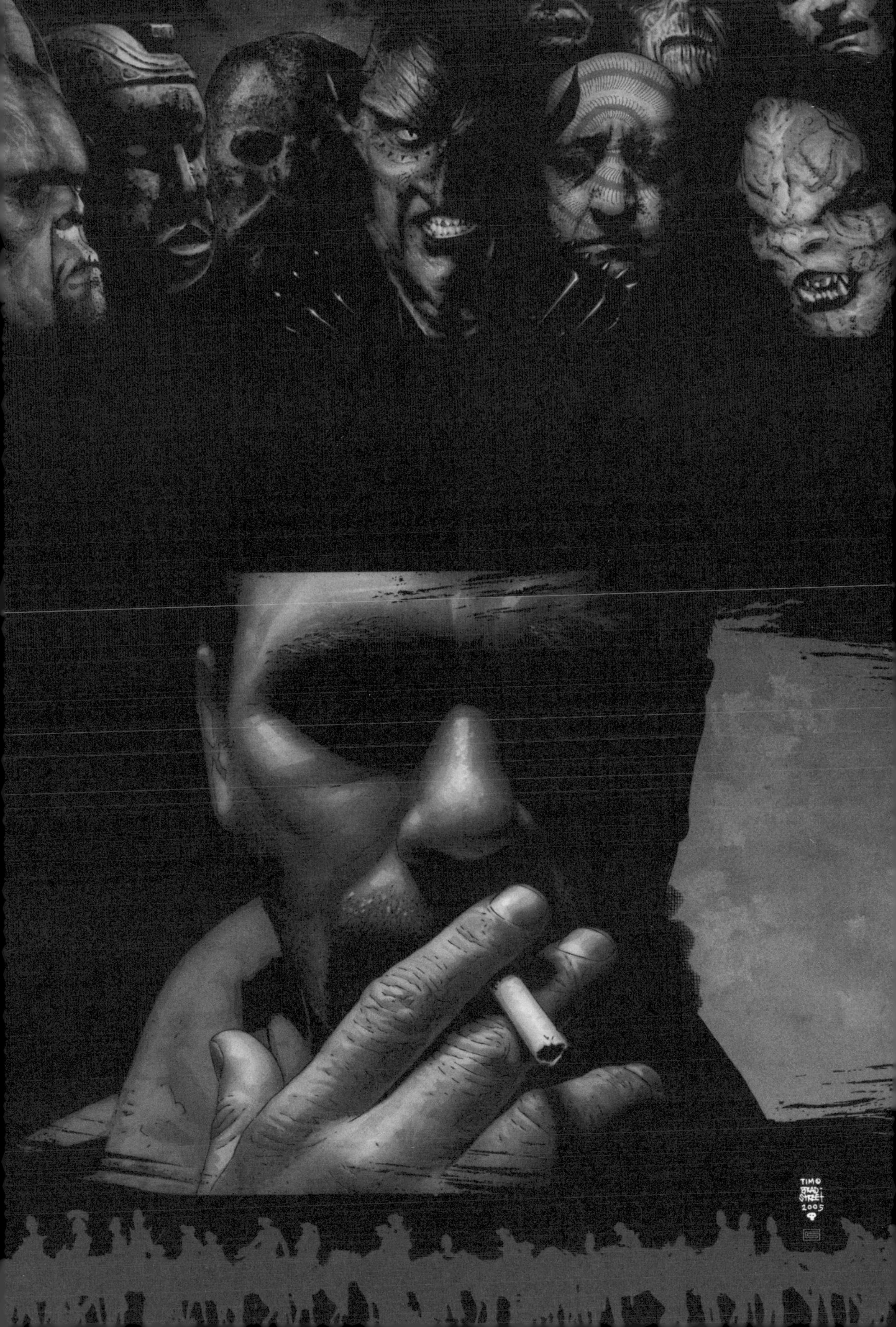

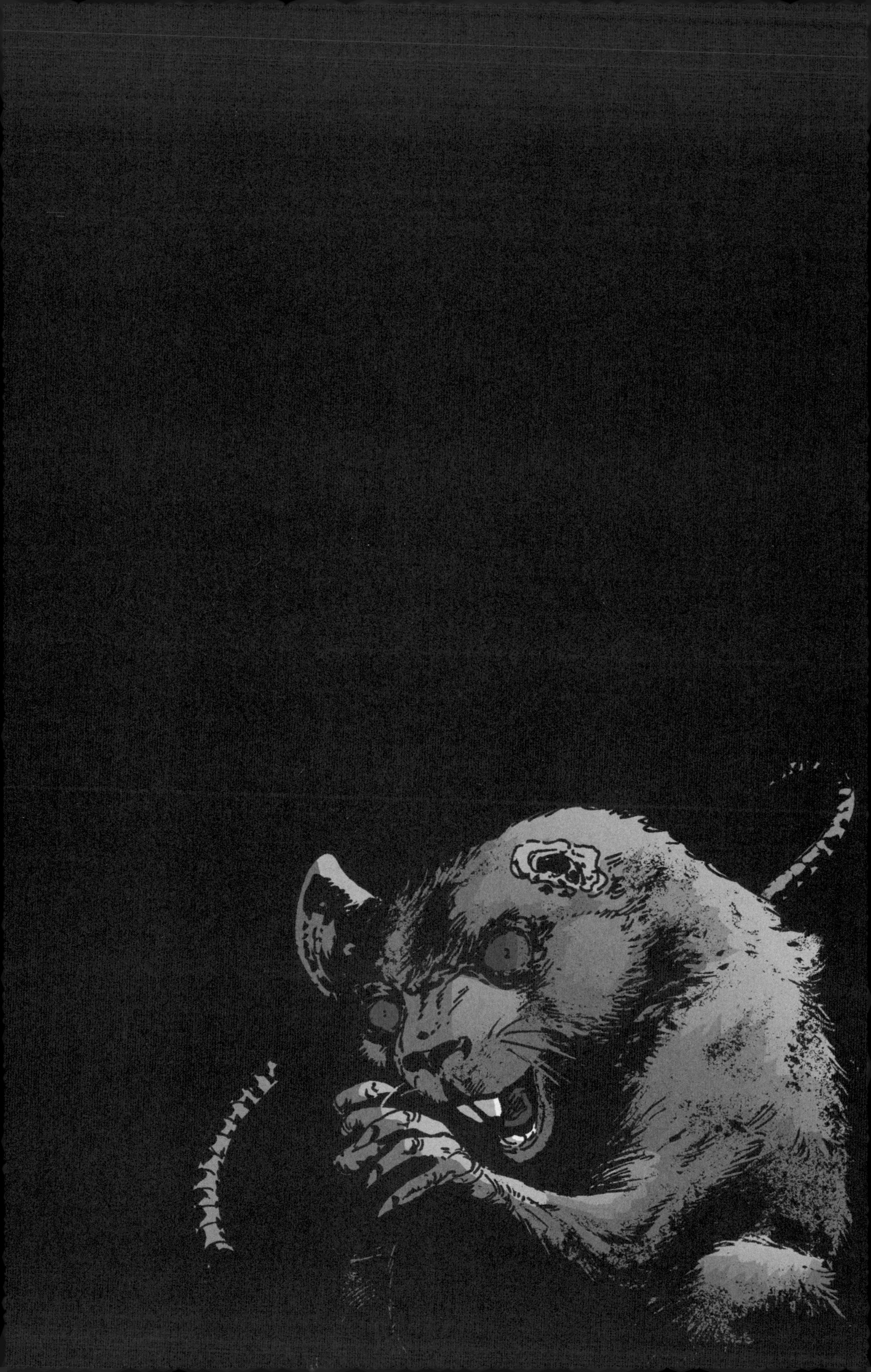

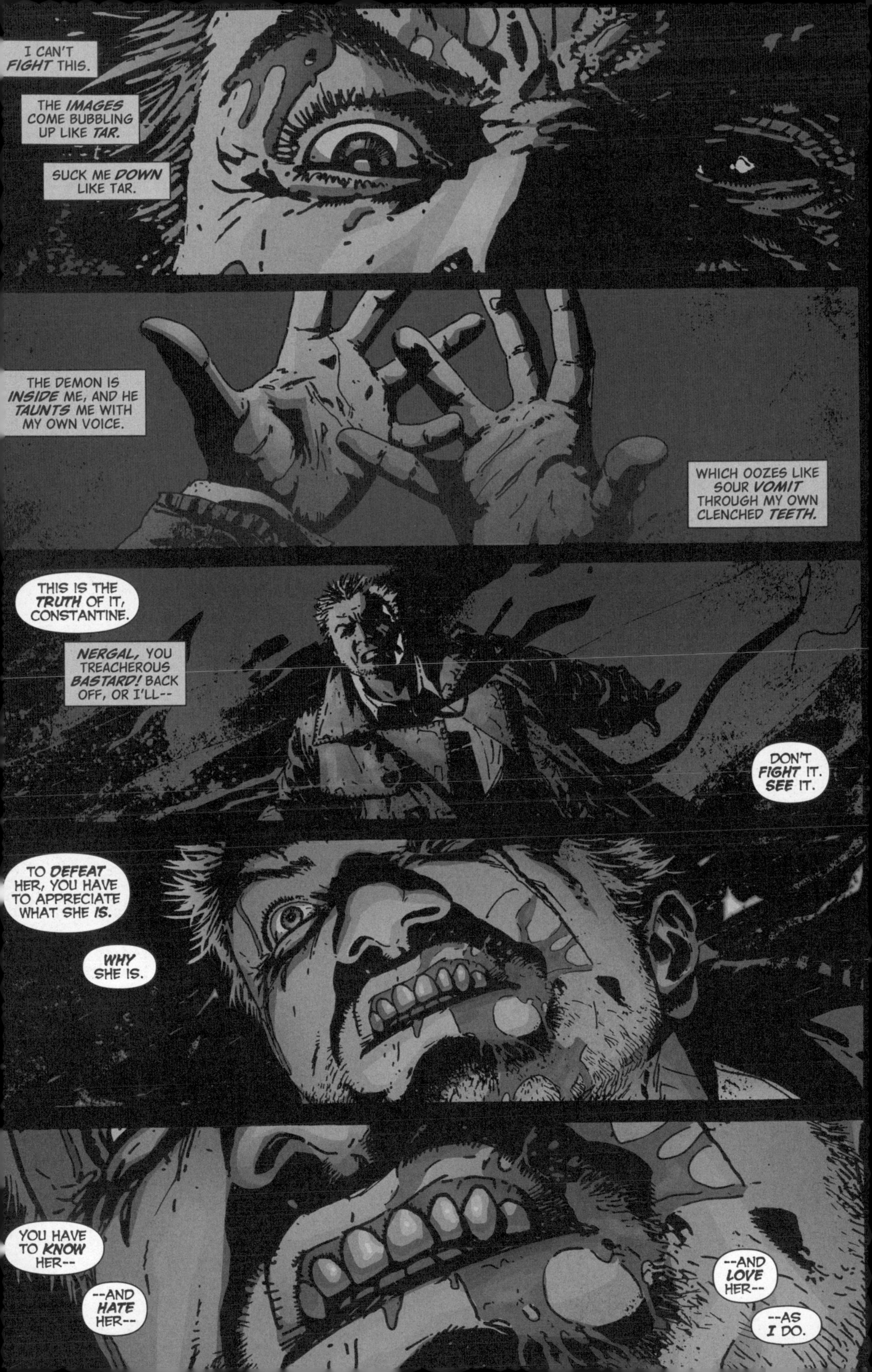
I CAN'T FIGHT THIS.
THE IMAGES COME BUBBLING UP LIKE TAR.
SUCK ME DOWN LIKE TAR.
THE DEMON IS INSIDE ME, AND HE TAUNTS ME WITH MY OWN VOICE.
WHICH OOZES LIKE SOUR VOMIT THROUGH MY OWN CLENCHED TEETH.
THIS IS THE TRUTH OF IT, CONSTANTINE.
NERGAL, YOU TREACHEROUS BASTARD! BACK OFF, OR I'LL--
DON'T FIGHT IT. SEE IT.
TO DEFEAT HER, YOU HAVE TO APPRECIATE WHAT SHE IS.
WHY SHE IS.
YOU HAVE TO KNOW HER--
--AND HATE HER--
--AND LOVE HER--
--AS I DO.

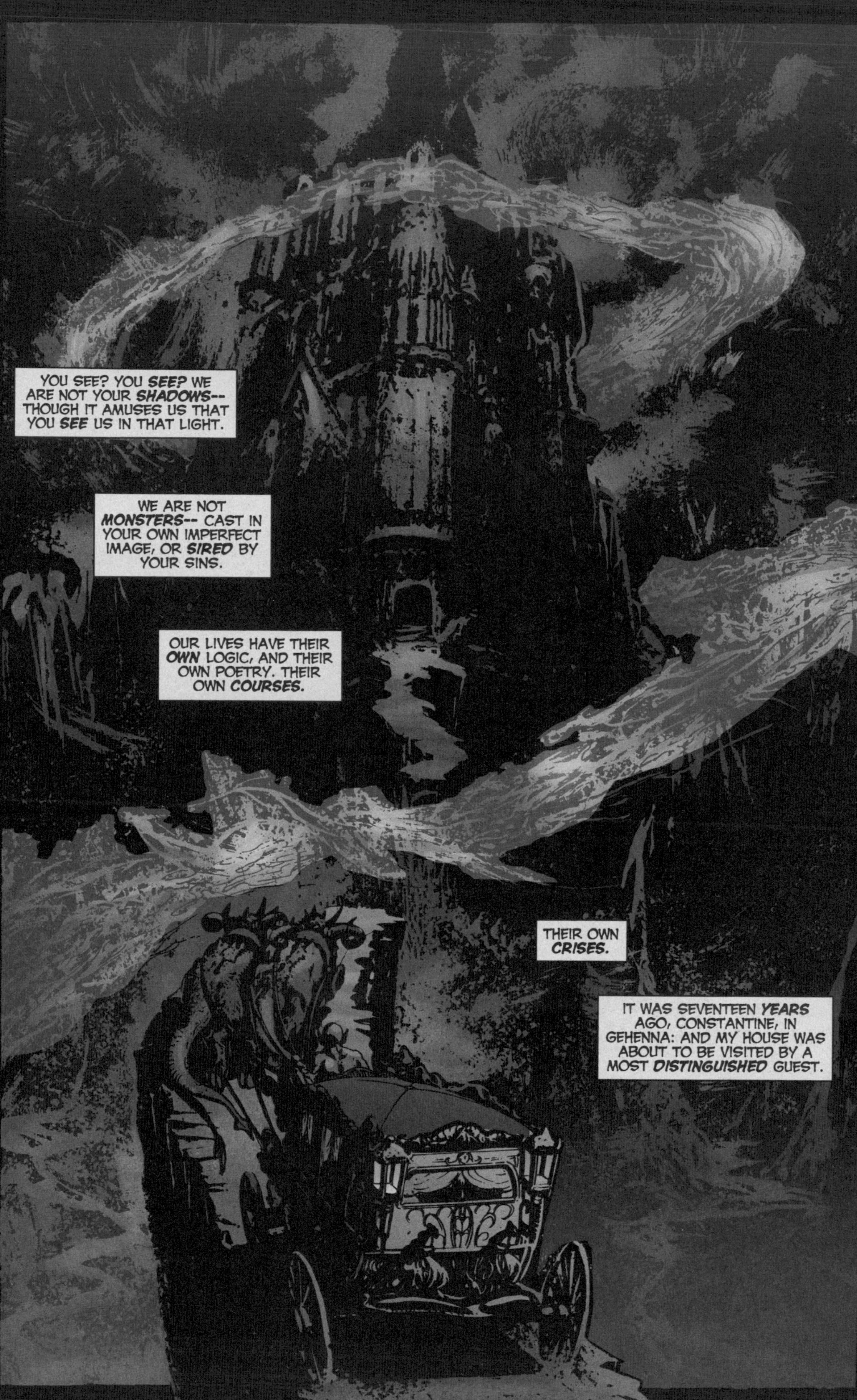
YOU SEE? YOU SEE? WE ARE NOT YOUR SHADOWS-- THOUGH IT AMUSES US THAT YOU SEE US IN THAT LIGHT.
WE ARE NOT MONSTERS-- CAST IN YOUR OWN IMPERFECT IMAGE, OR SIRED BY YOUR SINS.
OUR LIVES HAVE THEIR OWN LOGIC, AND THEIR OWN POETRY. THEIR OWN COURSES.
THEIR OWN CRISES.
IT WAS SEVENTEEN YEARS AGO, CONSTANTINE, IN GEHENNA: AND MY HOUSE WAS ABOUT TO BE VISITED BY A MOST DISTINGUISHED GUEST.

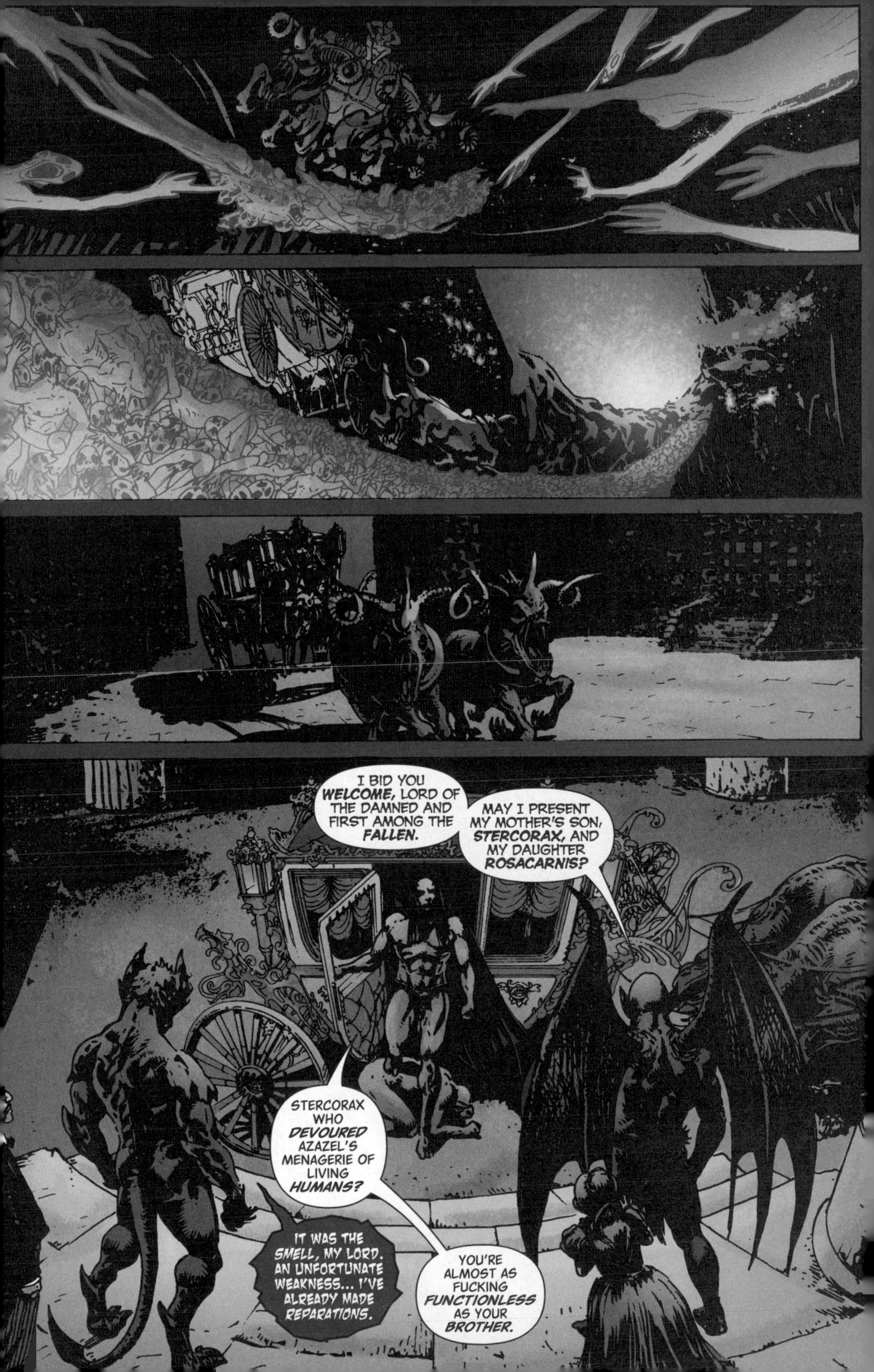
I BID YOU WELCOME, LORD OF THE DAMNED AND FIRST AMONG THE FALLEN.
MAY I PRESENT MY MOTHER'S SON, STERCORAX, AND MY DAUGHTER ROSACARNIS?
STERCORAX WHO DEVOURED AZAZEL'S MENAGERIE OF LIVING HUMANS?
IT WAS THE SMELL, MY LORD. AN UNFORTUNATE WEAKNESS... I'VE ALREADY MADE REPARATIONS.
YOU'RE ALMOST AS FUCKING FUNCTIONLESS AS YOUR BROTHER.

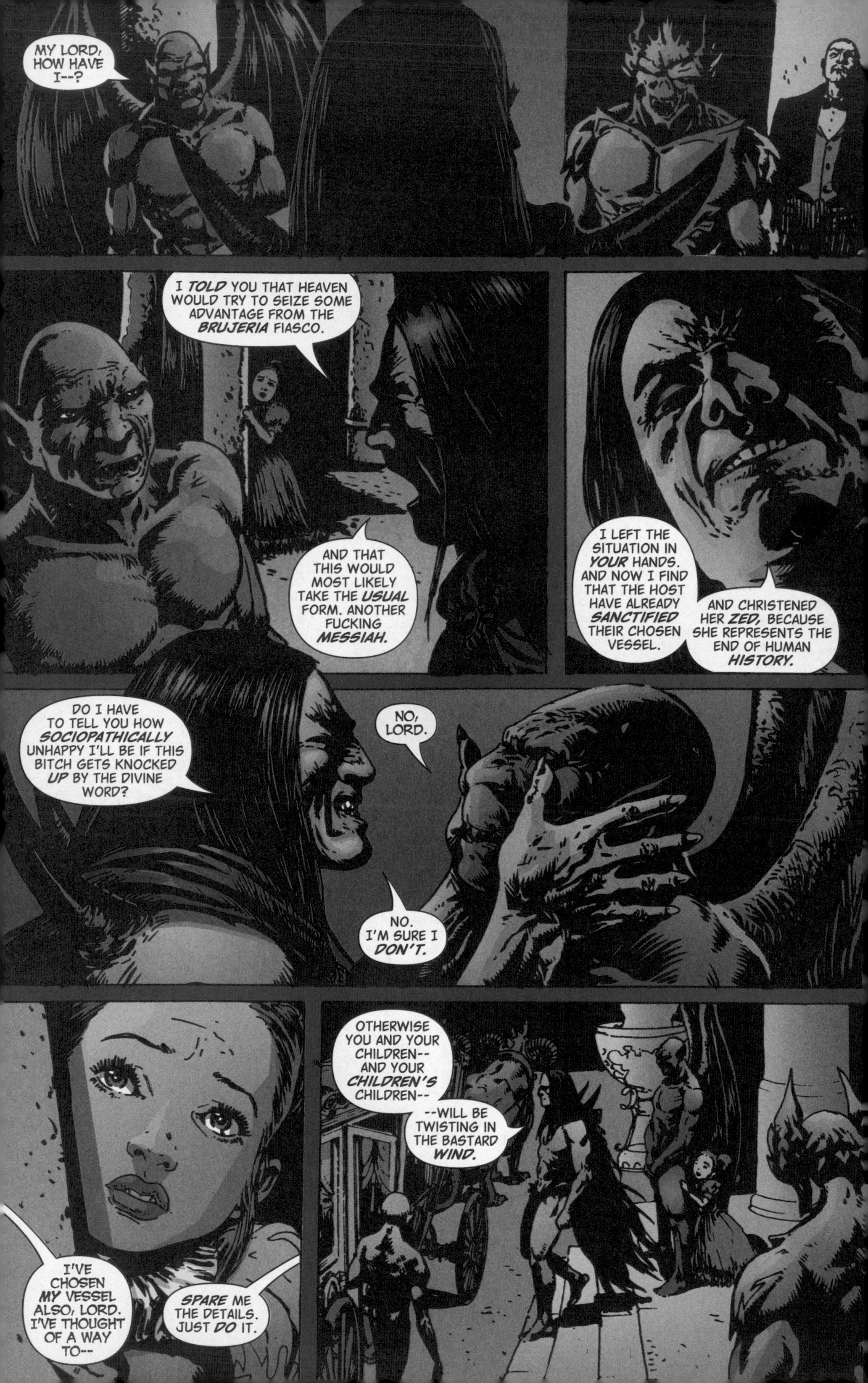
MY LORD, HOW HAVE I--?
I TOLD YOU THAT HEAVEN WOULD TRY TO SEIZE SOME ADVANTAGE FROM THE BRUJERIA FIASCO.
AND THAT THIS WOULD MOST LIKELY TAKE THE USUAL FORM. ANOTHER FUCKING MESSIAH.
I LEFT THE SITUATION IN YOUR HANDS. AND NOW I FIND THAT THE HOST HAVE ALREADY SANCTIFIED THEIR CHOSEN VESSEL.
AND CHRISTENED HER ZED, BECAUSE SHE REPRESENTS THE END OF HUMAN HISTORY.
DO I HAVE TO TELL YOU HOW SOCIOPATHICALLY UNHAPPY I'LL BE IF THIS BITCH GETS KNOCKED UP BY THE DIVINE WORD?
NO, LORD.
NO. I'M SURE I DON'T.
OTHERWISE YOU AND YOUR CHILDREN-- AND YOUR CHILDREN'S CHILDREN--
--WILL BE TWISTING IN THE BASTARD WIND.
I'VE CHOSEN MY VESSEL ALSO, LORD. I'VE THOUGHT OF A WAY TO--
SPARE ME THE DETAILS. JUST DO IT.

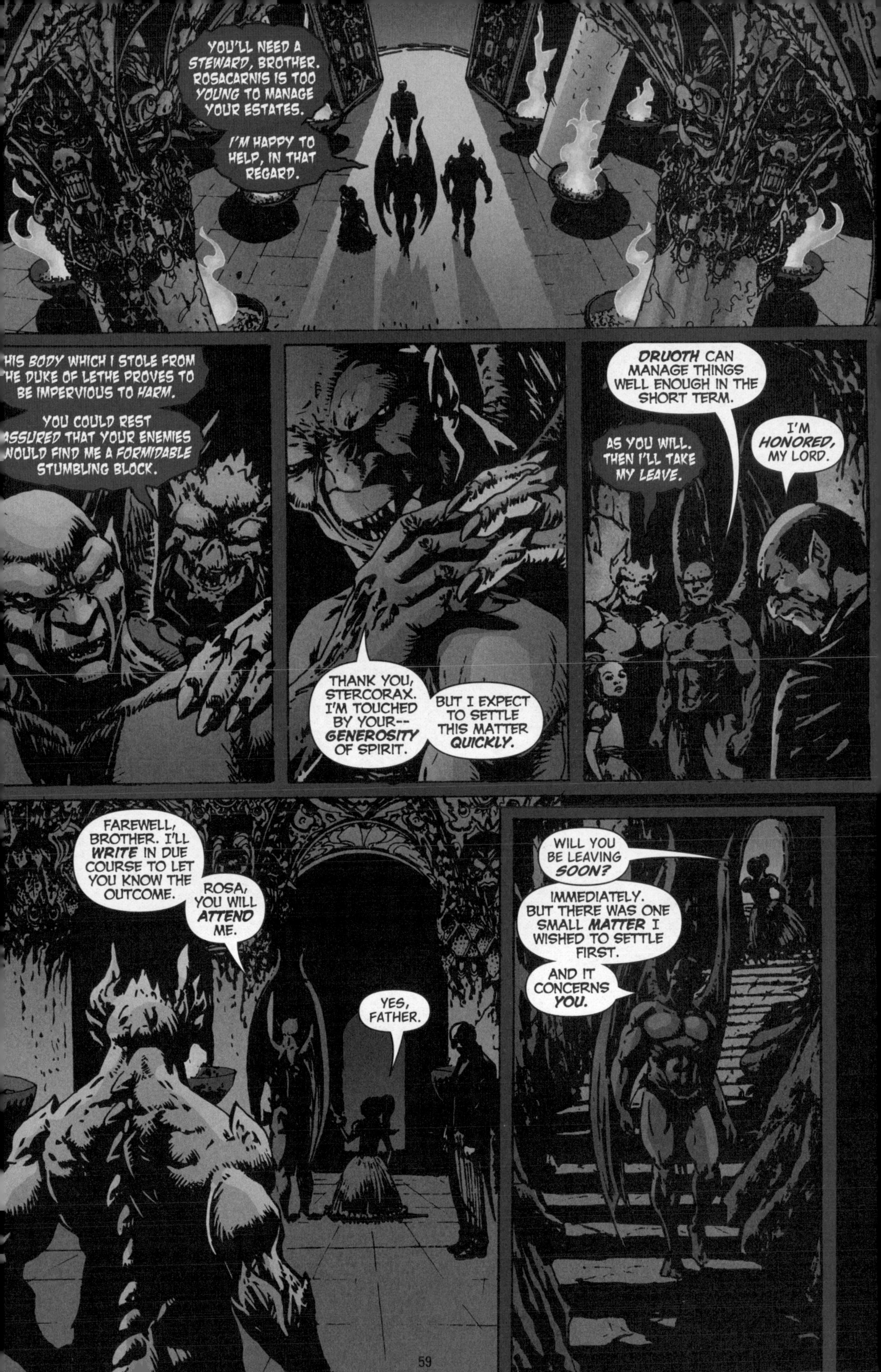

YOU'LL NEED A STEWARD, BROTHER. ROSACARNIS IS TOO YOUNG TO MANAGE YOUR ESTATES.
I'M HAPPY TO HELP, IN THAT REGARD.
HIS BODY WHICH I STOLE FROM THE DUKE OF LETHE PROVES TO BE IMPERVIOUS TO HARM.
YOU COULD REST ASSURED THAT YOUR ENEMIES WOULD FIND ME A FORMIDABLE STUMBLING BLOCK.
THANK YOU, STERCORAX. I'M TOUCHED BY YOUR-- GENEROSITY OF SPIRIT.
BUT I EXPECT TO SETTLE THIS MATTER QUICKLY.
DRUOTH CAN MANAGE THINGS WELL ENOUGH IN THE SHORT TERM.
AS YOU WILL. THEN I'LL TAKE MY LEAVE.
I'M HONORED, MY LORD.
FAREWELL, BROTHER. I'LL WRITE IN DUE COURSE TO LET YOU KNOW THE OUTCOME.
ROSA, YOU WILL ATTEND ME.
YES, FATHER.
WILL YOU BE LEAVING SOON?
IMMEDIATELY. BUT THERE WAS ONE SMALL MATTER I WISHED TO SETTLE FIRST.
AND IT CONCERNS YOU.

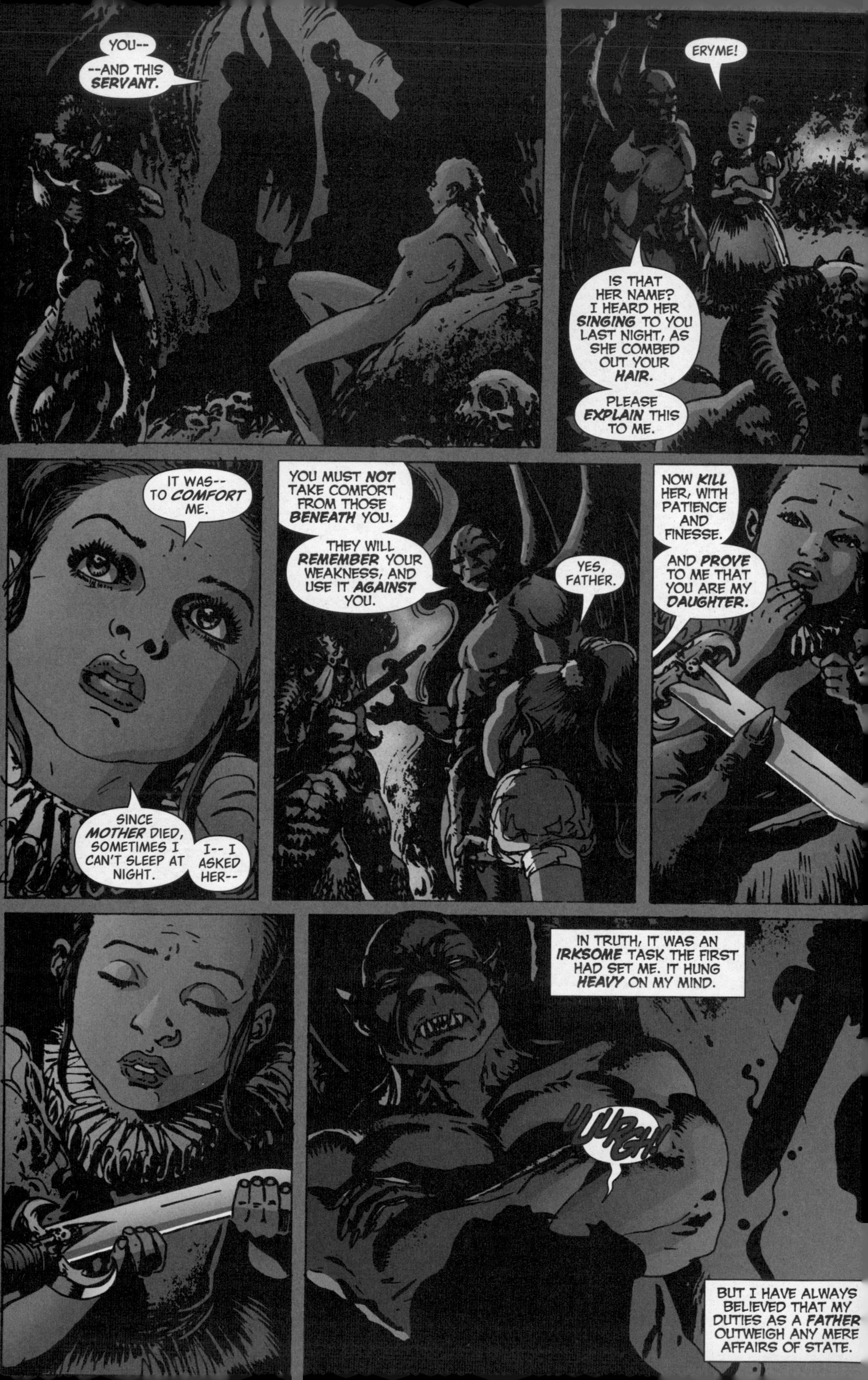
YOU--
--AND THIS SERVANT.
ERYME!
IS THAT HER NAME? I HEARD HER SINGING TO YOU LAST NIGHT, AS SHE COMBED OUT YOUR HAIR.
PLEASE EXPLAIN THIS TO ME.
IT WAS-- TO COMFORT ME.
SINCE MOTHER DIED, SOMETIMES I CAN'T SLEEP AT NIGHT.
I-- I ASKED HER--
YOU MUST NOT TAKE COMFORT FROM THOSE BENEATH YOU.
THEY WILL REMEMBER YOUR WEAKNESS, AND USE IT AGAINST YOU.
YES, FATHER.
NOW KILL HER, WITH PATIENCE AND FINESSE.
AND PROVE TO ME THAT YOU ARE MY DAUGHTER.
IN TRUTH, IT WAS AN IRKSOME TASK THE FIRST HAD SET ME. IT HUNG HEAVY ON MY MIND.
UURGH!
BUT I HAVE ALWAYS BELIEVED THAT MY DUTIES AS A FATHER OUTWEIGH ANY MERE AFFAIRS OF STATE.

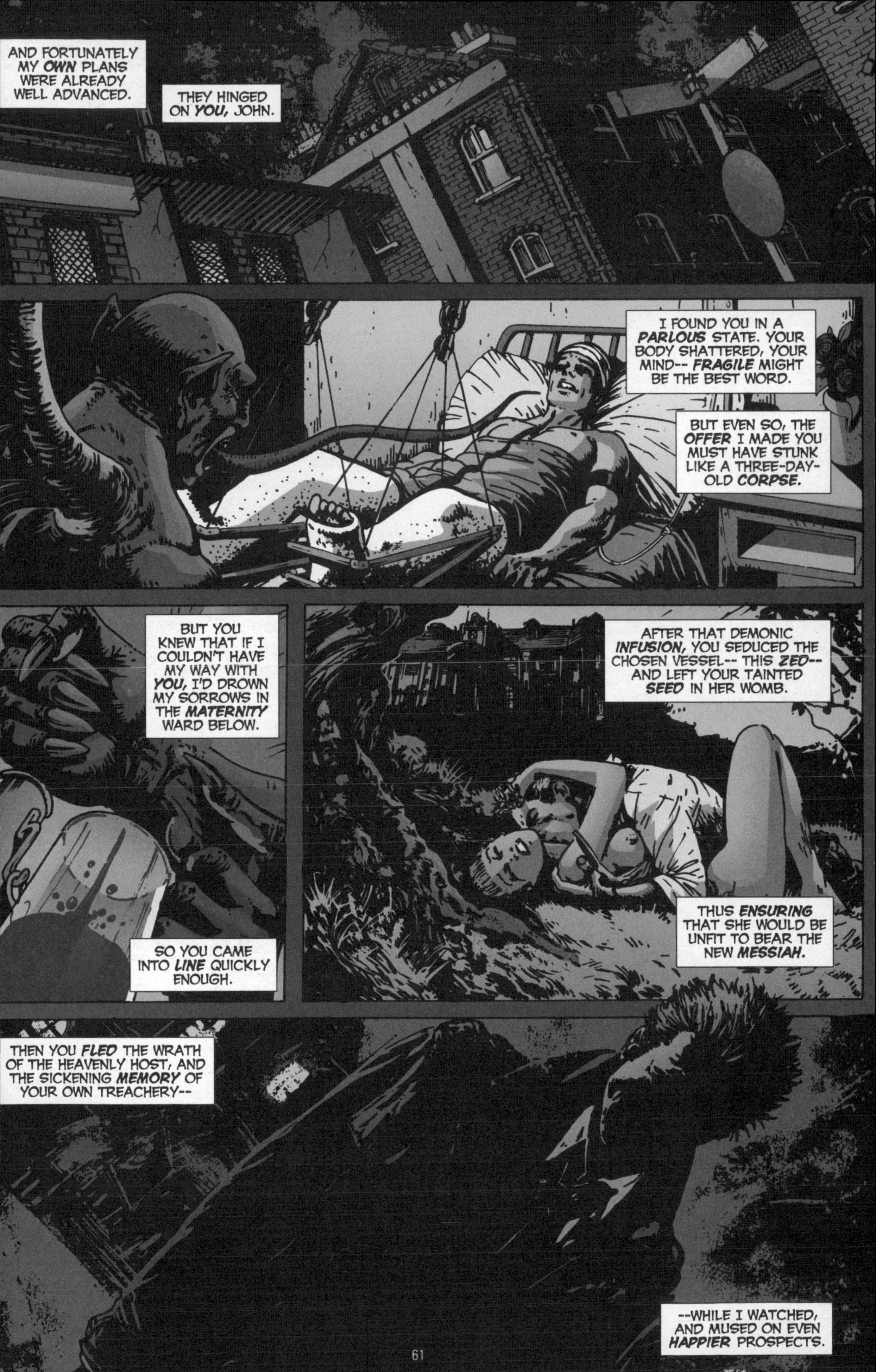

AND FORTUNATELY MY OWN PLANS WERE ALREADY WELL ADVANCED.
THEY HINGED ON YOU, JOHN.
I FOUND YOU IN A PARLOUS STATE. YOUR BODY SHATTERED, YOUR MIND-- FRAGILE MIGHT BE THE BEST WORD.
BUT EVEN SO, THE OFFER I MADE YOU MUST HAVE STUNK LIKE A THREE-DAY-OLD CORPSE.
BUT YOU KNEW THAT IF I COULDN'T HAVE MY WAY WITH YOU, I'D DROWN MY SORROWS IN THE MATERNITY WARD BELOW.
SO YOU CAME INTO LINE QUICKLY ENOUGH.
AFTER THAT DEMONIC INFUSION, YOU SEDUCED THE CHOSEN VESSEL-- THIS ZED-- AND LEFT YOUR TAINTED SEED IN HER WOMB.
THUS ENSURING THAT SHE WOULD BE UNFIT TO BEAR THE NEW MESSIAH.
THEN YOU FLED THE WRATH OF THE HEAVENLY HOST, AND THE SICKENING MEMORY OF YOUR OWN TREACHERY--
--WHILE I WATCHED, AND MUSED ON EVEN HAPPIER PROSPECTS.

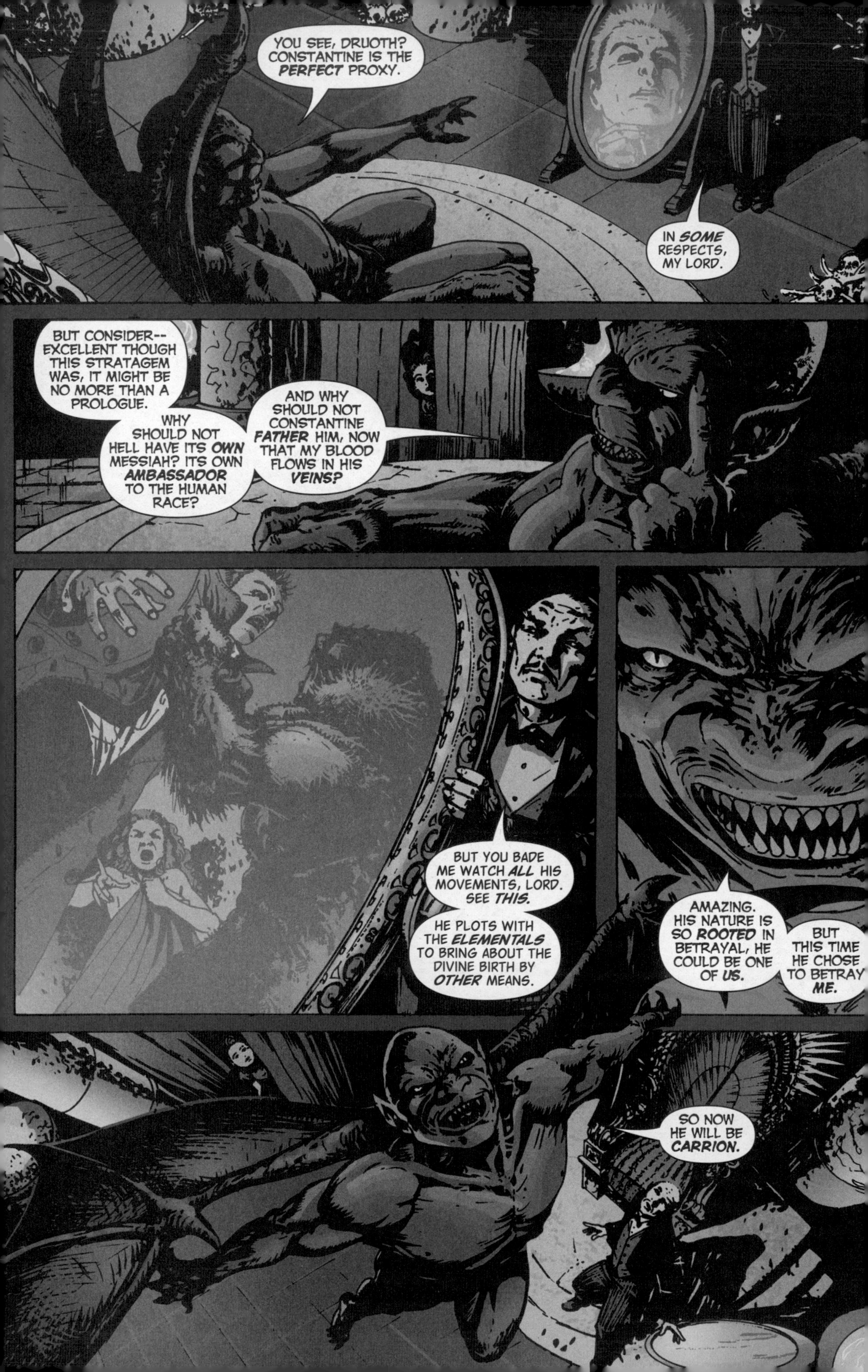

YOU SEE, DRUOTH? CONSTANTINE IS THE PERFECT PROXY.
IN SOME RESPECTS, MY LORD.
BUT CONSIDER-- EXCELLENT THOUGH THIS STRATAGEM WAS, IT MIGHT BE NO MORE THAN A PROLOGUE.
WHY SHOULD NOT HELL HAVE ITS OWN MESSIAH? ITS OWN AMBASSADOR TO THE HUMAN RACE?
AND WHY SHOULD NOT CONSTANTINE FATHER HIM, NOW THAT MY BLOOD FLOWS IN HIS VEINS?
BUT YOU BADE ME WATCH ALL HIS MOVEMENTS, LORD. SEE THIS.
HE PLOTS WITH THE ELEMENTALS TO BRING ABOUT THE DIVINE BIRTH BY OTHER MEANS.
AMAZING. HIS NATURE IS SO ROOTED IN BETRAYAL, HE COULD BE ONE OF US.
BUT THIS TIME HE CHOSE TO BETRAY ME.
SO NOW HE WILL BE CARRION.

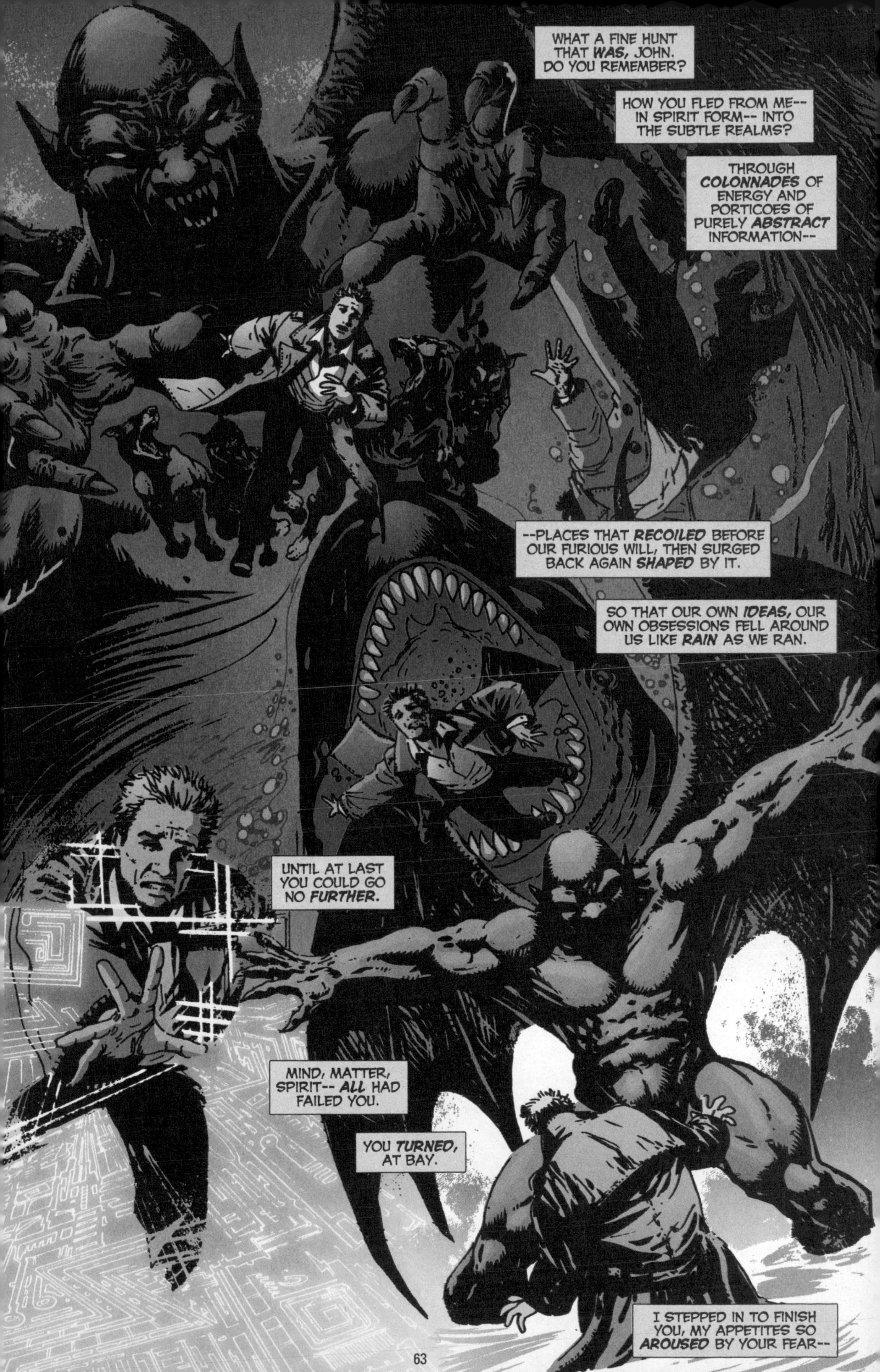
WHAT A FINE HUNT THAT WAS, JOHN. DO YOU REMEMBER?
HOW YOU FLED FROM ME-- IN SPIRIT FORM-- INTO THE SUBTLE REALMS?
THROUGH COLONNADES OF ENERGY AND PORTICOES OF PURELY ABSTRACT INFORMATION--
--PLACES THAT RECOILED BEFORE OUR FURIOUS WILL, THEN SURGED BACK AGAIN SHAPED BY IT.
SO THAT OUR OWN IDEAS, OUR OWN OBSESSIONS FELL AROUND US LIKE RAIN AS WE RAN.
UNTIL AT LAST YOU COULD GO NO FURTHER.
MIND, MATTER, SPIRIT-- ALL HAD FAILED YOU.
YOU TURNED, AT BAY.
I STEPPED IN TO FINISH YOU, MY APPETITES SO AROUSED BY YOUR FEAR--

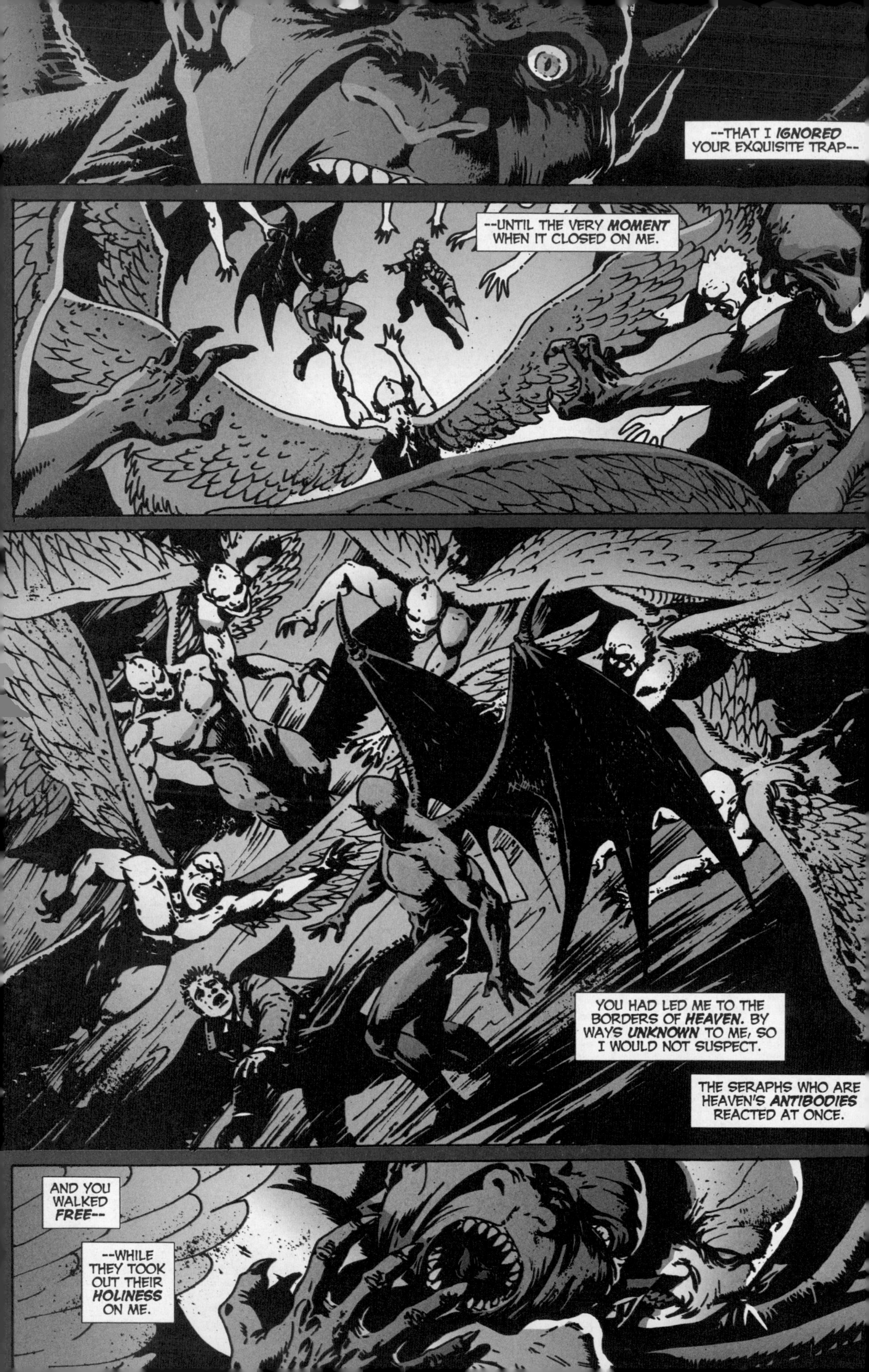
--THAT I IGNORED YOUR EXQUISITE TRAP--
--UNTIL THE VERY MOMENT WHEN IT CLOSED ON ME.
YOU HAD LED ME TO THE BORDERS OF HEAVEN. BY WAYS UNKNOWN TO ME, SO I WOULD NOT SUSPECT.
THE SERAPHS WHO ARE HEAVEN'S ANTIBODIES REACTED AT ONCE.
AND YOU WALKED FREE--
--WHILE THEY TOOK OUT THEIR HOLINESS ON ME.

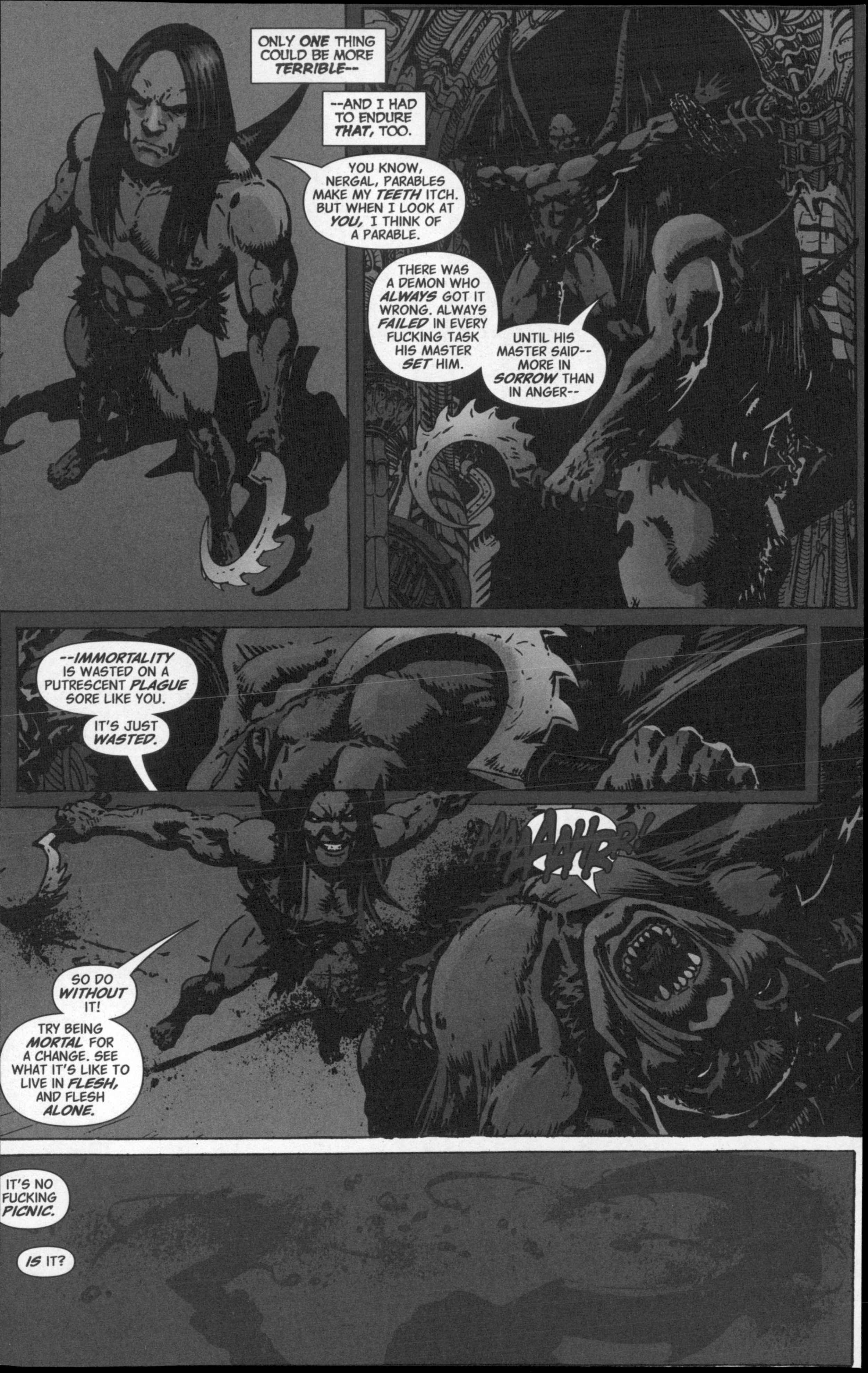
ONLY ONE THING COULD BE MORE TERRIBLE--
--AND I HAD TO ENDURE THAT, TOO.
YOU KNOW, NERGAL, PARABLES MAKE MY TEETH ITCH. BUT WHEN I LOOK AT YOU, I THINK OF A PARABLE.
THERE WAS A DEMON WHO ALWAYS GOT IT WRONG. ALWAYS FAILED IN EVERY FUCKING TASK HIS MASTER SET HIM.
UNTIL HIS MASTER SAID-- MORE IN SORROW THAN IN ANGER--
--IMMORTALITY IS WASTED ON A PUTRESCENT PLAGUE SORE LIKE YOU.
IT'S JUST WASTED.
AAAAAHR!
SO DO WITHOUT IT!
TRY BEING MORTAL FOR A CHANGE. SEE WHAT IT'S LIKE TO LIVE IN FLESH, AND FLESH ALONE.
IT'S NO FUCKING PICNIC.
IS IT?

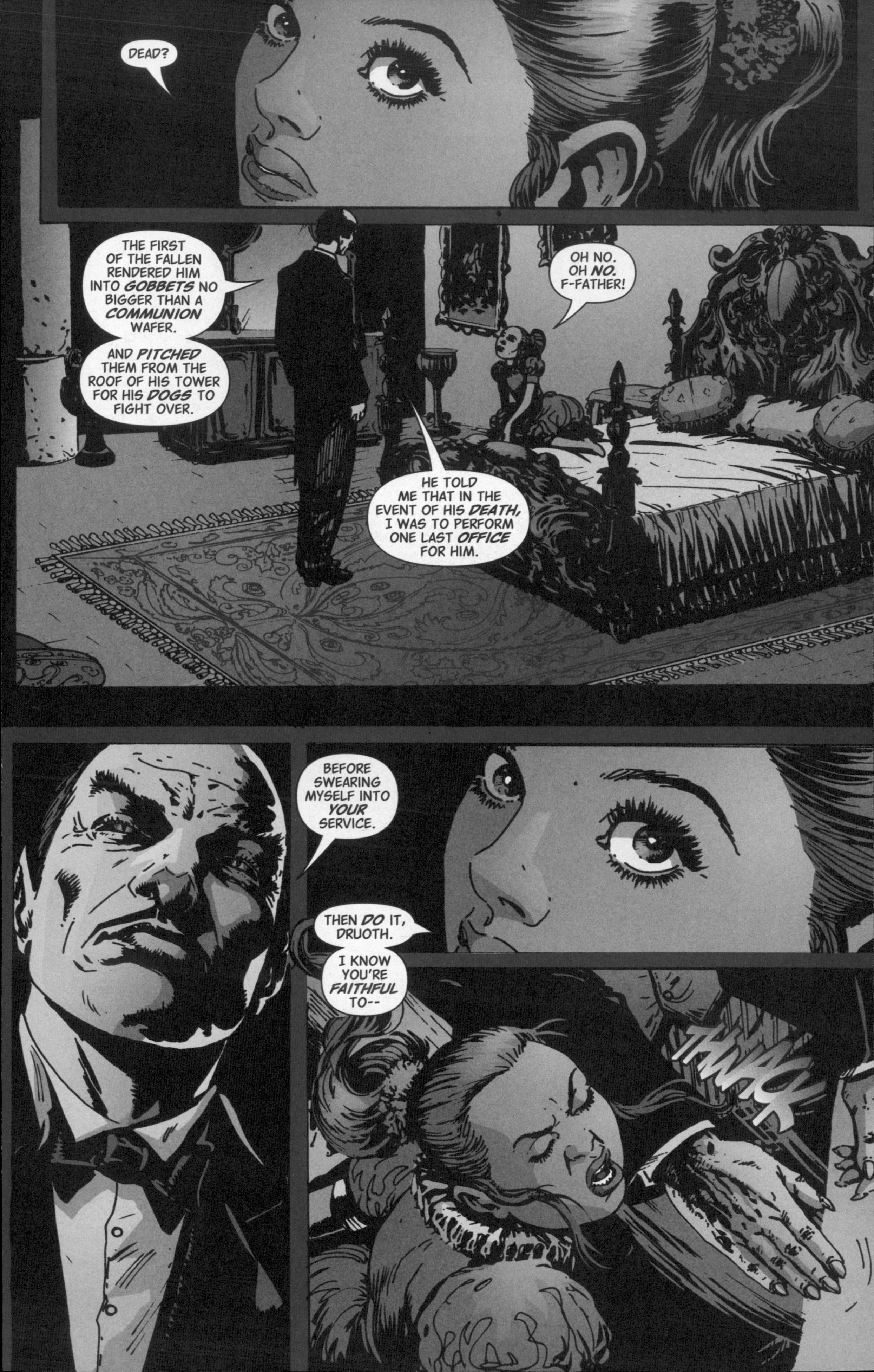
DEAD?
THE FIRST OF THE FALLEN RENDERED HIM INTO GOBBETS NO BIGGER THAN A COMMUNION WAFER.
AND PITCHED THEM FROM THE ROOF OF HIS TOWER FOR HIS DOGS TO FIGHT OVER.
OH NO. OH NO. F-FATHER!
HE TOLD ME THAT IN THE EVENT OF HIS DEATH, I WAS TO PERFORM ONE LAST OFFICE FOR HIM.
BEFORE SWEARING MYSELF INTO YOUR SERVICE.
THEN DO IT, DRUOTH.
I KNOW YOU'RE FAITHFUL TO--
THWACK

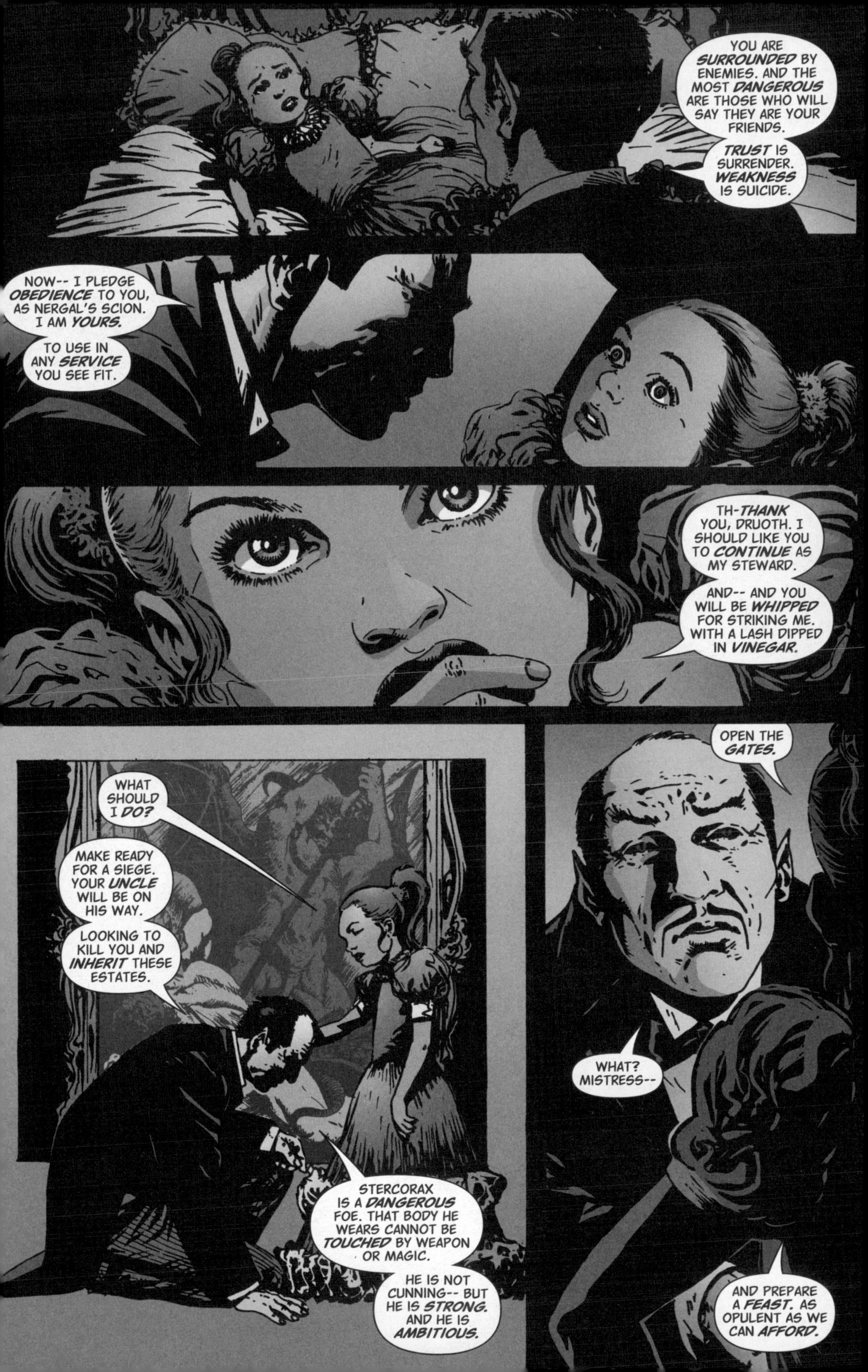
YOU ARE SURROUNDED BY ENEMIES. AND THE MOST DANGEROUS ARE THOSE WHO WILL SAY THEY ARE YOUR FRIENDS.
TRUST IS SURRENDER. WEAKNESS IS SUICIDE.
NOW-- I PLEDGE OBEDIENCE TO YOU, AS NERGAL'S SCION. I AM YOURS.
TO USE IN ANY SERVICE YOU SEE FIT.
TH-THANK YOU, DRUOTH. I SHOULD LIKE YOU TO CONTINUE AS MY STEWARD.
AND-- AND YOU WILL BE WHIPPED FOR STRIKING ME. WITH A LASH DIPPED IN VINEGAR.
WHAT SHOULD I DO?
MAKE READY FOR A SIEGE. YOUR UNCLE WILL BE ON HIS WAY.
LOOKING TO KILL YOU AND INHERIT THESE ESTATES.
STERCORAX IS A DANGEROUS FOE. THAT BODY HE WEARS CANNOT BE TOUCHED BY WEAPON OR MAGIC.
HE IS NOT CUNNING-- BUT HE IS STRONG. AND HE IS AMBITIOUS.
OPEN THE GATES.
WHAT? MISTRESS--
AND PREPARE A FEAST. AS OPULENT AS WE CAN AFFORD.

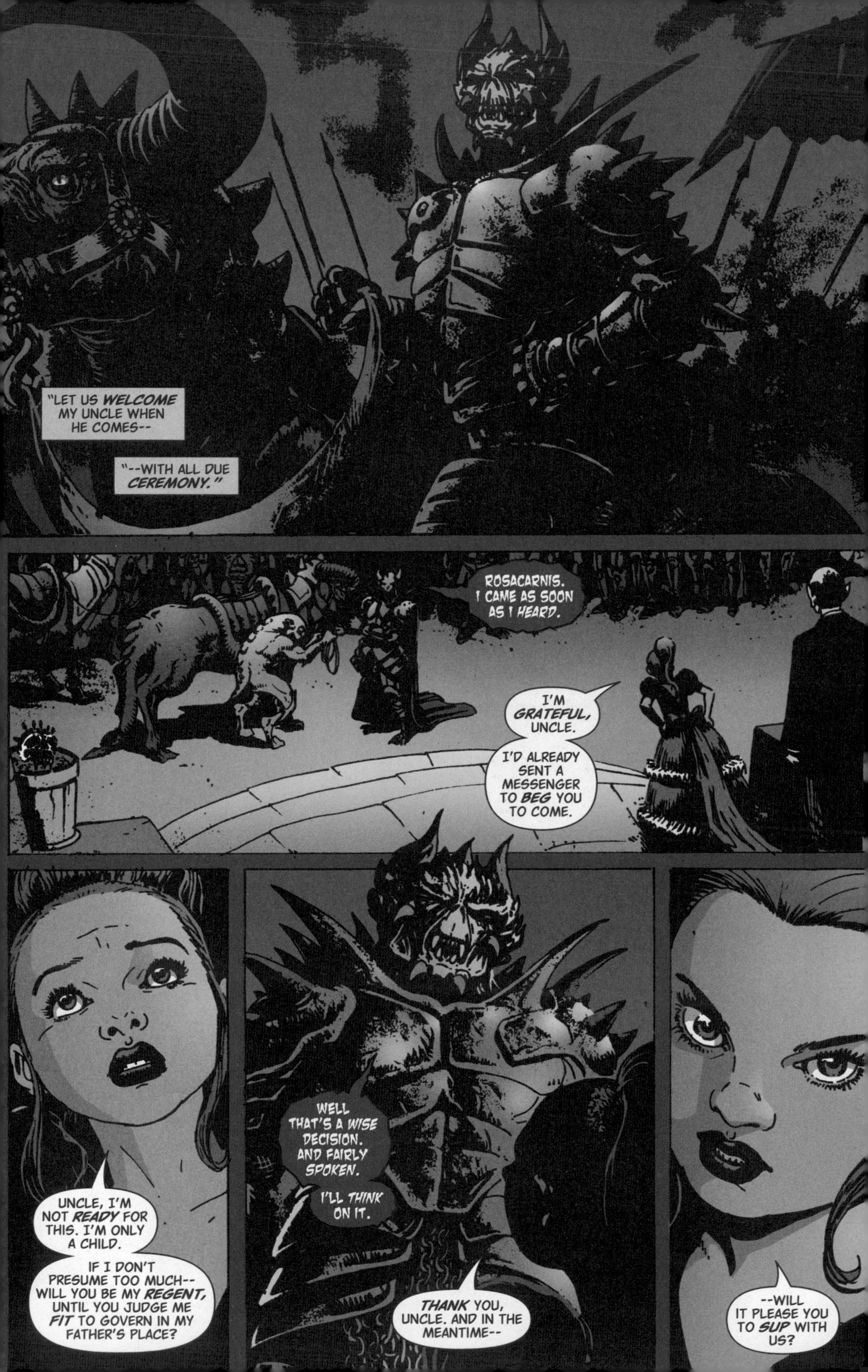
"LET US WELCOME MY UNCLE WHEN HE COMES--
"--WITH ALL DUE CEREMONY."
ROSACARNIS. I CAME AS SOON AS I HEARD.
I'M GRATEFUL, UNCLE.
I'D ALREADY SENT A MESSENGER TO BEG YOU TO COME.
UNCLE, I'M NOT READY FOR THIS. I'M ONLY A CHILD.
IF I DON'T PRESUME TOO MUCH-- WILL YOU BE MY REGENT, UNTIL YOU JUDGE ME FIT TO GOVERN IN MY FATHER'S PLACE?
WELL THAT'S A WISE DECISION. AND FAIRLY SPOKEN.
I'LL THINK ON IT.
THANK YOU, UNCLE. AND IN THE MEANTIME--
--WILL IT PLEASE YOU TO SUP WITH US?

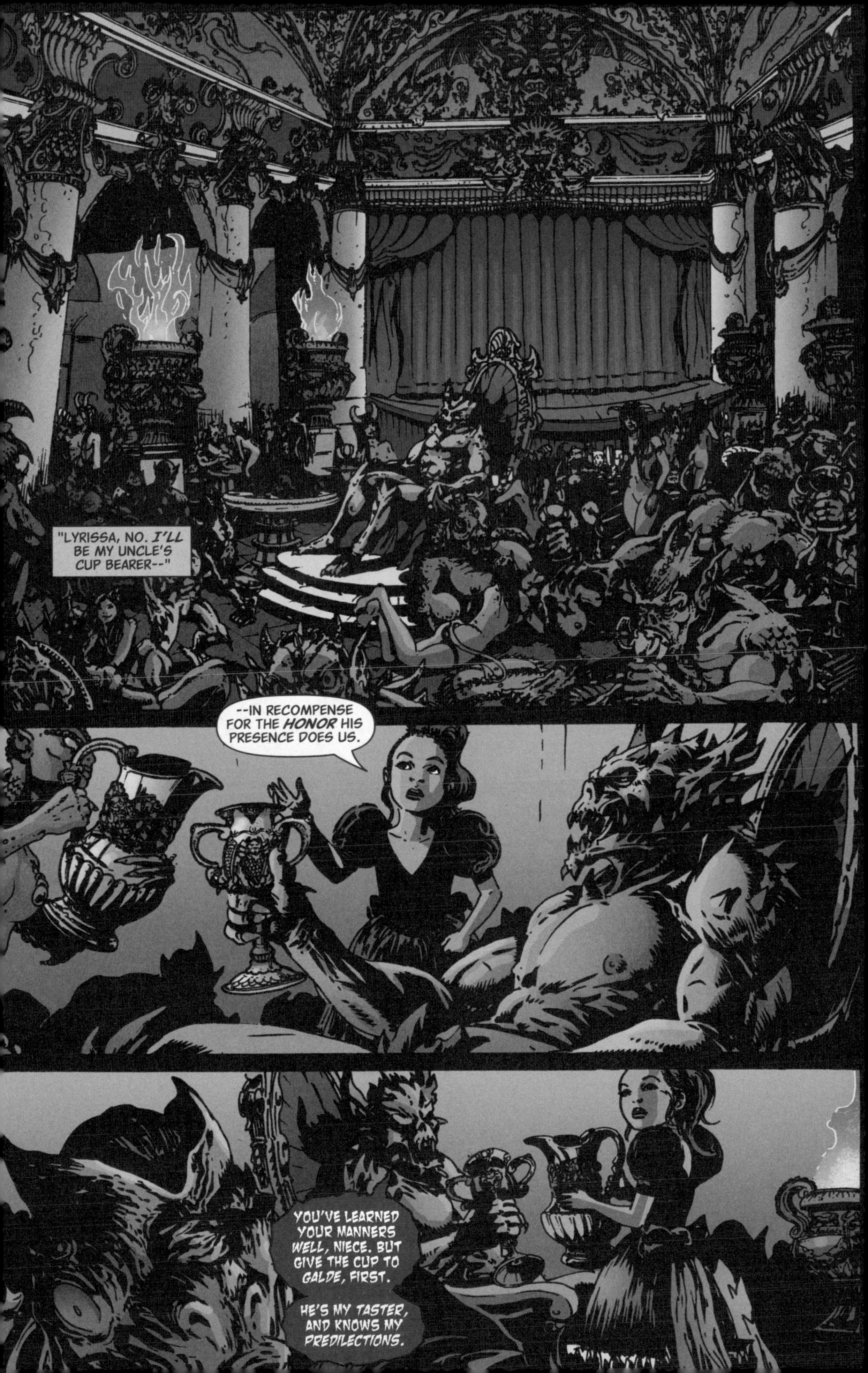
"LYRISSA, NO. I'LL BE MY UNCLE'S CUP BEARER--"
--IN RECOMPENSE FOR THE HONOR HIS PRESENCE DOES US.
YOU'VE LEARNED YOUR MANNERS WELL, NIECE. BUT GIVE THE CUP TO GALDE, FIRST.
HE'S MY TASTER, AND KNOWS MY PREDILECTIONS.

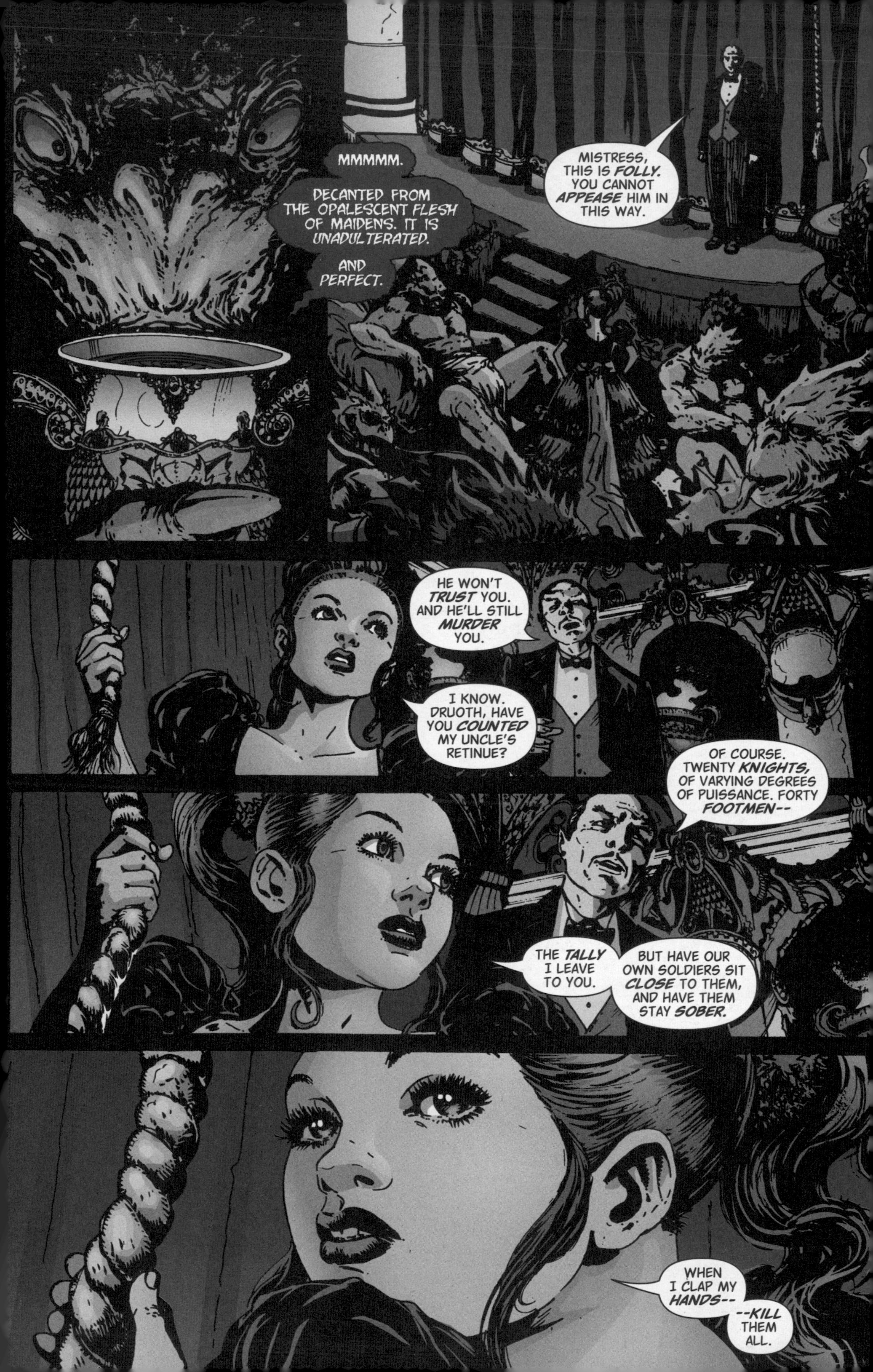
MMMMM.
DECANTED FROM THE OPALESCENT FLESH OF MAIDENS. IT IS UNADULTERATED.
AND PERFECT.
MISTRESS, THIS IS FOLLY. YOU CANNOT APPEASE HIM IN THIS WAY.
HE WON'T TRUST YOU. AND HE'LL STILL MURDER YOU.
I KNOW. DRUOTH, HAVE YOU COUNTED MY UNCLE'S RETINUE?
OF COURSE. TWENTY KNIGHTS, OF VARYING DEGREES OF PUISSANCE. FORTY FOOTMEN--
THE TALLY I LEAVE TO YOU.
BUT HAVE OUR OWN SOLDIERS SIT CLOSE TO THEM, AND HAVE THEM STAY SOBER.
WHEN I CLAP MY HANDS--
--KILL THEM ALL.

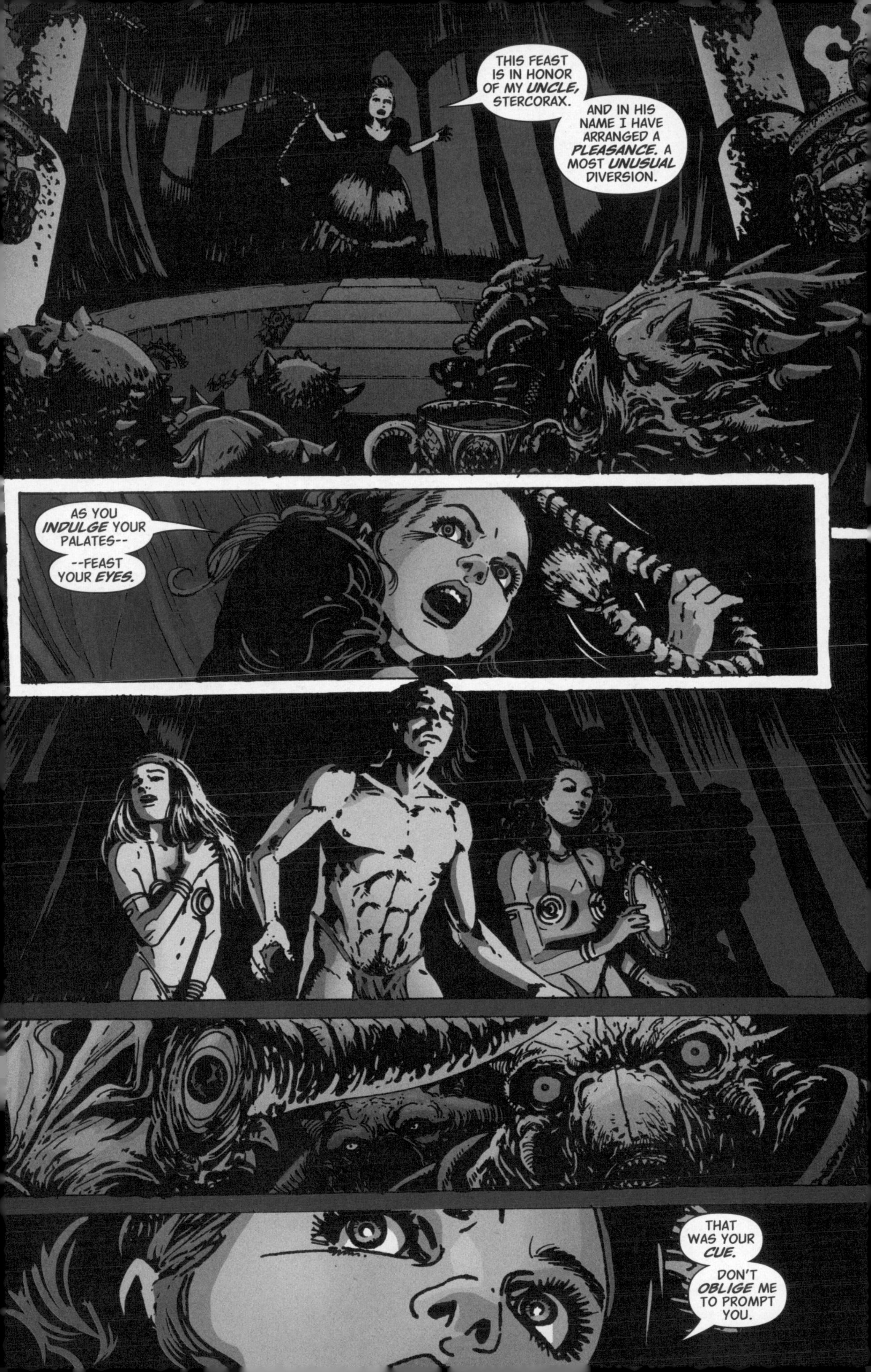

THIS FEAST IS IN HONOR OF MY UNCLE, STERCORAX.
AND IN HIS NAME I HAVE ARRANGED A PLEASANCE. A MOST UNUSUAL DIVERSION.
AS YOU INDULGE YOUR PALATES--
--FEAST YOUR EYES.
THAT WAS YOUR CUE.
DON'T OBLIGE ME TO PROMPT YOU.

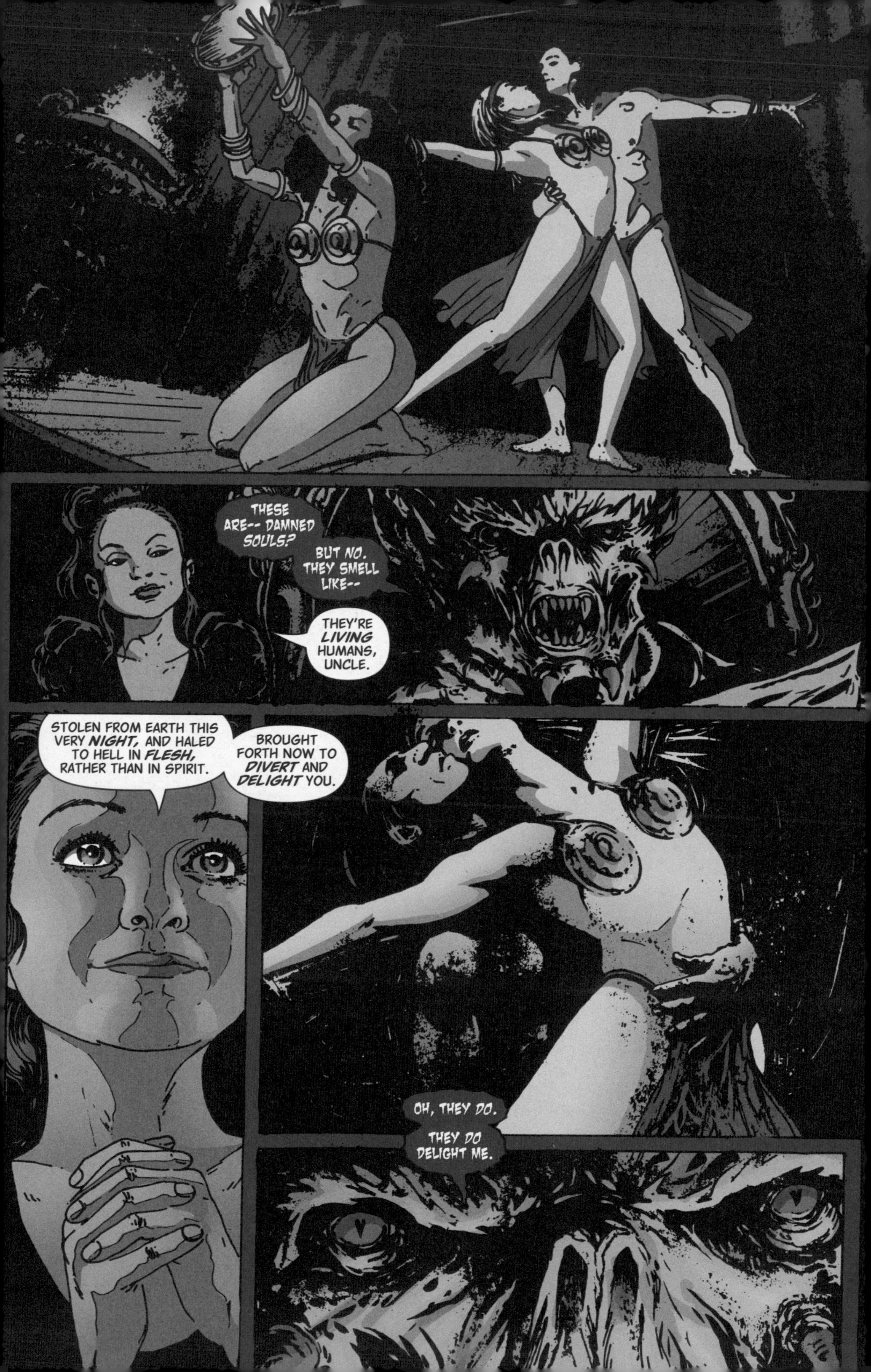
THESE ARE-- DAMNED SOULS?
BUT NO. THEY SMELL LIKE--
THEY'RE LIVING HUMANS, UNCLE.
STOLEN FROM EARTH THIS VERY NIGHT, AND HALED TO HELL IN FLESH, RATHER THAN IN SPIRIT.
BROUGHT FORTH NOW TO DIVERT AND DELIGHT YOU.
OH, THEY DO.
THEY DO DELIGHT ME.

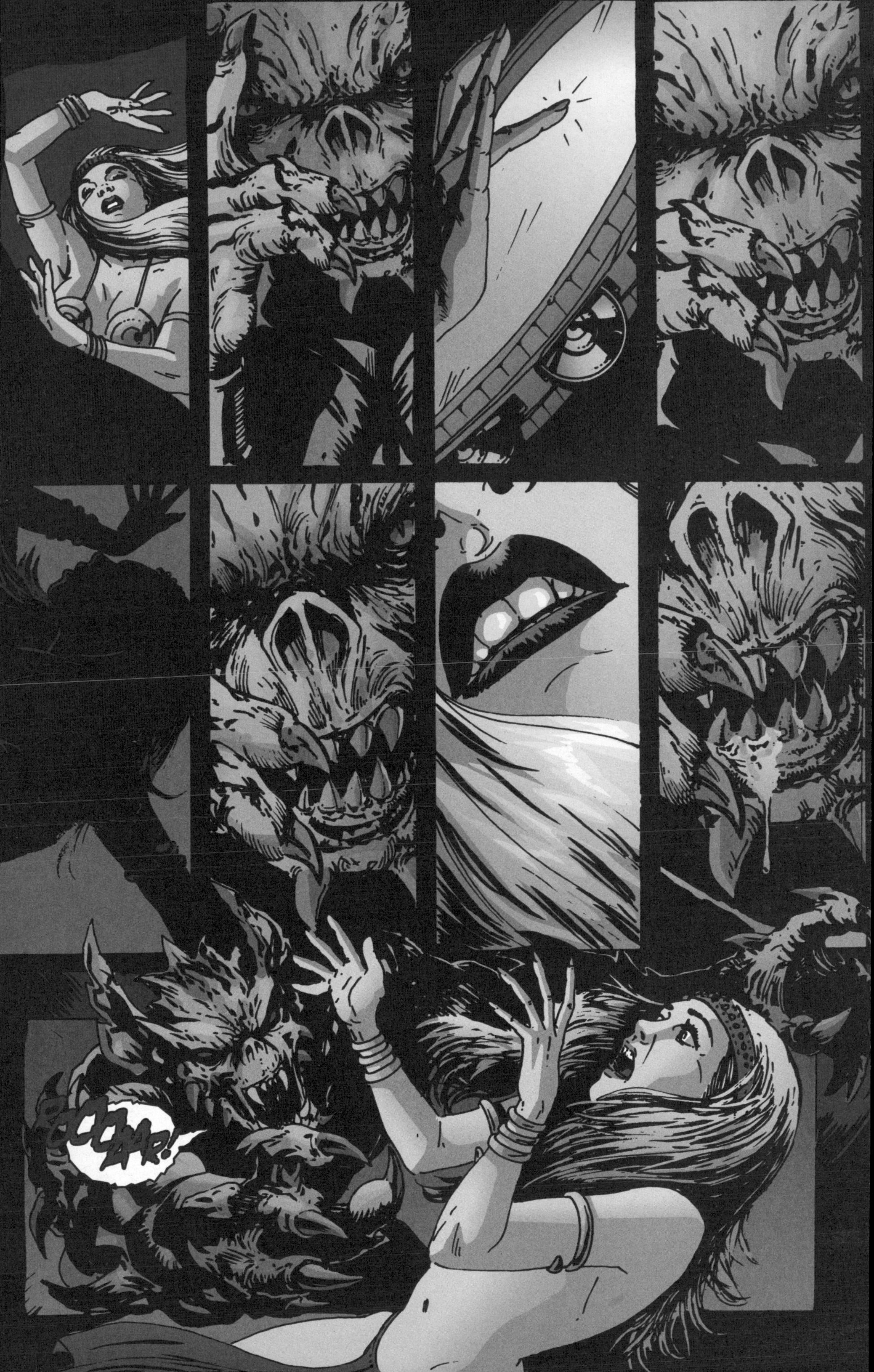

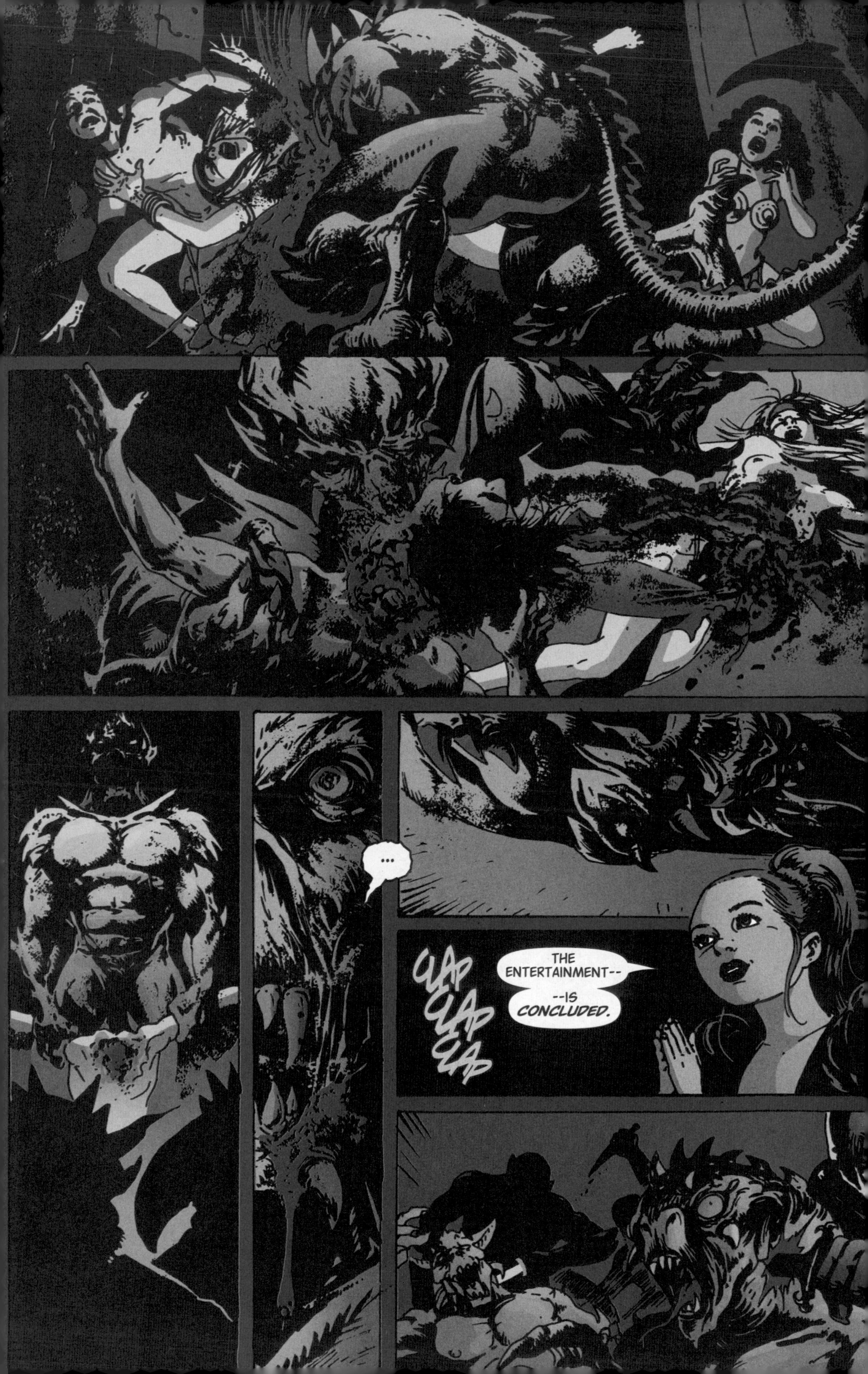
...
CLAP CLAP CLAP
THE ENTERTAINMENT--
--IS CONCLUDED.

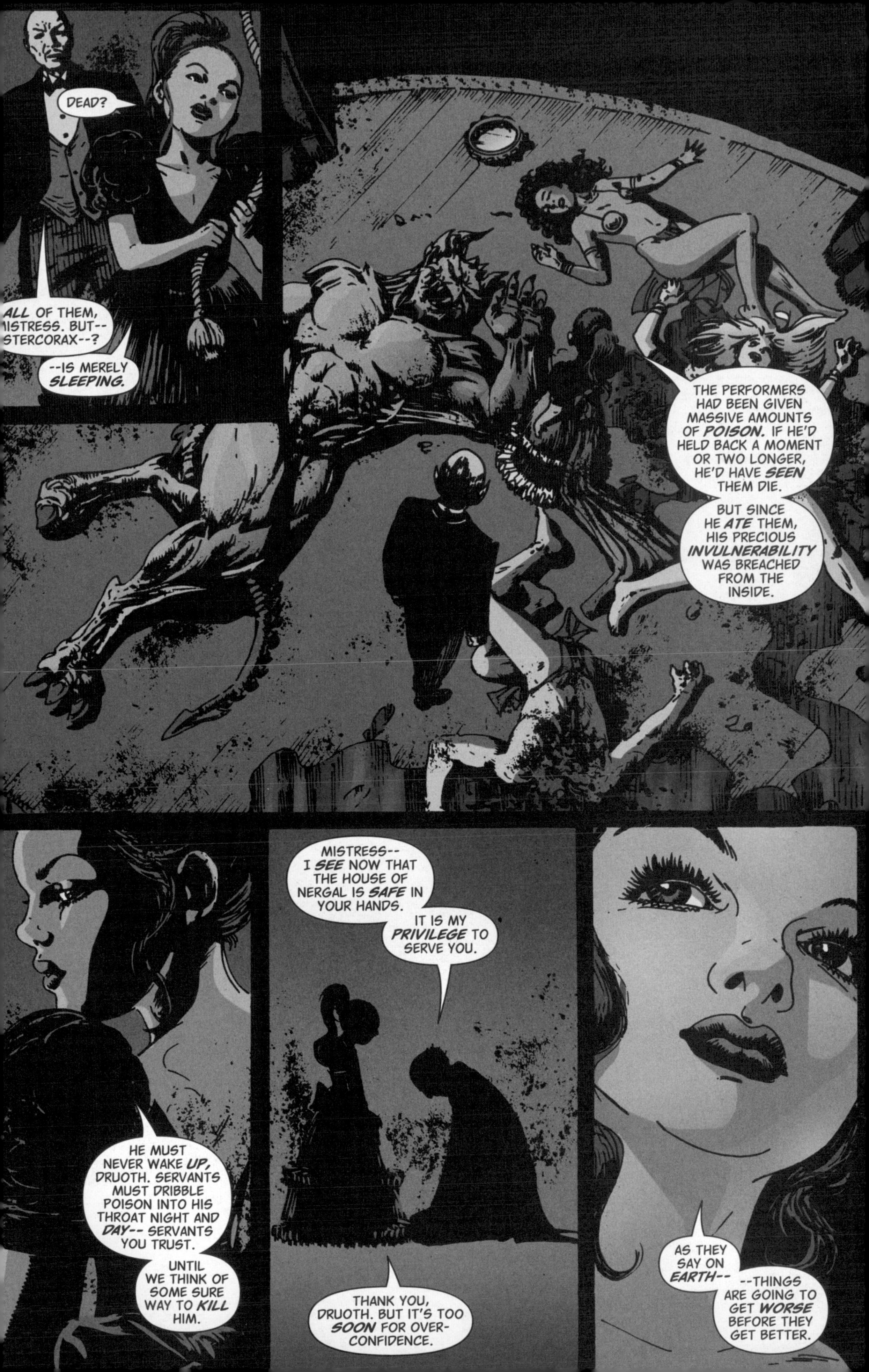
DEAD?
ALL OF THEM, MISTRESS. BUT-- STERCORAX--?
--IS MERELY SLEEPING.
THE PERFORMERS HAD BEEN GIVEN MASSIVE AMOUNTS OF POISON. IF HE'D HELD BACK A MOMENT OR TWO LONGER, HE'D HAVE SEEN THEM DIE.
BUT SINCE HE ATE THEM, HIS PRECIOUS INVULNERABILITY WAS BREACHED FROM THE INSIDE.
HE MUST NEVER WAKE UP, DRUOTH. SERVANTS MUST DRIBBLE POISON INTO HIS THROAT NIGHT AND DAY-- SERVANTS YOU TRUST.
UNTIL WE THINK OF SOME SURE WAY TO KILL HIM.
MISTRESS-- I SEE NOW THAT THE HOUSE OF NERGAL IS SAFE IN YOUR HANDS.
IT IS MY PRIVILEGE TO SERVE YOU.
THANK YOU, DRUOTH. BUT IT'S TOO SOON FOR OVER-CONFIDENCE.
AS THEY SAY ON EARTH--
--THINGS ARE GOING TO GET WORSE BEFORE THEY GET BETTER.

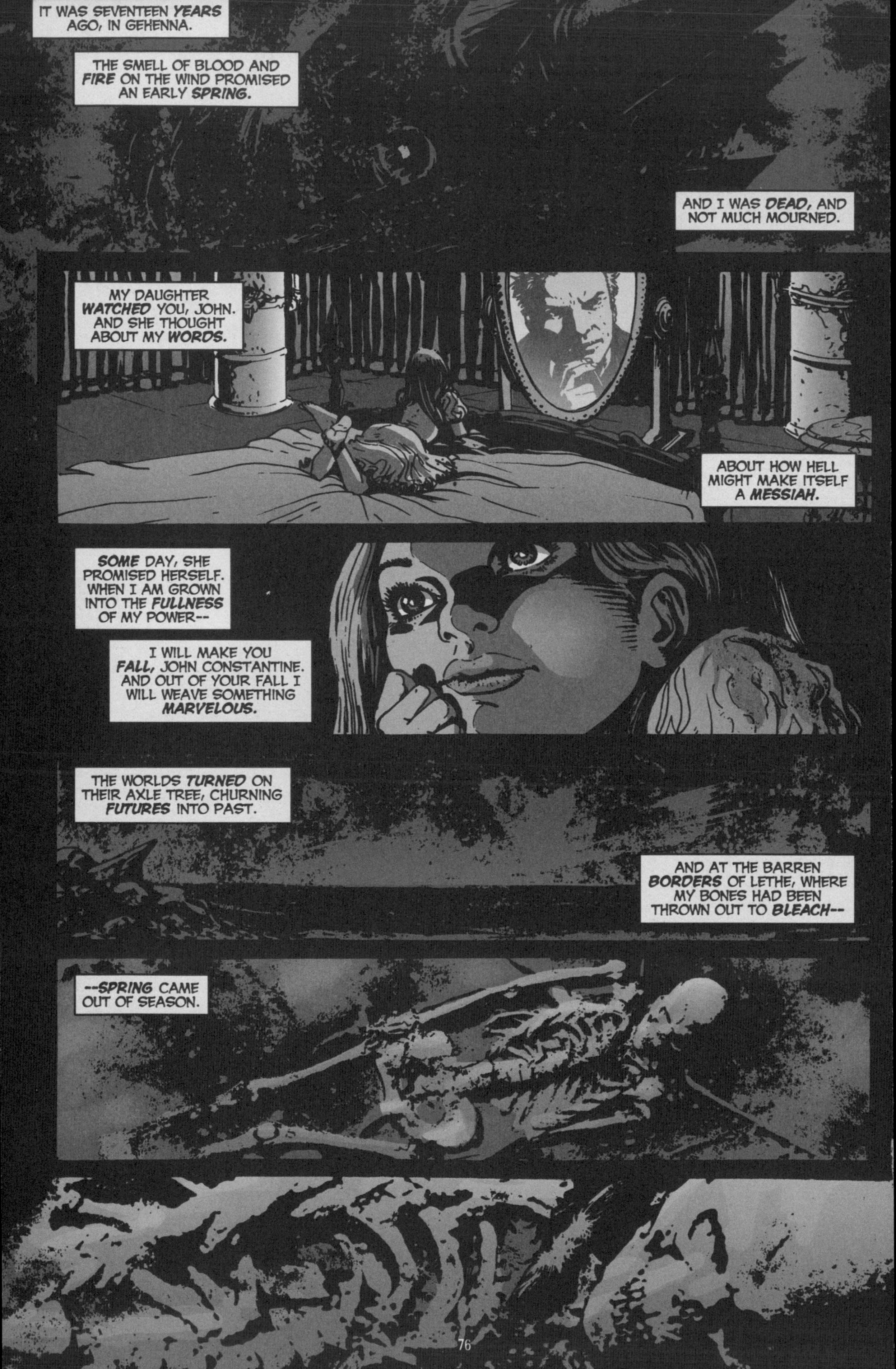
IT WAS SEVENTEEN YEARS AGO, IN GEHENNA.
THE SMELL OF BLOOD AND FIRE ON THE WIND PROMISED AN EARLY SPRING.
AND I WAS DEAD, AND NOT MUCH MOURNED.
MY DAUGHTER WATCHED YOU, JOHN. AND SHE THOUGHT ABOUT MY WORDS.
ABOUT HOW HELL MIGHT MAKE ITSELF A MESSIAH.
SOME DAY, SHE PROMISED HERSELF. WHEN I AM GROWN INTO THE FULLNESS OF MY POWER--
I WILL MAKE YOU FALL, JOHN CONSTANTINE. AND OUT OF YOUR FALL I WILL WEAVE SOMETHING MARVELOUS.
THE WORLDS TURNED ON THEIR AXLE TREE, CHURNING FUTURES INTO PAST.
AND AT THE BARREN BORDERS OF LETHE, WHERE MY BONES HAD BEEN THROWN OUT TO BLEACH--
--SPRING CAME OUT OF SEASON.

Down in the Ground Where the Dead Men Go CHAPTER FOUR

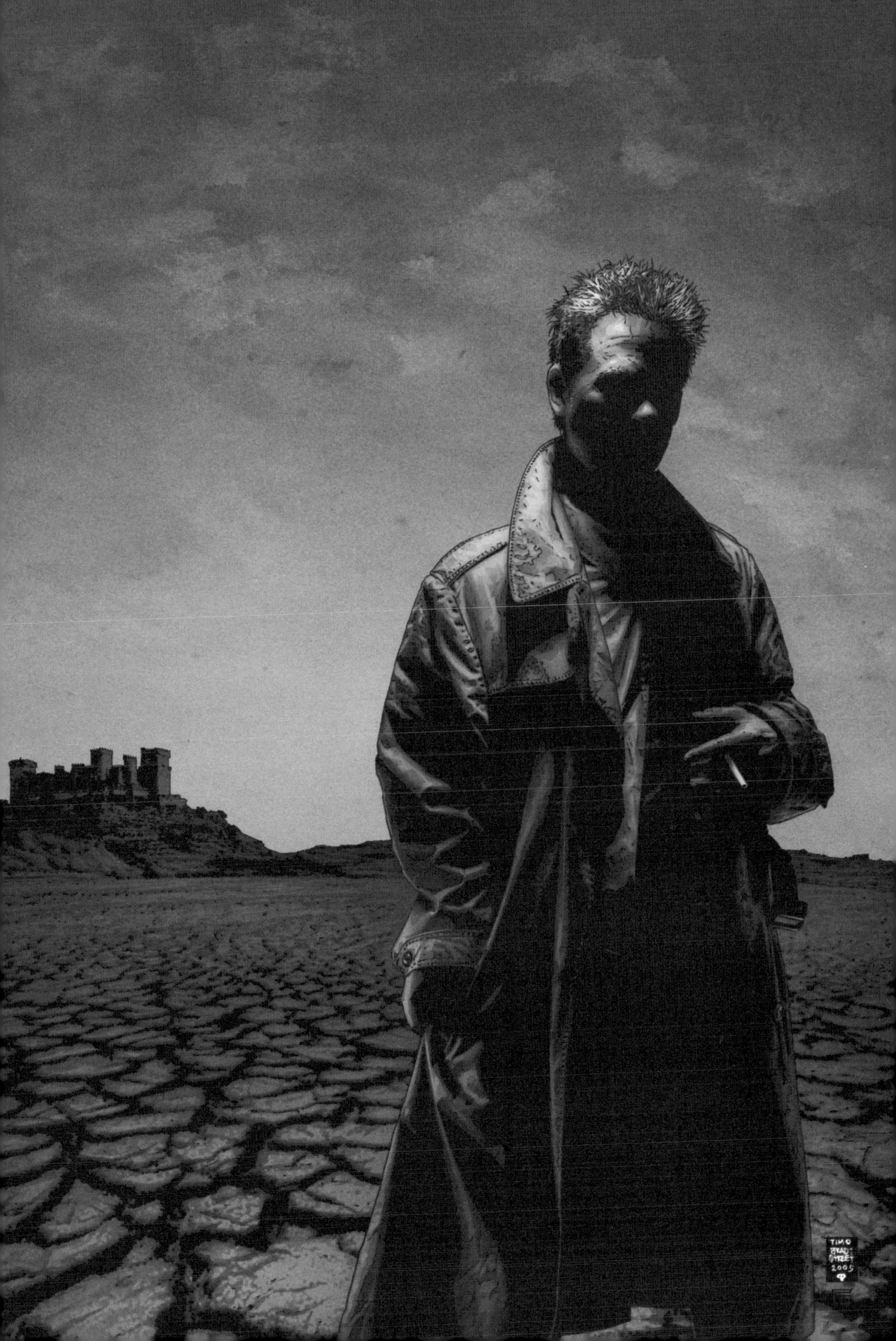
TIMO
BRAD-
STREET
2005

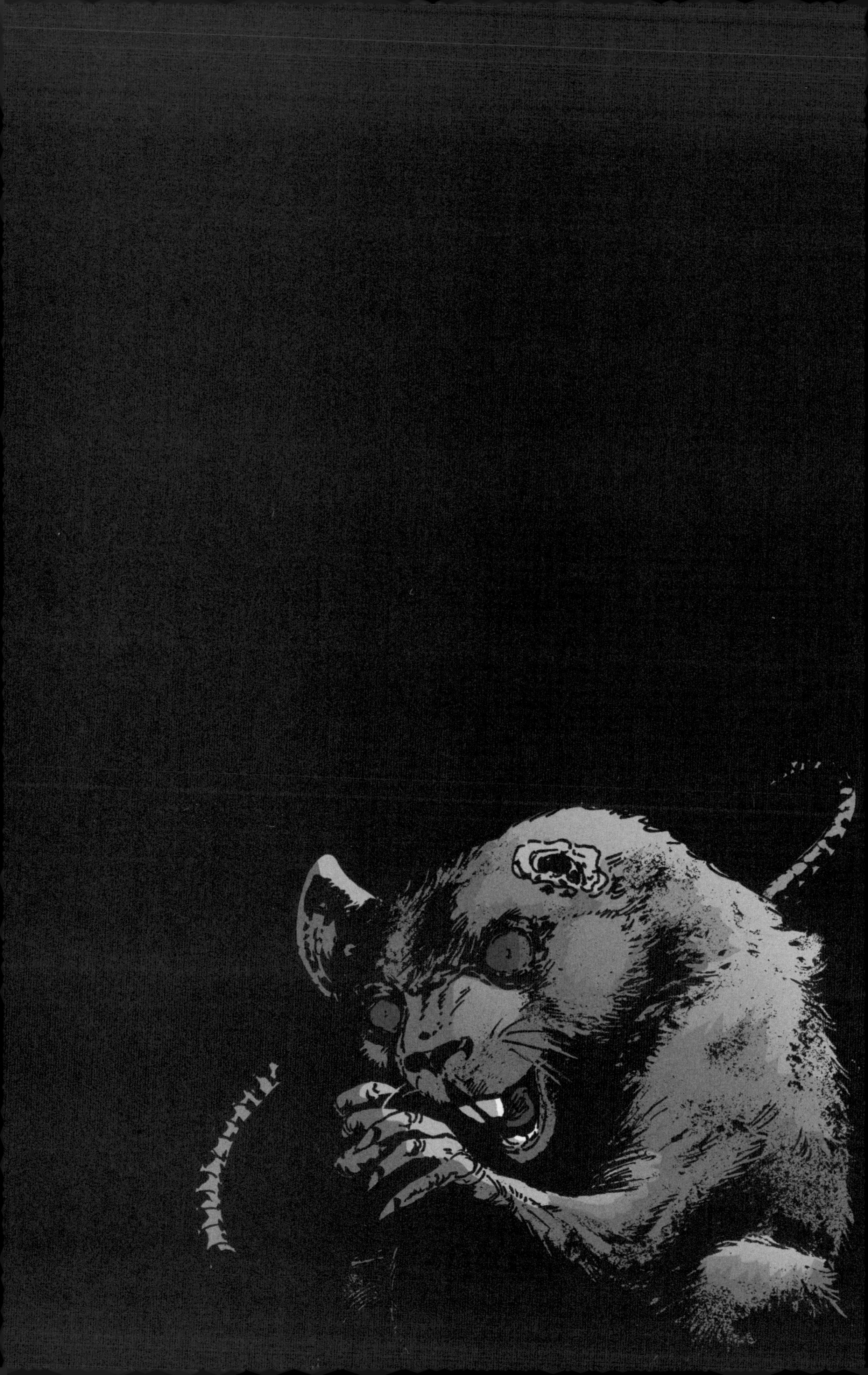

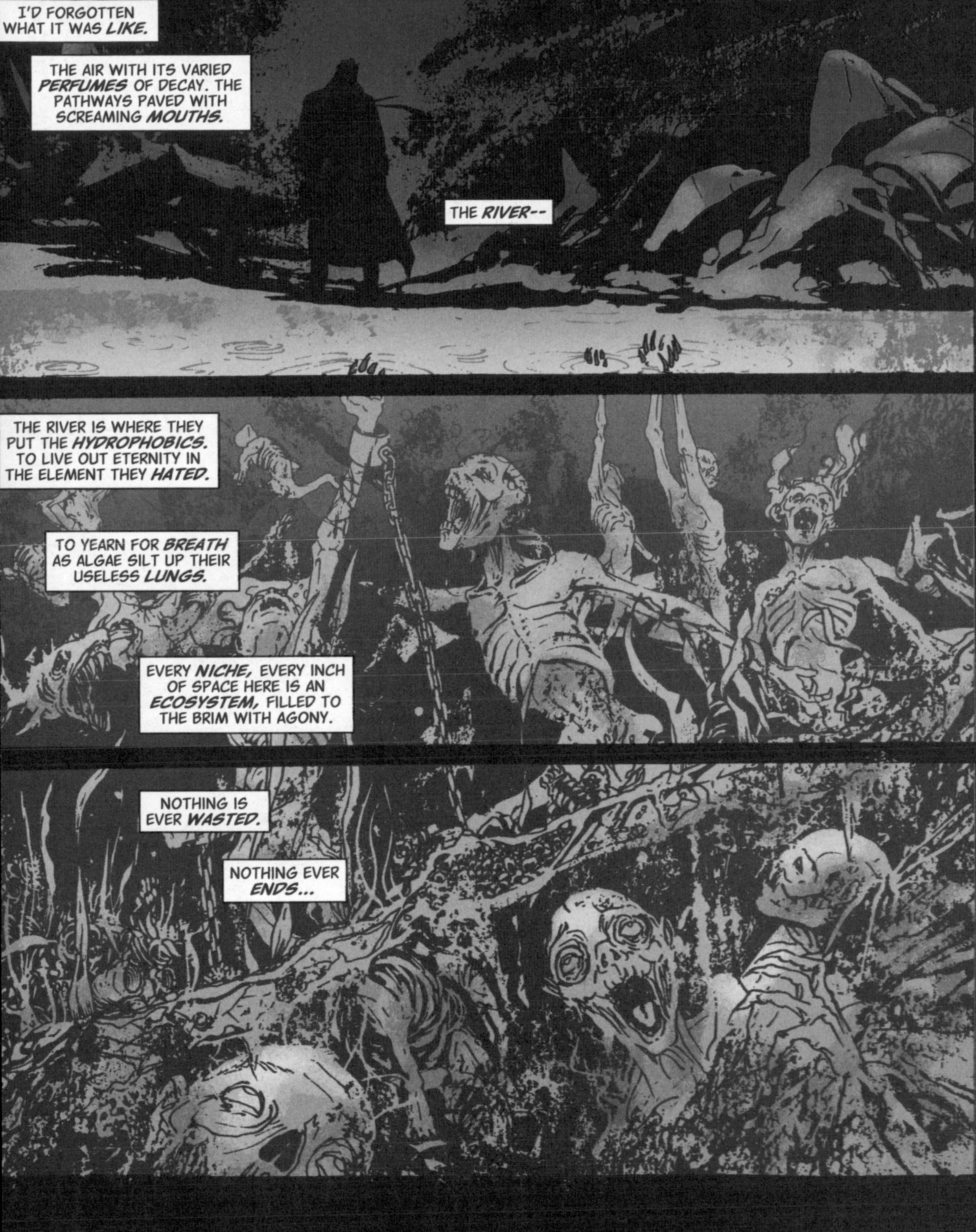

I'D FORGOTTEN WHAT IT WAS LIKE.
THE AIR WITH ITS VARIED PERFUMES OF DECAY. THE PATHWAYS PAVED WITH SCREAMING MOUTHS.
THE RIVER--
THE RIVER IS WHERE THEY PUT THE HYDROPHOBICS. TO LIVE OUT ETERNITY IN THE ELEMENT THEY HATED.
TO YEARN FOR BREATH AS ALGAE SILT UP THEIR USELESS LUNGS.
EVERY NICHE, EVERY INCH OF SPACE HERE IS AN ECOSYSTEM, FILLED TO THE BRIM WITH AGONY.
NOTHING IS EVER WASTED.
NOTHING EVER ENDS...

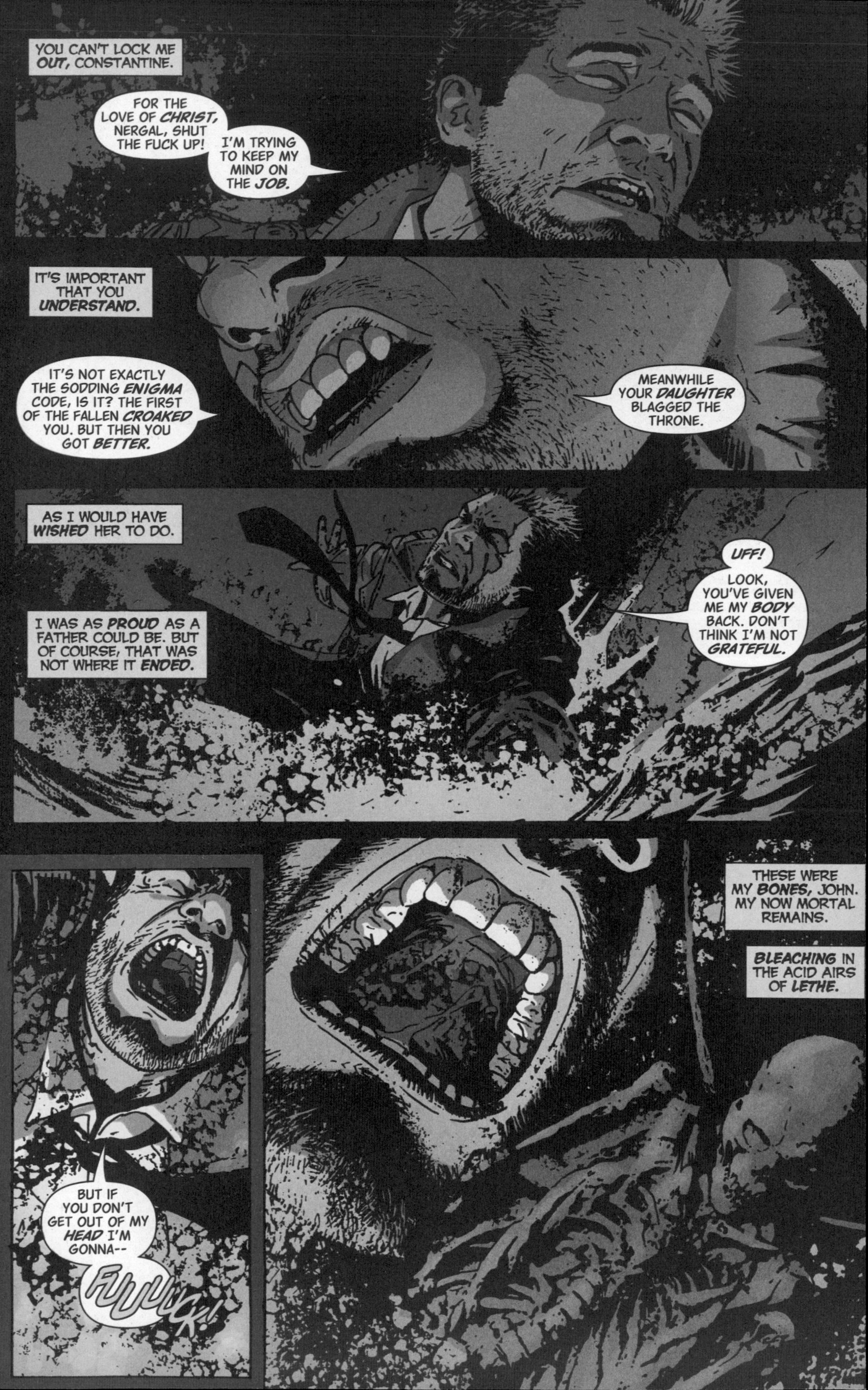
YOU CAN'T LOCK ME OUT, CONSTANTINE.
FOR THE LOVE OF CHRIST, NERGAL, SHUT THE FUCK UP!
I'M TRYING TO KEEP MY MIND ON THE JOB.
IT'S IMPORTANT THAT YOU UNDERSTAND.
IT'S NOT EXACTLY THE SODDING ENIGMA CODE, IS IT? THE FIRST OF THE FALLEN CROAKED YOU. BUT THEN YOU GOT BETTER.
MEANWHILE YOUR DAUGHTER BLAGGED THE THRONE.
AS I WOULD HAVE WISHED HER TO DO.
I WAS AS PROUD AS A FATHER COULD BE. BUT OF COURSE, THAT WAS NOT WHERE IT ENDED.
UFF!
LOOK, YOU'VE GIVEN ME MY BODY BACK. DON'T THINK I'M NOT GRATEFUL.
THESE WERE MY BONES, JOHN. MY NOW MORTAL REMAINS.
BLEACHING IN THE ACID AIRS OF LETHE.
BUT IF YOU DON'T GET OUT OF MY HEAD I'M GONNA--
FUUUUCK!

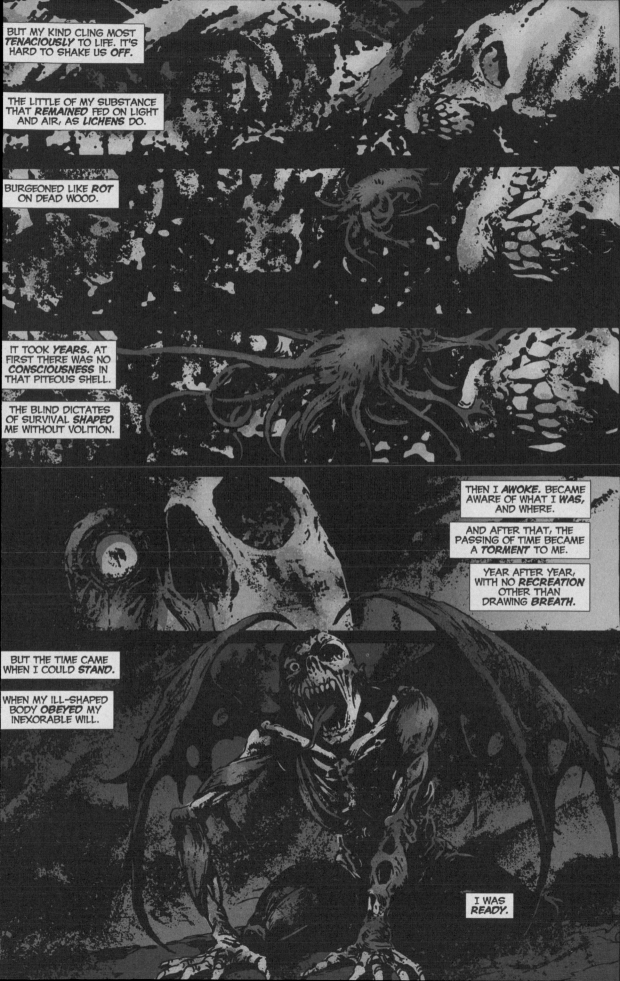

BUT MY KIND CLING MOST *TENACIOUSLY* TO LIFE. IT'S HARD TO SHAKE US *OFF.*

THE LITTLE OF MY SUBSTANCE THAT *REMAINED* FED ON LIGHT AND AIR, AS *LICHENS* DO.

BURGEONED LIKE *ROT* ON DEAD WOOD.

IT TOOK *YEARS.* AT FIRST THERE WAS NO *CONSCIOUSNESS* IN THAT PITEOUS SHELL.

THE BLIND DICTATES OF SURVIVAL *SHAPED* ME WITHOUT VOLITION.

THEN I *AWOKE.* BECAME AWARE OF WHAT I *WAS,* AND WHERE.

AND AFTER THAT, THE PASSING OF TIME BECAME A *TORMENT* TO ME.

YEAR AFTER YEAR, WITH NO *RECREATION* OTHER THAN DRAWING *BREATH.*

BUT THE TIME CAME WHEN I COULD *STAND.*

WHEN MY ILL-SHAPED BODY *OBEYED* MY INEXORABLE WILL.

I WAS *READY.*

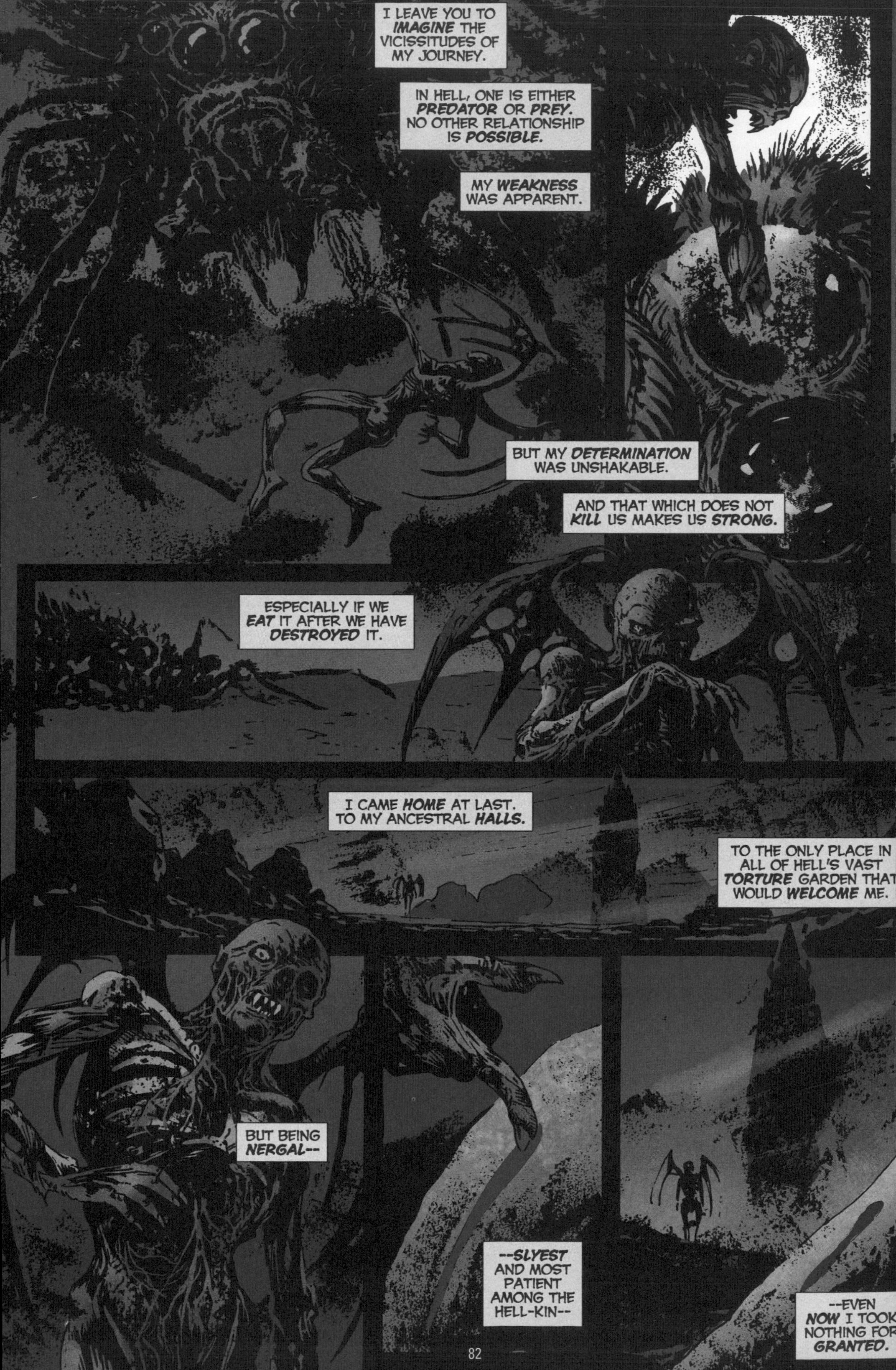

I LEAVE YOU TO IMAGINE THE VICISSITUDES OF MY JOURNEY.
IN HELL, ONE IS EITHER PREDATOR OR PREY. NO OTHER RELATIONSHIP IS POSSIBLE.
MY WEAKNESS WAS APPARENT.
BUT MY DETERMINATION WAS UNSHAKABLE.
AND THAT WHICH DOES NOT KILL US MAKES US STRONG.
ESPECIALLY IF WE EAT IT AFTER WE HAVE DESTROYED IT.
I CAME HOME AT LAST. TO MY ANCESTRAL HALLS.
TO THE ONLY PLACE IN ALL OF HELL'S VAST TORTURE GARDEN THAT WOULD WELCOME ME.
BUT BEING NERGAL--
--SLYEST AND MOST PATIENT AMONG THE HELL-KIN--
--EVEN NOW I TOOK NOTHING FOR GRANTED.

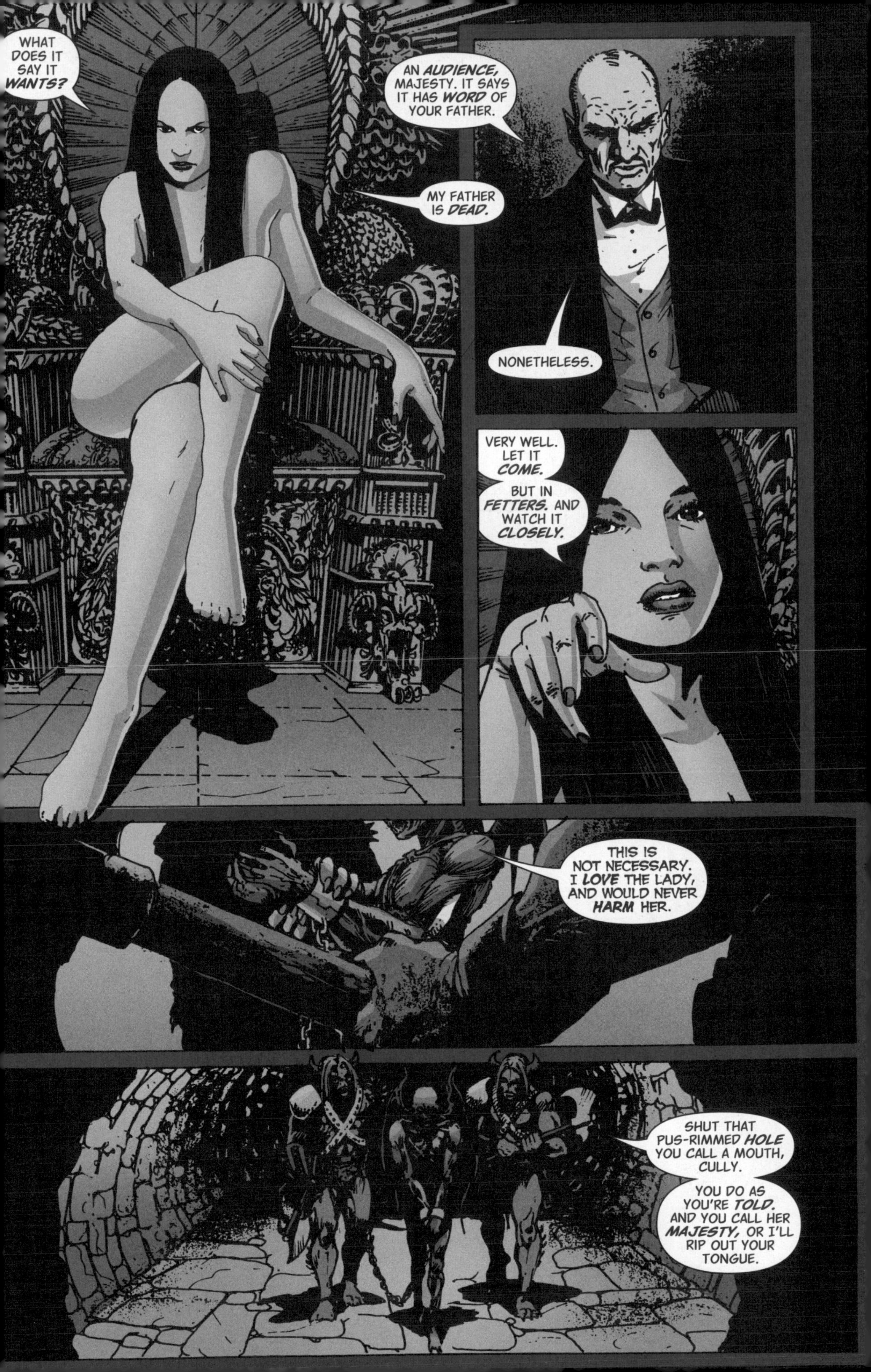
WHAT DOES IT SAY IT *WANTS?*
AN *AUDIENCE,* MAJESTY. IT SAYS IT HAS *WORD* OF YOUR FATHER.
MY FATHER IS *DEAD.*
NONETHELESS.
VERY WELL. LET IT *COME.*
BUT IN *FETTERS.* AND WATCH IT *CLOSELY.*
THIS IS NOT NECESSARY. I *LOVE* THE LADY, AND WOULD NEVER *HARM* HER.
SHUT THAT PUS-RIMMED *HOLE* YOU CALL A MOUTH, CULLY.
YOU DO AS YOU'RE *TOLD.* AND YOU CALL HER *MAJESTY,* OR I'LL RIP OUT YOUR TONGUE.

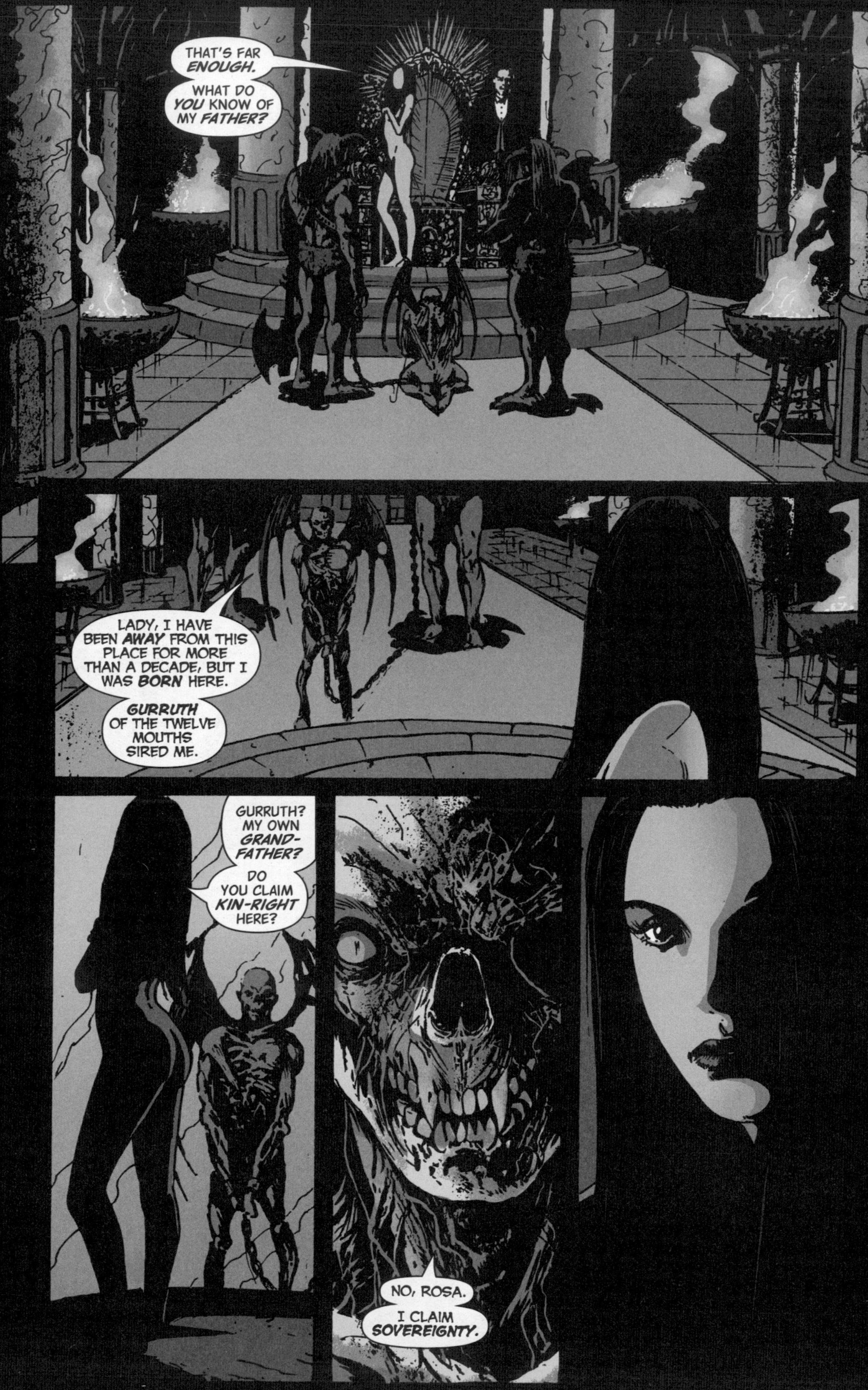
THAT'S FAR ENOUGH.
WHAT DO YOU KNOW OF MY FATHER?
LADY, I HAVE BEEN AWAY FROM THIS PLACE FOR MORE THAN A DECADE, BUT I WAS BORN HERE.
GURRUTH OF THE TWELVE MOUTHS SIRED ME.
GURRUTH? MY OWN GRAND-FATHER?
DO YOU CLAIM KIN-RIGHT HERE?
NO, ROSA.
I CLAIM SOVEREIGNTY.

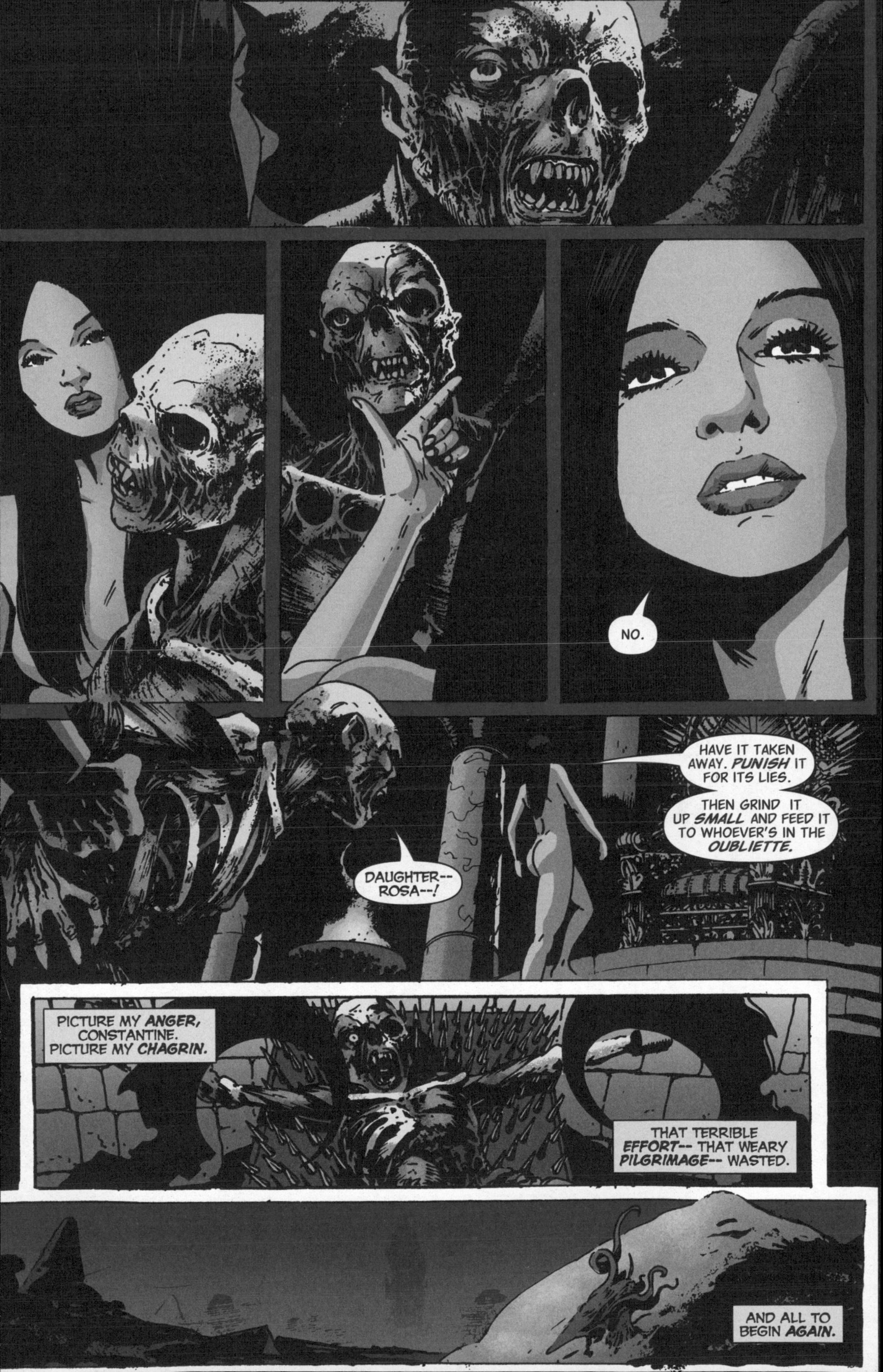
NO.
DAUGHTER-- ROSA--!
HAVE IT TAKEN AWAY. PUNISH IT FOR ITS LIES.
THEN GRIND IT UP SMALL AND FEED IT TO WHOEVER'S IN THE OUBLIETTE.
PICTURE MY ANGER, CONSTANTINE. PICTURE MY CHAGRIN.
THAT TERRIBLE EFFORT-- THAT WEARY PILGRIMAGE-- WASTED.
AND ALL TO BEGIN AGAIN.

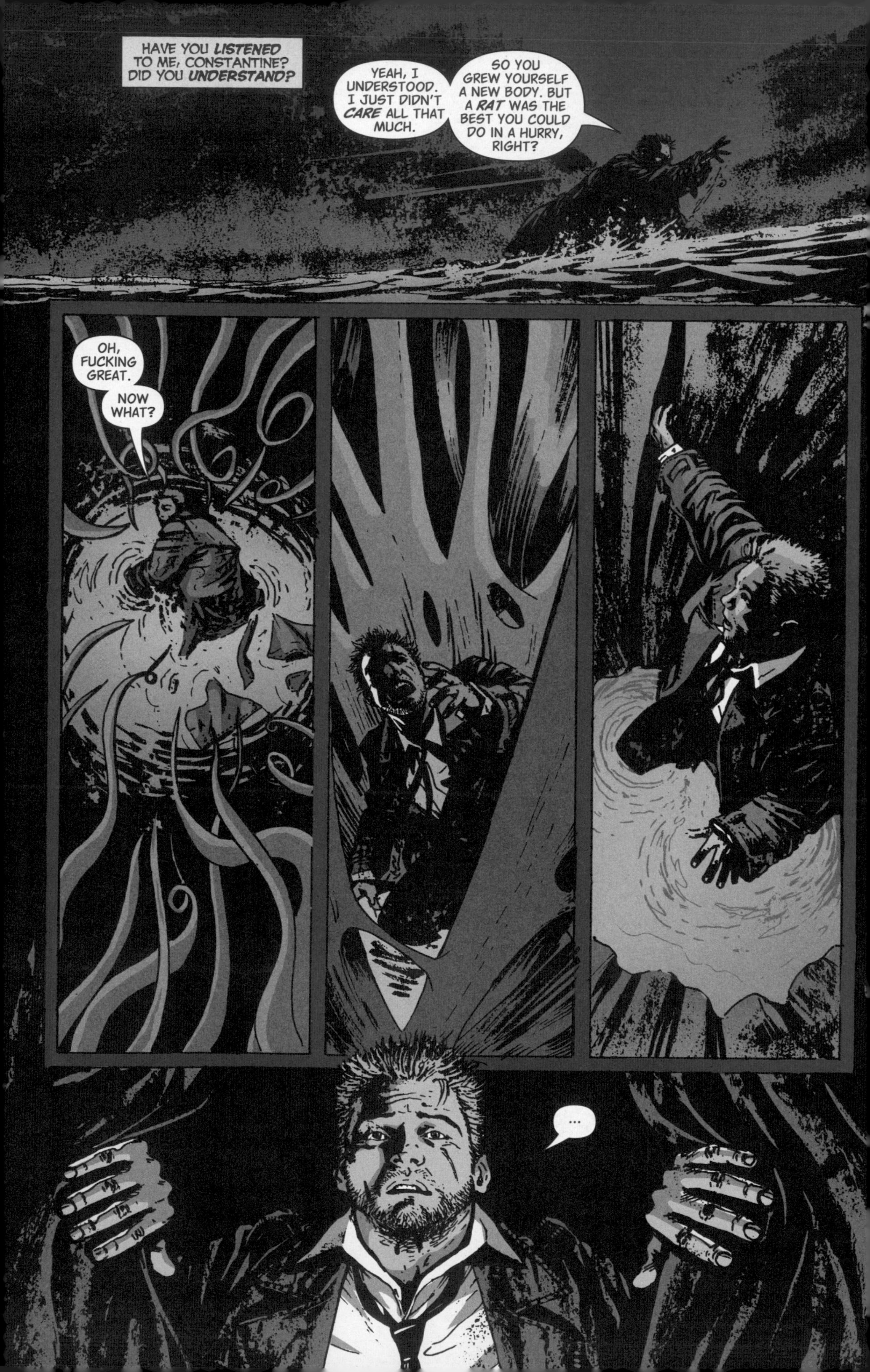
HAVE YOU LISTENED TO ME, CONSTANTINE? DID YOU UNDERSTAND?
YEAH, I UNDERSTOOD. I JUST DIDN'T CARE ALL THAT MUCH.
SO YOU GREW YOURSELF A NEW BODY. BUT A RAT WAS THE BEST YOU COULD DO IN A HURRY, RIGHT?
OH, FUCKING GREAT.
NOW WHAT?
...

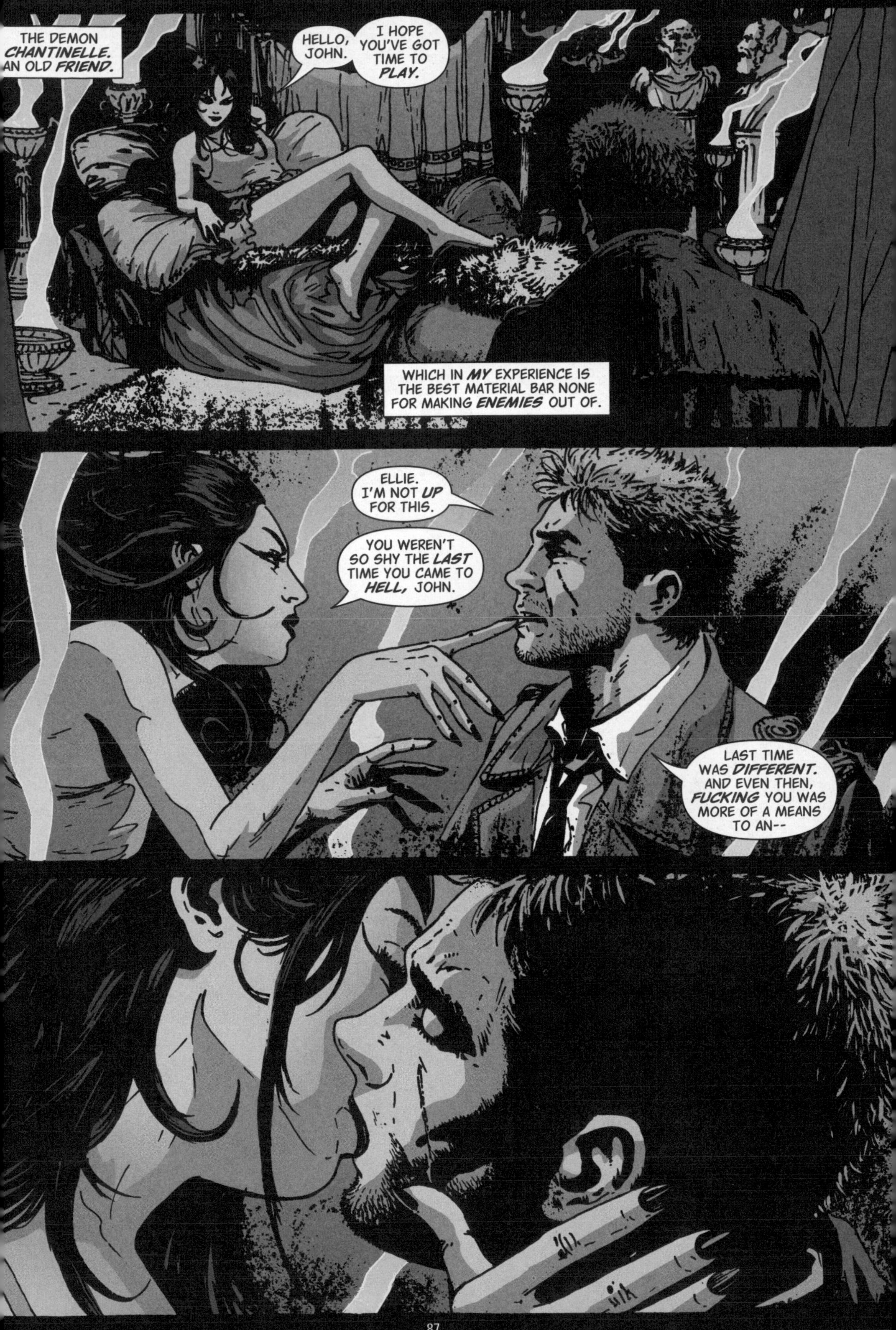
THE DEMON CHANTINELLE. AN OLD FRIEND.
HELLO, JOHN.
I HOPE YOU'VE GOT TIME TO PLAY.
WHICH IN MY EXPERIENCE IS THE BEST MATERIAL BAR NONE FOR MAKING ENEMIES OUT OF.
ELLIE. I'M NOT UP FOR THIS.
YOU WEREN'T SO SHY THE LAST TIME YOU CAME TO HELL, JOHN.
LAST TIME WAS DIFFERENT. AND EVEN THEN, FUCKING YOU WAS MORE OF A MEANS TO AN--

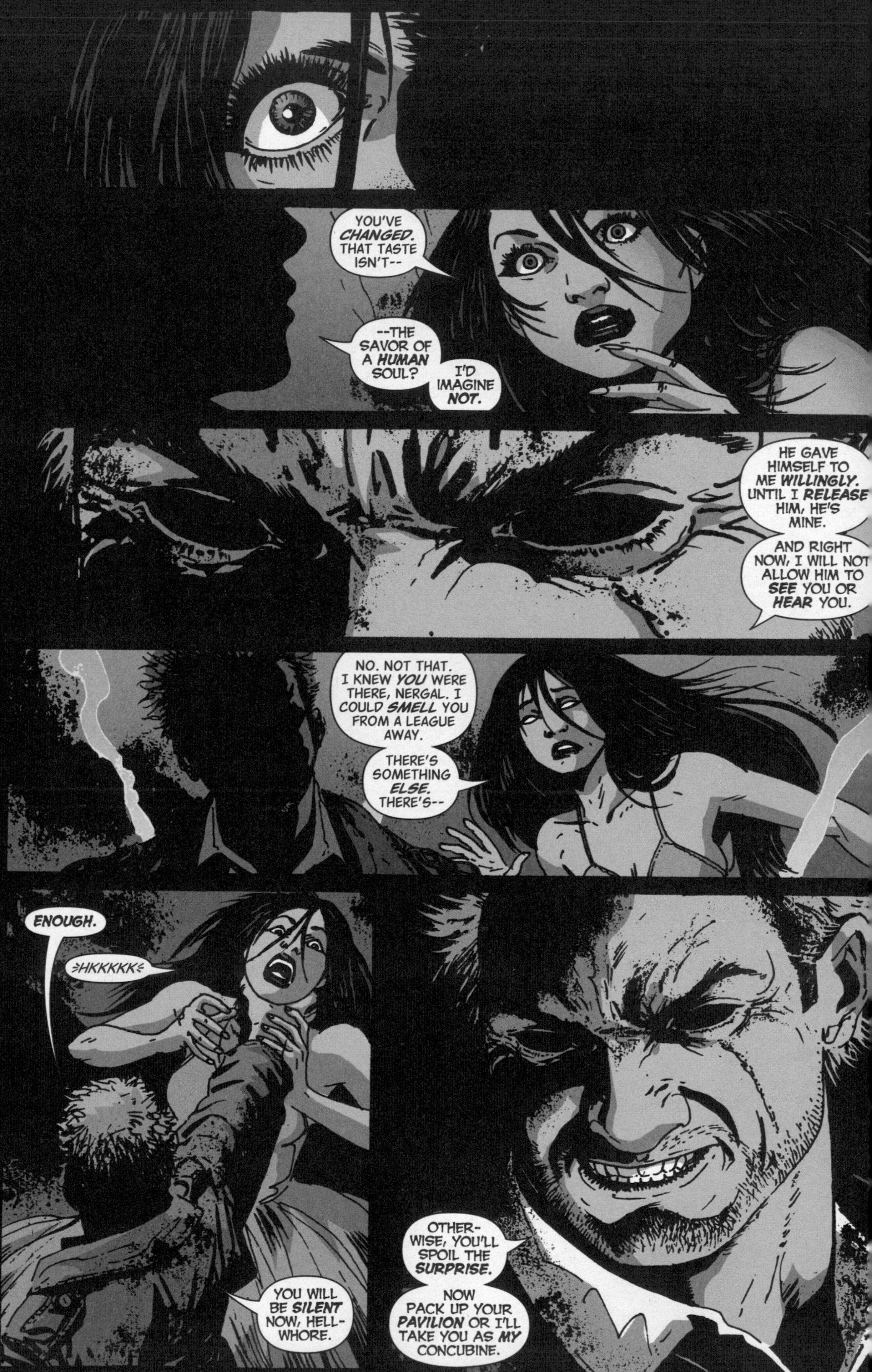

YOU'VE CHANGED. THAT TASTE ISN'T--
--THE SAVOR OF A HUMAN SOUL?
I'D IMAGINE NOT.
HE GAVE HIMSELF TO ME WILLINGLY. UNTIL I RELEASE HIM, HE'S MINE.
AND RIGHT NOW, I WILL NOT ALLOW HIM TO SEE YOU OR HEAR YOU.
NO. NOT THAT. I KNEW YOU WERE THERE, NERGAL. I COULD SMELL YOU FROM A LEAGUE AWAY.
THERE'S SOMETHING ELSE. THERE'S--
ENOUGH.
HKKKKK
YOU WILL BE SILENT NOW, HELL-WHORE.
OTHER-WISE, YOU'LL SPOIL THE SURPRISE.
NOW PACK UP YOUR PAVILION OR I'LL TAKE YOU AS MY CONCUBINE.

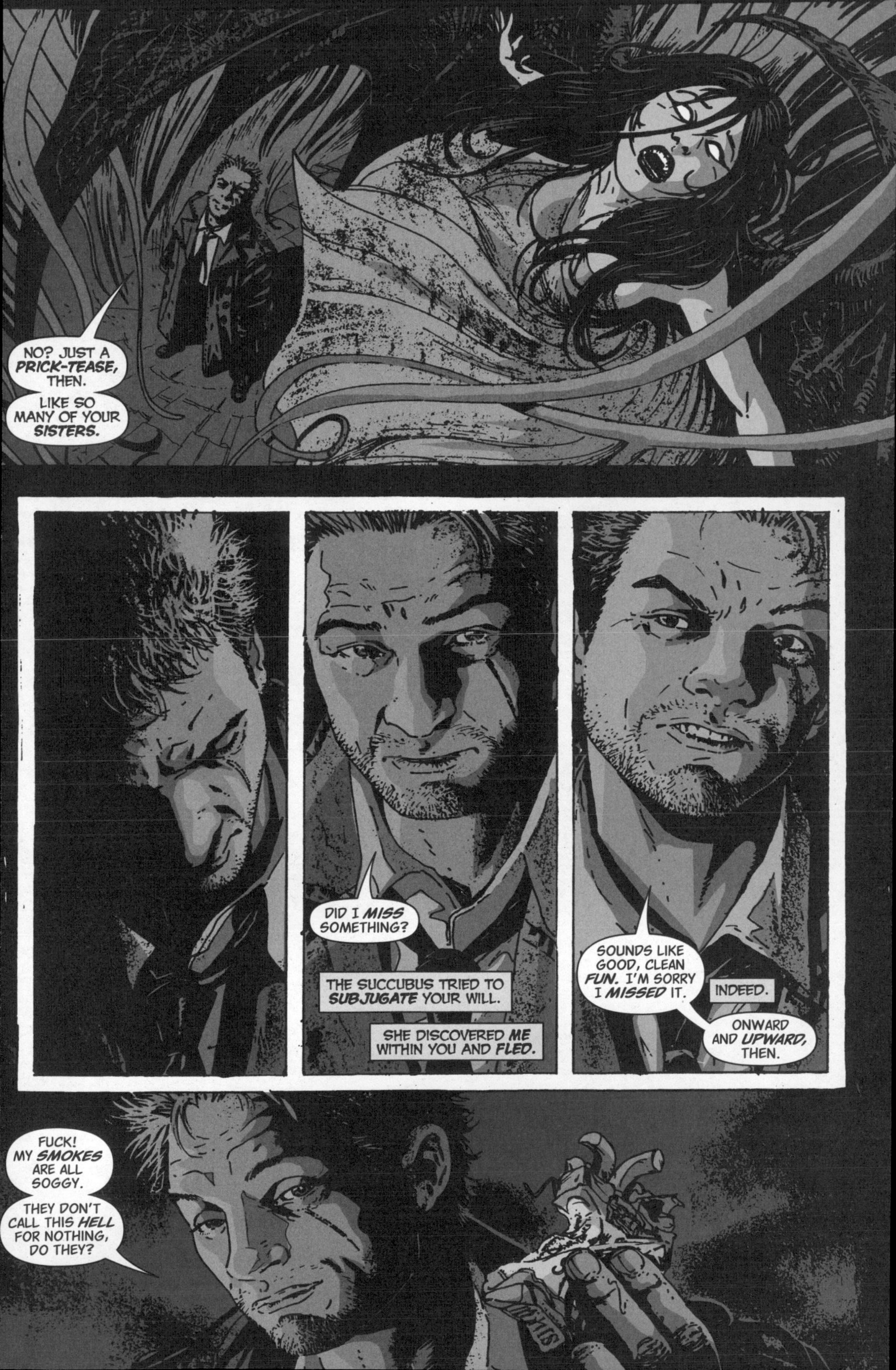

NO? JUST A *PRICK-TEASE*, THEN.
LIKE SO MANY OF YOUR *SISTERS*.
DID I *MISS* SOMETHING?
THE SUCCUBUS TRIED TO *SUBJUGATE* YOUR WILL.
SHE DISCOVERED *ME* WITHIN YOU AND *FLED*.
SOUNDS LIKE GOOD, CLEAN *FUN*. I'M SORRY I *MISSED* IT.
INDEED.
ONWARD AND *UPWARD*, THEN.
FUCK! MY *SMOKES* ARE ALL SOGGY.
THEY DON'T CALL THIS *HELL* FOR NOTHING, DO THEY?

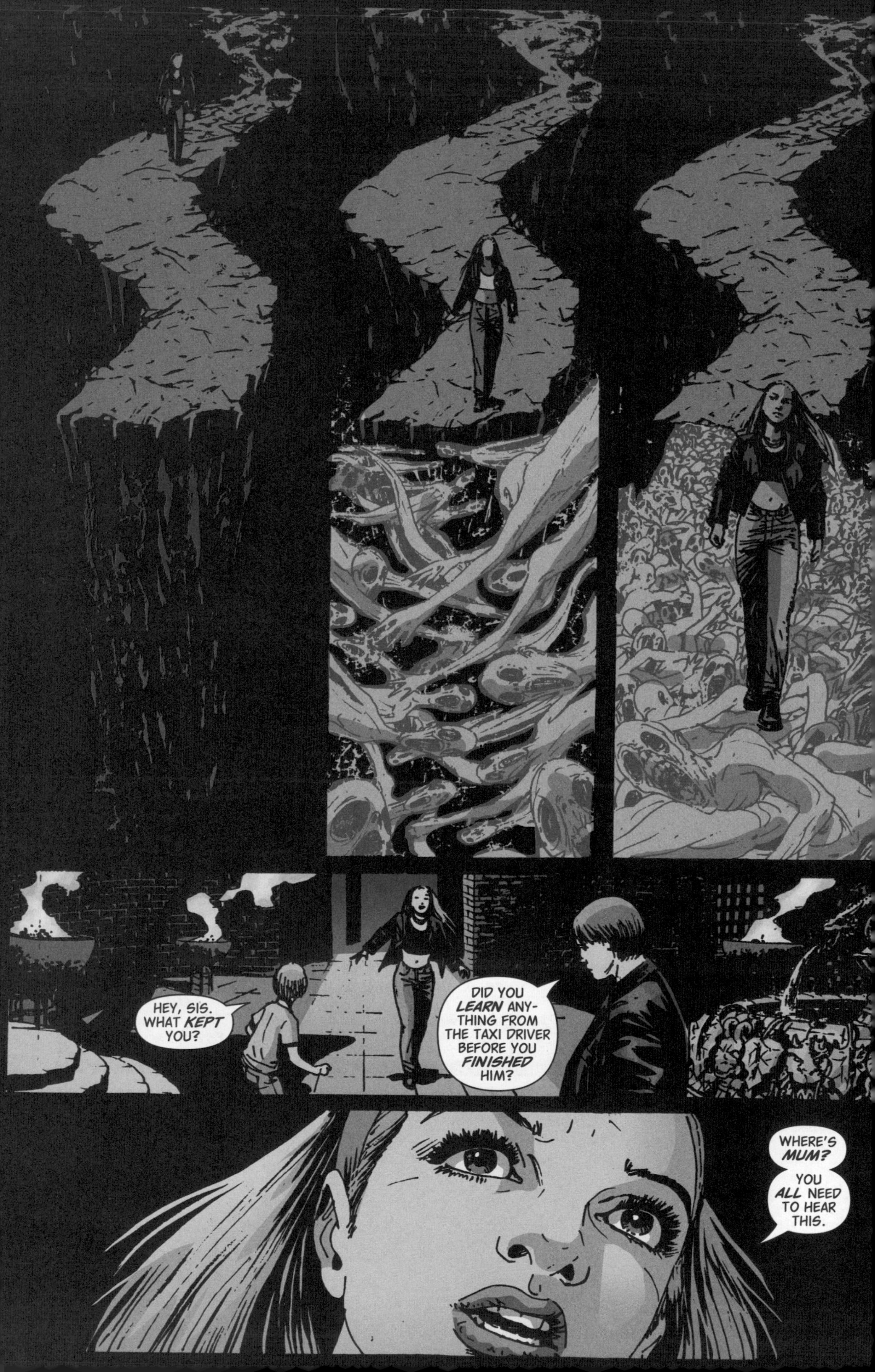
HEY, SIS. WHAT KEPT YOU?
DID YOU LEARN ANYTHING FROM THE TAXI DRIVER BEFORE YOU FINISHED HIM?
WHERE'S MUM?
YOU ALL NEED TO HEAR THIS.

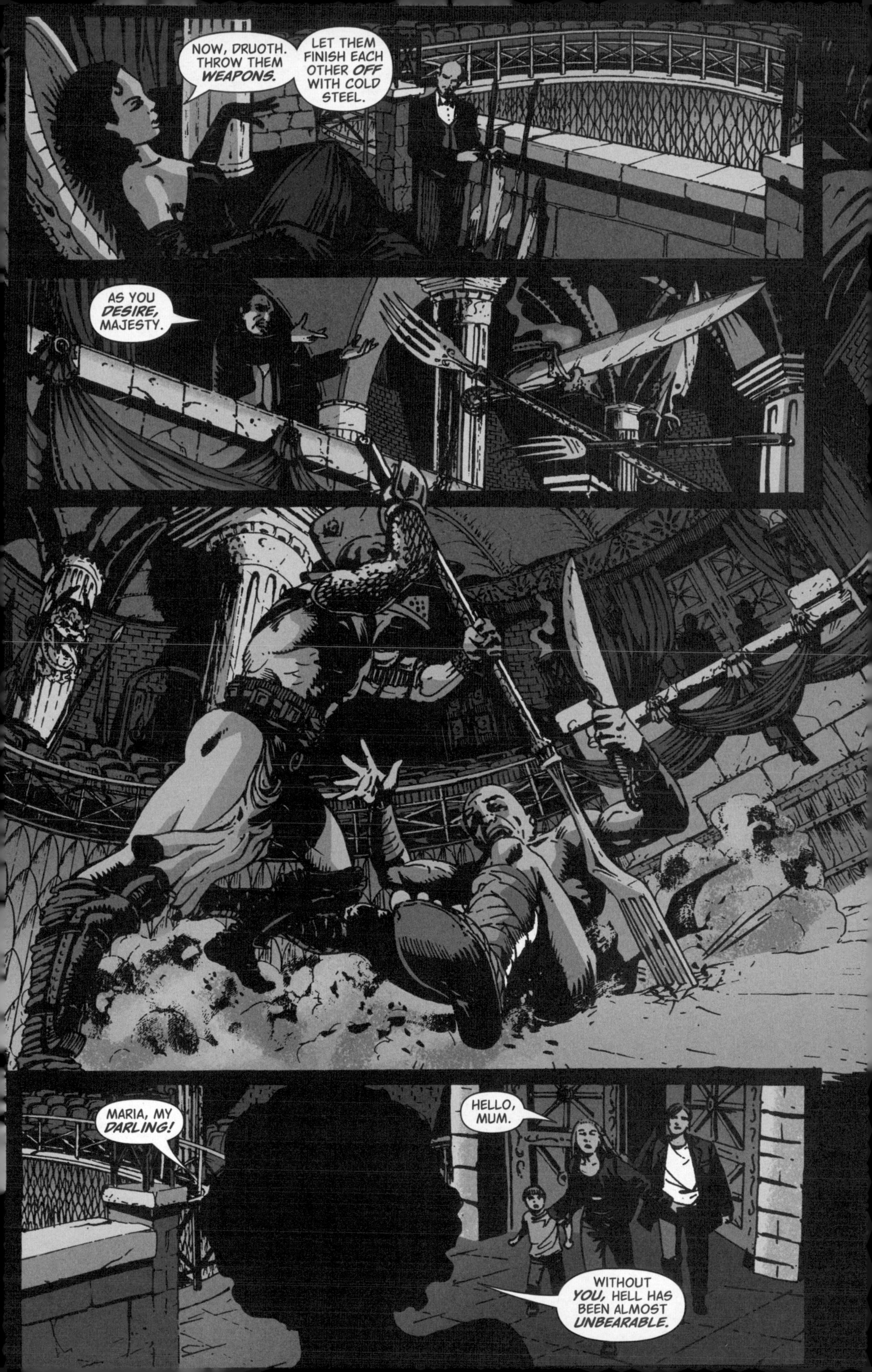
NOW, DRUOTH. THROW THEM WEAPONS.
LET THEM FINISH EACH OTHER OFF WITH COLD STEEL.
AS YOU DESIRE, MAJESTY.
MARIA, MY DARLING!
HELLO, MUM.
WITHOUT YOU, HELL HAS BEEN ALMOST UNBEARABLE.

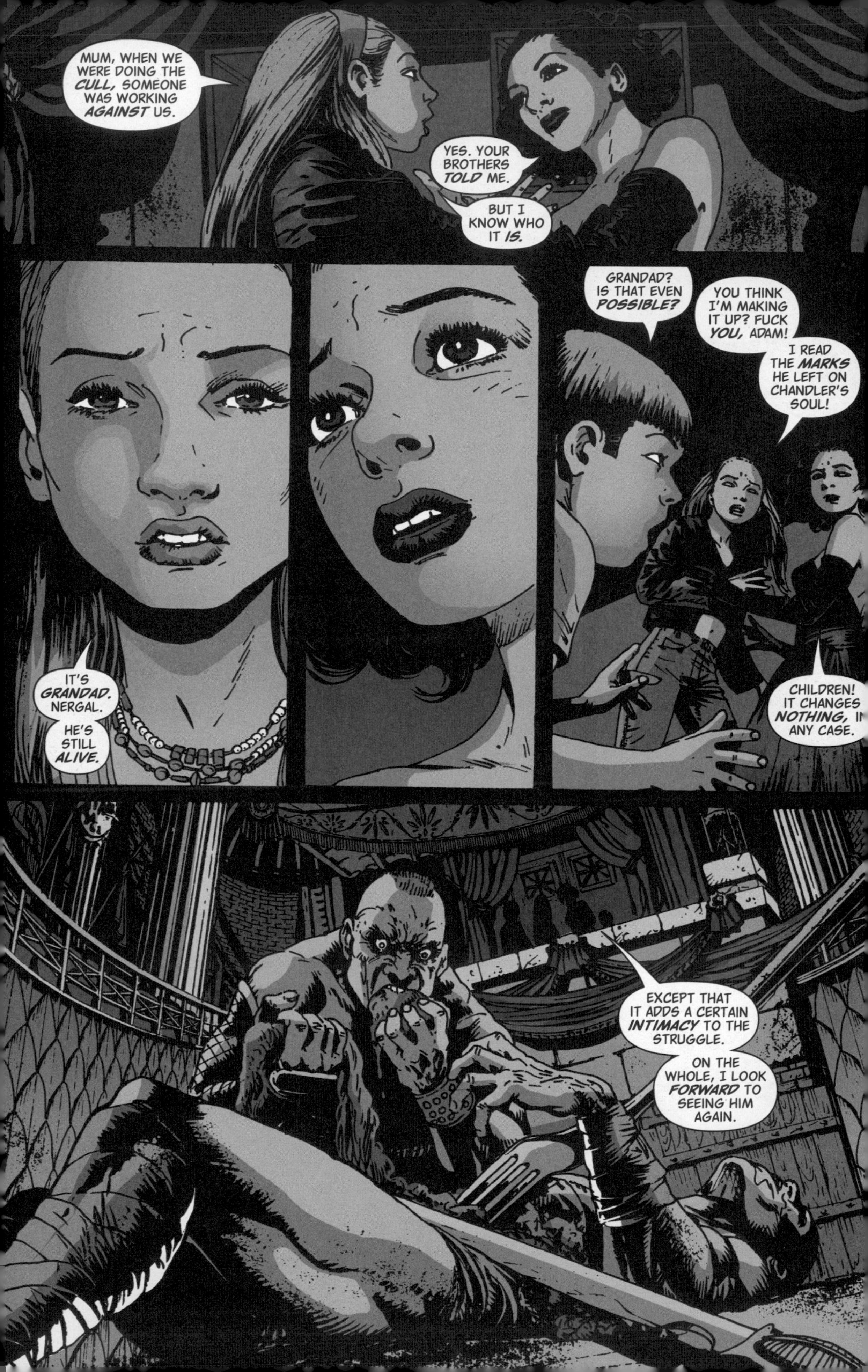
MUM, WHEN WE WERE DOING THE CULL, SOMEONE WAS WORKING AGAINST US.
YES. YOUR BROTHERS TOLD ME.
BUT I KNOW WHO IT IS.
IT'S GRANDAD. NERGAL.
HE'S STILL ALIVE.
GRANDAD? IS THAT EVEN POSSIBLE?
YOU THINK I'M MAKING IT UP? FUCK YOU, ADAM!
I READ THE MARKS HE LEFT ON CHANDLER'S SOUL!
CHILDREN! IT CHANGES NOTHING, IN ANY CASE.
EXCEPT THAT IT ADDS A CERTAIN INTIMACY TO THE STRUGGLE.
ON THE WHOLE, I LOOK FORWARD TO SEEING HIM AGAIN.

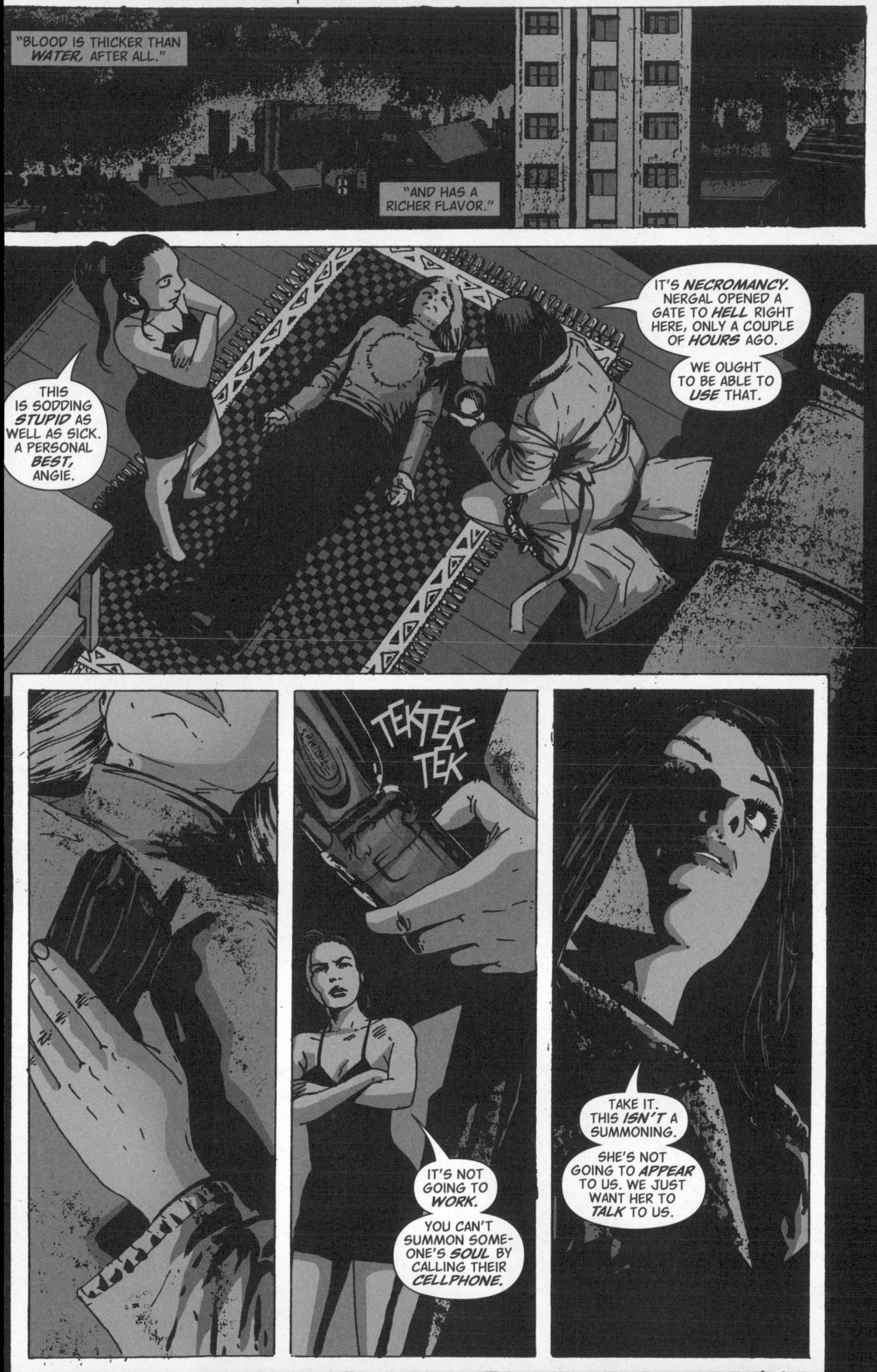

"BLOOD IS THICKER THAN WATER, AFTER ALL."
"AND HAS A RICHER FLAVOR."
IT'S NECROMANCY. NERGAL OPENED A GATE TO HELL RIGHT HERE, ONLY A COUPLE OF HOURS AGO.
WE OUGHT TO BE ABLE TO USE THAT.
THIS IS SODDING STUPID AS WELL AS SICK. A PERSONAL BEST, ANGIE.
TEKTEK TEK
IT'S NOT GOING TO WORK.
YOU CAN'T SUMMON SOME-ONE'S SOUL BY CALLING THEIR CELLPHONE.
TAKE IT. THIS ISN'T A SUMMONING.
SHE'S NOT GOING TO APPEAR TO US. WE JUST WANT HER TO TALK TO US.

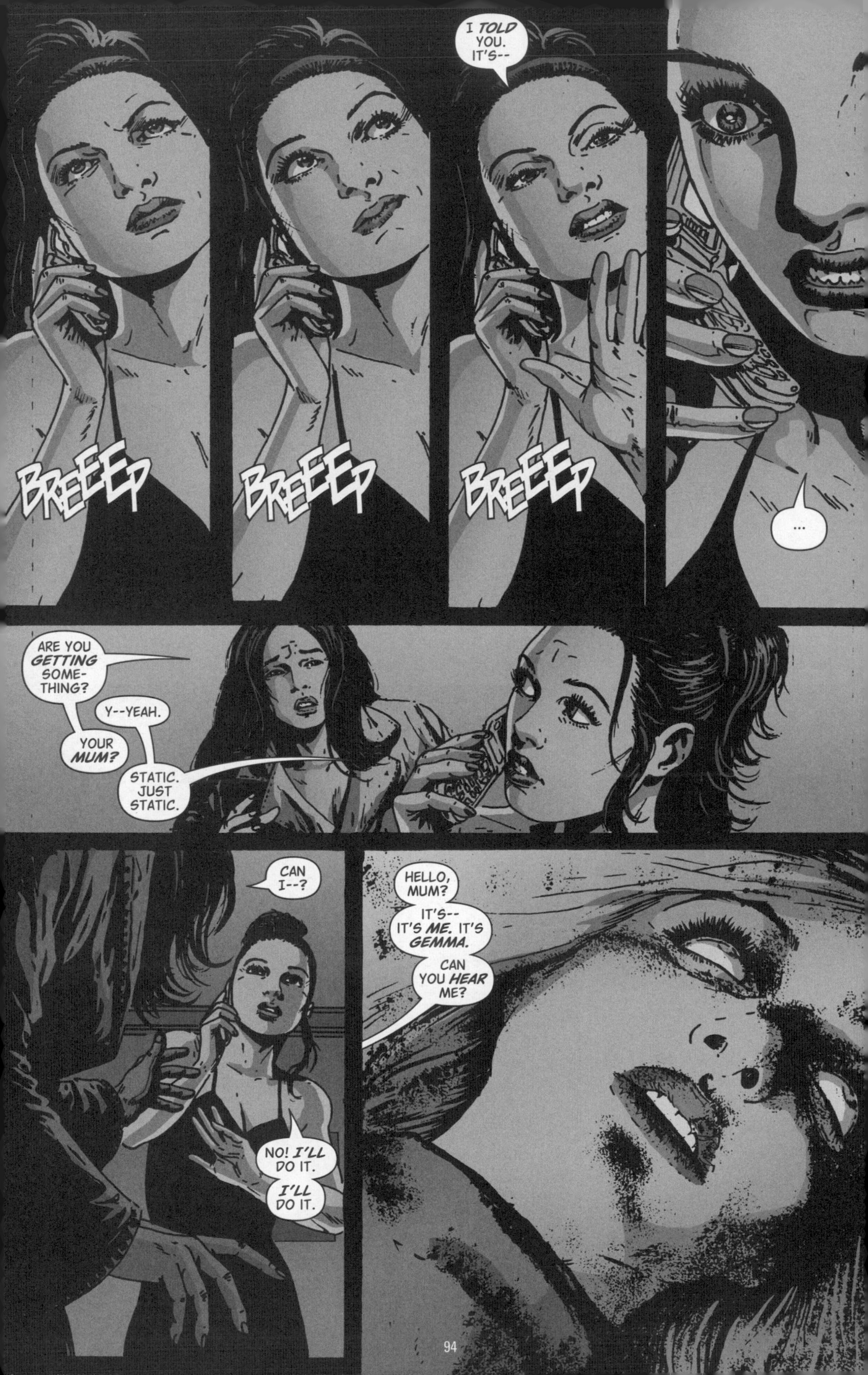

BREEEP
BREEEP
I TOLD YOU. IT'S--
BREEEP
...
ARE YOU GETTING SOME-THING?
Y--YEAH.
YOUR MUM?
STATIC. JUST STATIC.
CAN I--?
NO! I'LL DO IT.
I'LL DO IT.
HELLO, MUM?
IT'S-- IT'S ME. IT'S GEMMA.
CAN YOU HEAR ME?

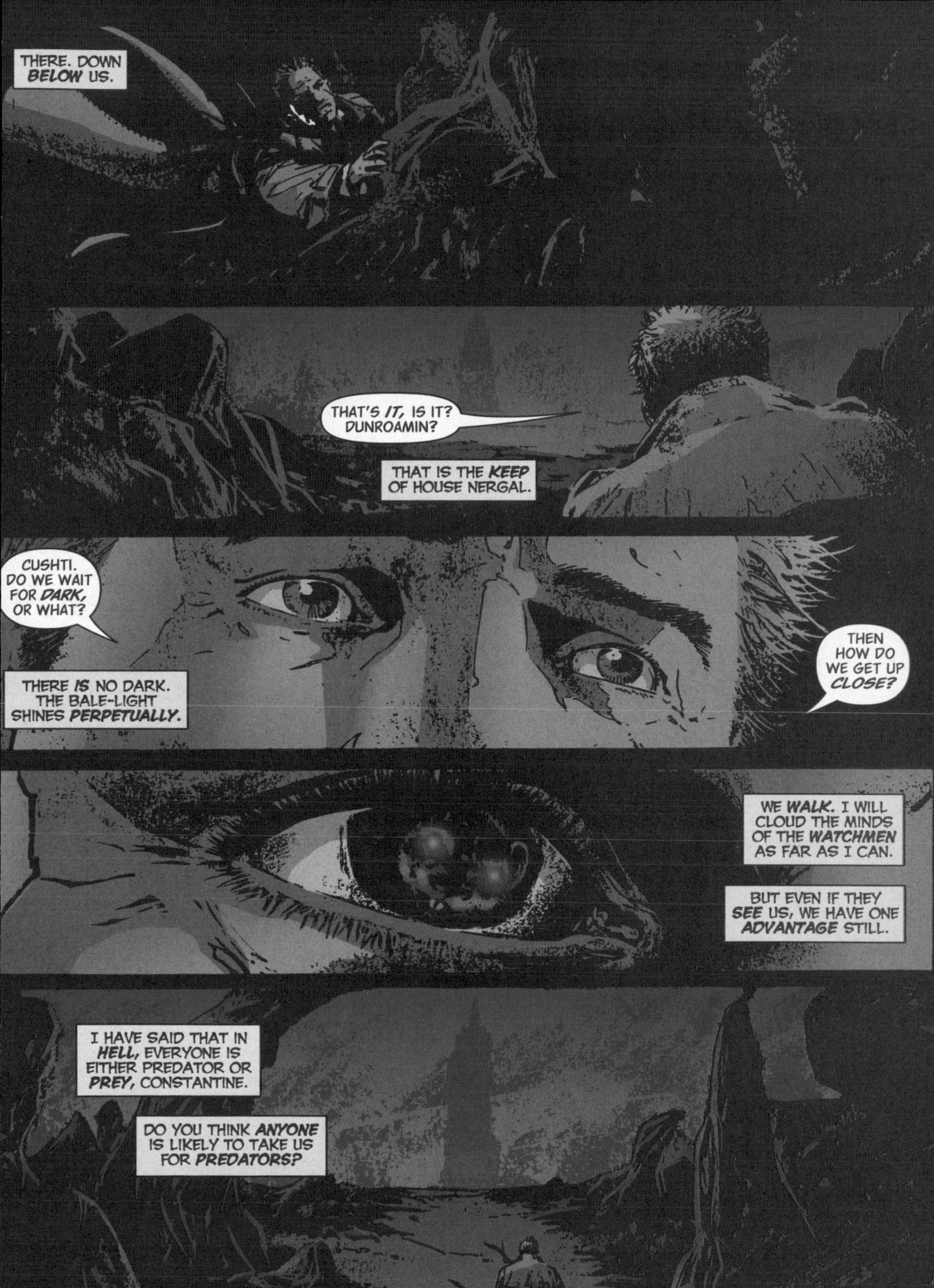

THERE. DOWN BELOW US.
THAT'S IT, IS IT? DUNROAMIN?
THAT IS THE KEEP OF HOUSE NERGAL.
CUSHTI. DO WE WAIT FOR DARK, OR WHAT?
THERE IS NO DARK. THE BALE-LIGHT SHINES PERPETUALLY.
THEN HOW DO WE GET UP CLOSE?
WE WALK. I WILL CLOUD THE MINDS OF THE WATCHMEN AS FAR AS I CAN.
BUT EVEN IF THEY SEE US, WE HAVE ONE ADVANTAGE STILL.
I HAVE SAID THAT IN HELL, EVERYONE IS EITHER PREDATOR OR PREY, CONSTANTINE.
DO YOU THINK ANYONE IS LIKELY TO TAKE US FOR PREDATORS?

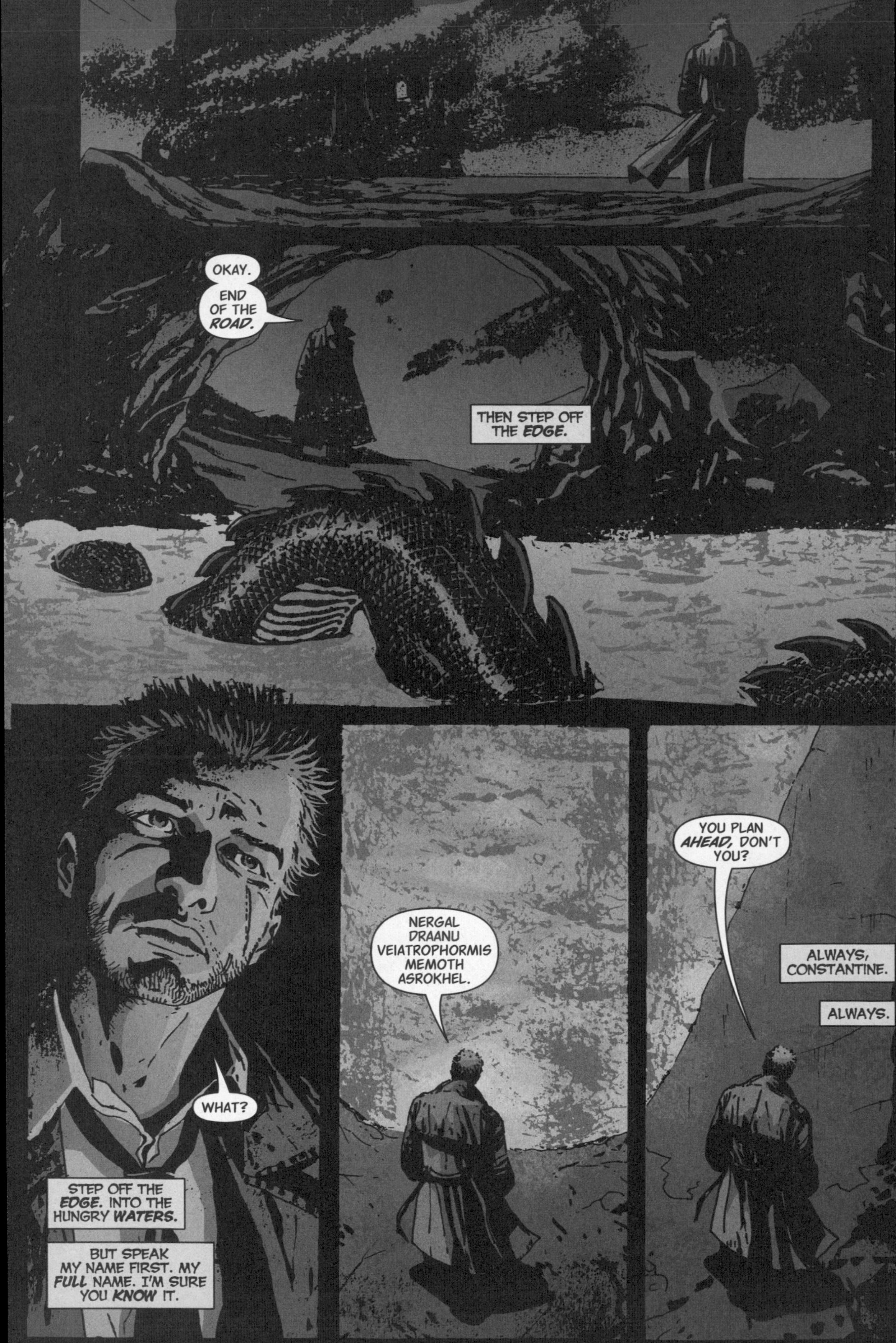
OKAY.
END OF THE ROAD.
THEN STEP OFF THE EDGE.
WHAT?
STEP OFF THE EDGE. INTO THE HUNGRY WATERS.
BUT SPEAK MY NAME FIRST. MY FULL NAME. I'M SURE YOU KNOW IT.
NERGAL DRAANU VEIATROPHORMIS MEMOTH ASROKHEL.
YOU PLAN AHEAD, DON'T YOU?
ALWAYS, CONSTANTINE.
ALWAYS.

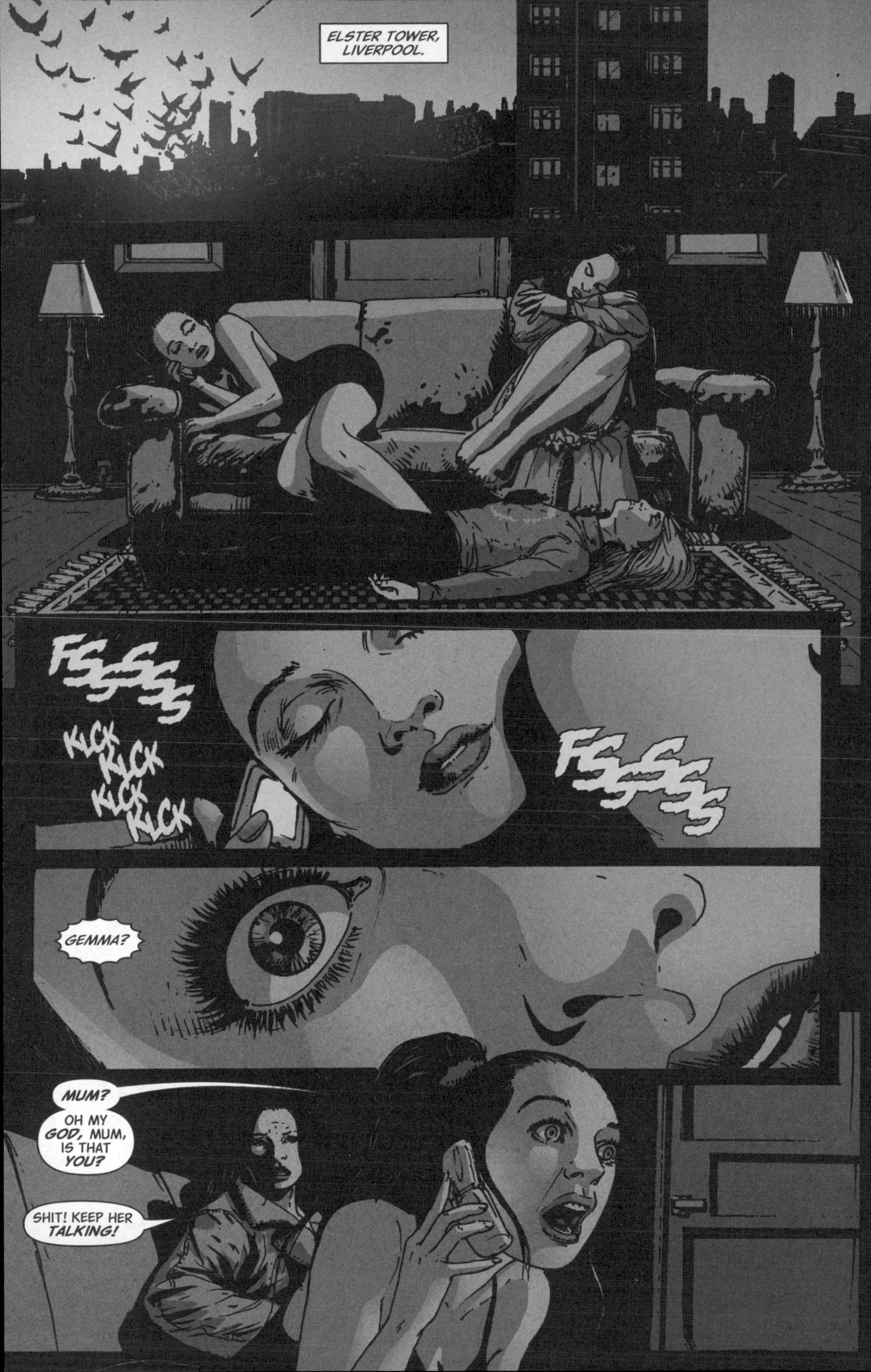
ELSTER TOWER, LIVERPOOL.
FSSSSS
KLICK KLICK KLICK KLICK
FSSSSS
GEMMA?
MUM?
OH MY GOD, MUM, IS THAT YOU?
SHIT! KEEP HER TALKING!

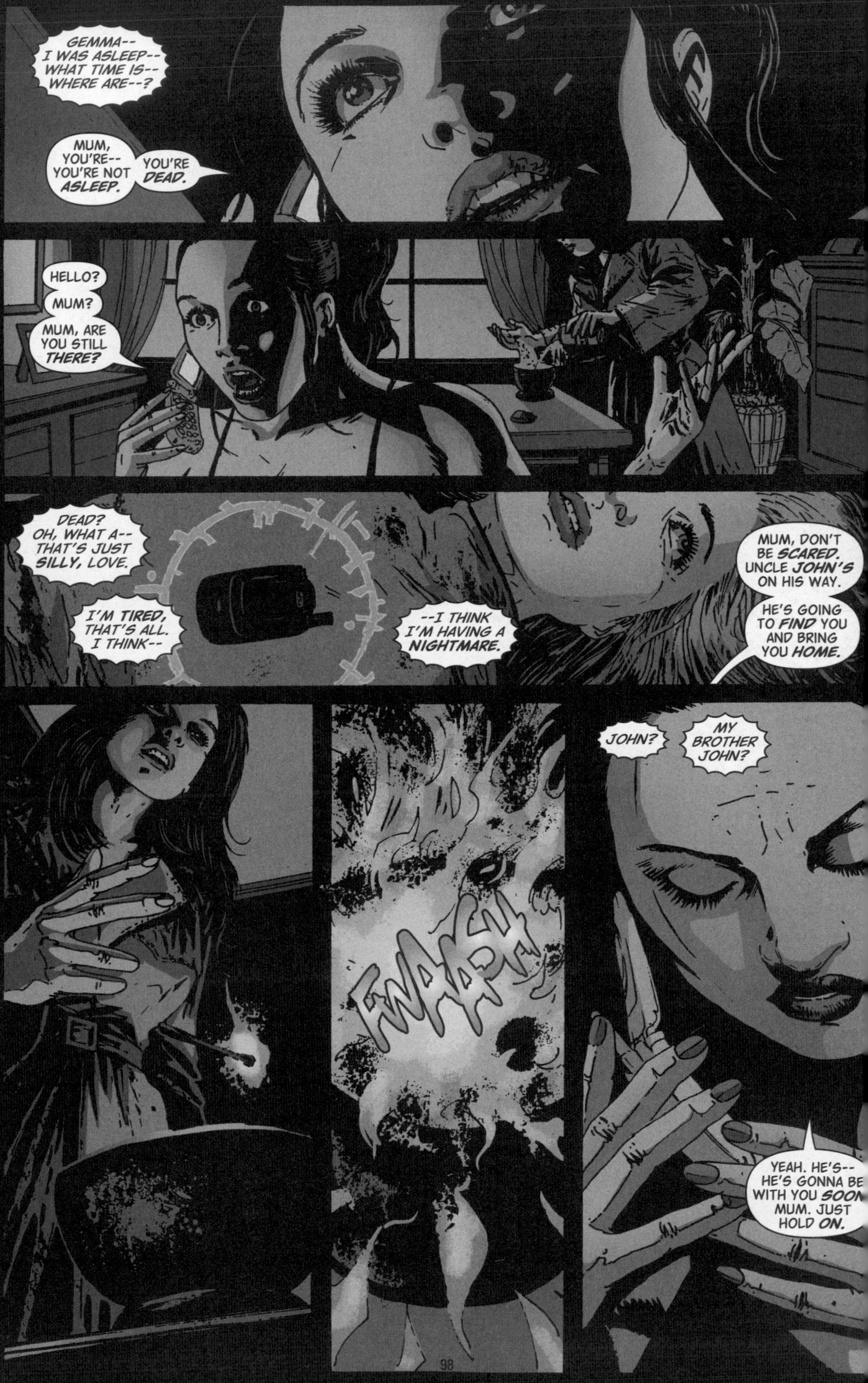
GEMMA-- I WAS ASLEEP-- WHAT TIME IS-- WHERE ARE--?
MUM, YOU'RE-- YOU'RE NOT ASLEEP.
YOU'RE DEAD.
HELLO?
MUM?
MUM, ARE YOU STILL THERE?
DEAD? OH, WHAT A-- THAT'S JUST SILLY, LOVE.
I'M TIRED, THAT'S ALL. I THINK--
--I THINK I'M HAVING A NIGHTMARE.
MUM, DON'T BE SCARED. UNCLE JOHN'S ON HIS WAY.
HE'S GOING TO FIND YOU AND BRING YOU HOME.
FWASH
JOHN?
MY BROTHER JOHN?
YEAH. HE'S-- HE'S GONNA BE WITH YOU SOON MUM. JUST HOLD ON.

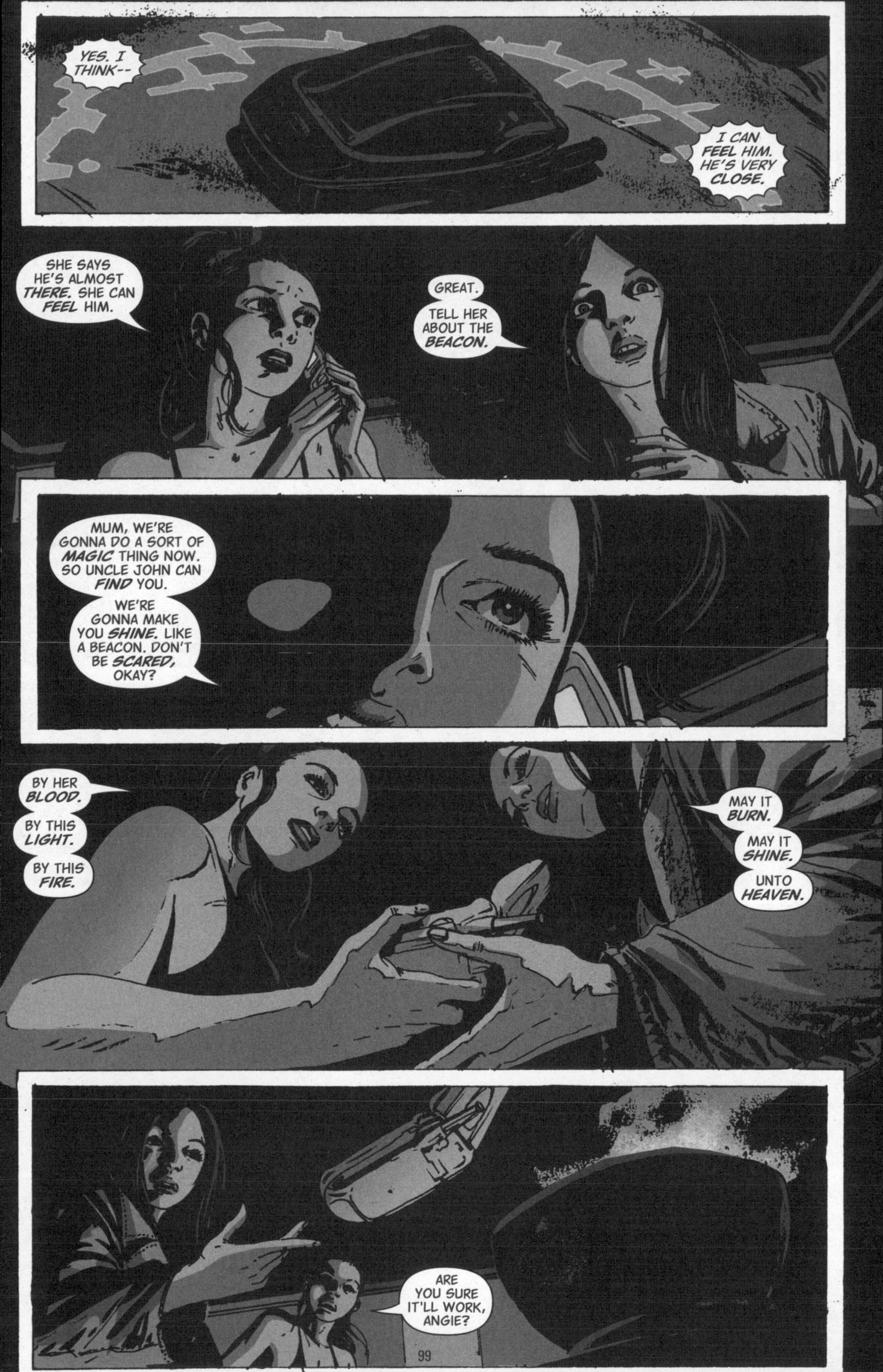

YES. I THINK--
I CAN FEEL HIM. HE'S VERY CLOSE.
SHE SAYS HE'S ALMOST THERE. SHE CAN FEEL HIM.
GREAT.
TELL HER ABOUT THE BEACON.
MUM, WE'RE GONNA DO A SORT OF MAGIC THING NOW. SO UNCLE JOHN CAN FIND YOU.
WE'RE GONNA MAKE YOU SHINE. LIKE A BEACON. DON'T BE SCARED, OKAY?
BY HER BLOOD.
BY THIS LIGHT.
BY THIS FIRE.
MAY IT BURN.
MAY IT SHINE.
UNTO HEAVEN.
ARE YOU SURE IT'LL WORK, ANGIE?

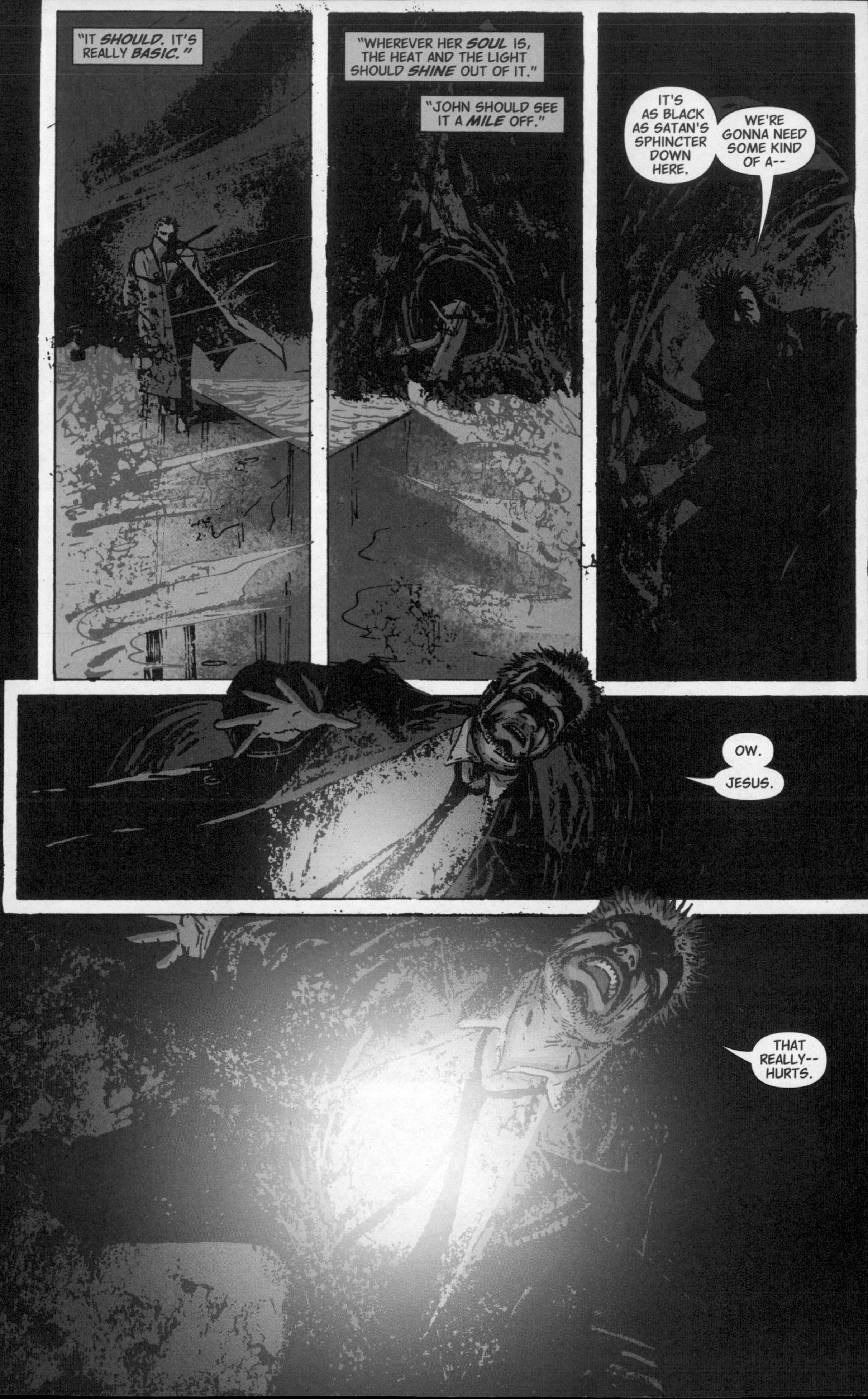
"IT SHOULD. IT'S REALLY BASIC."
"WHEREVER HER SOUL IS, THE HEAT AND THE LIGHT SHOULD SHINE OUT OF IT."
"JOHN SHOULD SEE IT A MILE OFF."
IT'S AS BLACK AS SATAN'S SPHINCTER DOWN HERE.
WE'RE GONNA NEED SOME KIND OF A--
OW.
JESUS.
THAT REALLY-- HURTS.

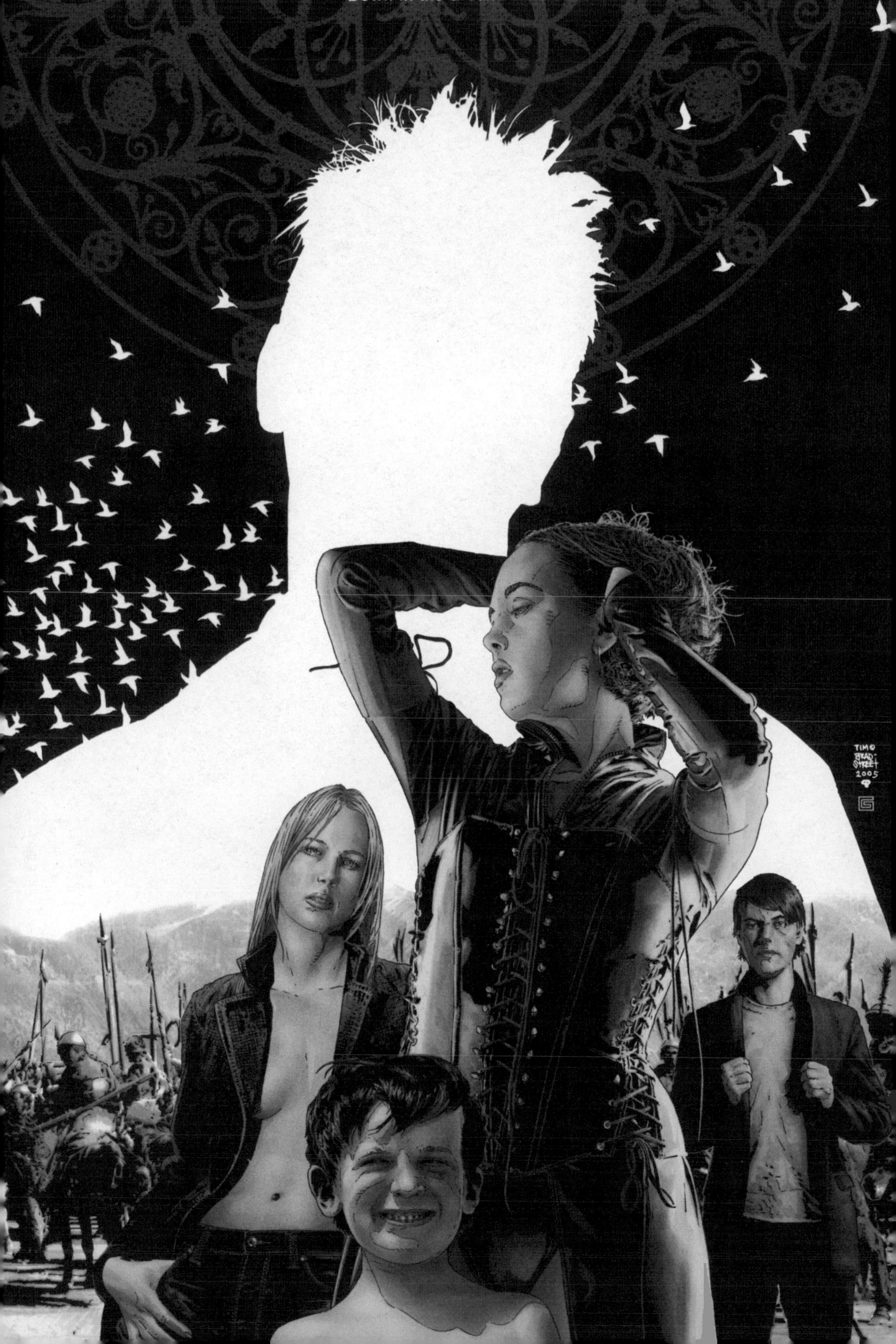
TIMO
BRAD-
STREET
2005

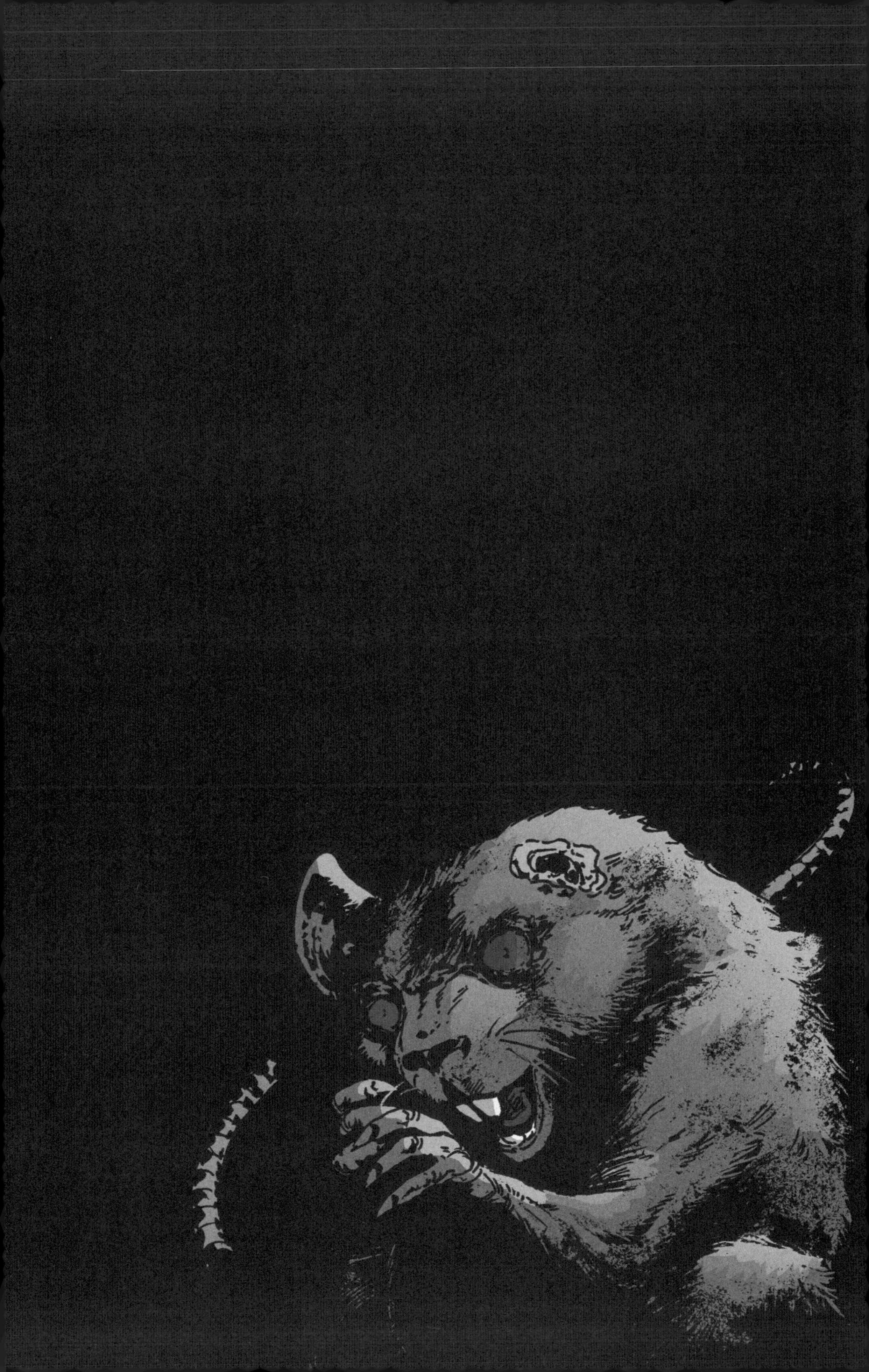

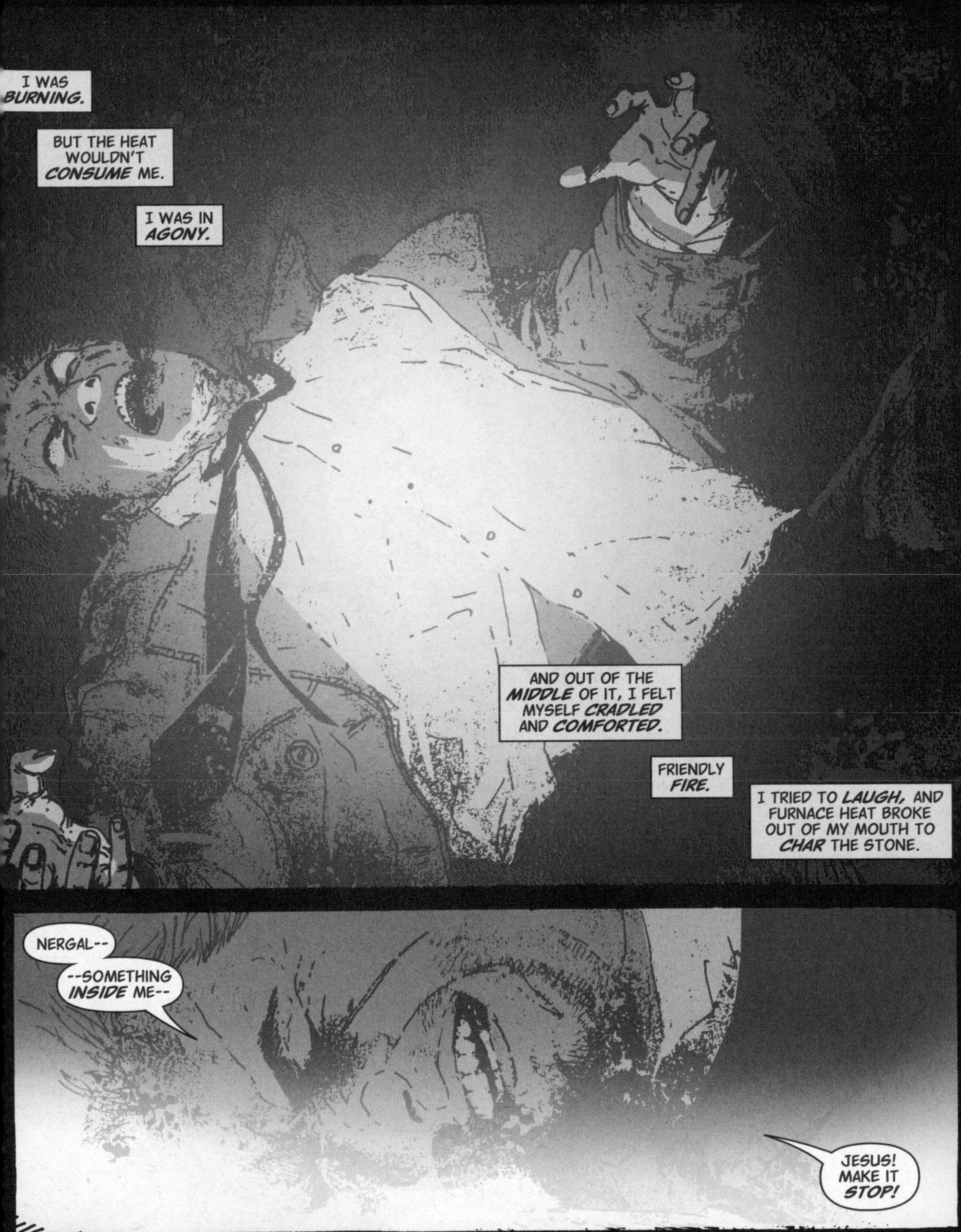
I WAS BURNING.
BUT THE HEAT WOULDN'T CONSUME ME.
I WAS IN AGONY.
AND OUT OF THE MIDDLE OF IT, I FELT MYSELF CRADLED AND COMFORTED.
FRIENDLY FIRE.
I TRIED TO LAUGH, AND FURNACE HEAT BROKE OUT OF MY MOUTH TO CHAR THE STONE.
NERGAL--
--SOMETHING INSIDE ME--
JESUS! MAKE IT STOP!

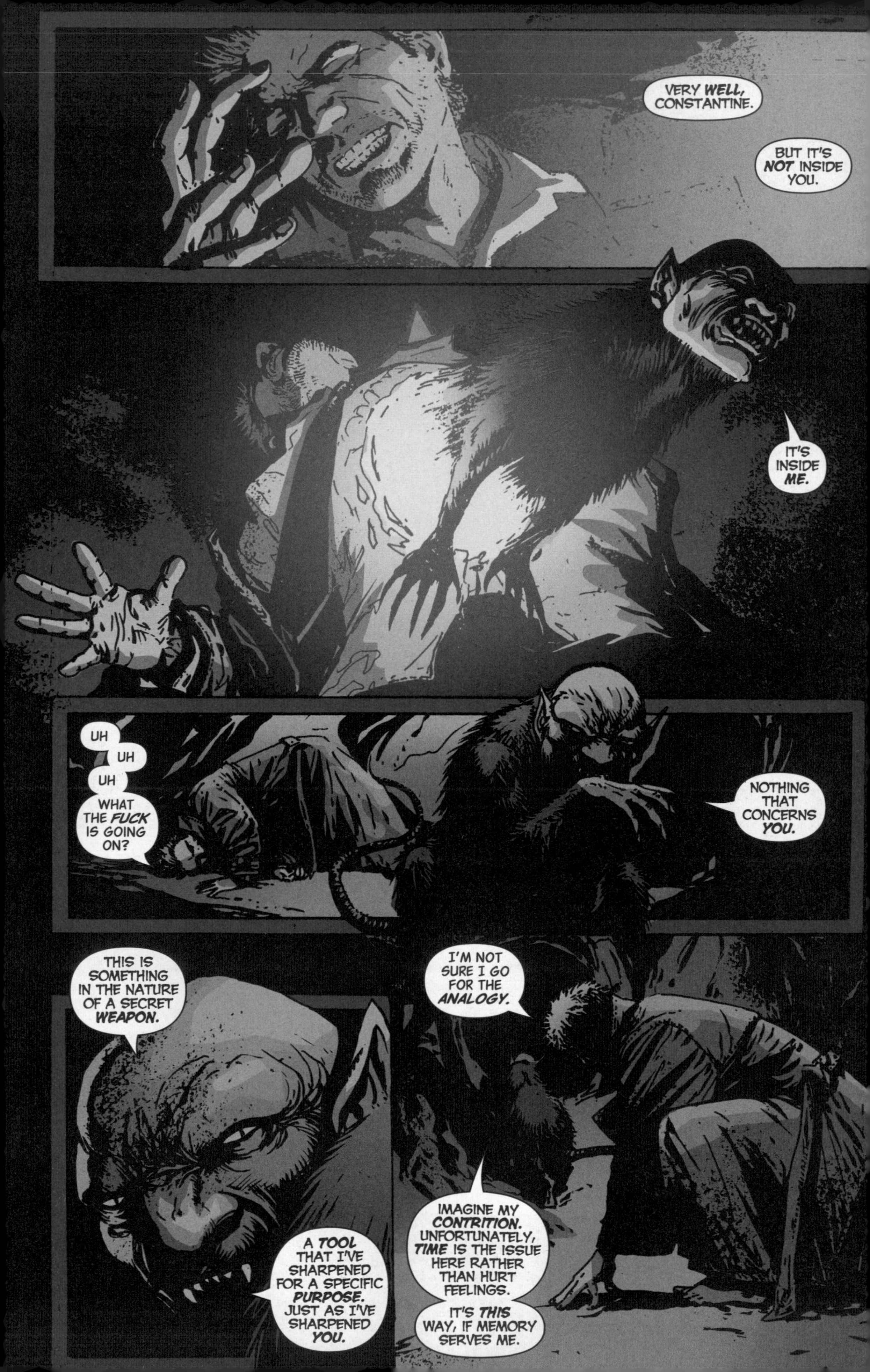
VERY WELL, CONSTANTINE.
BUT IT'S NOT INSIDE YOU.
IT'S INSIDE ME.
UH
UH
UH
WHAT THE FUCK IS GOING ON?
NOTHING THAT CONCERNS YOU.
THIS IS SOMETHING IN THE NATURE OF A SECRET WEAPON.
I'M NOT SURE I GO FOR THE ANALOGY.
A TOOL THAT I'VE SHARPENED FOR A SPECIFIC PURPOSE. JUST AS I'VE SHARPENED YOU.
IMAGINE MY CONTRITION. UNFORTUNATELY, TIME IS THE ISSUE HERE RATHER THAN HURT FEELINGS.
IT'S THIS WAY, IF MEMORY SERVES ME.

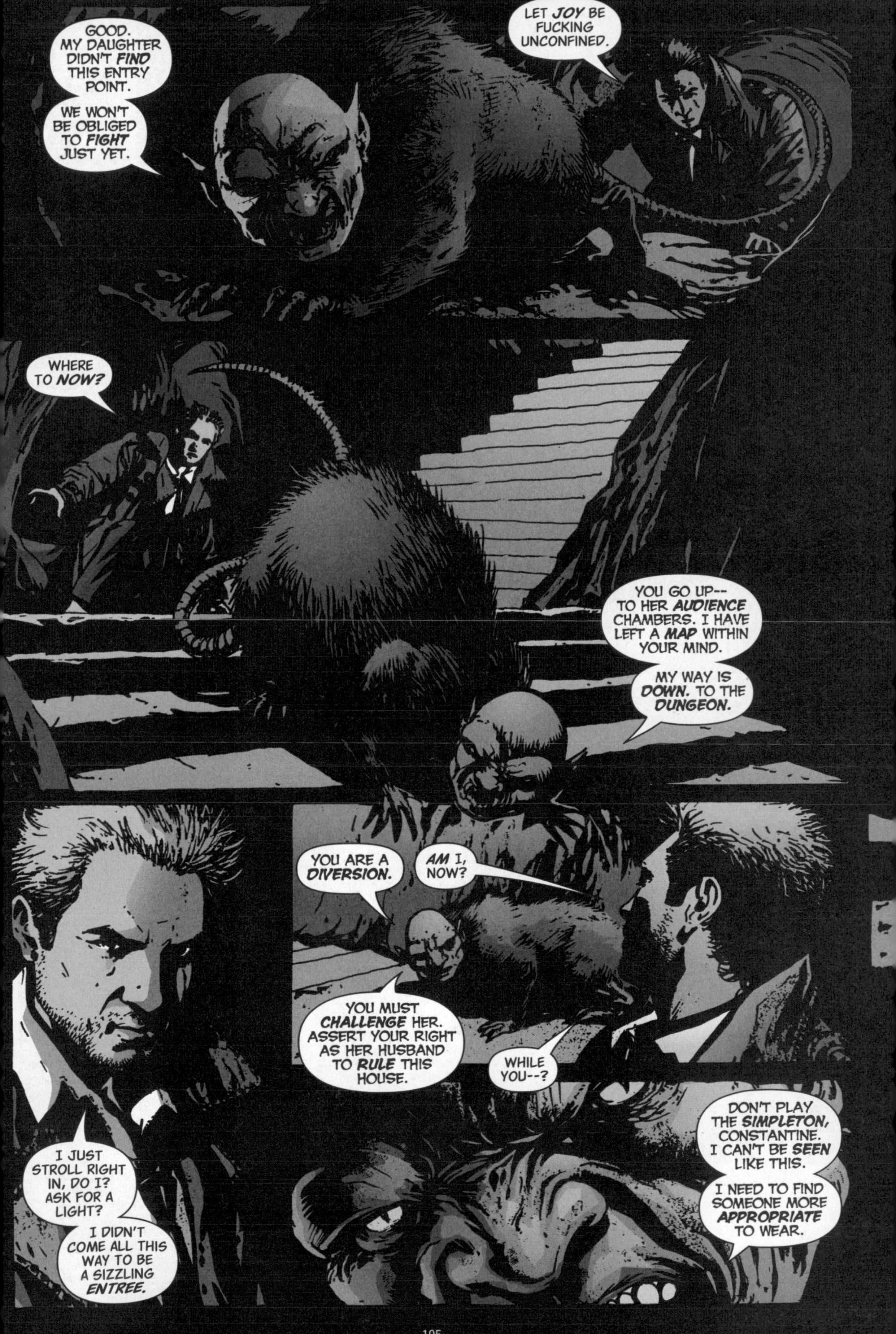
GOOD. MY DAUGHTER DIDN'T FIND THIS ENTRY POINT.
WE WON'T BE OBLIGED TO FIGHT JUST YET.
LET JOY BE FUCKING UNCONFINED.
WHERE TO NOW?
YOU GO UP-- TO HER AUDIENCE CHAMBERS. I HAVE LEFT A MAP WITHIN YOUR MIND.
MY WAY IS DOWN. TO THE DUNGEON.
YOU ARE A DIVERSION.
AM I, NOW?
YOU MUST CHALLENGE HER. ASSERT YOUR RIGHT AS HER HUSBAND TO RULE THIS HOUSE.
WHILE YOU--?
I JUST STROLL RIGHT IN, DO I? ASK FOR A LIGHT?
I DIDN'T COME ALL THIS WAY TO BE A SIZZLING ENTREE.
DON'T PLAY THE SIMPLETON, CONSTANTINE. I CAN'T BE SEEN LIKE THIS.
I NEED TO FIND SOMEONE MORE APPROPRIATE TO WEAR.

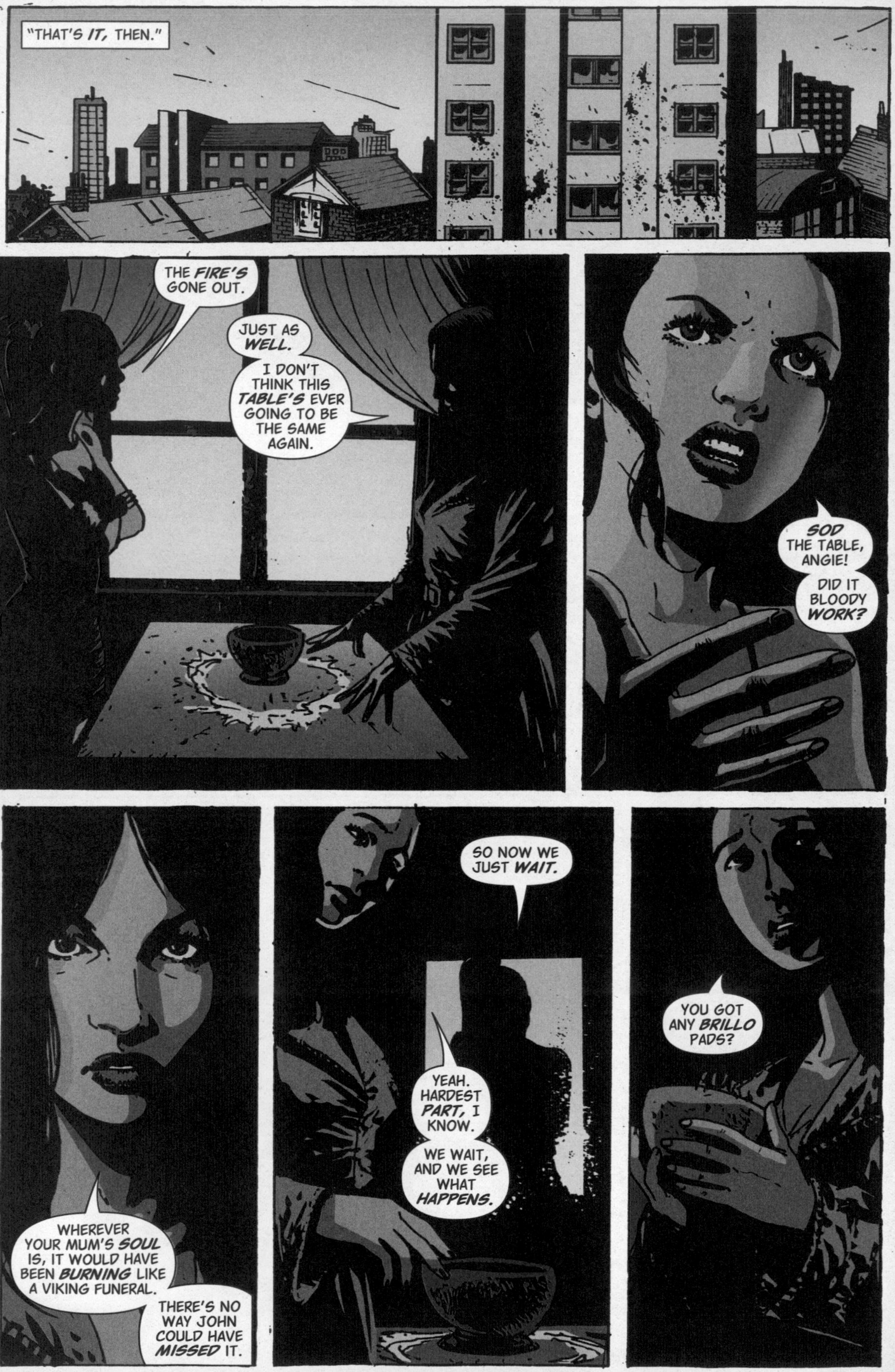
"THAT'S IT, THEN."
THE FIRE'S GONE OUT.
JUST AS WELL.
I DON'T THINK THIS TABLE'S EVER GOING TO BE THE SAME AGAIN.
SOD THE TABLE, ANGIE!
DID IT BLOODY WORK?
WHEREVER YOUR MUM'S SOUL IS, IT WOULD HAVE BEEN BURNING LIKE A VIKING FUNERAL.
THERE'S NO WAY JOHN COULD HAVE MISSED IT.
SO NOW WE JUST WAIT.
YEAH. HARDEST PART, I KNOW.
WE WAIT, AND WE SEE WHAT HAPPENS.
YOU GOT ANY BRILLO PADS?

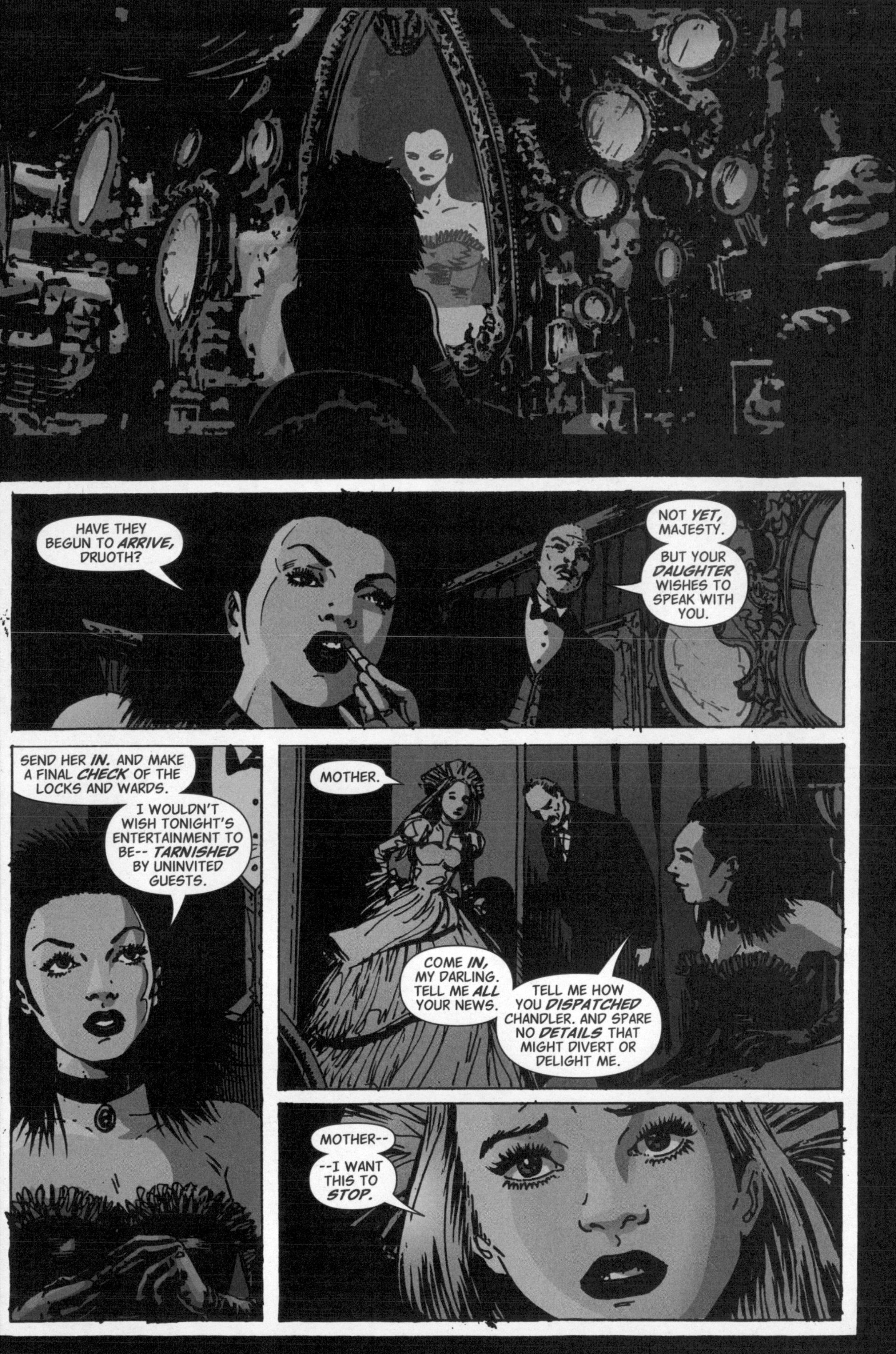
HAVE THEY BEGUN TO ARRIVE, DRUOTH?
NOT YET, MAJESTY.
BUT YOUR DAUGHTER WISHES TO SPEAK WITH YOU.
SEND HER IN. AND MAKE A FINAL CHECK OF THE LOCKS AND WARDS.
I WOULDN'T WISH TONIGHT'S ENTERTAINMENT TO BE-- TARNISHED BY UNINVITED GUESTS.
MOTHER.
COME IN, MY DARLING. TELL ME ALL YOUR NEWS.
TELL ME HOW YOU DISPATCHED CHANDLER. AND SPARE NO DETAILS THAT MIGHT DIVERT OR DELIGHT ME.
MOTHER--
--I WANT THIS TO STOP.

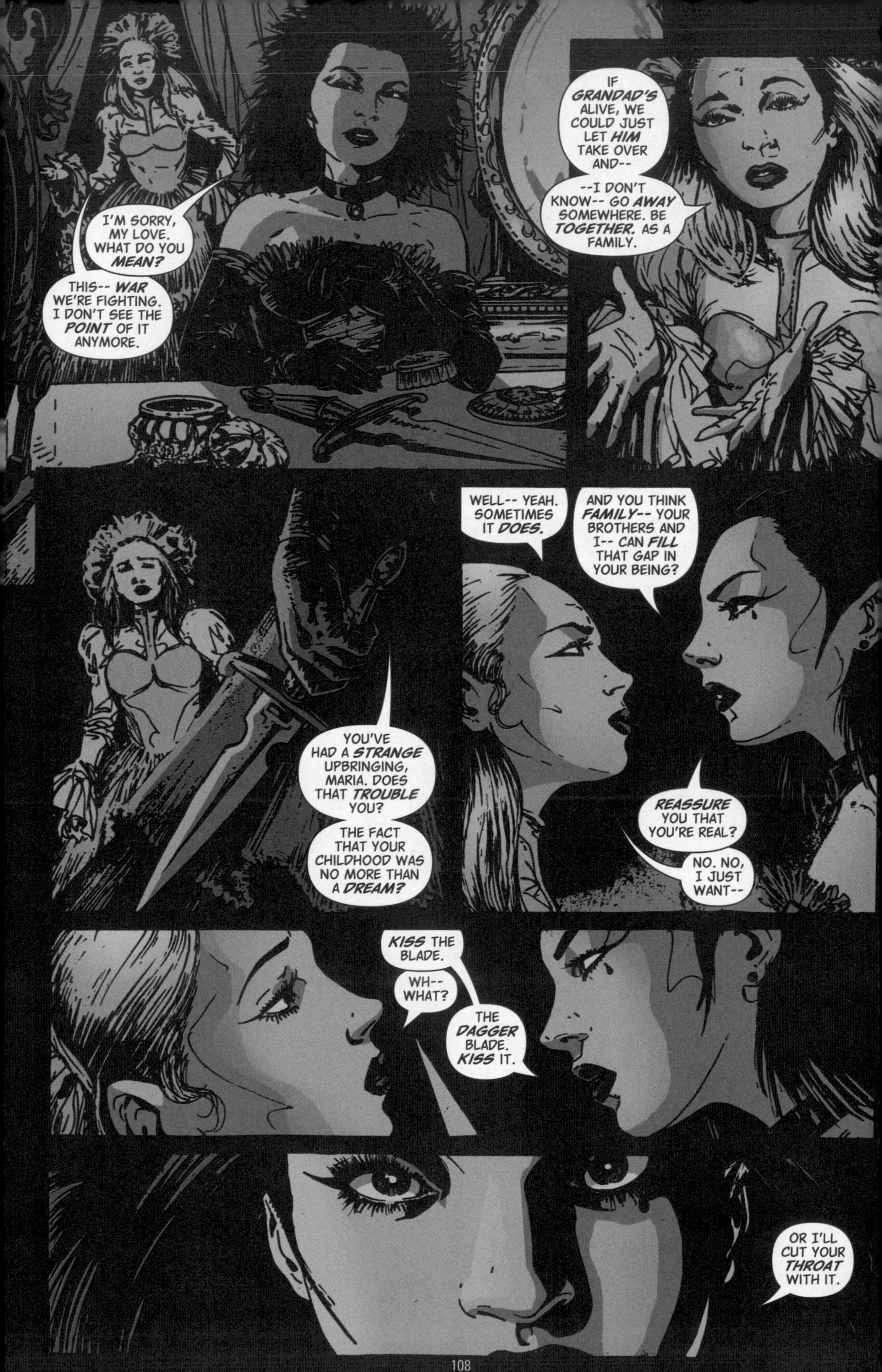

I'M SORRY, MY LOVE. WHAT DO YOU MEAN?
THIS-- WAR WE'RE FIGHTING. I DON'T SEE THE POINT OF IT ANYMORE.
IF GRANDAD'S ALIVE, WE COULD JUST LET HIM TAKE OVER AND--
--I DON'T KNOW-- GO AWAY SOMEWHERE. BE TOGETHER. AS A FAMILY.
YOU'VE HAD A STRANGE UPBRINGING, MARIA. DOES THAT TROUBLE YOU?
THE FACT THAT YOUR CHILDHOOD WAS NO MORE THAN A DREAM?
WELL-- YEAH. SOMETIMES IT DOES.
AND YOU THINK FAMILY-- YOUR BROTHERS AND I-- CAN FILL THAT GAP IN YOUR BEING?
REASSURE YOU THAT YOU'RE REAL?
NO. NO, I JUST WANT--
KISS THE BLADE.
WH-- WHAT?
THE DAGGER BLADE. KISS IT.
OR I'LL CUT YOUR THROAT WITH IT.

AS THOUGH YOU *LOVE* IT.

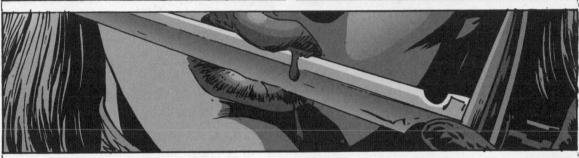

MY FATHER WOULD NOT *ACCEPT* A TRUCE.

HE'D SPIT IN MY *FACE* IF I OFFERED IT. *THINK* ON THAT.

WHEN YOU'RE READY TO ASK MY *FORGIVENESS*, THEN YOU MAY COME TO ME AGAIN.

AND IN THE MEANTIME--

--I SUGGEST YOU *KEEP* THE KNIFE.

AS AN AID TO *MEDITATION*.

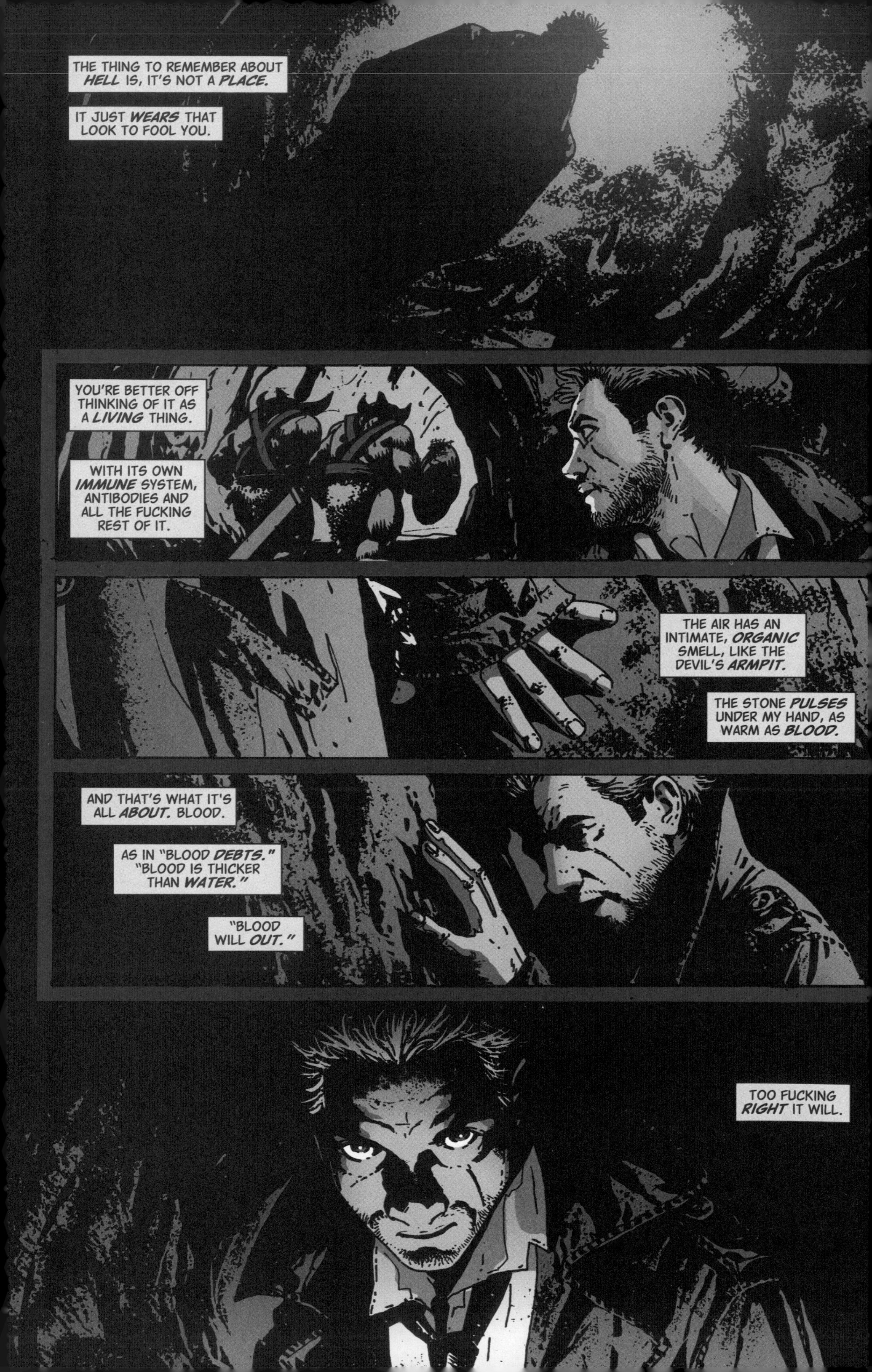
THE THING TO REMEMBER ABOUT HELL IS, IT'S NOT A PLACE.
IT JUST WEARS THAT LOOK TO FOOL YOU.
YOU'RE BETTER OFF THINKING OF IT AS A LIVING THING.
WITH ITS OWN IMMUNE SYSTEM, ANTIBODIES AND ALL THE FUCKING REST OF IT.
THE AIR HAS AN INTIMATE, ORGANIC SMELL, LIKE THE DEVIL'S ARMPIT.
THE STONE PULSES UNDER MY HAND, AS WARM AS BLOOD.
AND THAT'S WHAT IT'S ALL ABOUT. BLOOD.
AS IN "BLOOD DEBTS." "BLOOD IS THICKER THAN WATER."
"BLOOD WILL OUT."
TOO FUCKING RIGHT IT WILL.

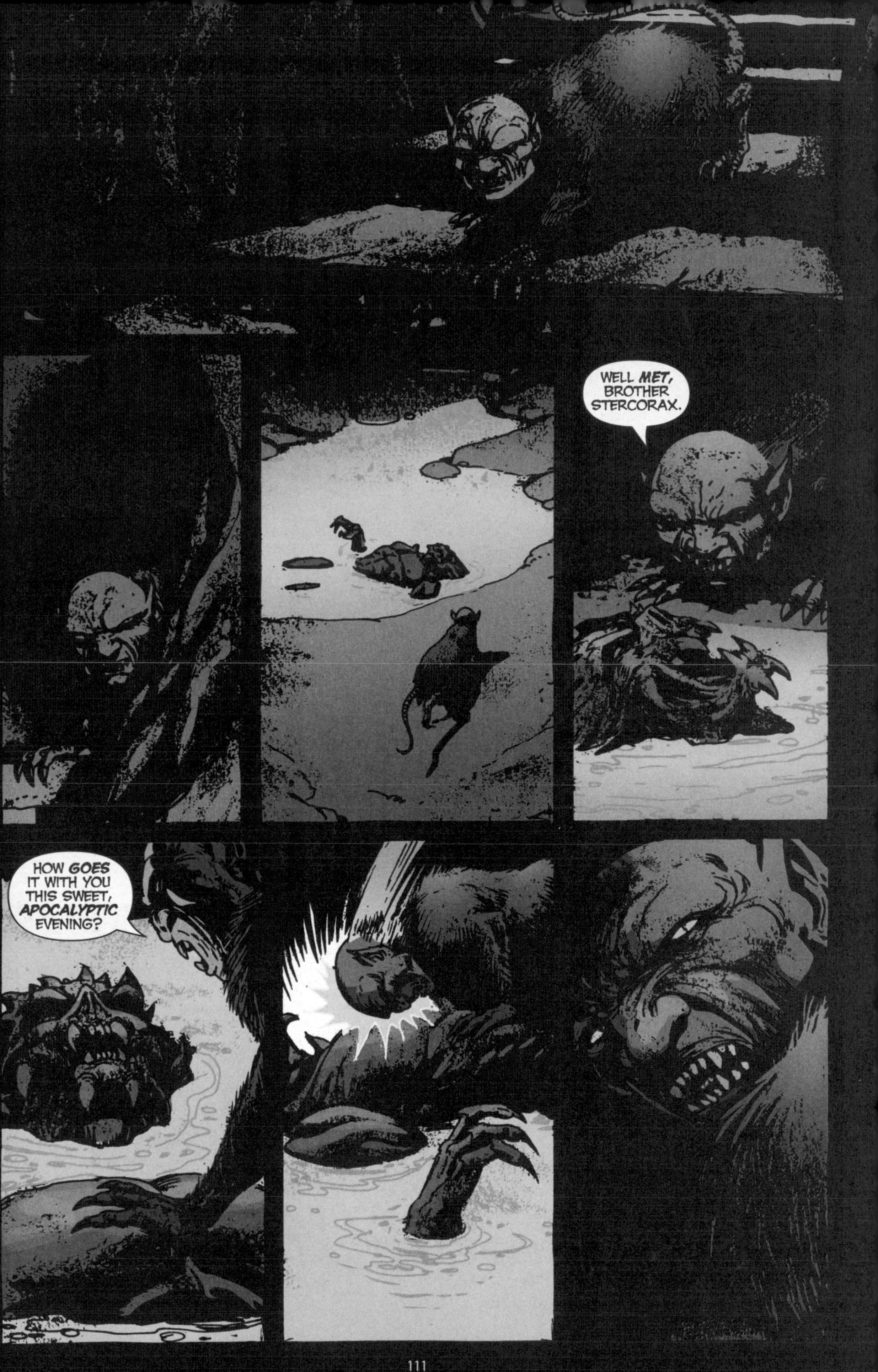
WELL MET, BROTHER STERCORAX.
HOW GOES IT WITH YOU THIS SWEET, APOCALYPTIC EVENING?

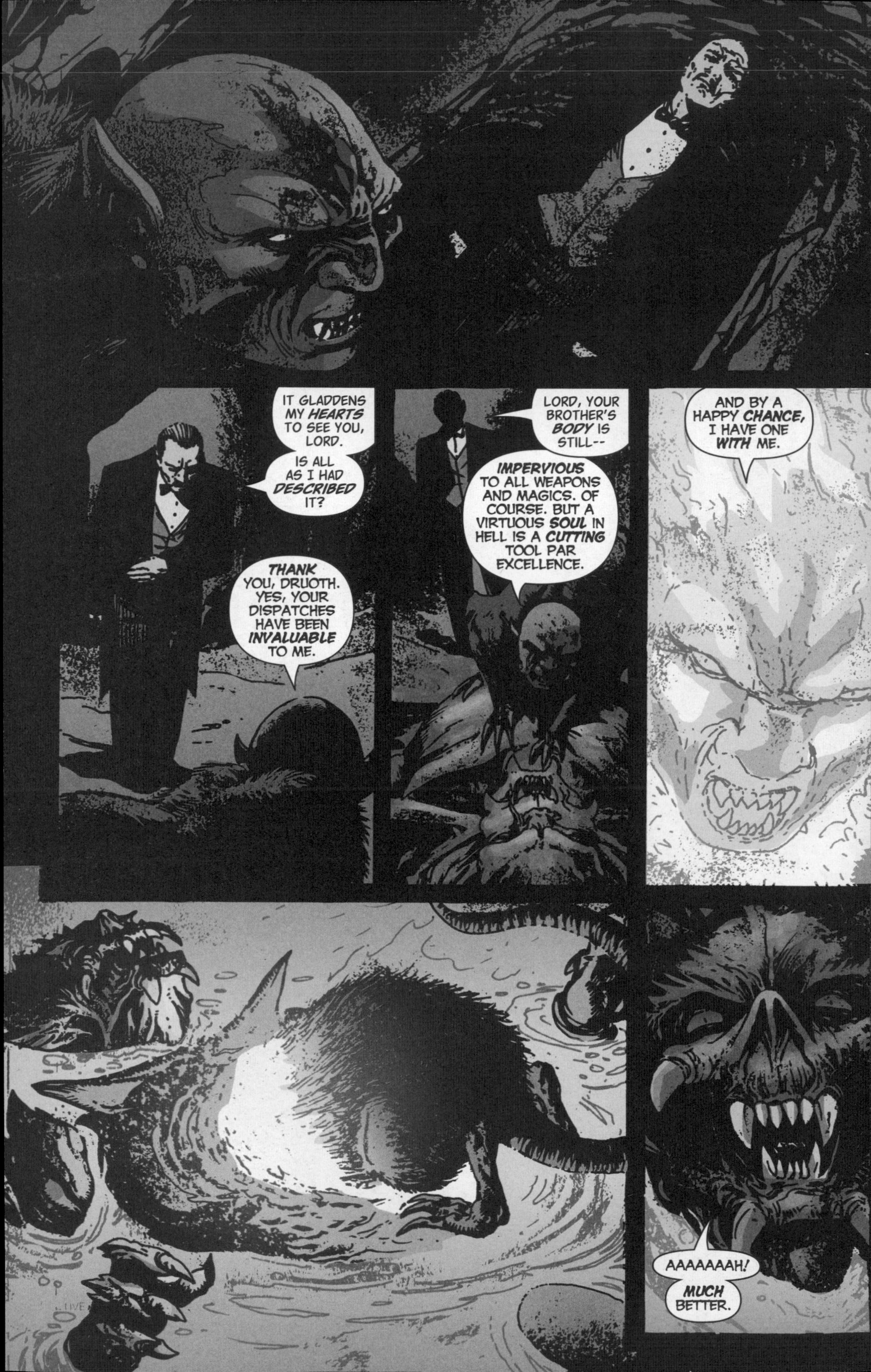
IT GLADDENS MY HEARTS TO SEE YOU, LORD.
IS ALL AS I HAD DESCRIBED IT?
THANK YOU, DRUOTH. YES, YOUR DISPATCHES HAVE BEEN INVALUABLE TO ME.
LORD, YOUR BROTHER'S BODY IS STILL--
IMPERVIOUS TO ALL WEAPONS AND MAGICS. OF COURSE. BUT A VIRTUOUS SOUL IN HELL IS A CUTTING TOOL PAR EXCELLENCE.
AND BY A HAPPY CHANCE, I HAVE ONE WITH ME.
AAAAAAAH!
MUCH BETTER.

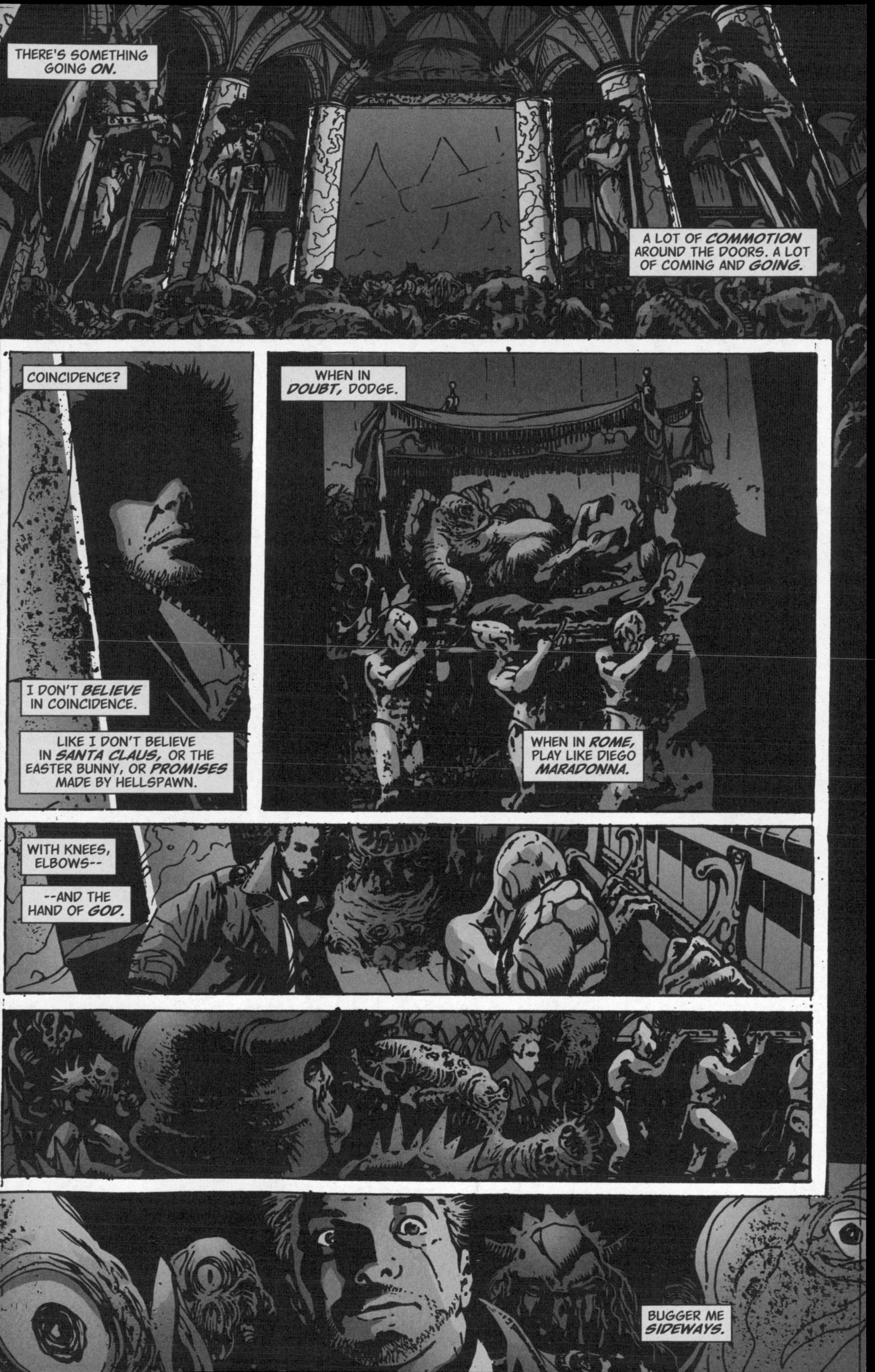
THERE'S SOMETHING GOING ON.
A LOT OF COMMOTION AROUND THE DOORS. A LOT OF COMING AND GOING.
COINCIDENCE?
I DON'T BELIEVE IN COINCIDENCE.
LIKE I DON'T BELIEVE IN SANTA CLAUS, OR THE EASTER BUNNY, OR PROMISES MADE BY HELLSPAWN.
WHEN IN DOUBT, DODGE.
WHEN IN ROME, PLAY LIKE DIEGO MARADONNA.
WITH KNEES, ELBOWS--
--AND THE HAND OF GOD.
BUGGER ME SIDEWAYS.

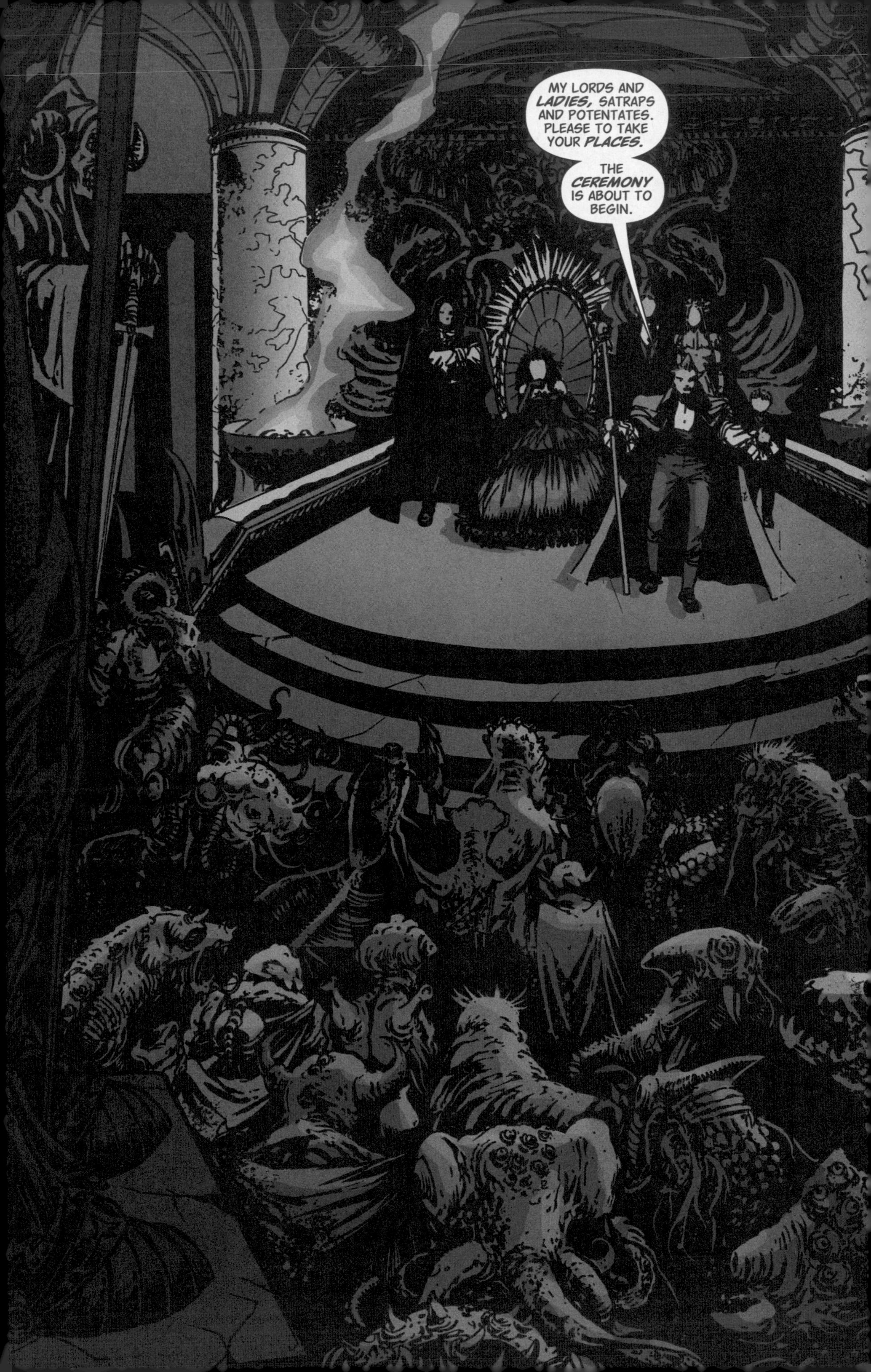
MY LORDS AND LADIES, SATRAPS AND POTENTATES. PLEASE TO TAKE YOUR PLACES.
THE CEREMONY IS ABOUT TO BEGIN.

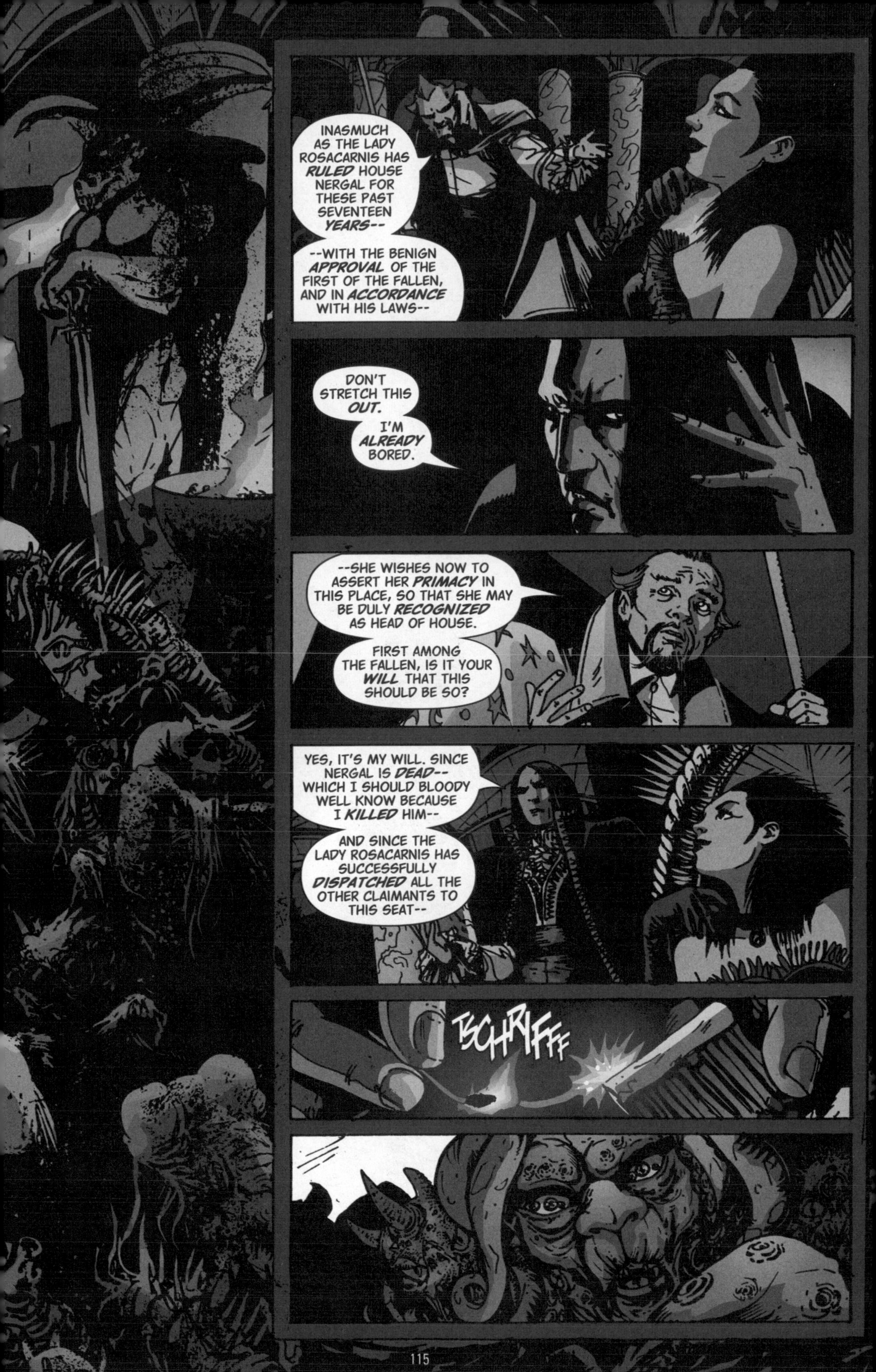
INASMUCH AS THE LADY ROSACARNIS HAS *RULED* HOUSE NERGAL FOR THESE PAST SEVENTEEN *YEARS*--
--WITH THE BENIGN *APPROVAL* OF THE FIRST OF THE FALLEN, AND IN *ACCORDANCE* WITH HIS LAWS--
DON'T STRETCH THIS *OUT*.
I'M *ALREADY* BORED.
--SHE WISHES NOW TO ASSERT HER *PRIMACY* IN THIS PLACE, SO THAT SHE MAY BE DULY *RECOGNIZED* AS HEAD OF HOUSE.
FIRST AMONG THE FALLEN, IS IT YOUR *WILL* THAT THIS SHOULD BE SO?
YES, IT'S MY WILL. SINCE NERGAL IS *DEAD*-- WHICH I SHOULD BLOODY WELL KNOW BECAUSE I *KILLED* HIM--
AND SINCE THE LADY ROSACARNIS HAS SUCCESSFULLY *DISPATCHED* ALL THE OTHER CLAIMANTS TO THIS SEAT--
TSCHRIFFF

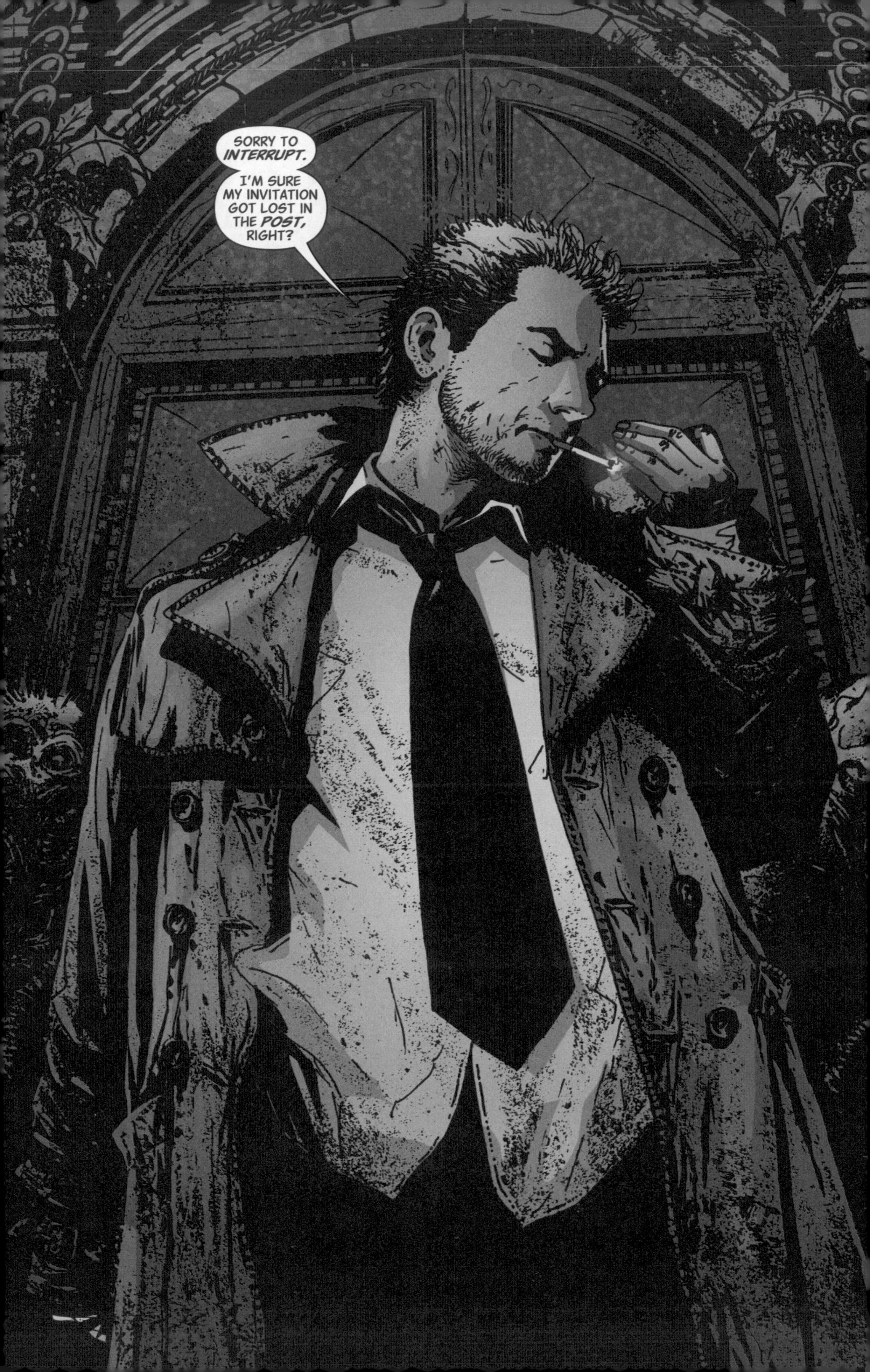
SORRY TO *INTERRUPT.*
I'M SURE MY INVITATION GOT LOST IN THE *POST,* RIGHT?

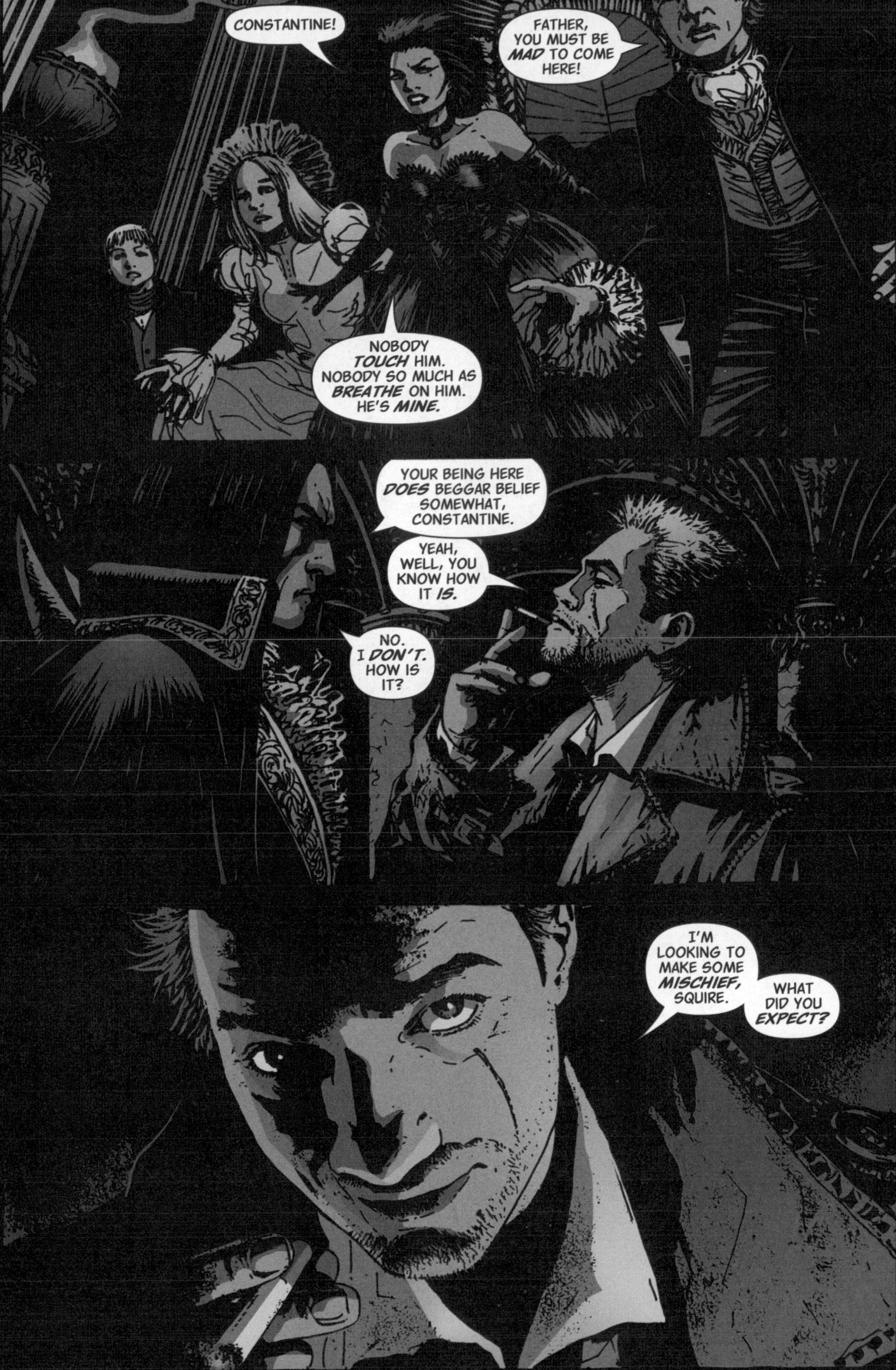
CONSTANTINE!
FATHER, YOU MUST BE MAD TO COME HERE!
NOBODY TOUCH HIM. NOBODY SO MUCH AS BREATHE ON HIM. HE'S MINE.
YOUR BEING HERE DOES BEGGAR BELIEF SOMEWHAT, CONSTANTINE.
YEAH, WELL, YOU KNOW HOW IT IS.
NO. I DON'T. HOW IS IT?
I'M LOOKING TO MAKE SOME MISCHIEF, SQUIRE.
WHAT DID YOU EXPECT?

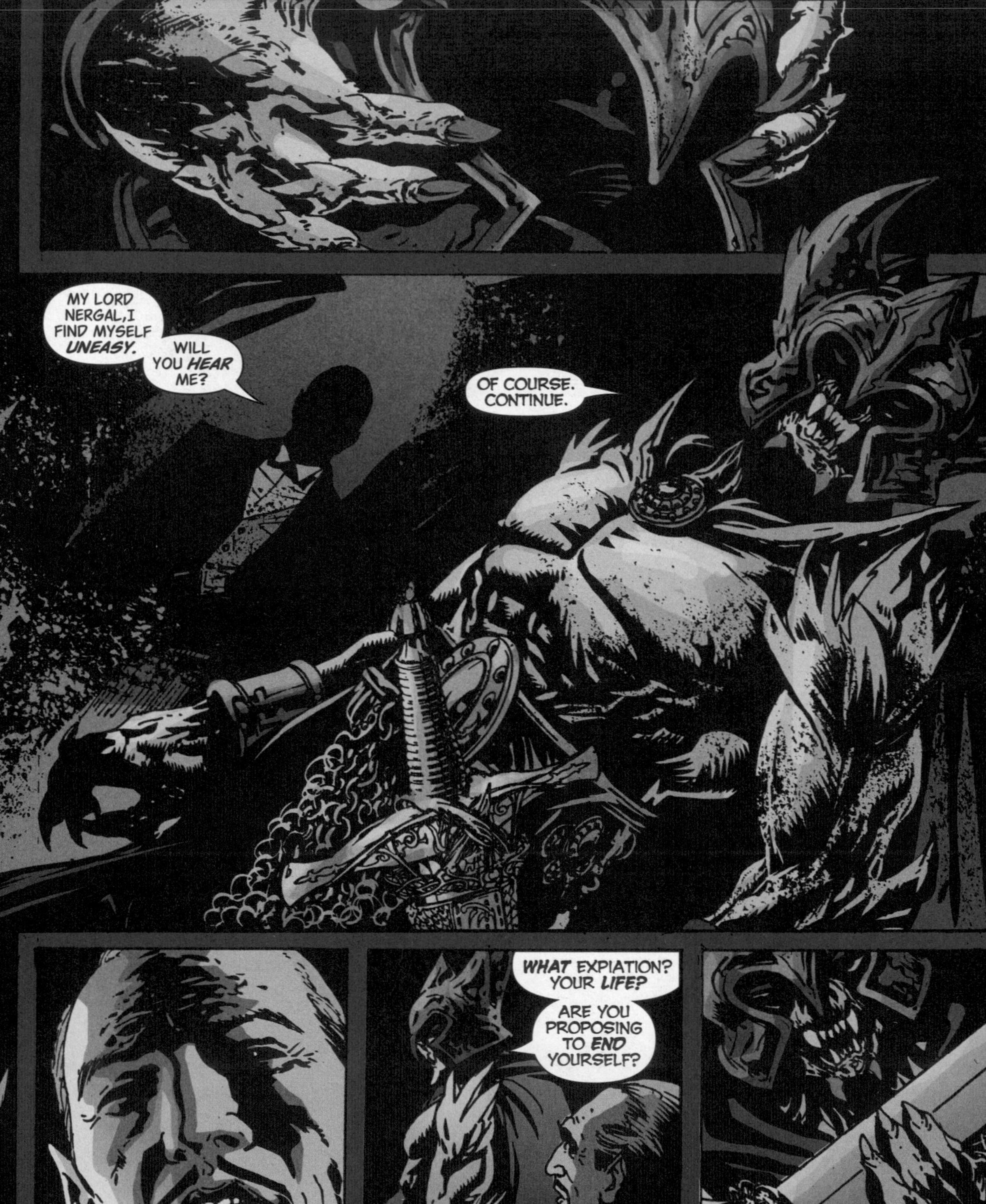
MY LORD NERGAL, I FIND MYSELF *UNEASY*.
WILL YOU *HEAR* ME?
OF COURSE. CONTINUE.
WHAT EXPIATION? YOUR *LIFE?*
ARE YOU PROPOSING TO *END* YOURSELF?

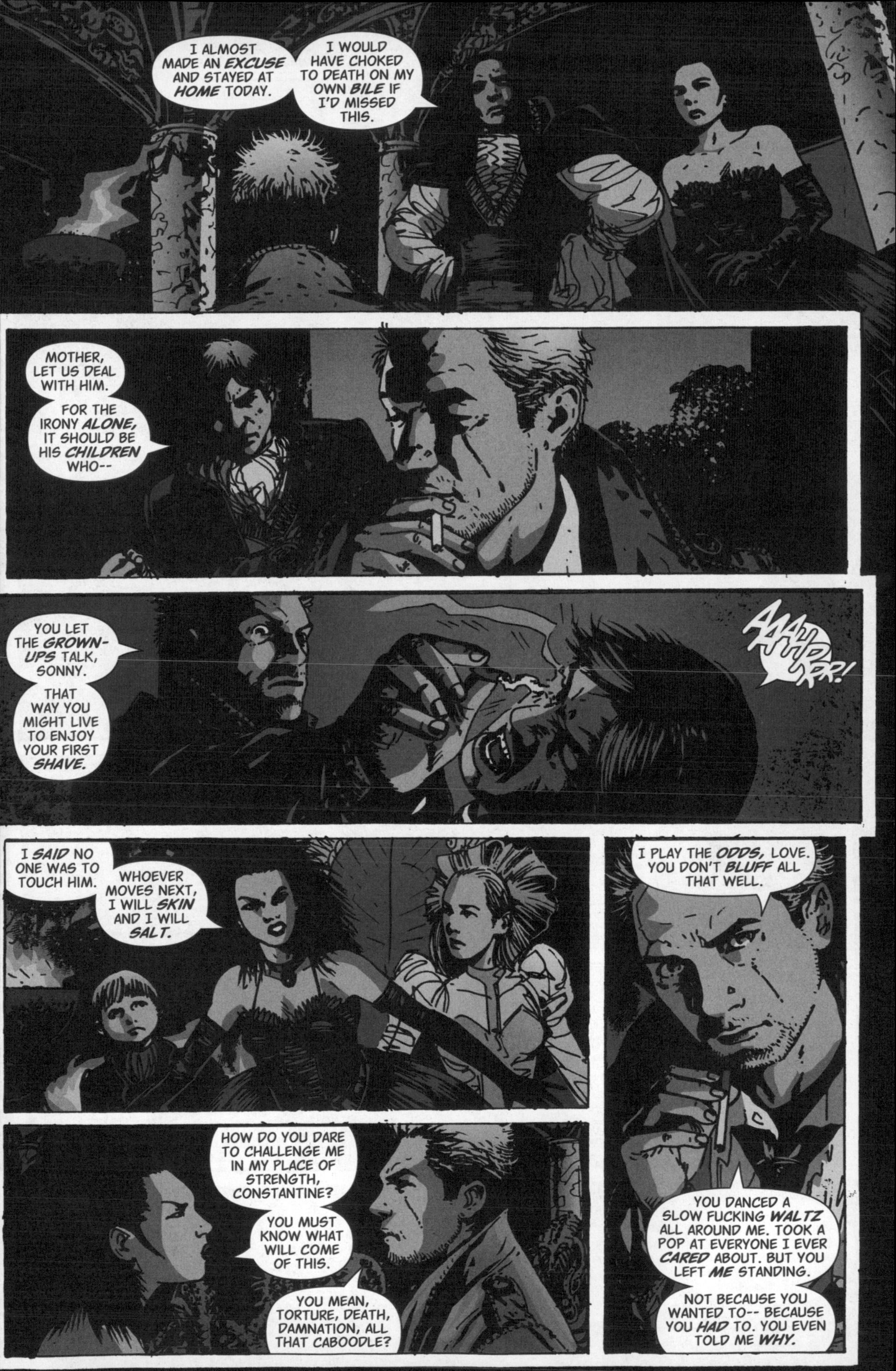
I ALMOST MADE AN *EXCUSE* AND STAYED AT *HOME* TODAY.
I WOULD HAVE CHOKED TO DEATH ON MY OWN *BILE* IF I'D MISSED THIS.
MOTHER, LET US DEAL WITH HIM.
FOR THE IRONY *ALONE,* IT SHOULD BE HIS *CHILDREN* WHO--
YOU LET THE *GROWN-UPS* TALK, SONNY.
THAT WAY YOU MIGHT LIVE TO ENJOY YOUR FIRST *SHAVE.*
AAAHURRR!
I *SAID* NO ONE WAS TO TOUCH HIM.
WHOEVER MOVES NEXT, I WILL *SKIN* AND I WILL *SALT.*
HOW DO YOU DARE TO CHALLENGE ME IN MY PLACE OF STRENGTH, CONSTANTINE?
YOU MUST KNOW WHAT WILL COME OF THIS.
YOU MEAN, TORTURE, DEATH, DAMNATION, ALL THAT CABOODLE?
I PLAY THE *ODDS,* LOVE. YOU DON'T *BLUFF* ALL THAT WELL.
YOU DANCED A SLOW FUCKING *WALTZ* ALL AROUND ME. TOOK A POP AT EVERYONE I EVER *CARED* ABOUT. BUT YOU LEFT *ME* STANDING.
NOT BECAUSE YOU WANTED TO-- BECAUSE YOU *HAD* TO. YOU EVEN TOLD ME *WHY.*

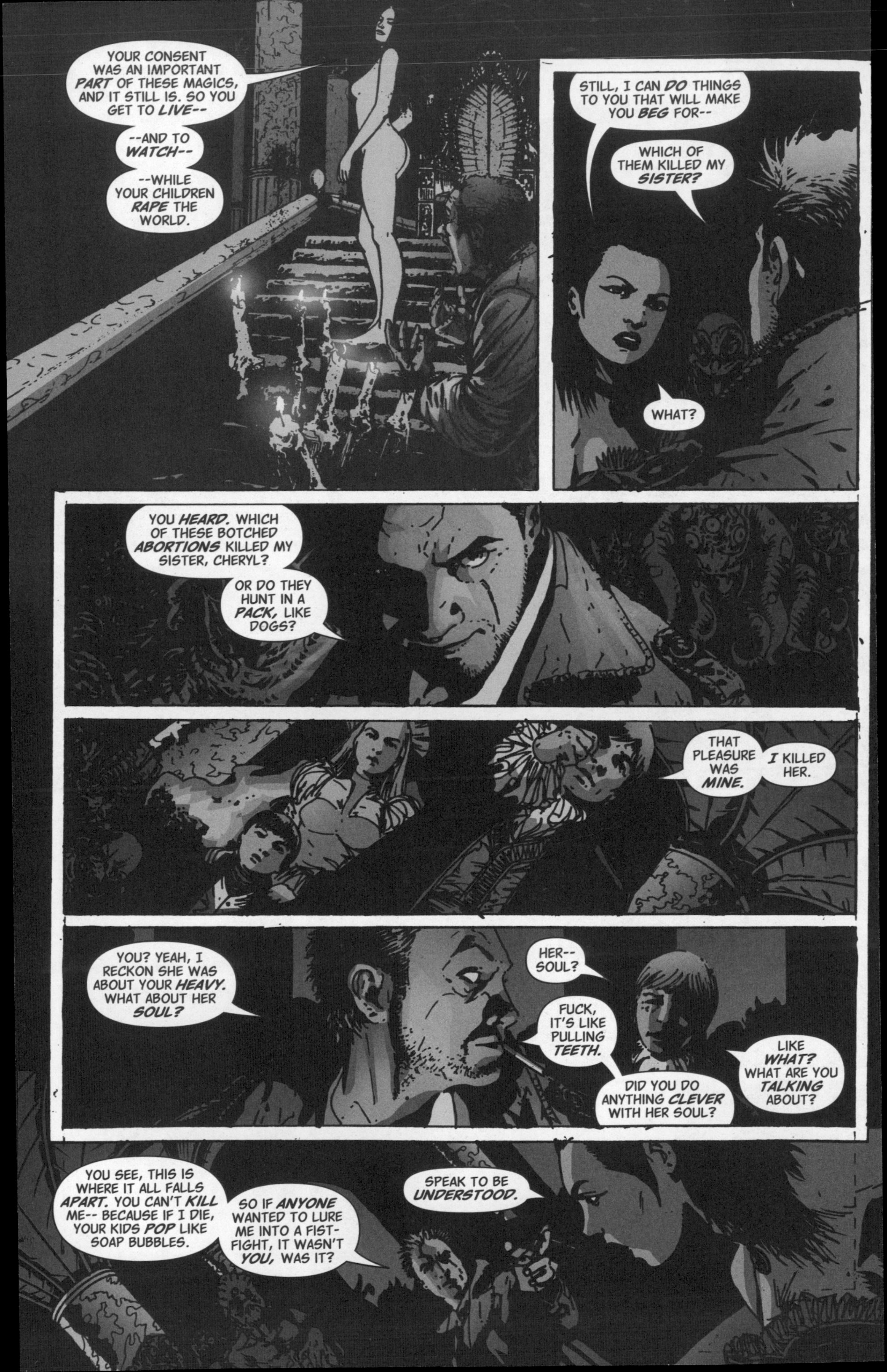
YOUR CONSENT WAS AN IMPORTANT PART OF THESE MAGICS, AND IT STILL IS. SO YOU GET TO LIVE--
--AND TO WATCH--
--WHILE YOUR CHILDREN RAPE THE WORLD.
STILL, I CAN DO THINGS TO YOU THAT WILL MAKE YOU BEG FOR--
WHICH OF THEM KILLED MY SISTER?
WHAT?
YOU HEARD. WHICH OF THESE BOTCHED ABORTIONS KILLED MY SISTER, CHERYL?
OR DO THEY HUNT IN A PACK, LIKE DOGS?
THAT PLEASURE WAS MINE.
I KILLED HER.
YOU? YEAH, I RECKON SHE WAS ABOUT YOUR HEAVY. WHAT ABOUT HER SOUL?
HER-- SOUL?
FUCK, IT'S LIKE PULLING TEETH.
DID YOU DO ANYTHING CLEVER WITH HER SOUL?
LIKE WHAT? WHAT ARE YOU TALKING ABOUT?
YOU SEE, THIS IS WHERE IT ALL FALLS APART. YOU CAN'T KILL ME-- BECAUSE IF I DIE, YOUR KIDS POP LIKE SOAP BUBBLES.
SO IF ANYONE WANTED TO LURE ME INTO A FIST-FIGHT, IT WASN'T YOU, WAS IT?
SPEAK TO BE UNDERSTOOD.

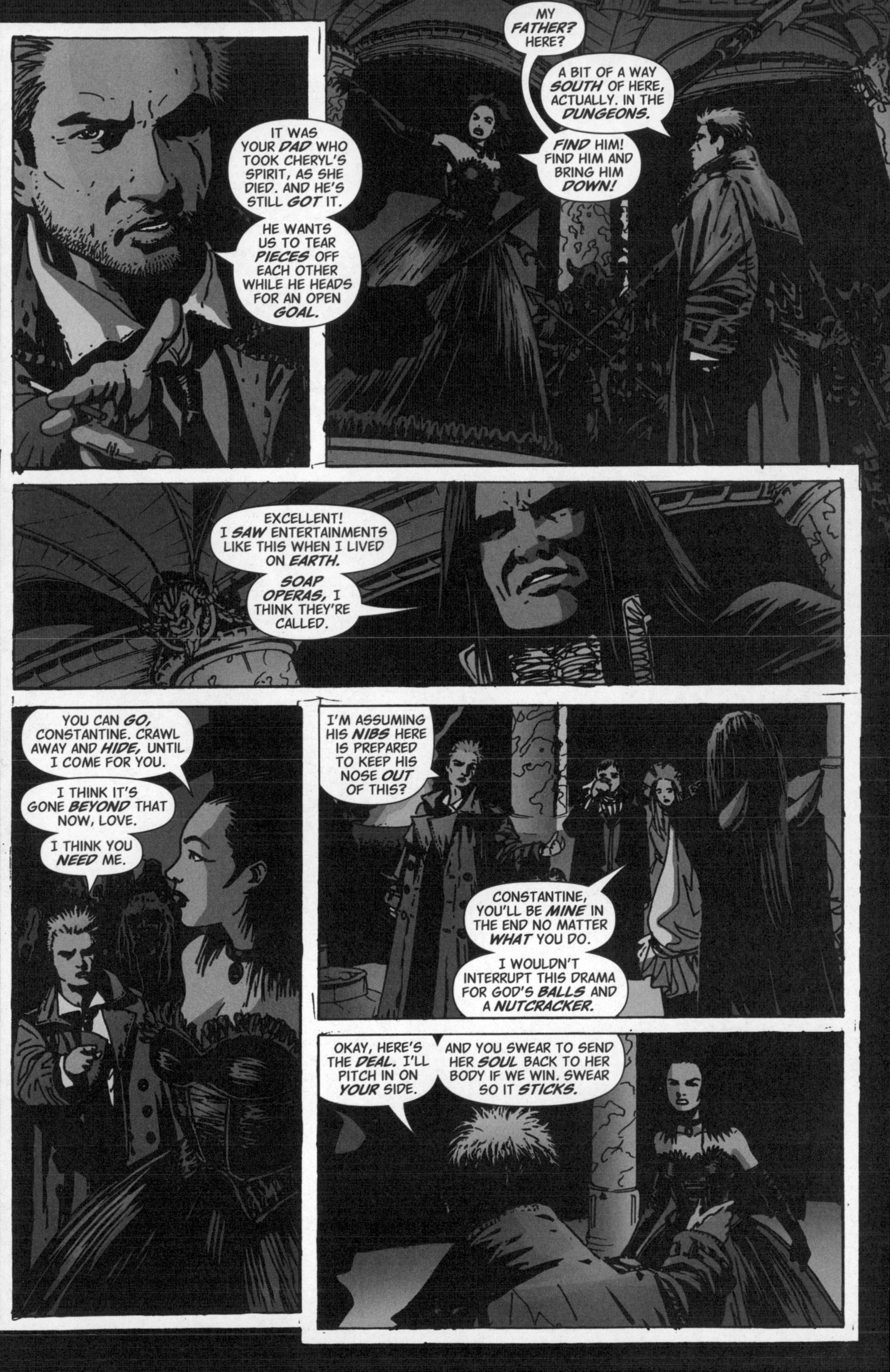
IT WAS YOUR DAD WHO TOOK CHERYL'S SPIRIT, AS SHE DIED. AND HE'S STILL GOT IT.
HE WANTS US TO TEAR PIECES OFF EACH OTHER WHILE HE HEADS FOR AN OPEN GOAL.
MY FATHER? HERE?
A BIT OF A WAY SOUTH OF HERE, ACTUALLY. IN THE DUNGEONS.
FIND HIM! FIND HIM AND BRING HIM DOWN!
EXCELLENT! I SAW ENTERTAINMENTS LIKE THIS WHEN I LIVED ON EARTH.
SOAP OPERAS, I THINK THEY'RE CALLED.
YOU CAN GO, CONSTANTINE. CRAWL AWAY AND HIDE, UNTIL I COME FOR YOU.
I THINK IT'S GONE BEYOND THAT NOW, LOVE.
I THINK YOU NEED ME.
I'M ASSUMING HIS NIBS HERE IS PREPARED TO KEEP HIS NOSE OUT OF THIS?
CONSTANTINE, YOU'LL BE MINE IN THE END NO MATTER WHAT YOU DO.
I WOULDN'T INTERRUPT THIS DRAMA FOR GOD'S BALLS AND A NUTCRACKER.
OKAY, HERE'S THE DEAL. I'LL PITCH IN ON YOUR SIDE.
AND YOU SWEAR TO SEND HER SOUL BACK TO HER BODY IF WE WIN. SWEAR SO IT STICKS.

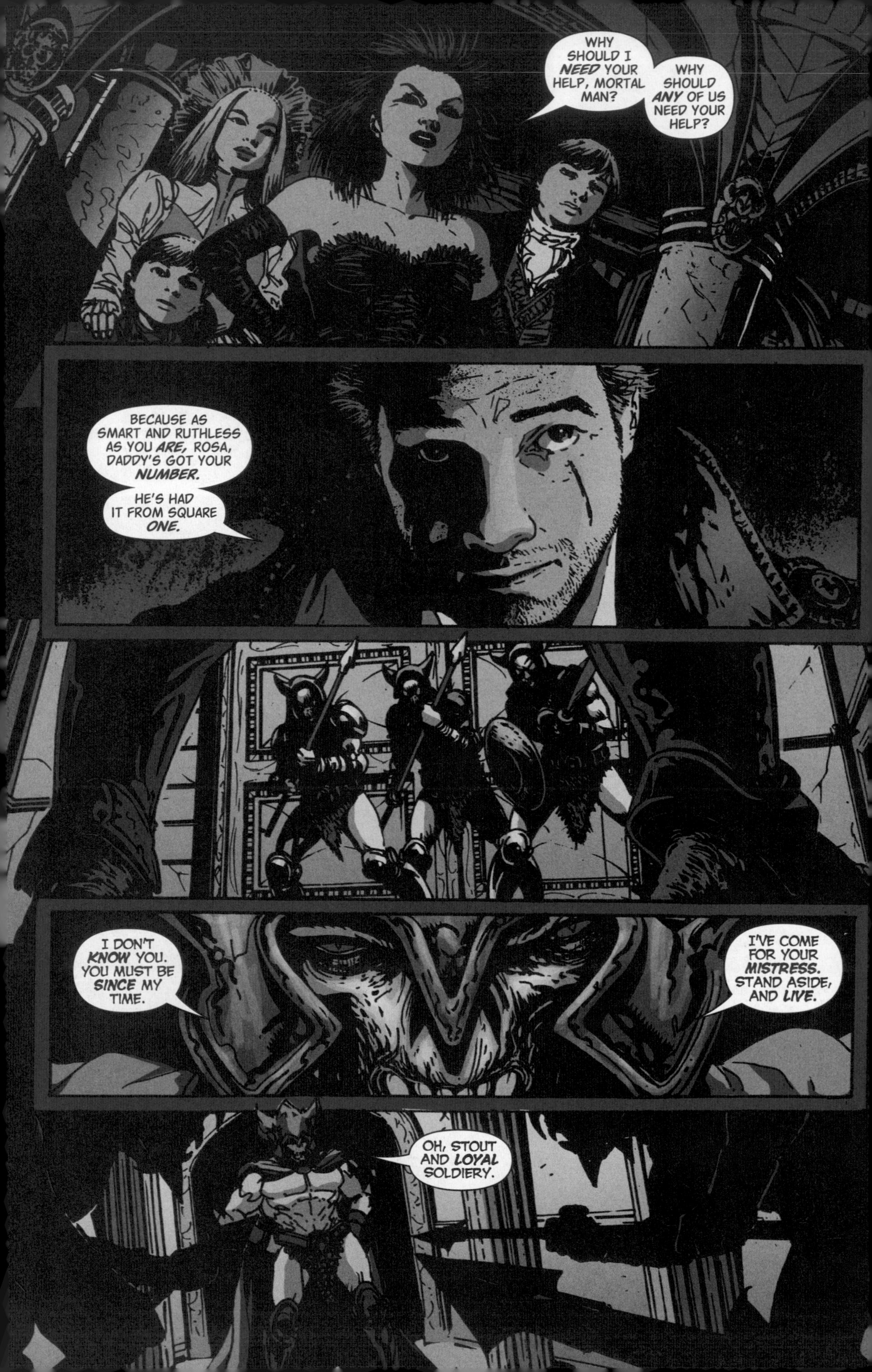
WHY SHOULD I NEED YOUR HELP, MORTAL MAN?
WHY SHOULD ANY OF US NEED YOUR HELP?
BECAUSE AS SMART AND RUTHLESS AS YOU ARE, ROSA, DADDY'S GOT YOUR NUMBER.
HE'S HAD IT FROM SQUARE ONE.
I'VE COME FOR YOUR MISTRESS. STAND ASIDE, AND LIVE.
I DON'T KNOW YOU. YOU MUST BE SINCE MY TIME.
OH, STOUT AND LOYAL SOLDIERY.

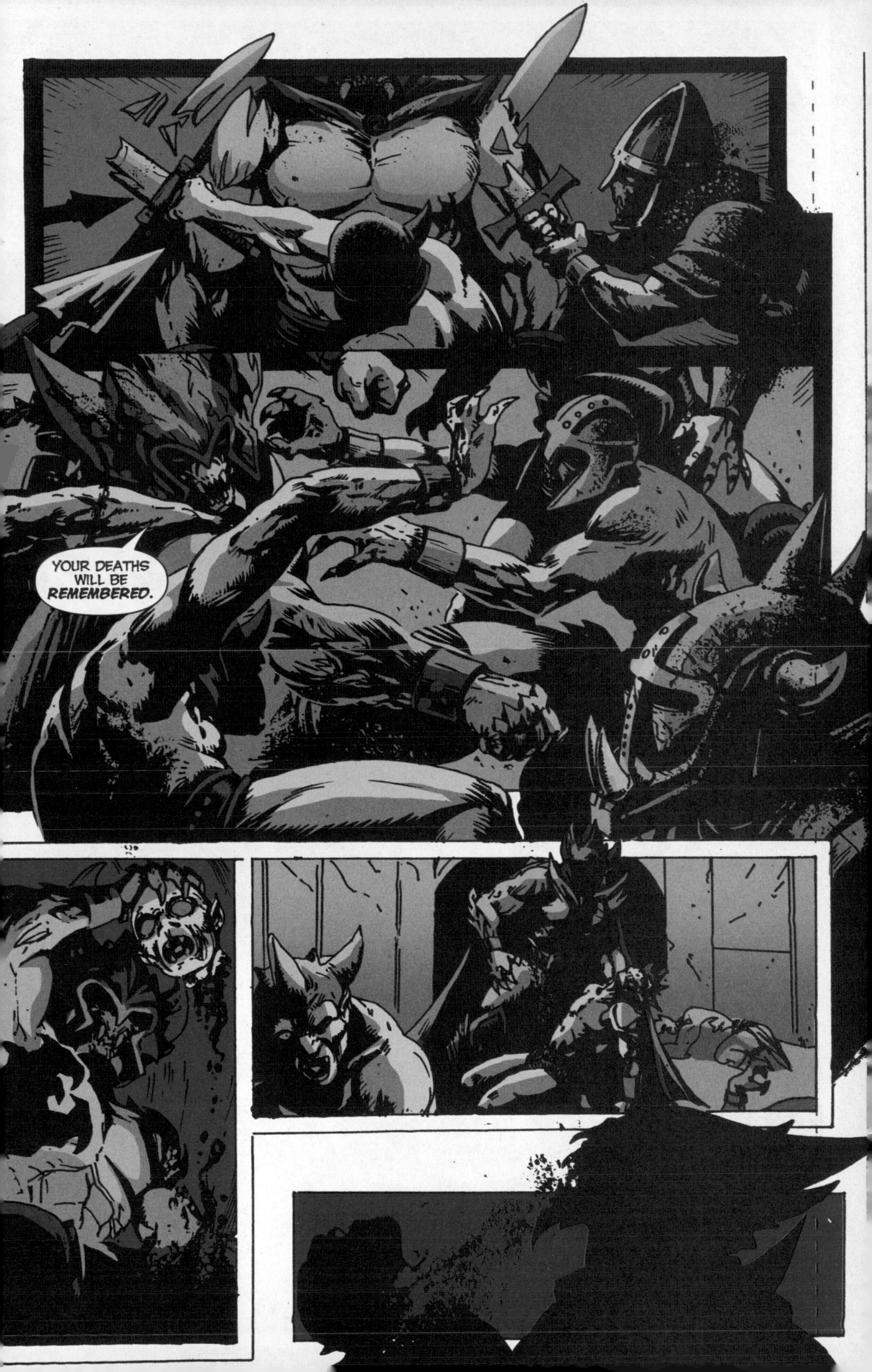
YOUR DEATHS WILL BE *REMEMBERED*.

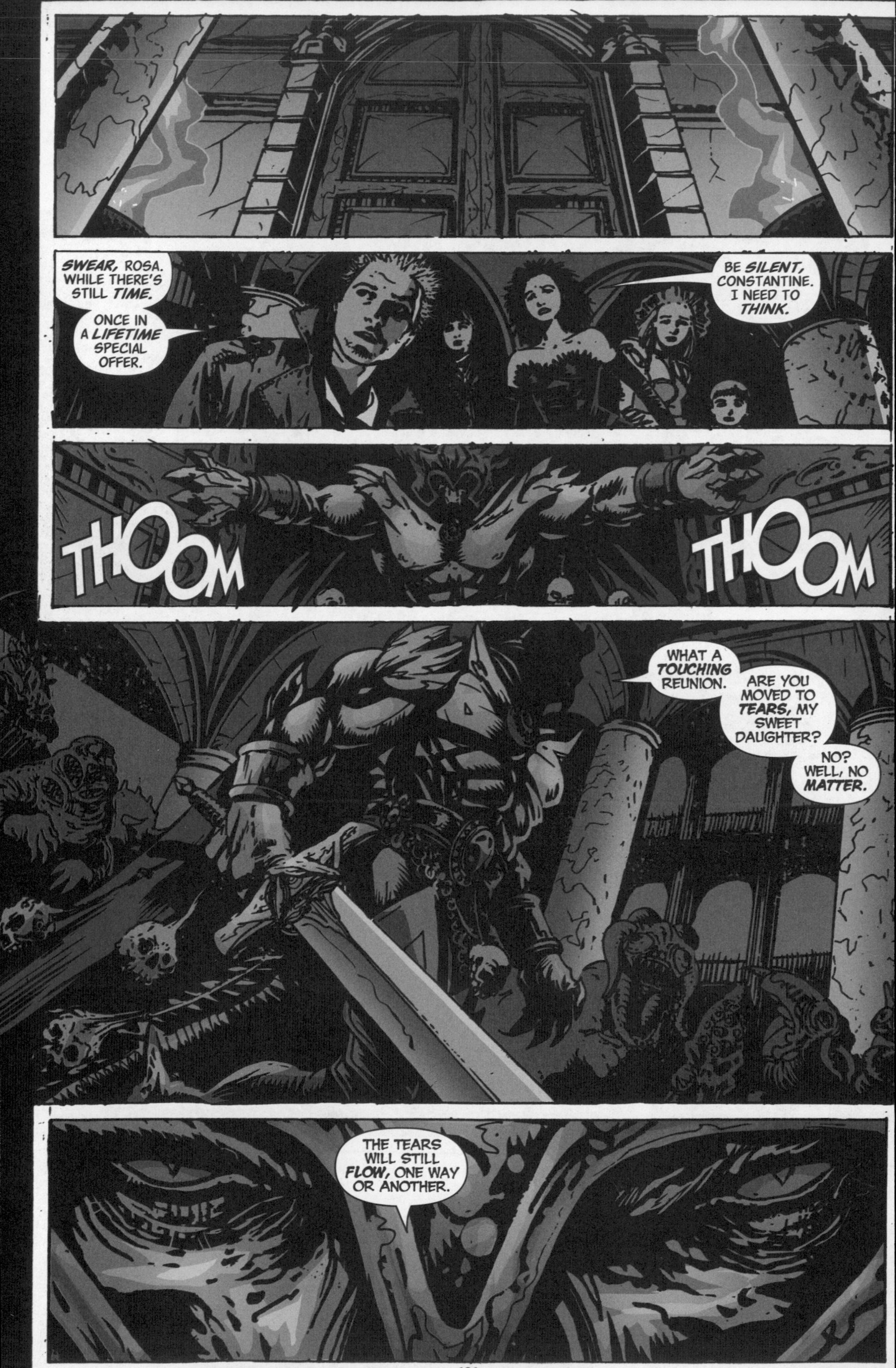
SWEAR, ROSA. WHILE THERE'S STILL TIME.
ONCE IN A LIFETIME SPECIAL OFFER.
BE SILENT, CONSTANTINE. I NEED TO THINK.
THOOM
THOOM
WHAT A TOUCHING REUNION.
ARE YOU MOVED TO TEARS, MY SWEET DAUGHTER?
NO? WELL, NO MATTER.
THE TEARS WILL STILL FLOW, ONE WAY OR ANOTHER.

Down in the Ground Where the Dead Men Go CHAPTER SIX

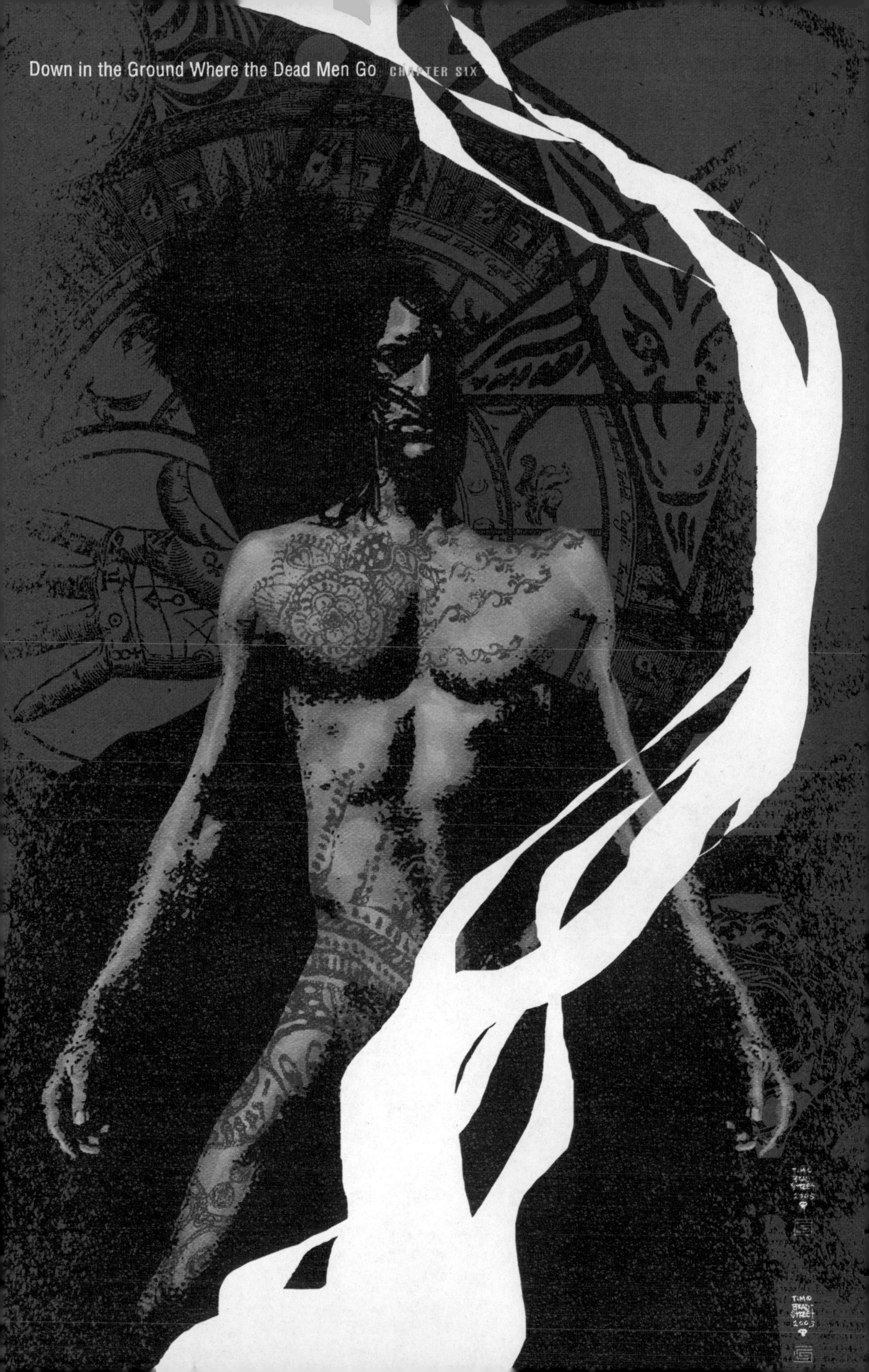

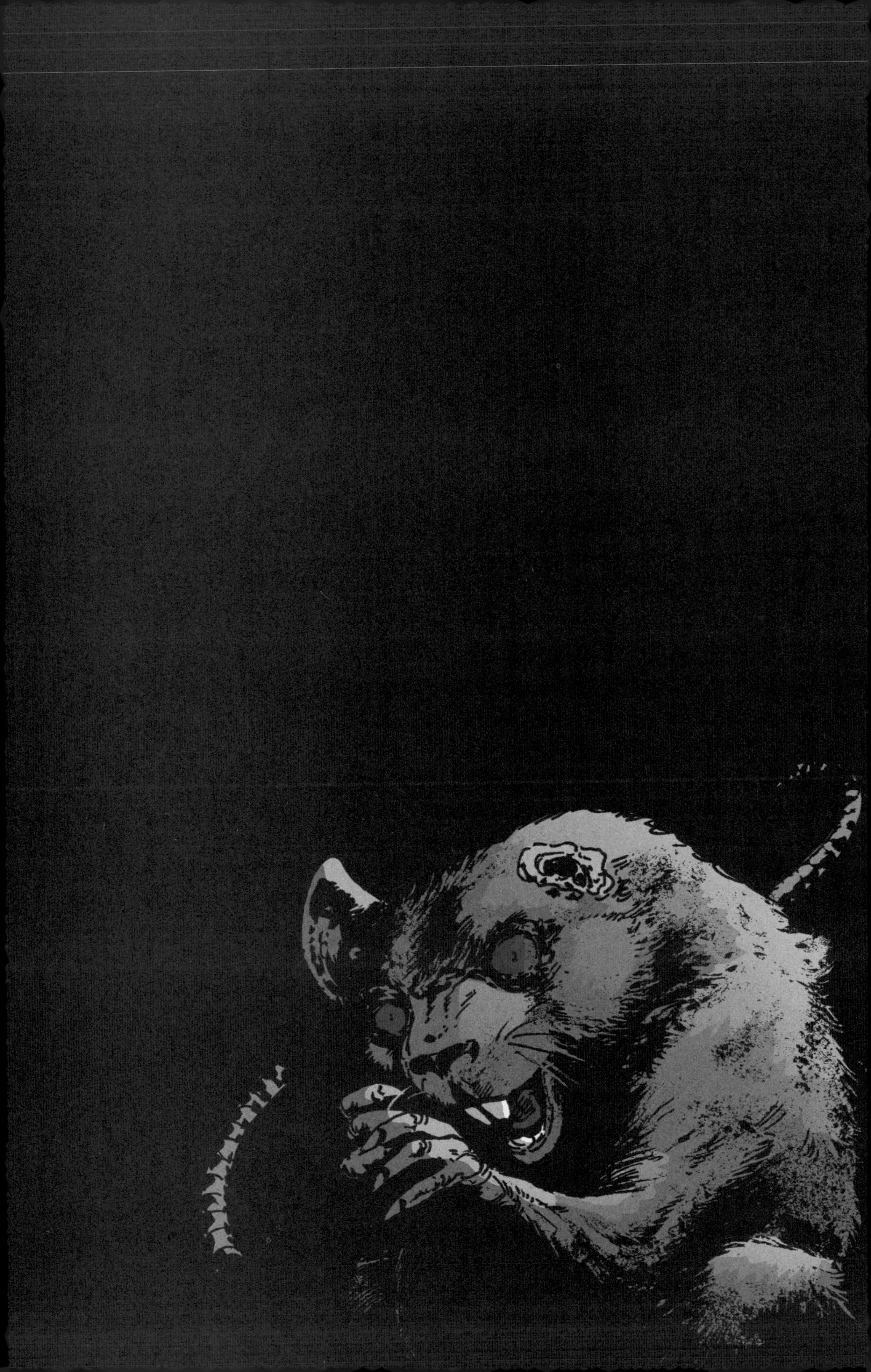

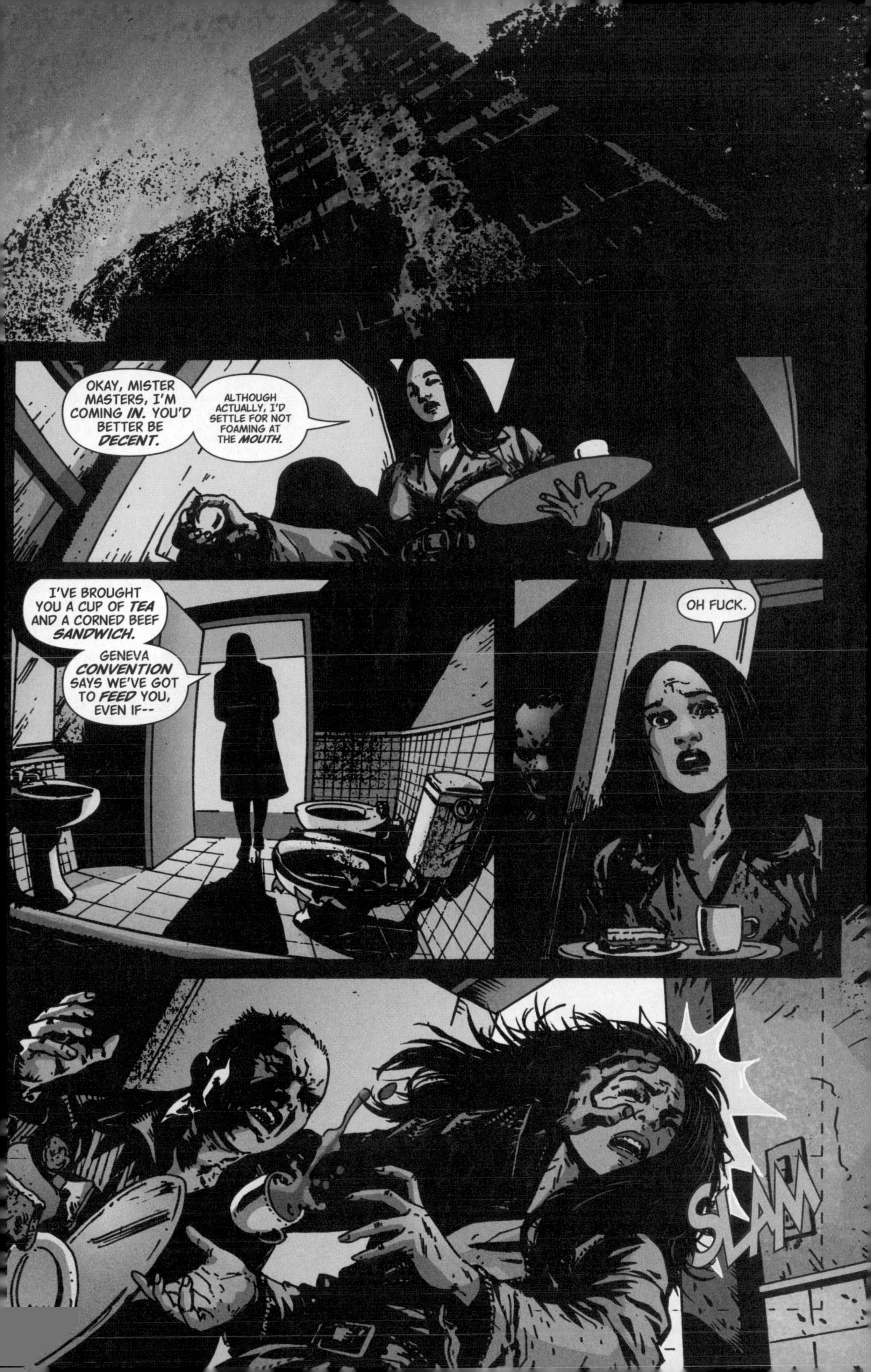
OKAY, MISTER MASTERS, I'M COMING *IN.* YOU'D BETTER BE *DECENT.*
ALTHOUGH ACTUALLY, I'D SETTLE FOR NOT FOAMING AT THE *MOUTH.*
I'VE BROUGHT YOU A CUP OF *TEA* AND A CORNED BEEF *SANDWICH.*
GENEVA *CONVENTION* SAYS WE'VE GOT TO *FEED* YOU, EVEN IF--
OH FUCK.
SLAM

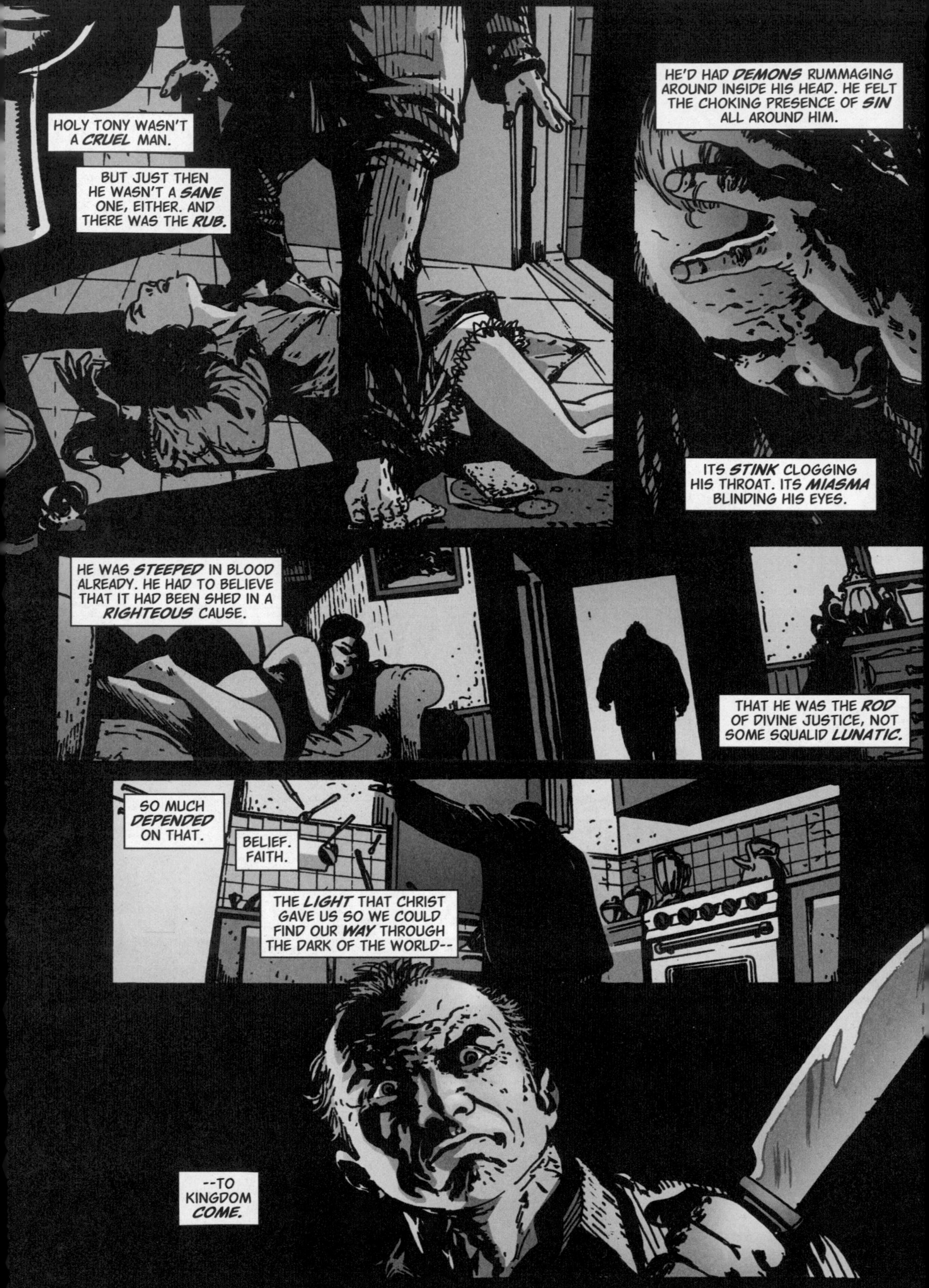
HOLY TONY WASN'T A CRUEL MAN.
BUT JUST THEN HE WASN'T A SANE ONE, EITHER. AND THERE WAS THE RUB.
HE'D HAD DEMONS RUMMAGING AROUND INSIDE HIS HEAD. HE FELT THE CHOKING PRESENCE OF SIN ALL AROUND HIM.
ITS STINK CLOGGING HIS THROAT. ITS MIASMA BLINDING HIS EYES.
HE WAS STEEPED IN BLOOD ALREADY. HE HAD TO BELIEVE THAT IT HAD BEEN SHED IN A RIGHTEOUS CAUSE.
THAT HE WAS THE ROD OF DIVINE JUSTICE, NOT SOME SQUALID LUNATIC.
SO MUCH DEPENDED ON THAT.
BELIEF. FAITH.
THE LIGHT THAT CHRIST GAVE US SO WE COULD FIND OUR WAY THROUGH THE DARK OF THE WORLD--
--TO KINGDOM COME.

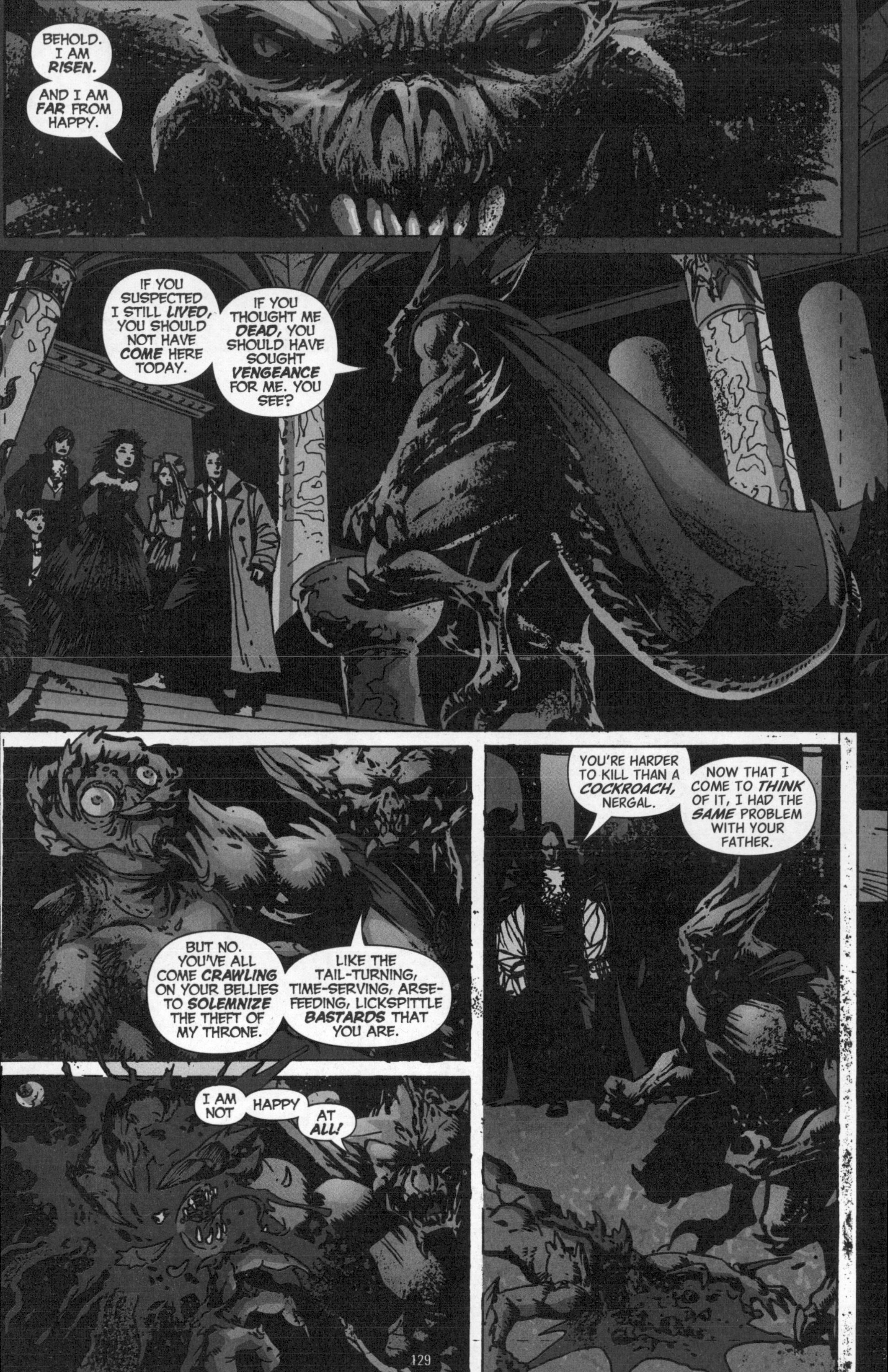
BEHOLD. I AM RISEN.
AND I AM FAR FROM HAPPY.
IF YOU SUSPECTED I STILL LIVED, YOU SHOULD NOT HAVE COME HERE TODAY.
IF YOU THOUGHT ME DEAD, YOU SHOULD HAVE SOUGHT VENGEANCE FOR ME. YOU SEE?
BUT NO. YOU'VE ALL COME CRAWLING ON YOUR BELLIES TO SOLEMNIZE THE THEFT OF MY THRONE.
LIKE THE TAIL-TURNING, TIME-SERVING, ARSE-FEEDING, LICKSPITTLE BASTARDS THAT YOU ARE.
I AM NOT
HAPPY
AT ALL!
YOU'RE HARDER TO KILL THAN A COCKROACH, NERGAL.
NOW THAT I COME TO THINK OF IT, I HAD THE SAME PROBLEM WITH YOUR FATHER.

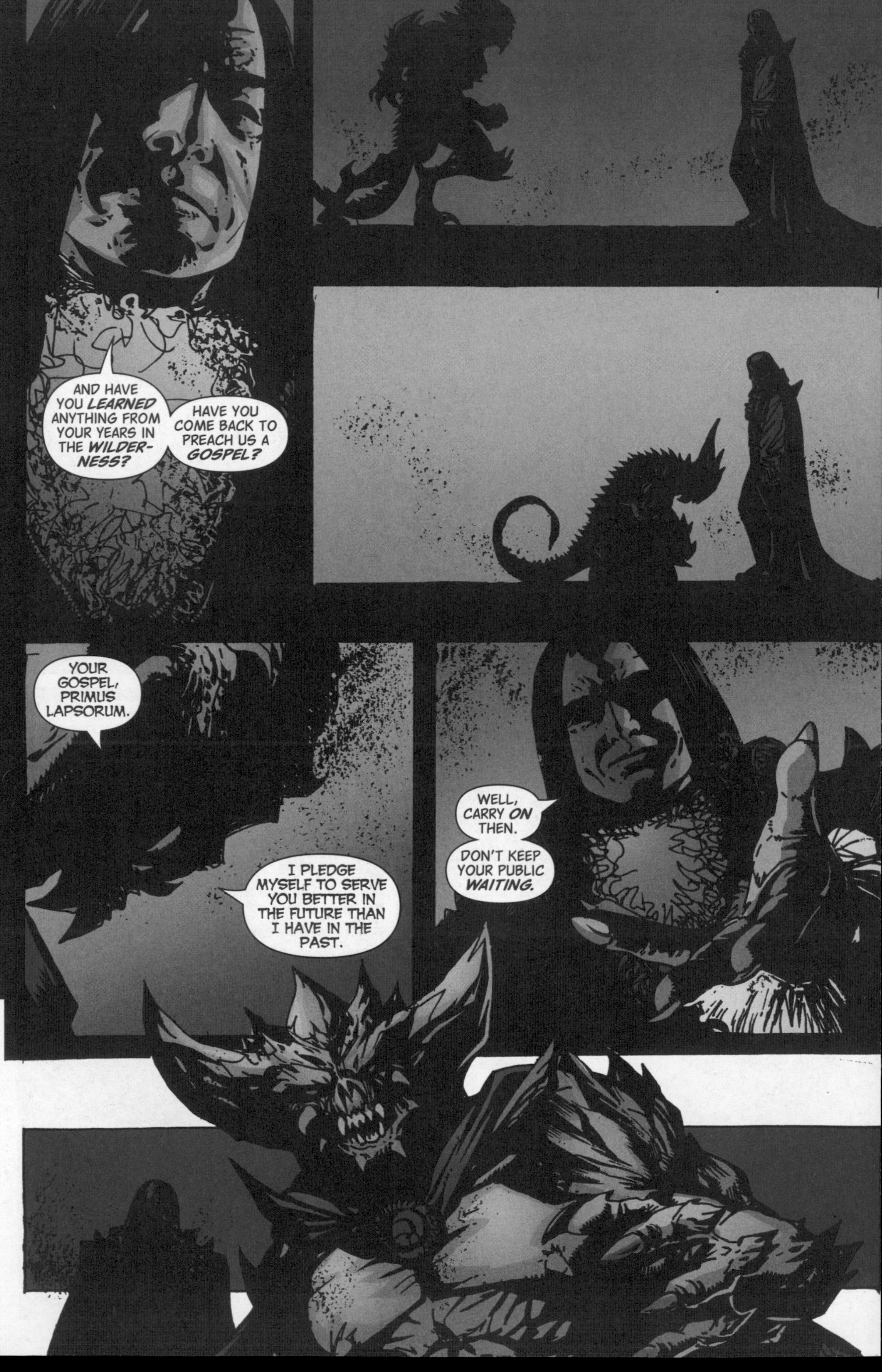
AND HAVE YOU LEARNED ANYTHING FROM YOUR YEARS IN THE WILDER-NESS?
HAVE YOU COME BACK TO PREACH US A GOSPEL?
YOUR GOSPEL, PRIMUS LAPSORUM.
I PLEDGE MYSELF TO SERVE YOU BETTER IN THE FUTURE THAN I HAVE IN THE PAST.
WELL, CARRY ON THEN.
DON'T KEEP YOUR PUBLIC WAITING.

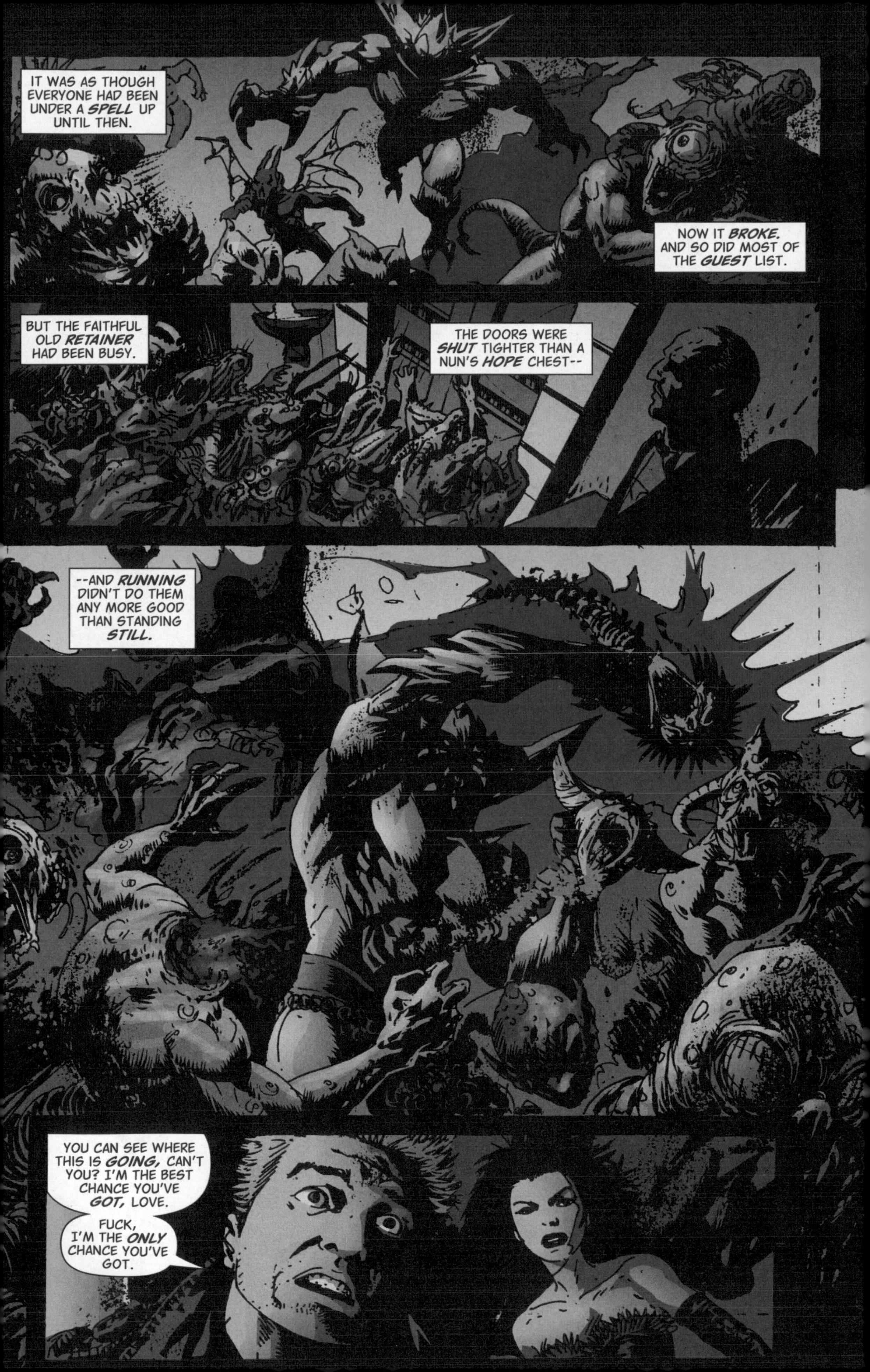
IT WAS AS THOUGH EVERYONE HAD BEEN UNDER A SPELL UP UNTIL THEN.
NOW IT BROKE. AND SO DID MOST OF THE GUEST LIST.
BUT THE FAITHFUL OLD RETAINER HAD BEEN BUSY.
THE DOORS WERE SHUT TIGHTER THAN A NUN'S HOPE CHEST--
--AND RUNNING DIDN'T DO THEM ANY MORE GOOD THAN STANDING STILL.
YOU CAN SEE WHERE THIS IS GOING, CAN'T YOU? I'M THE BEST CHANCE YOU'VE GOT, LOVE.
FUCK, I'M THE ONLY CHANCE YOU'VE GOT.

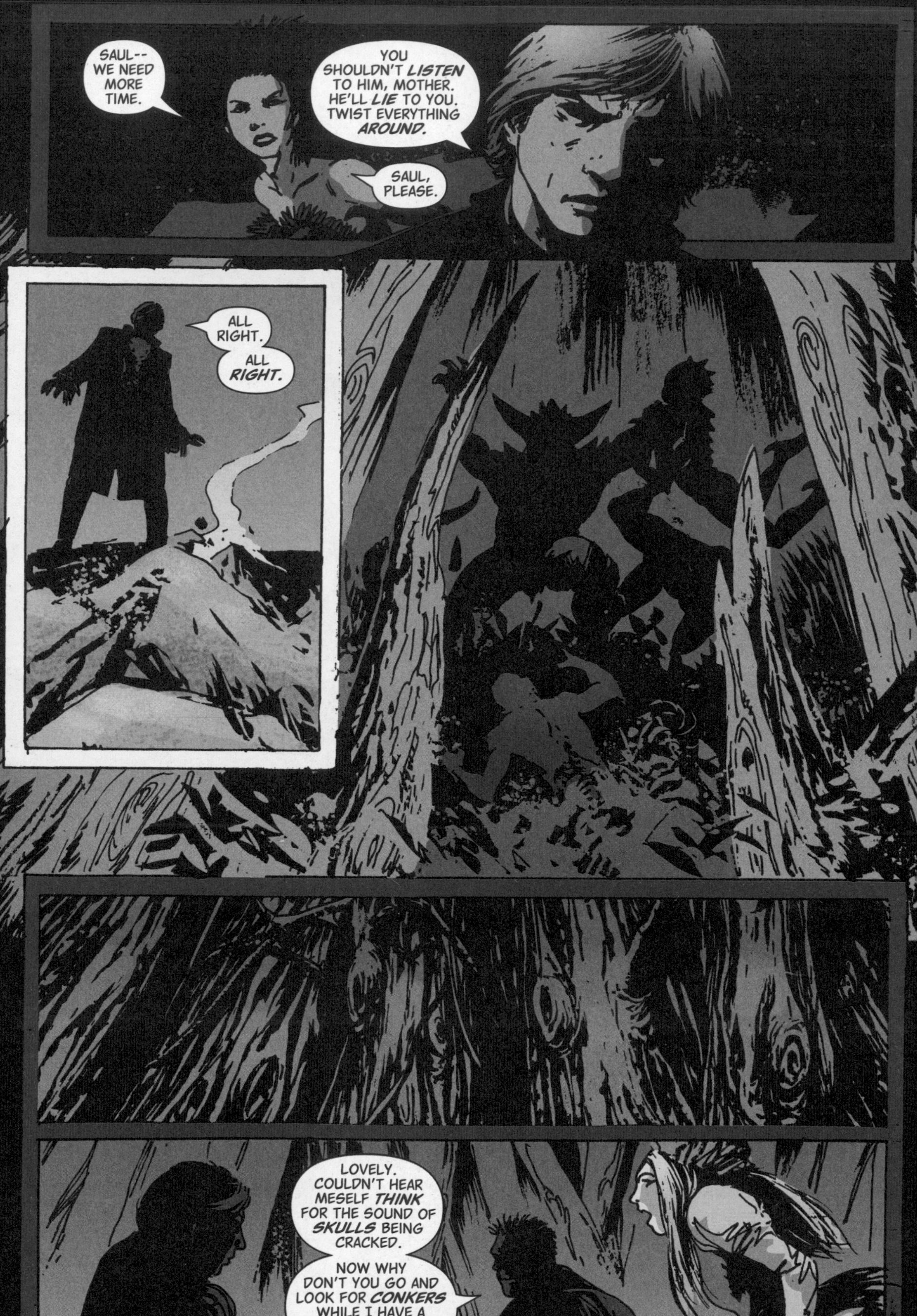
SAUL-- WE NEED MORE TIME.
YOU SHOULDN'T LISTEN TO HIM, MOTHER. HE'LL LIE TO YOU. TWIST EVERYTHING AROUND.
SAUL, PLEASE.
ALL RIGHT.
ALL RIGHT.
LOVELY. COULDN'T HEAR MESELF THINK FOR THE SOUND OF SKULLS BEING CRACKED.
NOW WHY DON'T YOU GO AND LOOK FOR CONKERS WHILE I HAVE A WORD WITH YOUR MUMMY?

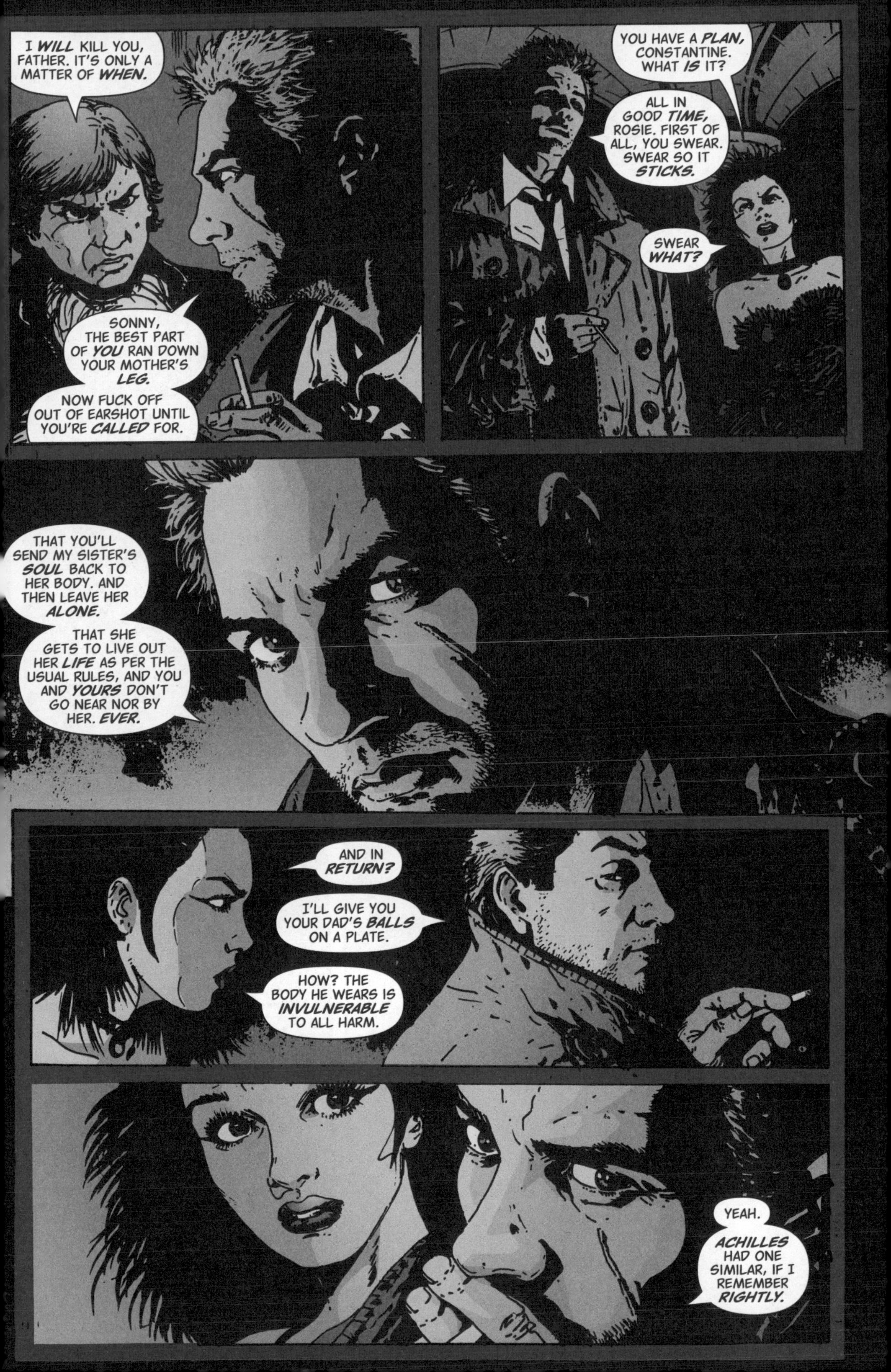

I WILL KILL YOU, FATHER. IT'S ONLY A MATTER OF WHEN.
SONNY, THE BEST PART OF YOU RAN DOWN YOUR MOTHER'S LEG.
NOW FUCK OFF OUT OF EARSHOT UNTIL YOU'RE CALLED FOR.
YOU HAVE A PLAN, CONSTANTINE. WHAT IS IT?
ALL IN GOOD TIME, ROSIE. FIRST OF ALL, YOU SWEAR. SWEAR SO IT STICKS.
SWEAR WHAT?
THAT YOU'LL SEND MY SISTER'S SOUL BACK TO HER BODY. AND THEN LEAVE HER ALONE.
THAT SHE GETS TO LIVE OUT HER LIFE AS PER THE USUAL RULES, AND YOU AND YOURS DON'T GO NEAR NOR BY HER. EVER.
AND IN RETURN?
I'LL GIVE YOU YOUR DAD'S BALLS ON A PLATE.
HOW? THE BODY HE WEARS IS INVULNERABLE TO ALL HARM.
YEAH.
ACHILLES HAD ONE SIMILAR, IF I REMEMBER RIGHTLY.

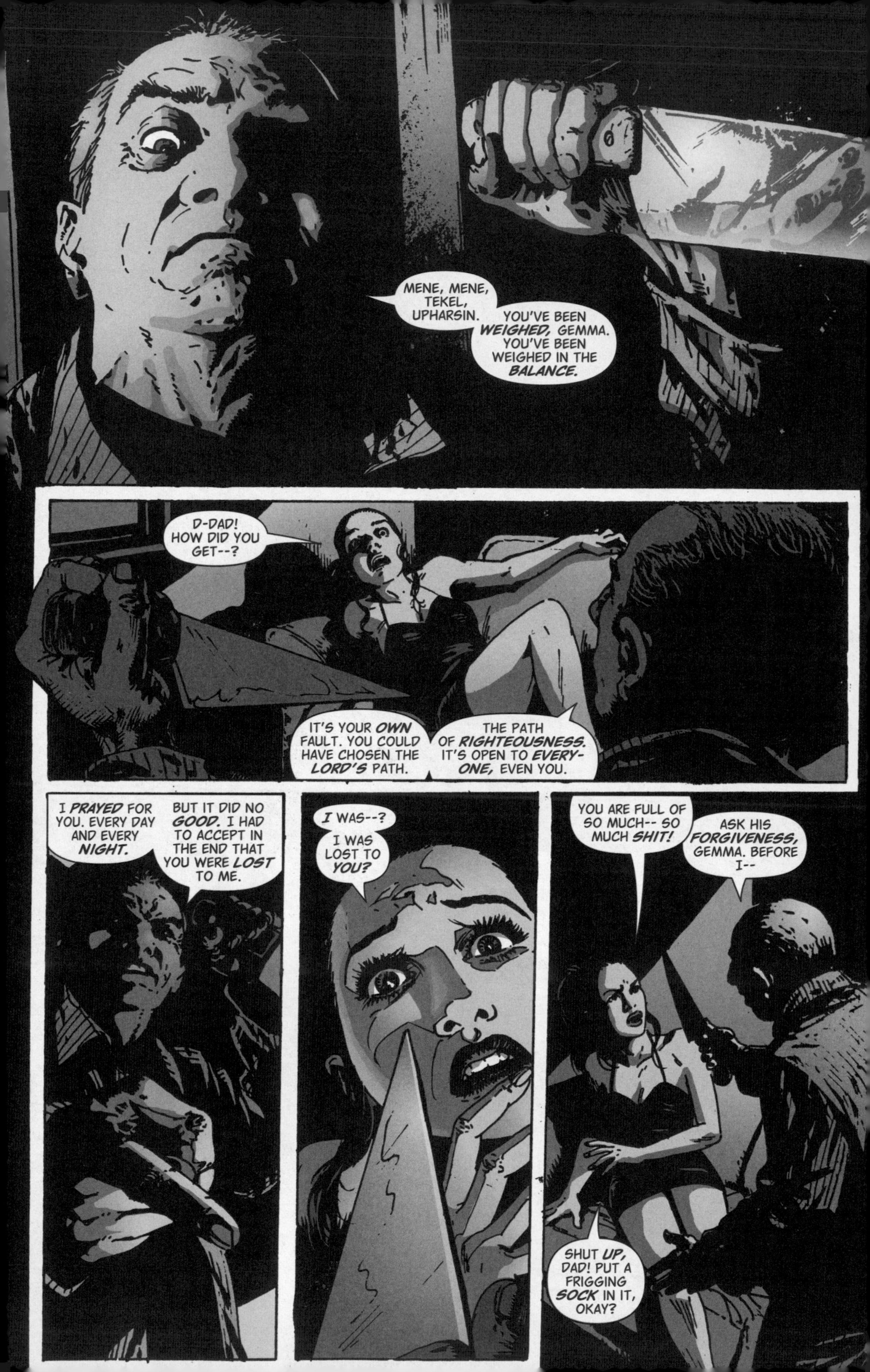

MENE, MENE, TEKEL, UPHARSIN.
YOU'VE BEEN *WEIGHED,* GEMMA. YOU'VE BEEN WEIGHED IN THE *BALANCE.*
D-DAD! HOW DID YOU GET--?
IT'S YOUR *OWN* FAULT. YOU COULD HAVE CHOSEN THE *LORD'S* PATH.
THE PATH OF *RIGHTEOUSNESS.* IT'S OPEN TO *EVERY-ONE,* EVEN YOU.
I *PRAYED* FOR YOU. EVERY DAY AND EVERY *NIGHT.*
BUT IT DID NO *GOOD.* I HAD TO ACCEPT IN THE END THAT YOU WERE *LOST* TO ME.
I WAS--?
I WAS LOST TO *YOU?*
YOU ARE FULL OF SO MUCH-- SO MUCH *SHIT!*
ASK HIS *FORGIVENESS,* GEMMA. BEFORE I--
SHUT *UP,* DAD! PUT A FRIGGING *SOCK* IN IT, OKAY?

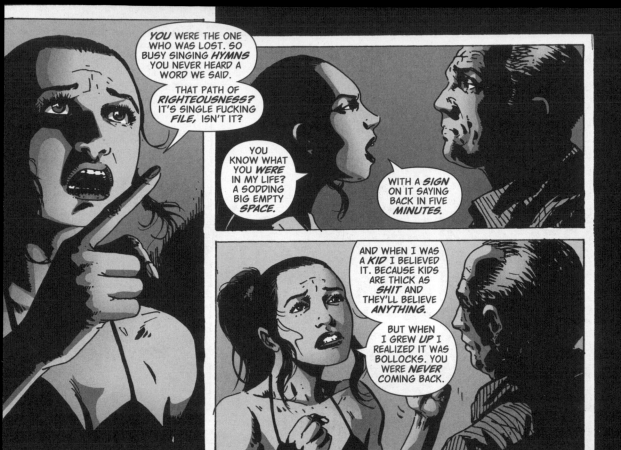

YOU WERE THE ONE WHO WAS LOST. SO BUSY SINGING *HYMNS* YOU NEVER HEARD A WORD WE SAID.

THAT PATH OF *RIGHTEOUSNESS?* IT'S SINGLE FUCKING *FILE*, ISN'T IT?

YOU KNOW WHAT YOU *WERE* IN MY LIFE? A SODDING BIG EMPTY *SPACE.*

WITH A *SIGN* ON IT SAYING BACK IN FIVE *MINUTES.*

AND WHEN I WAS A *KID* I BELIEVED IT. BECAUSE KIDS ARE THICK AS *SHIT* AND THEY'LL BELIEVE *ANYTHING.*

BUT WHEN I GREW *UP* I REALIZED IT WAS BOLLOCKS. YOU WERE *NEVER* COMING BACK.

IS THAT WHAT IT'S *LIKE* WHEN YOU'RE SNOGGING WITH *GOD,* DAD?

DOES NOTHING ELSE *MATTER?* IS NOBODY ELSE *REAL?*

YOU KILLED YOUR *WIFE!* HAS THAT SUNK *IN* YET? HAS THE PENNY *DROPPED?*

YOU *KILLED* YOUR *FUCKING* *WIFE!*

OKAY, DAD. IF YOUR DEFINITION OF TOUGH *LOVE* INCLUDES SLICING ME UP WITH A KITCHEN *DEVIL,* YOU GET STUCK IN.

I'M ALL *YOURS.*

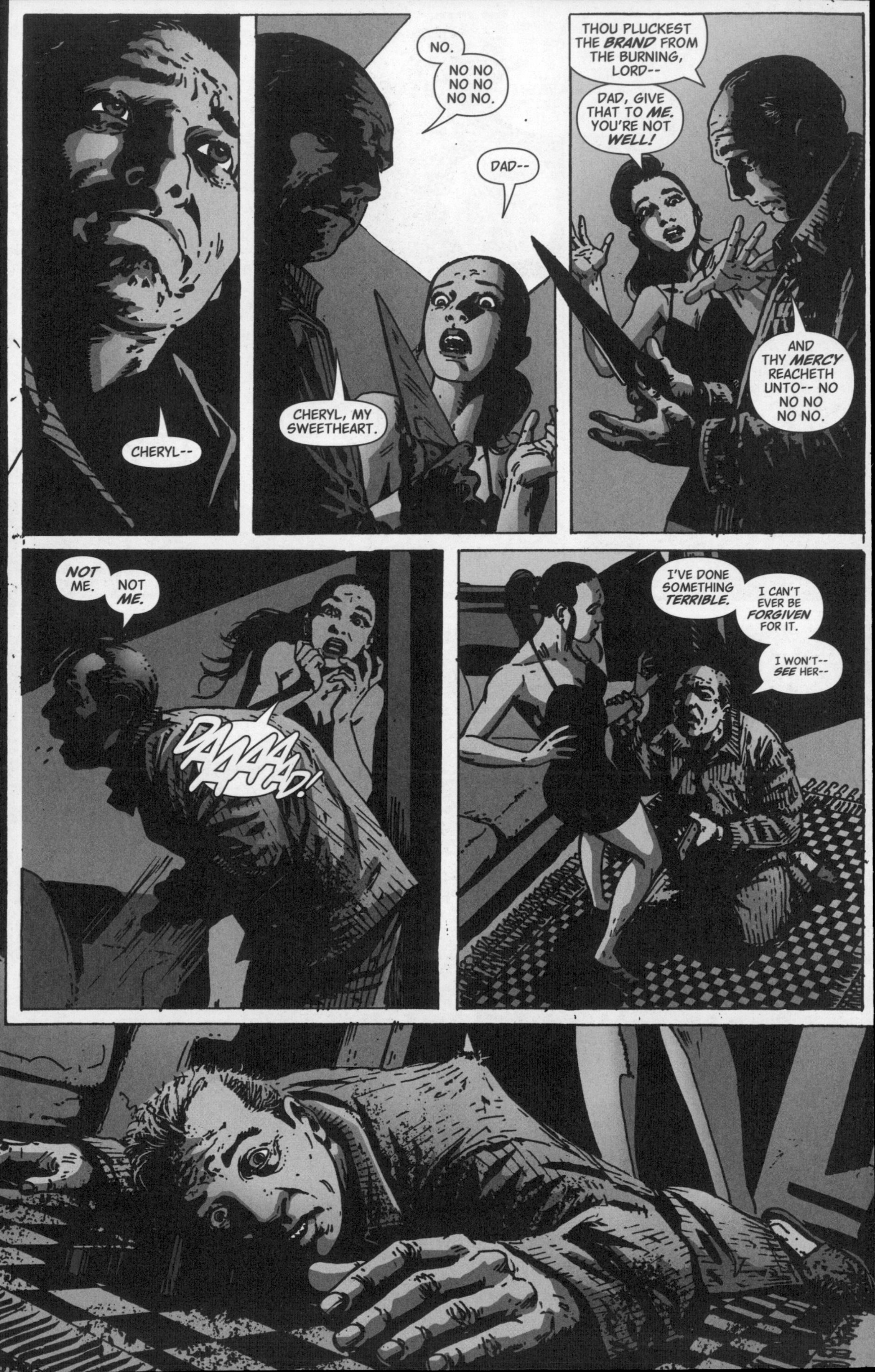
CHERYL--
NO.
NO NO NO NO NO NO.
DAD--
CHERYL, MY SWEETHEART.
THOU PLUCKEST THE BRAND FROM THE BURNING, LORD--
DAD, GIVE THAT TO ME. YOU'RE NOT WELL!
AND THY MERCY REACHETH UNTO-- NO NO NO NO NO.
NOT ME.
NOT ME.
DAAAAAAAAD!
I'VE DONE SOMETHING TERRIBLE.
I CAN'T EVER BE FORGIVEN FOR IT.
I WON'T-- SEE HER--

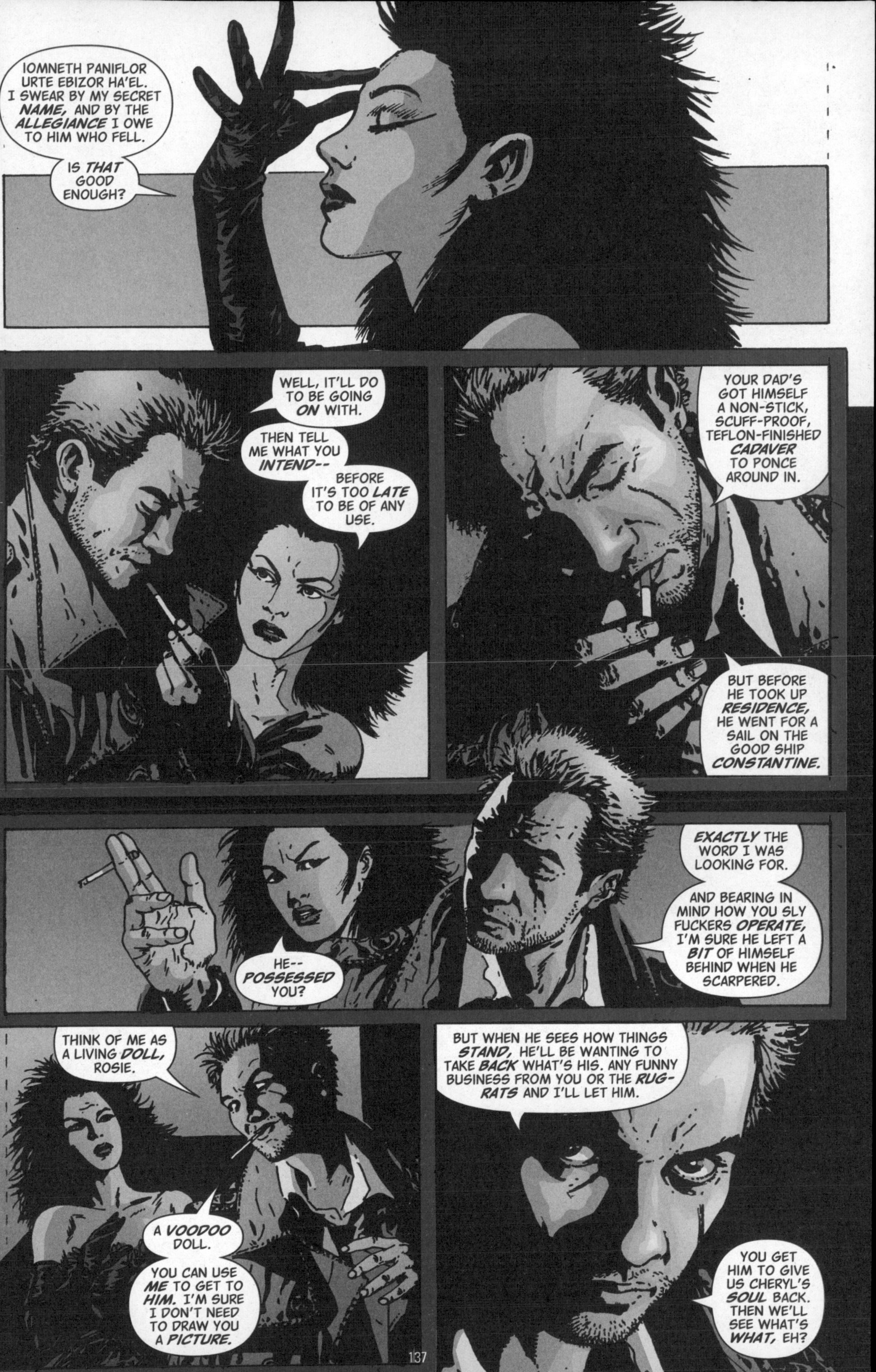
IOMNETH PANIFLOR URTE EBIZOR HA'EL. I SWEAR BY MY SECRET NAME, AND BY THE ALLEGIANCE I OWE TO HIM WHO FELL.
IS THAT GOOD ENOUGH?
WELL, IT'LL DO TO BE GOING ON WITH.
THEN TELL ME WHAT YOU INTEND--
BEFORE IT'S TOO LATE TO BE OF ANY USE.
YOUR DAD'S GOT HIMSELF A NON-STICK, SCUFF-PROOF, TEFLON-FINISHED CADAVER TO PONCE AROUND IN.
BUT BEFORE HE TOOK UP RESIDENCE, HE WENT FOR A SAIL ON THE GOOD SHIP CONSTANTINE.
HE-- POSSESSED YOU?
EXACTLY THE WORD I WAS LOOKING FOR.
AND BEARING IN MIND HOW YOU SLY FUCKERS OPERATE, I'M SURE HE LEFT A BIT OF HIMSELF BEHIND WHEN HE SCARPERED.
THINK OF ME AS A LIVING DOLL, ROSIE.
A VOODOO DOLL.
YOU CAN USE ME TO GET TO HIM. I'M SURE I DON'T NEED TO DRAW YOU A PICTURE.
BUT WHEN HE SEES HOW THINGS STAND, HE'LL BE WANTING TO TAKE BACK WHAT'S HIS. ANY FUNNY BUSINESS FROM YOU OR THE RUG-RATS AND I'LL LET HIM.
YOU GET HIM TO GIVE US CHERYL'S SOUL BACK. THEN WE'LL SEE WHAT'S WHAT, EH?

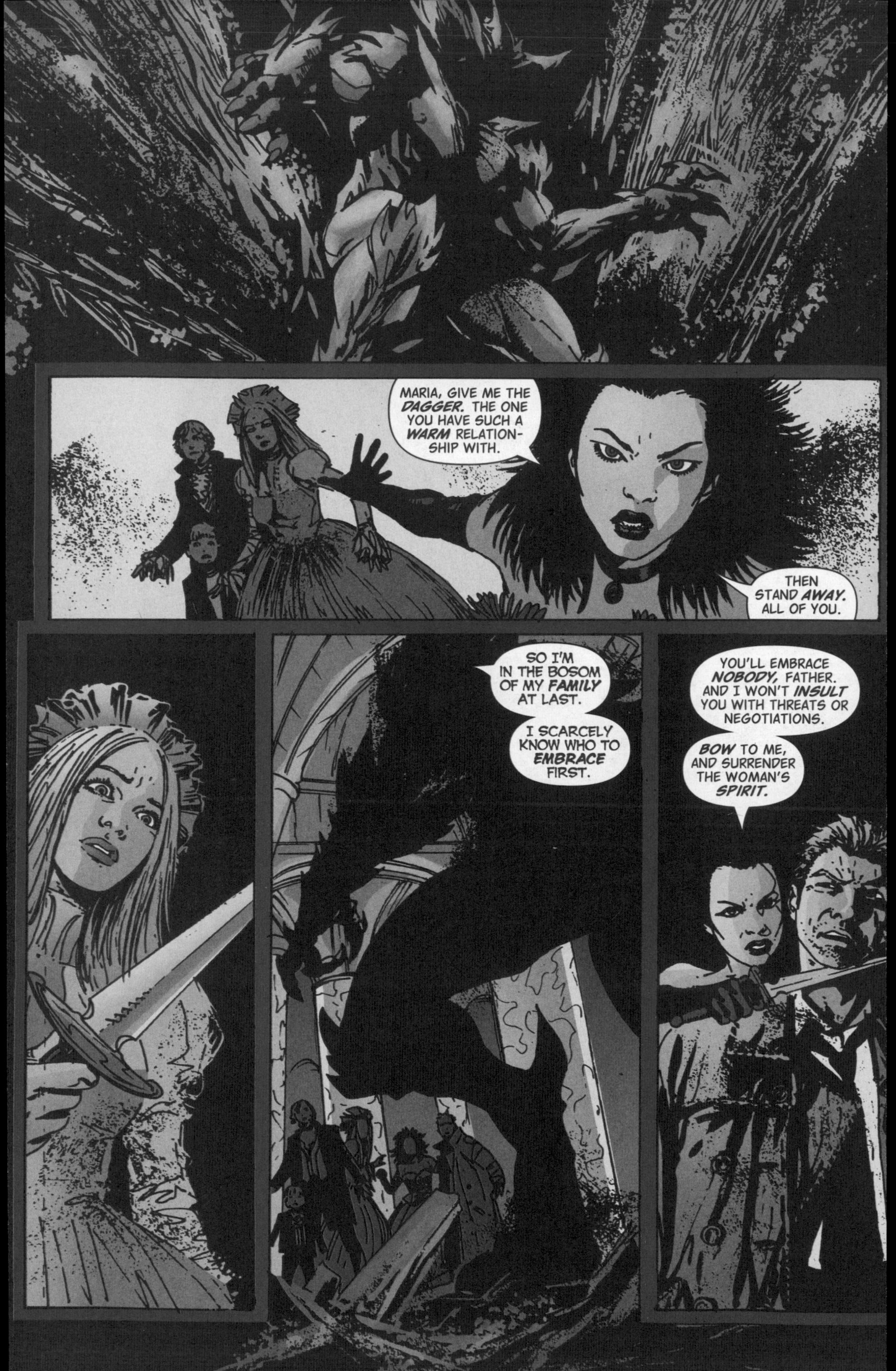
MARIA, GIVE ME THE DAGGER. THE ONE YOU HAVE SUCH A WARM RELATION-SHIP WITH.
THEN STAND AWAY. ALL OF YOU.
SO I'M IN THE BOSOM OF MY FAMILY AT LAST.
I SCARCELY KNOW WHO TO EMBRACE FIRST.
YOU'LL EMBRACE NOBODY, FATHER. AND I WON'T INSULT YOU WITH THREATS OR NEGOTIATIONS.
BOW TO ME, AND SURRENDER THE WOMAN'S SPIRIT.

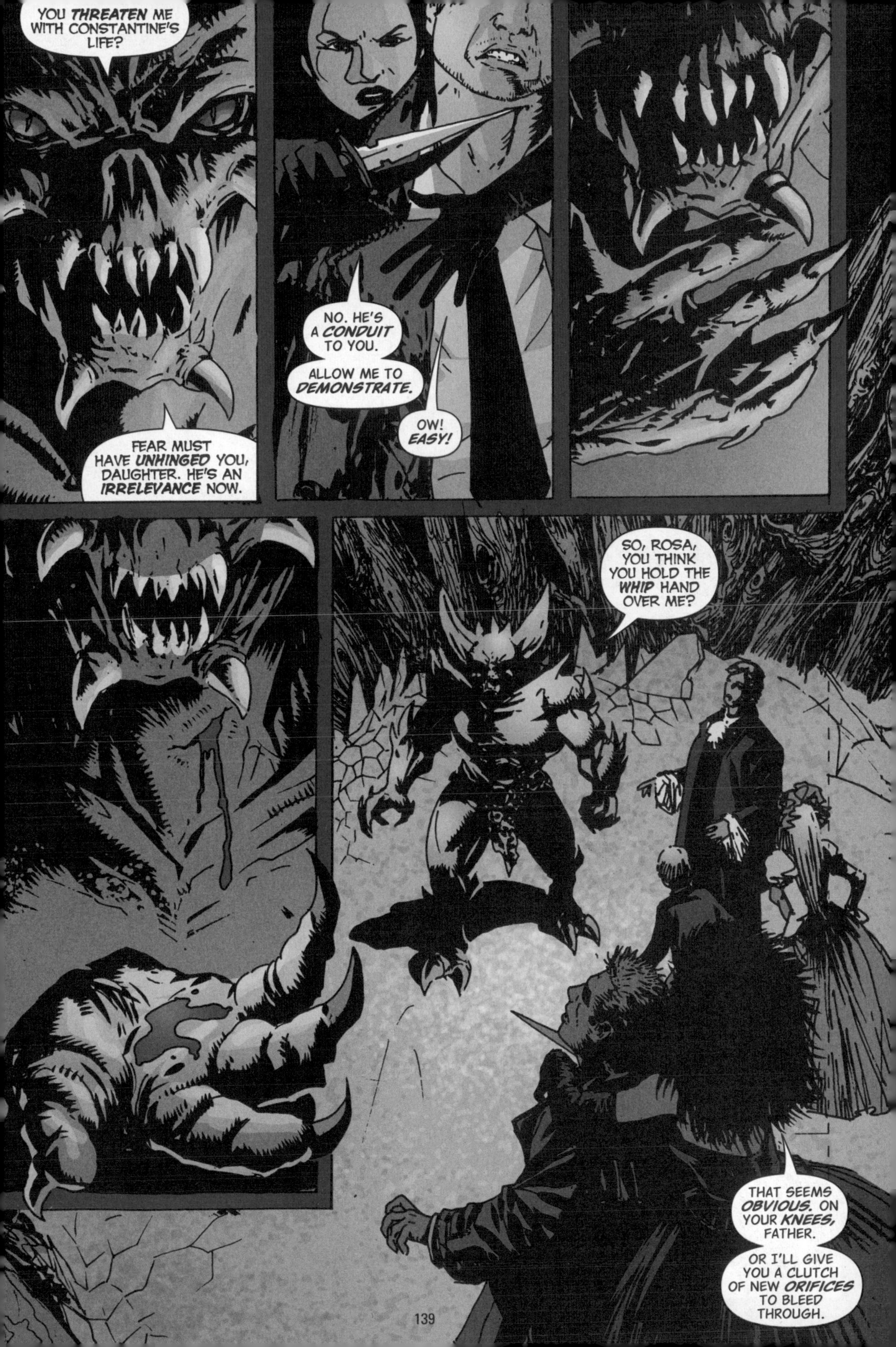
YOU THREATEN ME WITH CONSTANTINE'S LIFE?
FEAR MUST HAVE UNHINGED YOU, DAUGHTER. HE'S AN IRRELEVANCE NOW.
NO. HE'S A CONDUIT TO YOU.
ALLOW ME TO DEMONSTRATE.
OW! EASY!
SO, ROSA, YOU THINK YOU HOLD THE WHIP HAND OVER ME?
THAT SEEMS OBVIOUS. ON YOUR KNEES, FATHER.
OR I'LL GIVE YOU A CLUTCH OF NEW ORIFICES TO BLEED THROUGH.

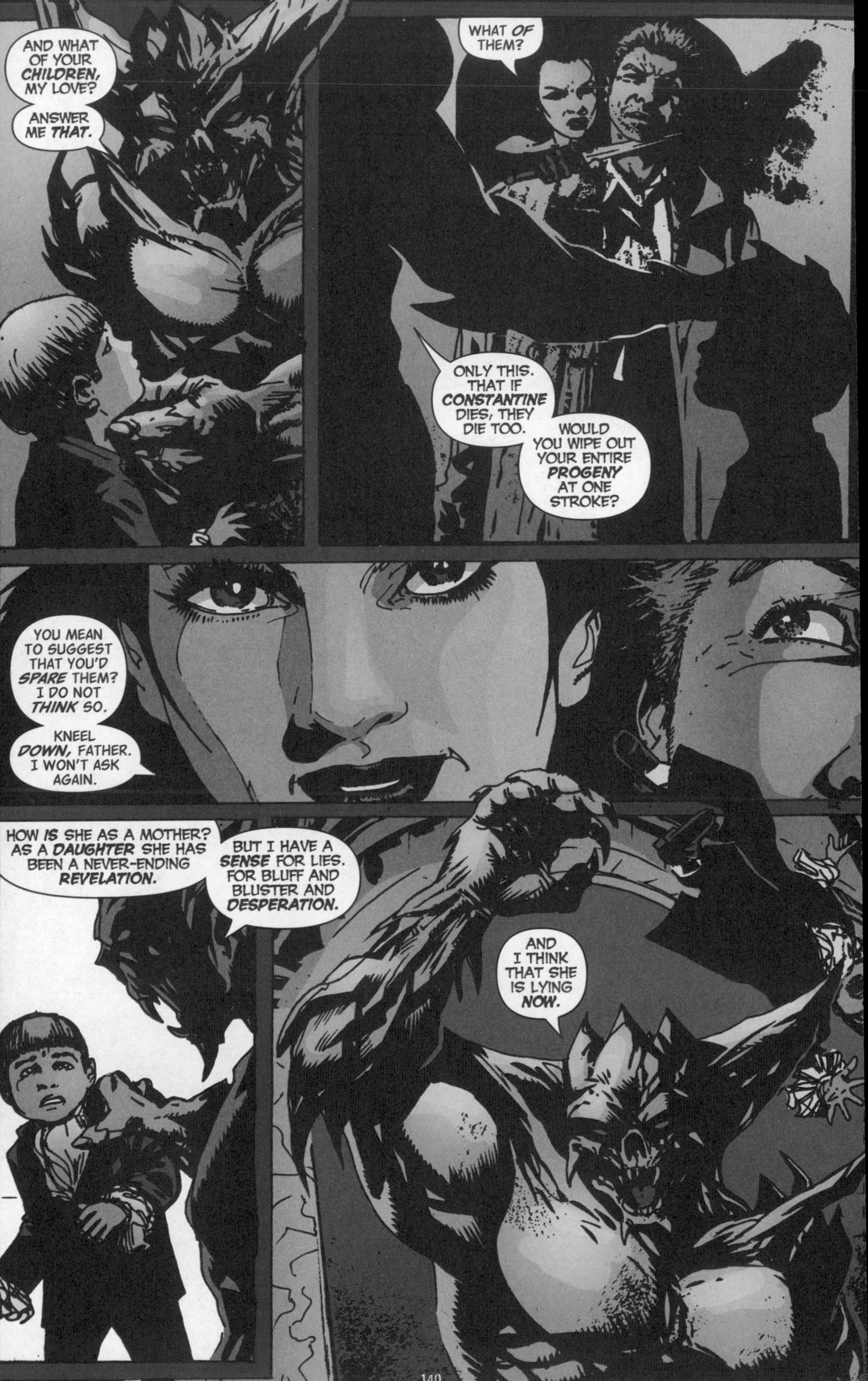
AND WHAT OF YOUR CHILDREN, MY LOVE?
ANSWER ME THAT.
WHAT OF THEM?
ONLY THIS. THAT IF CONSTANTINE DIES, THEY DIE TOO.
WOULD YOU WIPE OUT YOUR ENTIRE PROGENY AT ONE STROKE?
YOU MEAN TO SUGGEST THAT YOU'D SPARE THEM? I DO NOT THINK SO.
KNEEL DOWN, FATHER. I WON'T ASK AGAIN.
HOW IS SHE AS A MOTHER? AS A DAUGHTER SHE HAS BEEN A NEVER-ENDING REVELATION.
BUT I HAVE A SENSE FOR LIES. FOR BLUFF AND BLUSTER AND DESPERATION.
AND I THINK THAT SHE IS LYING NOW.

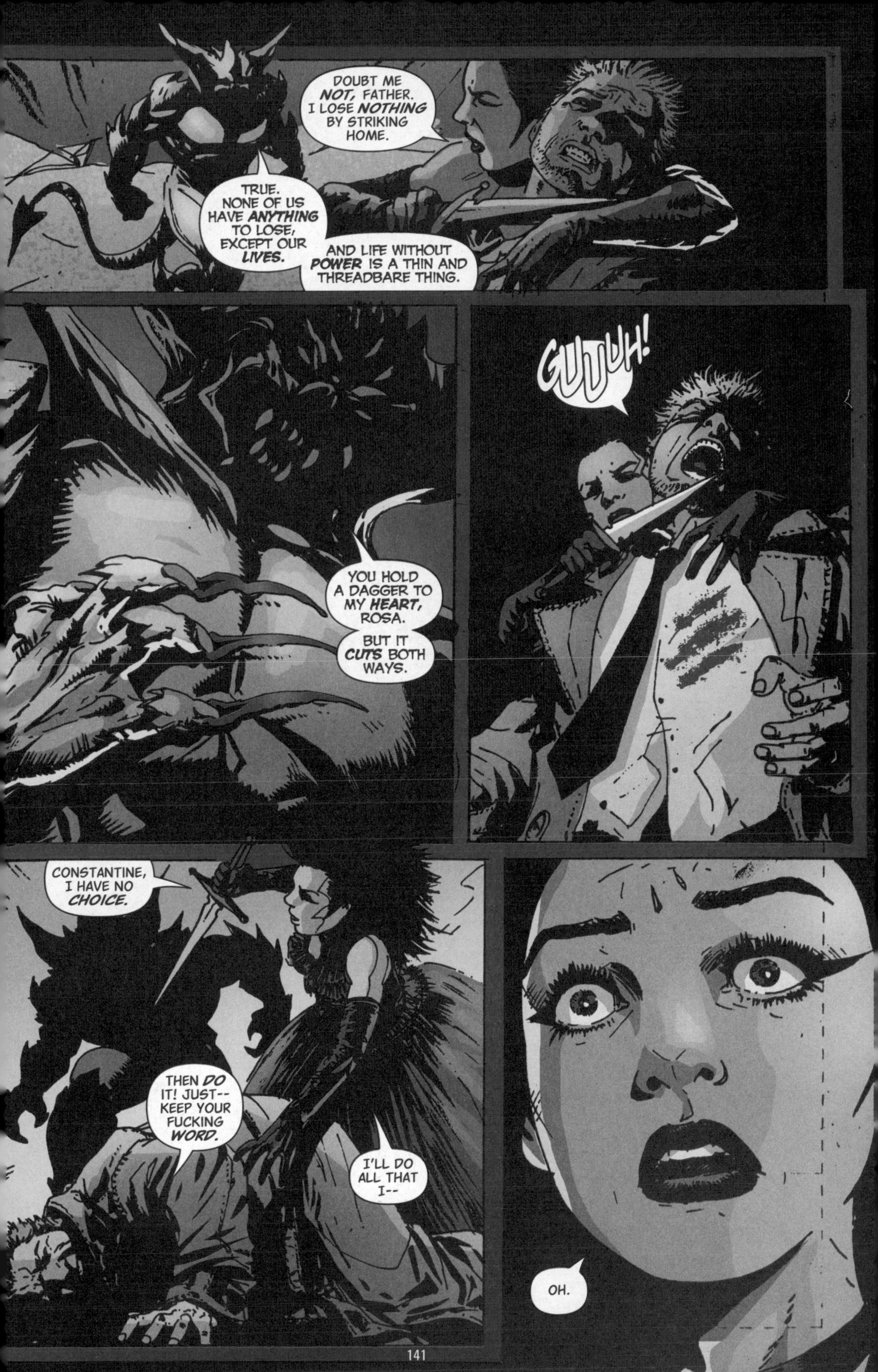
DOUBT ME NOT, FATHER. I LOSE NOTHING BY STRIKING HOME.
TRUE. NONE OF US HAVE ANYTHING TO LOSE, EXCEPT OUR LIVES.
AND LIFE WITHOUT POWER IS A THIN AND THREADBARE THING.
YOU HOLD A DAGGER TO MY HEART, ROSA.
BUT IT CUTS BOTH WAYS.
GUUUH!
CONSTANTINE, I HAVE NO CHOICE.
THEN DO IT! JUST-- KEEP YOUR FUCKING WORD.
I'LL DO ALL THAT I--
OH.

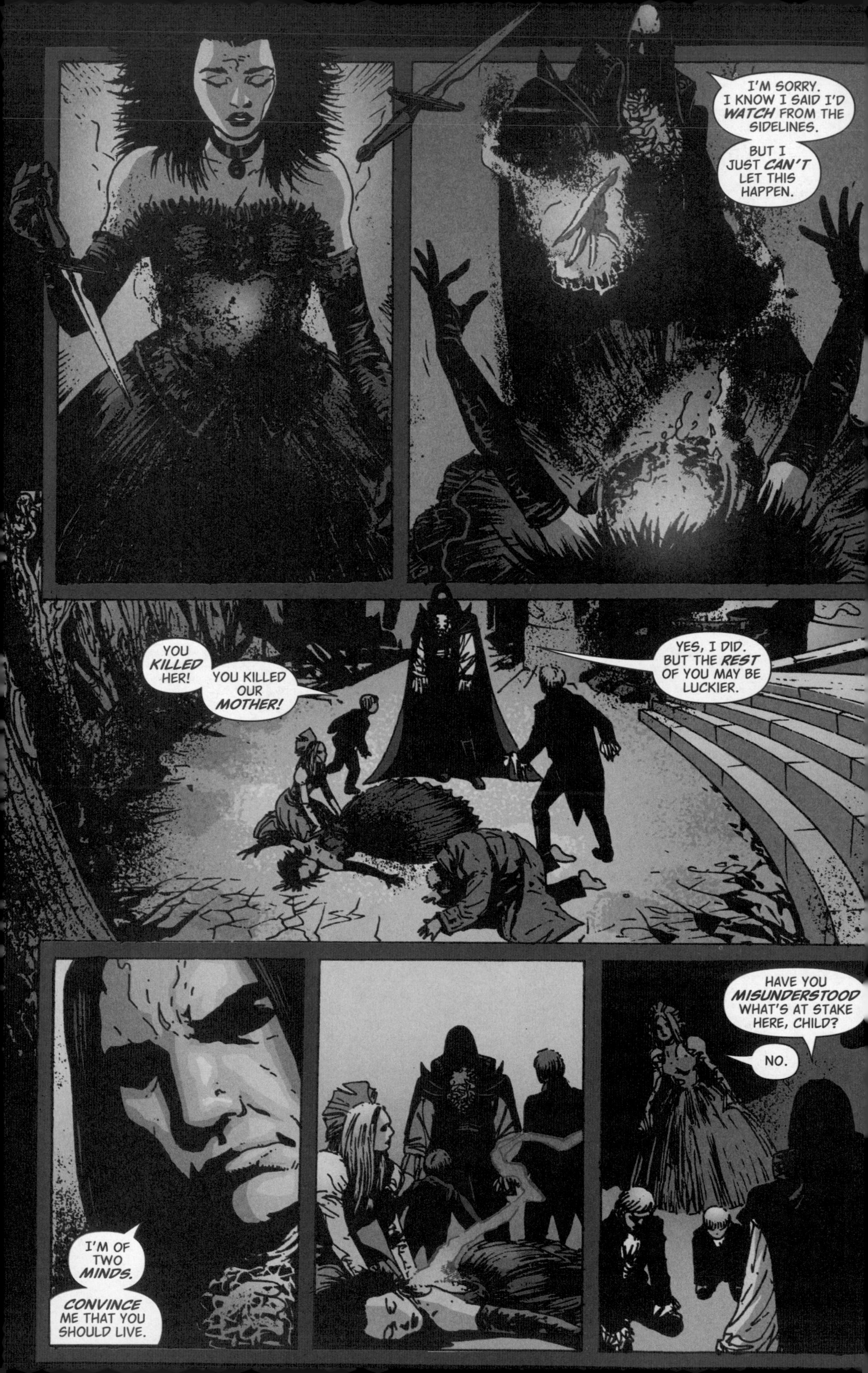
I'M SORRY. I KNOW I SAID I'D WATCH FROM THE SIDELINES.
BUT I JUST CAN'T LET THIS HAPPEN.
YOU KILLED HER!
YOU KILLED OUR MOTHER!
YES, I DID. BUT THE REST OF YOU MAY BE LUCKIER.
I'M OF TWO MINDS.
CONVINCE ME THAT YOU SHOULD LIVE.
HAVE YOU MISUNDERSTOOD WHAT'S AT STAKE HERE, CHILD?
NO.

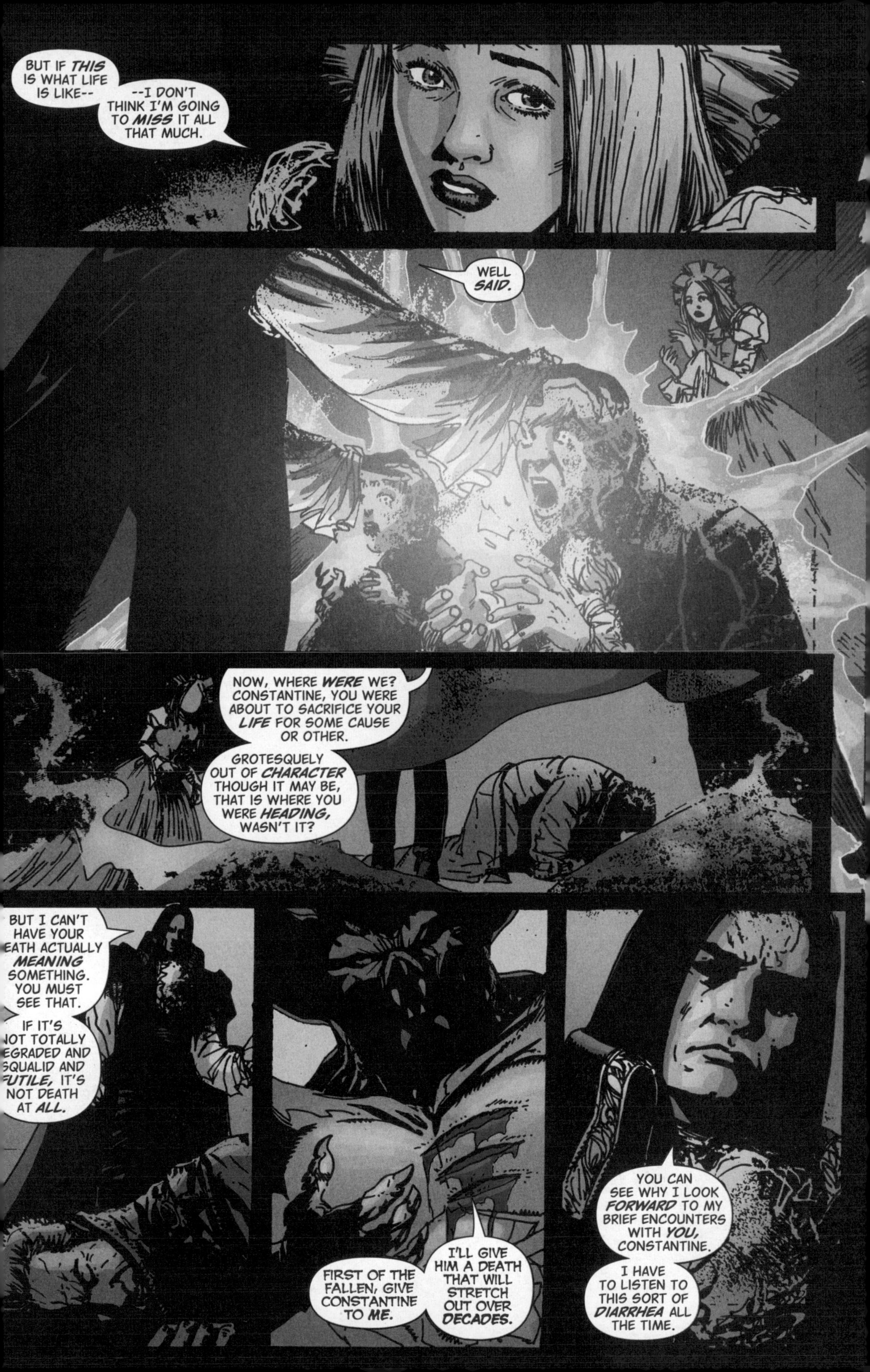
BUT IF *THIS* IS WHAT LIFE IS LIKE--
--I DON'T THINK I'M GOING TO *MISS* IT ALL THAT MUCH.
WELL *SAID.*
NOW, WHERE *WERE* WE? CONSTANTINE, YOU WERE ABOUT TO SACRIFICE YOUR *LIFE* FOR SOME CAUSE OR OTHER.
GROTESQUELY OUT OF *CHARACTER* THOUGH IT MAY BE, THAT IS WHERE YOU WERE *HEADING,* WASN'T IT?
BUT I CAN'T HAVE YOUR EATH ACTUALLY *MEANING* SOMETHING. YOU MUST SEE THAT.
IF IT'S NOT TOTALLY EGRADED AND SQUALID AND *FUTILE,* IT'S NOT DEATH AT *ALL.*
FIRST OF THE FALLEN, GIVE CONSTANTINE TO *ME.*
I'LL GIVE HIM A DEATH THAT WILL STRETCH OUT OVER *DECADES.*
YOU CAN SEE WHY I LOOK *FORWARD* TO MY BRIEF ENCOUNTERS WITH *YOU,* CONSTANTINE.
I HAVE TO LISTEN TO THIS SORT OF *DIARRHEA* ALL THE TIME.

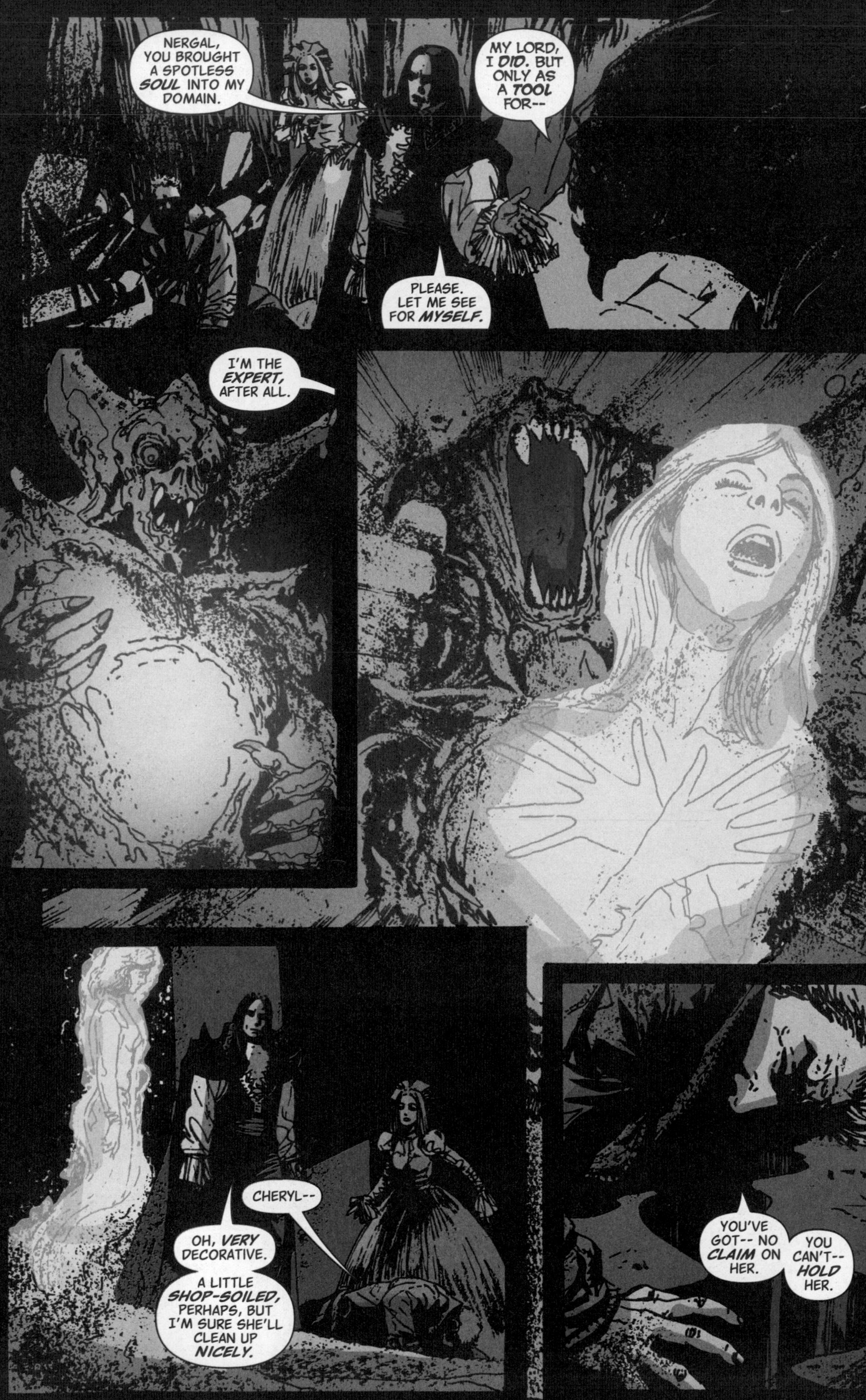
NERGAL, YOU BROUGHT A SPOTLESS *SOUL* INTO MY DOMAIN.
MY LORD, I *DID.* BUT ONLY AS A *TOOL* FOR--
PLEASE. LET ME SEE FOR *MYSELF.*
I'M THE *EXPERT,* AFTER ALL.
CHERYL--
OH, *VERY* DECORATIVE.
A LITTLE *SHOP-SOILED,* PERHAPS, BUT I'M SURE SHE'LL CLEAN UP *NICELY.*
YOU'VE GOT-- NO *CLAIM* ON HER.
YOU CAN'T-- *HOLD* HER.

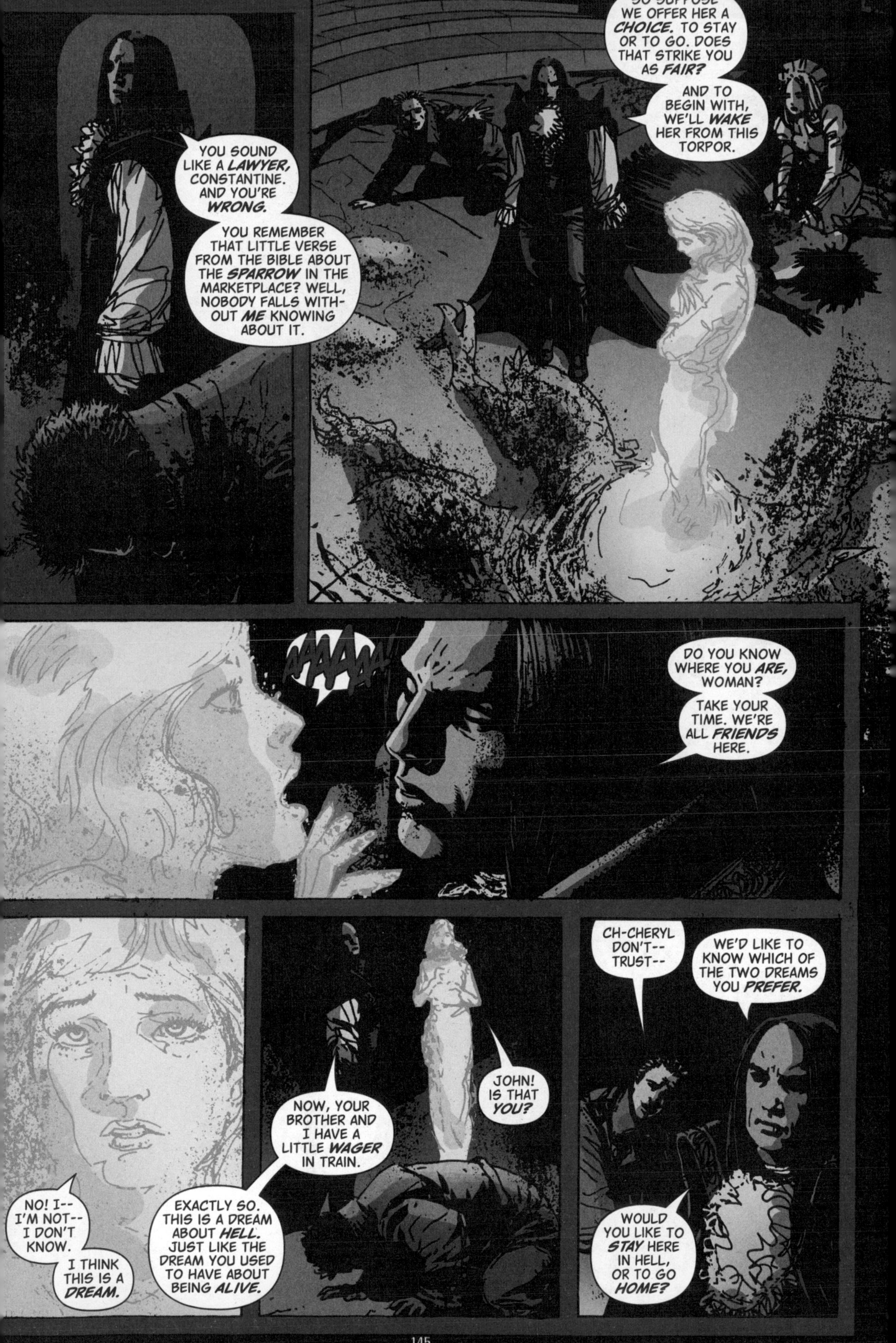

SO SUPPOSE WE OFFER HER A *CHOICE*. TO STAY OR TO GO. DOES THAT STRIKE YOU AS *FAIR?*
AND TO BEGIN WITH, WE'LL *WAKE* HER FROM THIS TORPOR.
YOU SOUND LIKE A *LAWYER*, CONSTANTINE. AND YOU'RE *WRONG.*
YOU REMEMBER THAT LITTLE VERSE FROM THE BIBLE ABOUT THE *SPARROW* IN THE MARKETPLACE? WELL, NOBODY FALLS WITH-OUT *ME* KNOWING ABOUT IT.
AAAAAA!
DO YOU KNOW WHERE YOU *ARE*, WOMAN?
TAKE YOUR TIME. WE'RE ALL *FRIENDS* HERE.
NO! I-- I'M NOT-- I DON'T KNOW.
I THINK THIS IS A *DREAM.*
EXACTLY SO. THIS IS A DREAM ABOUT *HELL*. JUST LIKE THE DREAM YOU USED TO HAVE ABOUT BEING *ALIVE.*
NOW, YOUR BROTHER AND I HAVE A LITTLE *WAGER* IN TRAIN.
JOHN! IS THAT *YOU?*
CH-CHERYL DON'T-- TRUST--
WE'D LIKE TO KNOW WHICH OF THE TWO DREAMS YOU *PREFER.*
WOULD YOU LIKE TO *STAY* HERE IN HELL, OR TO GO *HOME?*

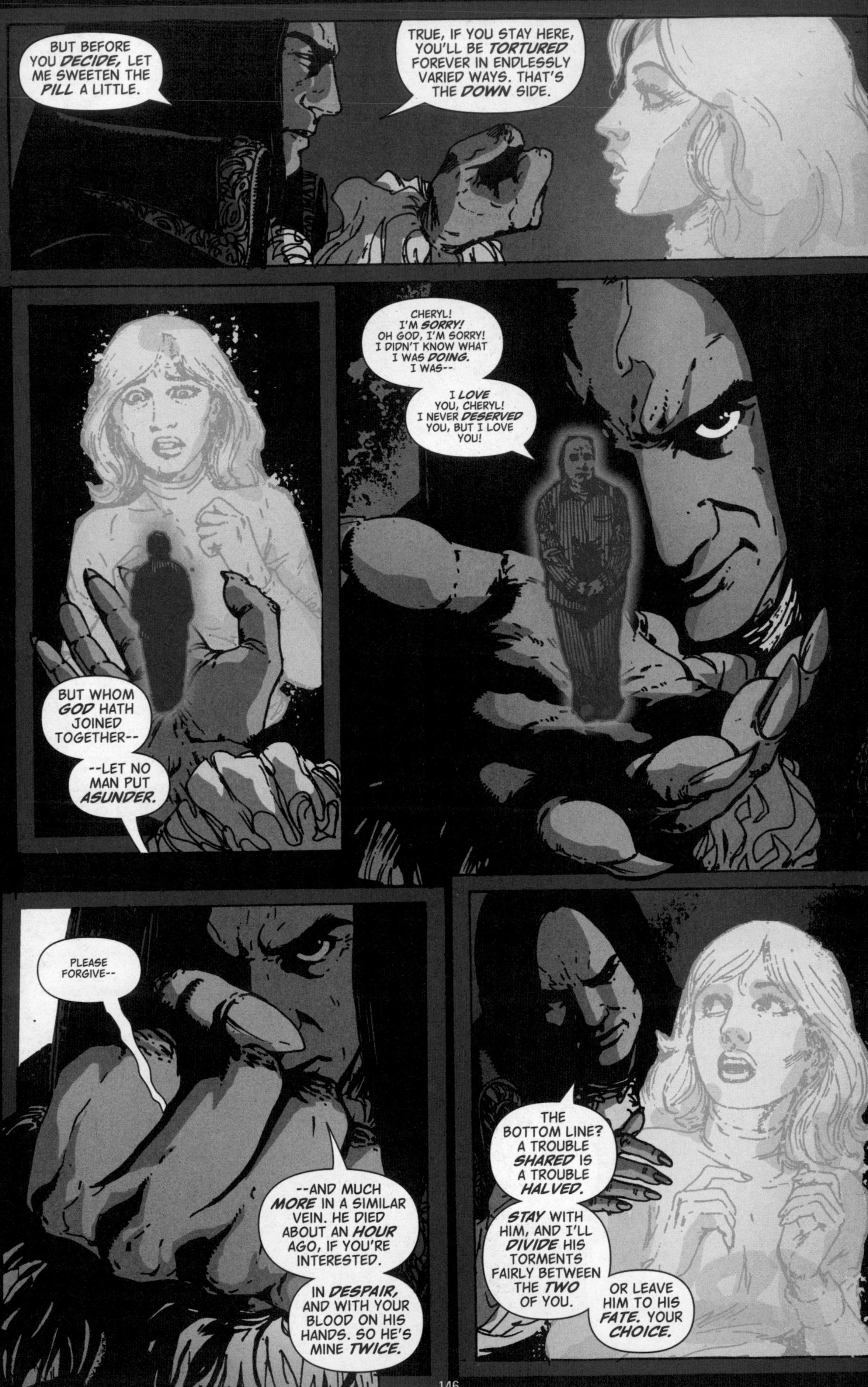
BUT BEFORE YOU DECIDE, LET ME SWEETEN THE PILL A LITTLE.
TRUE, IF YOU STAY HERE, YOU'LL BE TORTURED FOREVER IN ENDLESSLY VARIED WAYS. THAT'S THE DOWN SIDE.
CHERYL! I'M SORRY! OH GOD, I'M SORRY! I DIDN'T KNOW WHAT I WAS DOING. I WAS--
I LOVE YOU, CHERYL! I NEVER DESERVED YOU, BUT I LOVE YOU!
BUT WHOM GOD HATH JOINED TOGETHER--
--LET NO MAN PUT ASUNDER.
PLEASE FORGIVE--
--AND MUCH MORE IN A SIMILAR VEIN. HE DIED ABOUT AN HOUR AGO, IF YOU'RE INTERESTED.
IN DESPAIR, AND WITH YOUR BLOOD ON HIS HANDS. SO HE'S MINE TWICE.
THE BOTTOM LINE? A TROUBLE SHARED IS A TROUBLE HALVED.
STAY WITH HIM, AND I'LL DIVIDE HIS TORMENTS FAIRLY BETWEEN THE TWO OF YOU.
OR LEAVE HIM TO HIS FATE. YOUR CHOICE.

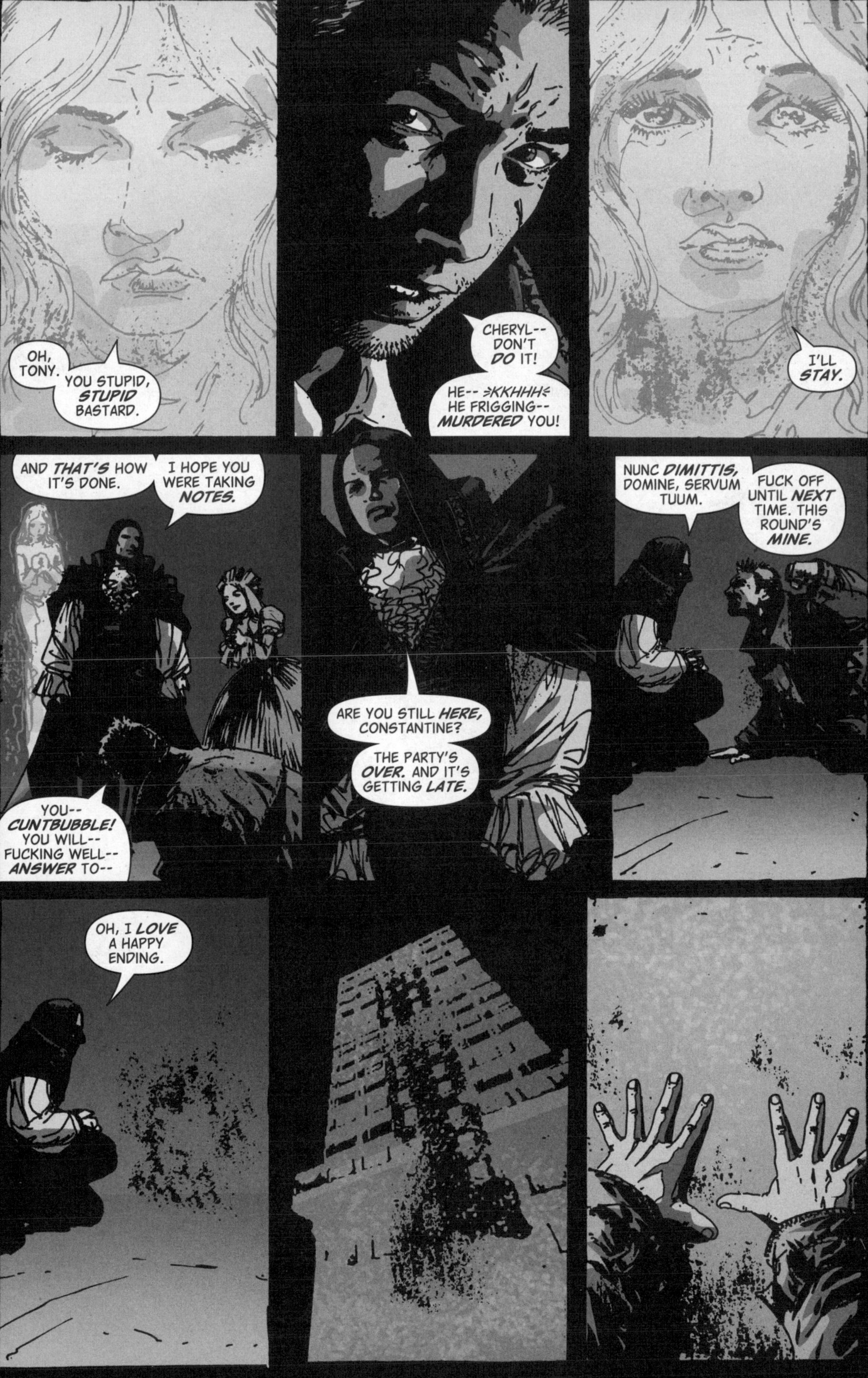

OH, TONY.
YOU STUPID, STUPID BASTARD.
CHERYL-- DON'T DO IT!
HE-- ≥KKHHH≤ HE FRIGGING-- MURDERED YOU!
I'LL STAY.
AND THAT'S HOW IT'S DONE.
I HOPE YOU WERE TAKING NOTES.
YOU-- CUNTBUBBLE! YOU WILL-- FUCKING WELL-- ANSWER TO--
ARE YOU STILL HERE, CONSTANTINE?
THE PARTY'S OVER. AND IT'S GETTING LATE.
NUNC DIMITTIS, DOMINE, SERVUM TUUM.
FUCK OFF UNTIL NEXT TIME. THIS ROUND'S MINE.
OH, I LOVE A HAPPY ENDING.

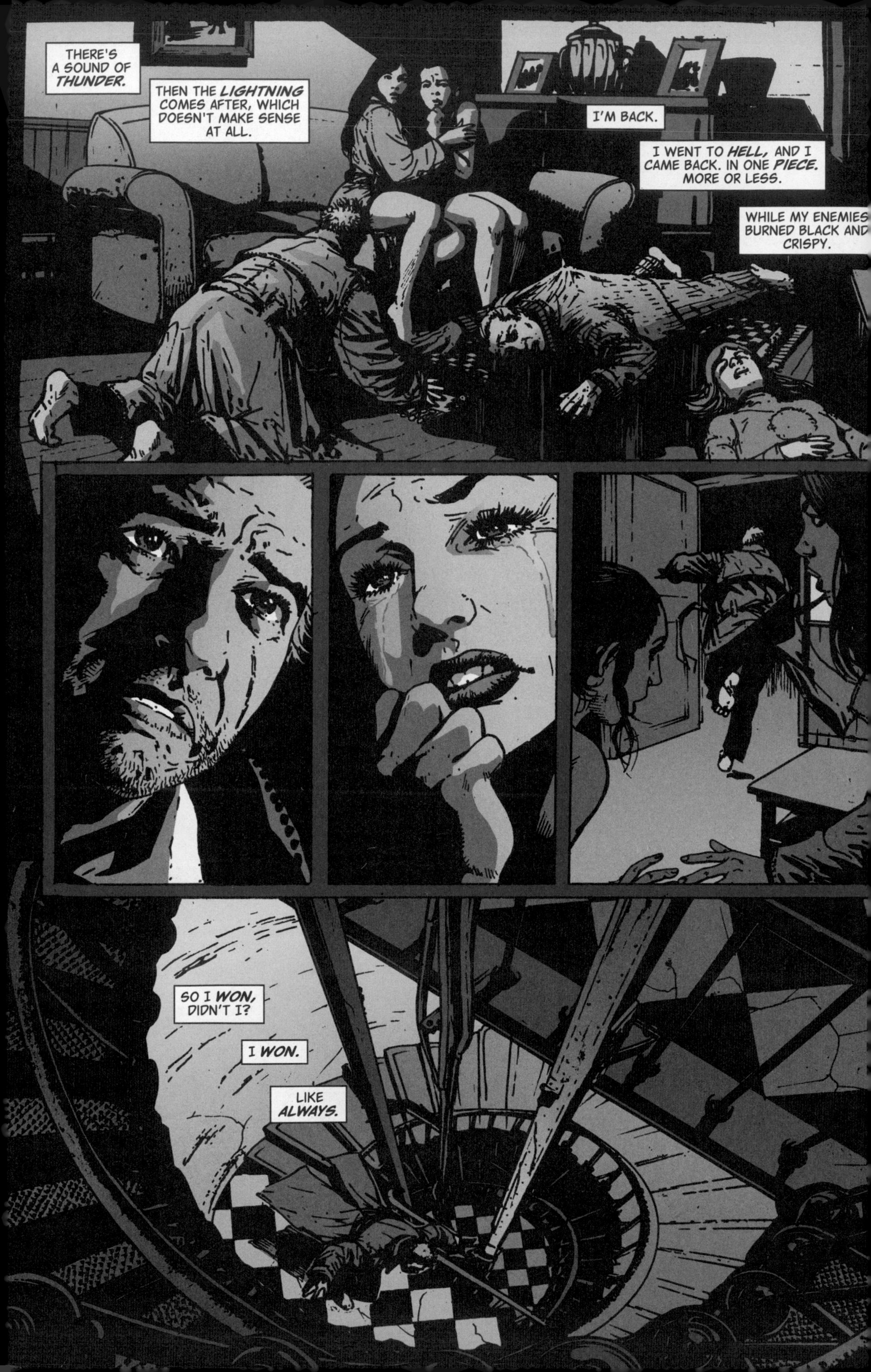

THERE'S A SOUND OF THUNDER.
THEN THE LIGHTNING COMES AFTER, WHICH DOESN'T MAKE SENSE AT ALL.
I'M BACK.
I WENT TO HELL, AND I CAME BACK. IN ONE PIECE. MORE OR LESS.
WHILE MY ENEMIES BURNED BLACK AND CRISPY.
SO I WON, DIDN'T I?
I WON.
LIKE ALWAYS.

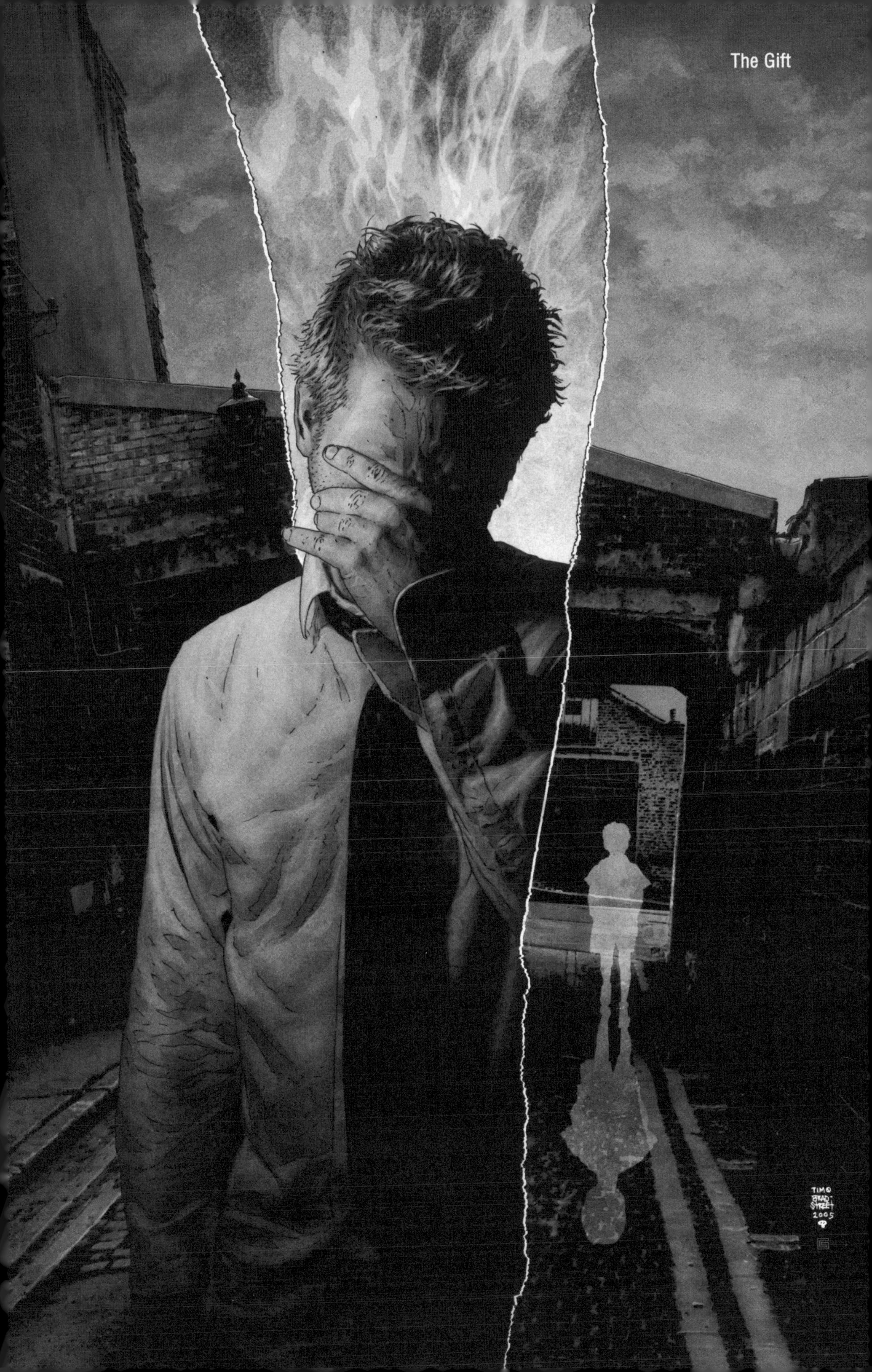
The Gift
TIMO BRADSTREET 2005

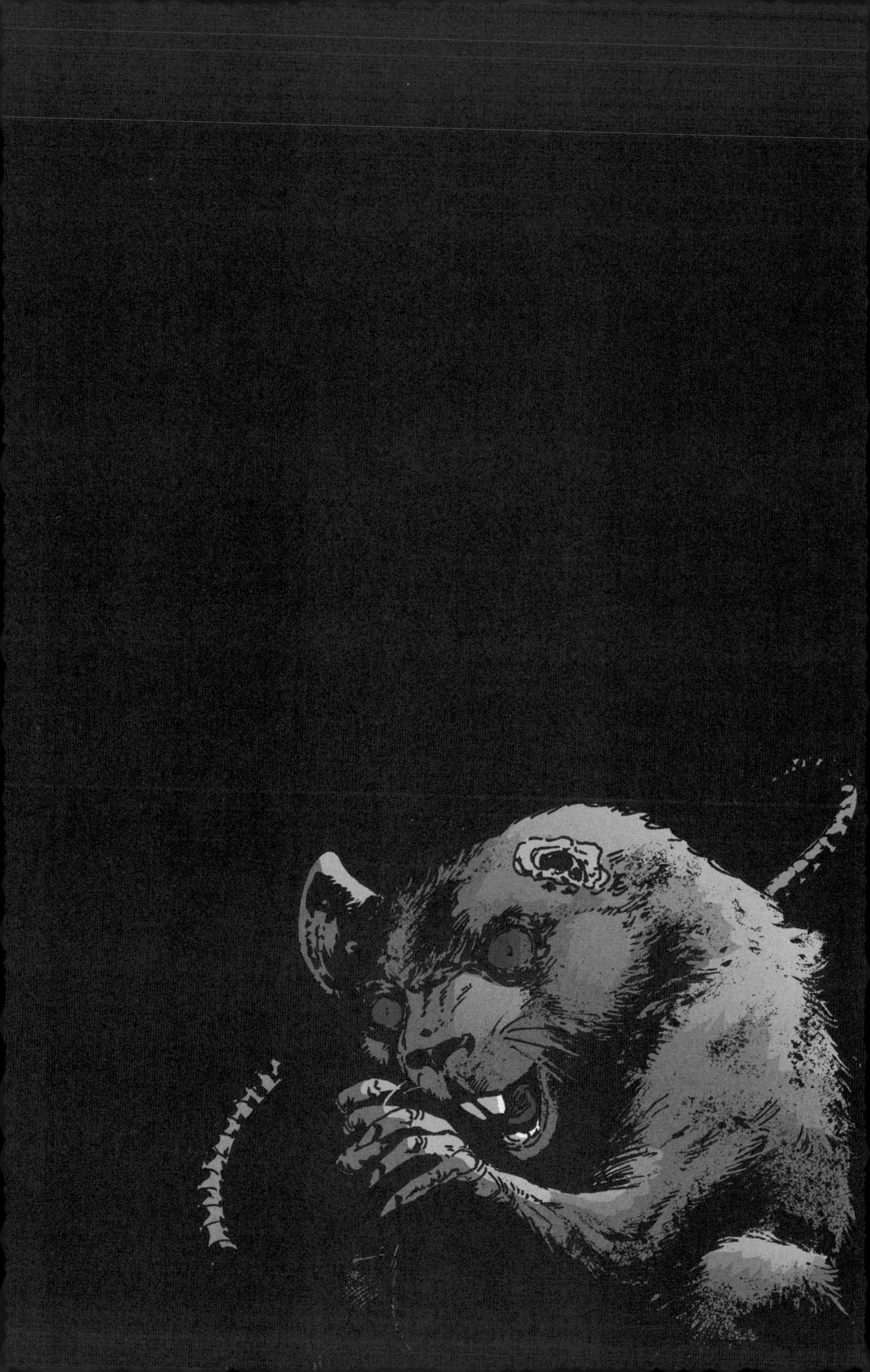

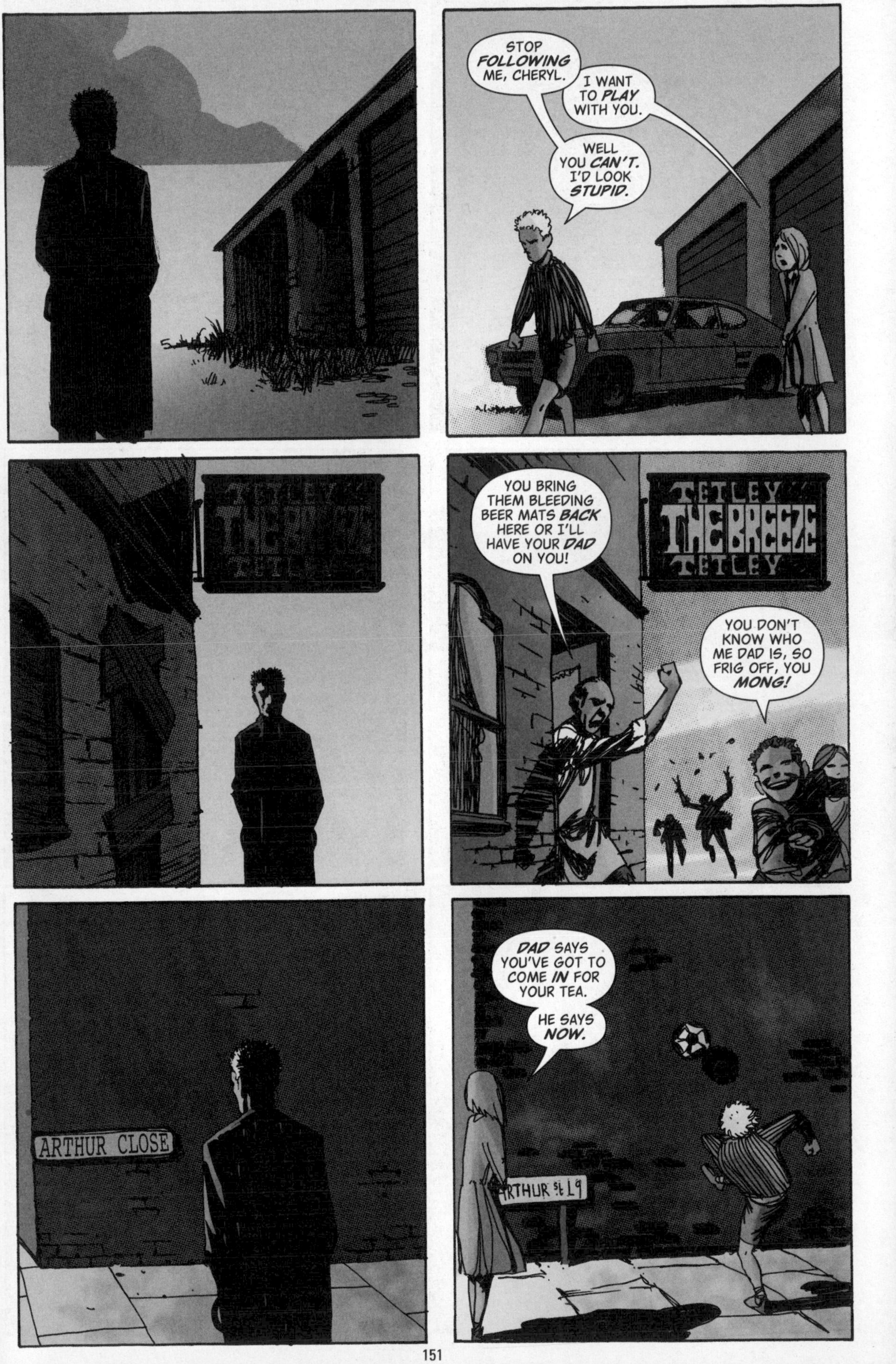
STOP FOLLOWING ME, CHERYL.
I WANT TO PLAY WITH YOU.
WELL YOU CAN'T. I'D LOOK STUPID.
TETLEY THE BREEZE TETLEY
YOU BRING THEM BLEEDING BEER MATS BACK HERE OR I'LL HAVE YOUR DAD ON YOU!
YOU DON'T KNOW WHO ME DAD IS, SO FRIG OFF, YOU MONG!
ARTHUR CLOSE
DAD SAYS YOU'VE GOT TO COME IN FOR YOUR TEA.
HE SAYS NOW.
ARTHUR St L9

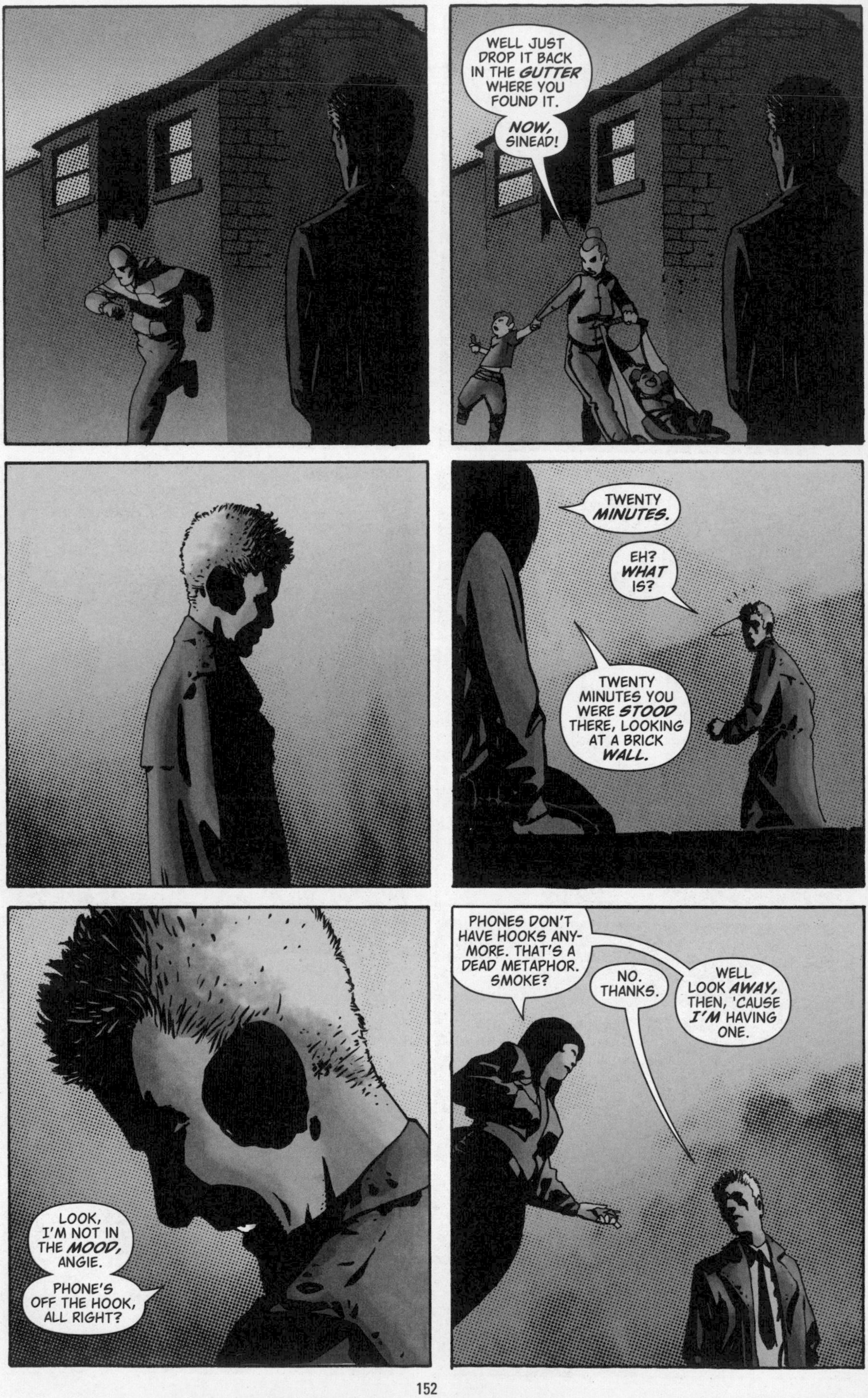
WELL JUST DROP IT BACK IN THE GUTTER WHERE YOU FOUND IT.
NOW, SINEAD!
TWENTY MINUTES.
EH? WHAT IS?
TWENTY MINUTES YOU WERE STOOD THERE, LOOKING AT A BRICK WALL.
LOOK, I'M NOT IN THE MOOD, ANGIE.
PHONE'S OFF THE HOOK, ALL RIGHT?
PHONES DON'T HAVE HOOKS ANY-MORE. THAT'S A DEAD METAPHOR. SMOKE?
NO. THANKS.
WELL LOOK AWAY, THEN, 'CAUSE I'M HAVING ONE.

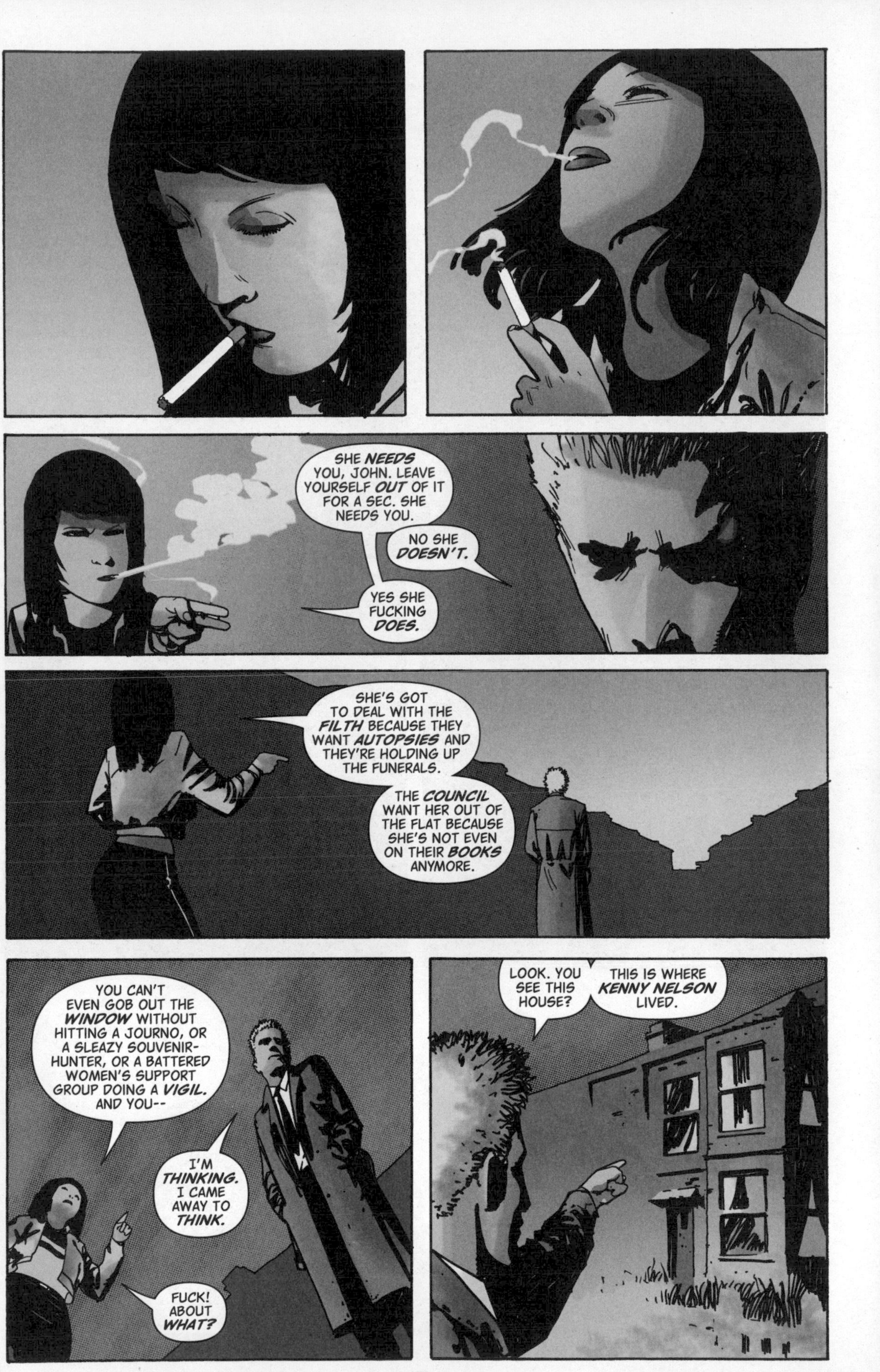
SHE NEEDS YOU, JOHN. LEAVE YOURSELF OUT OF IT FOR A SEC. SHE NEEDS YOU.
NO SHE DOESN'T.
YES SHE FUCKING DOES.
SHE'S GOT TO DEAL WITH THE FILTH BECAUSE THEY WANT AUTOPSIES AND THEY'RE HOLDING UP THE FUNERALS.
THE COUNCIL WANT HER OUT OF THE FLAT BECAUSE SHE'S NOT EVEN ON THEIR BOOKS ANYMORE.
YOU CAN'T EVEN GOB OUT THE WINDOW WITHOUT HITTING A JOURNO, OR A SLEAZY SOUVENIR-HUNTER, OR A BATTERED WOMEN'S SUPPORT GROUP DOING A VIGIL. AND YOU--
I'M THINKING. I CAME AWAY TO THINK.
FUCK! ABOUT WHAT?
LOOK. YOU SEE THIS HOUSE?
THIS IS WHERE KENNY NELSON LIVED.

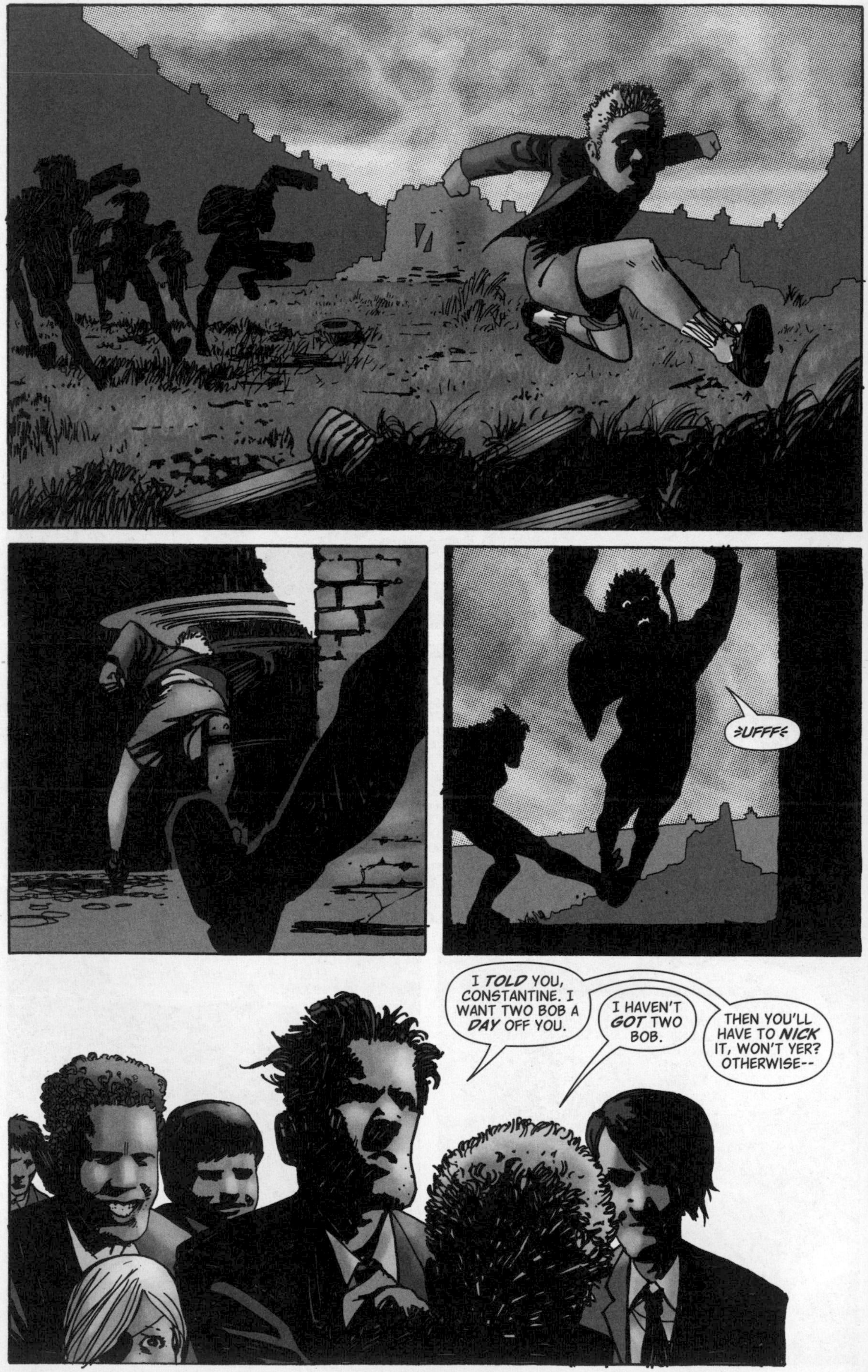
UFFF
I TOLD YOU, CONSTANTINE. I WANT TWO BOB A DAY OFF YOU.
I HAVEN'T GOT TWO BOB.
THEN YOU'LL HAVE TO NICK IT, WON'T YER? OTHERWISE--

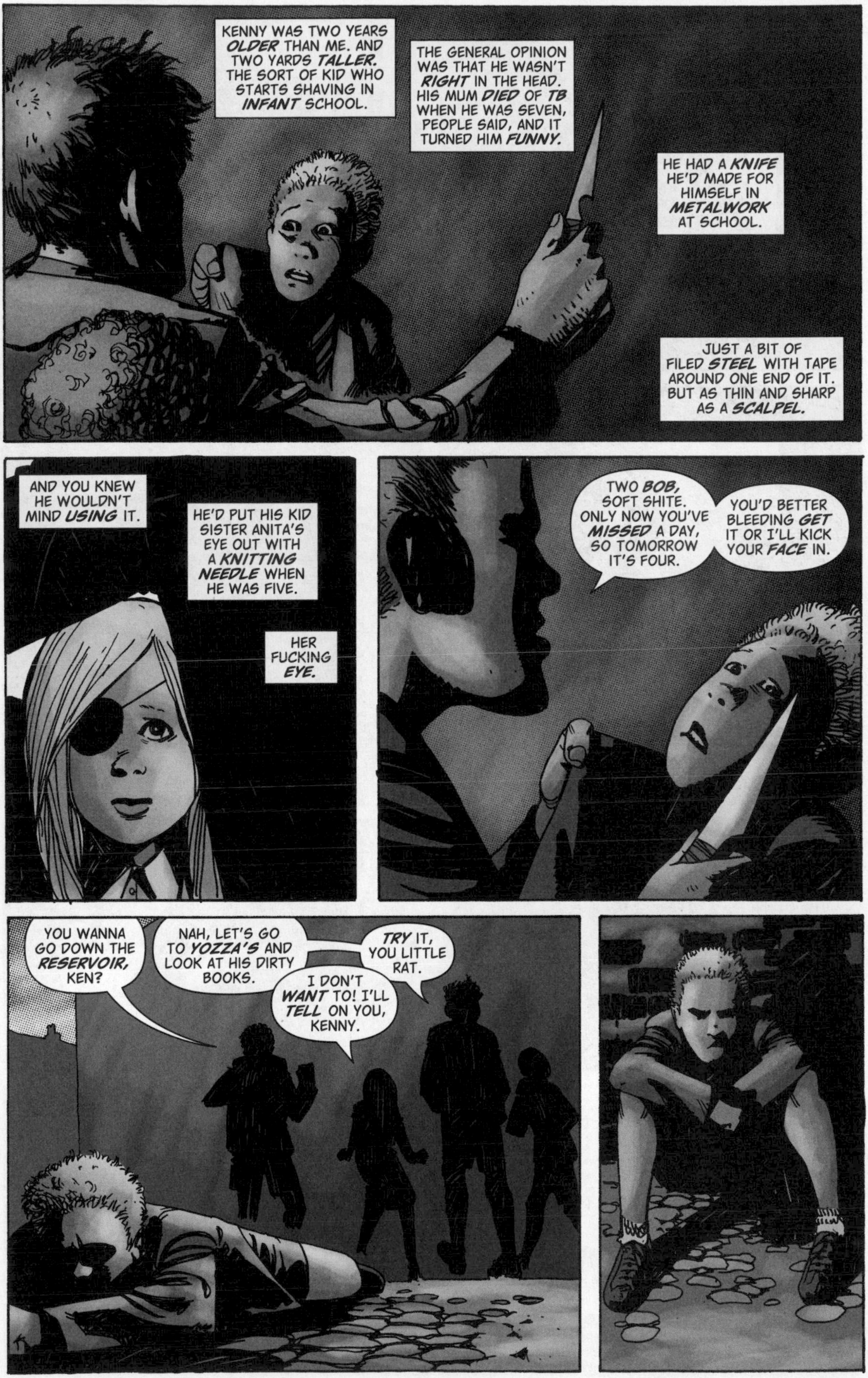
KENNY WAS TWO YEARS OLDER THAN ME. AND TWO YARDS TALLER. THE SORT OF KID WHO STARTS SHAVING IN INFANT SCHOOL.
THE GENERAL OPINION WAS THAT HE WASN'T RIGHT IN THE HEAD. HIS MUM DIED OF TB WHEN HE WAS SEVEN, PEOPLE SAID, AND IT TURNED HIM FUNNY.
HE HAD A KNIFE HE'D MADE FOR HIMSELF IN METALWORK AT SCHOOL.
JUST A BIT OF FILED STEEL WITH TAPE AROUND ONE END OF IT. BUT AS THIN AND SHARP AS A SCALPEL.
AND YOU KNEW HE WOULDN'T MIND USING IT.
HE'D PUT HIS KID SISTER ANITA'S EYE OUT WITH A KNITTING NEEDLE WHEN HE WAS FIVE.
HER FUCKING EYE.
TWO BOB, SOFT SHITE. ONLY NOW YOU'VE MISSED A DAY, SO TOMORROW IT'S FOUR.
YOU'D BETTER BLEEDING GET IT OR I'LL KICK YOUR FACE IN.
YOU WANNA GO DOWN THE RESERVOIR, KEN?
NAH, LET'S GO TO YOZZA'S AND LOOK AT HIS DIRTY BOOKS.
I DON'T WANT TO! I'LL TELL ON YOU, KENNY.
TRY IT, YOU LITTLE RAT.

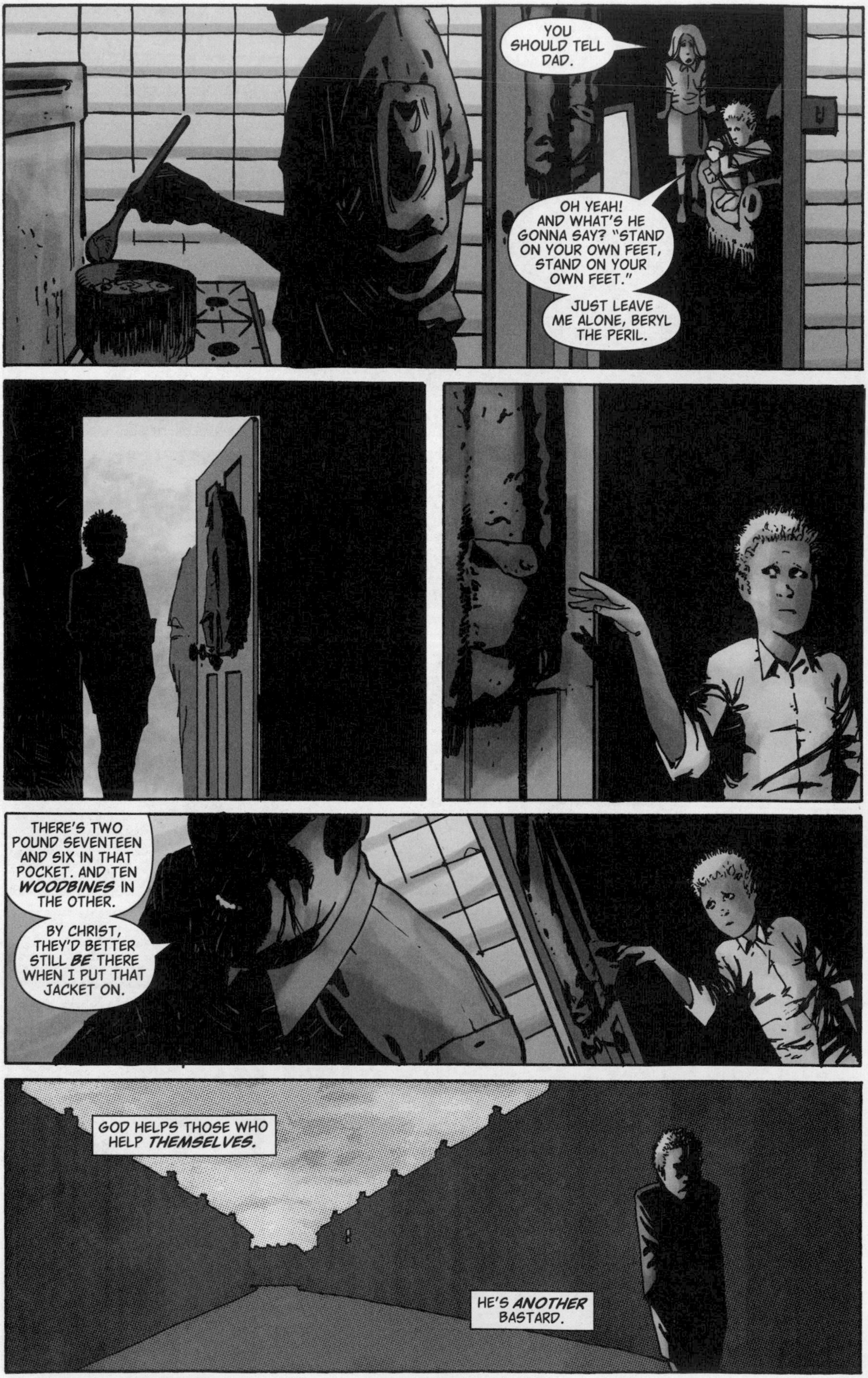
YOU SHOULD TELL DAD.
OH YEAH! AND WHAT'S HE GONNA SAY? "STAND ON YOUR OWN FEET, STAND ON YOUR OWN FEET."
JUST LEAVE ME ALONE, BERYL THE PERIL.
THERE'S TWO POUND SEVENTEEN AND SIX IN THAT POCKET. AND TEN WOODBINES IN THE OTHER.
BY CHRIST, THEY'D BETTER STILL BE THERE WHEN I PUT THAT JACKET ON.
GOD HELPS THOSE WHO HELP THEMSELVES.
HE'S ANOTHER BASTARD.

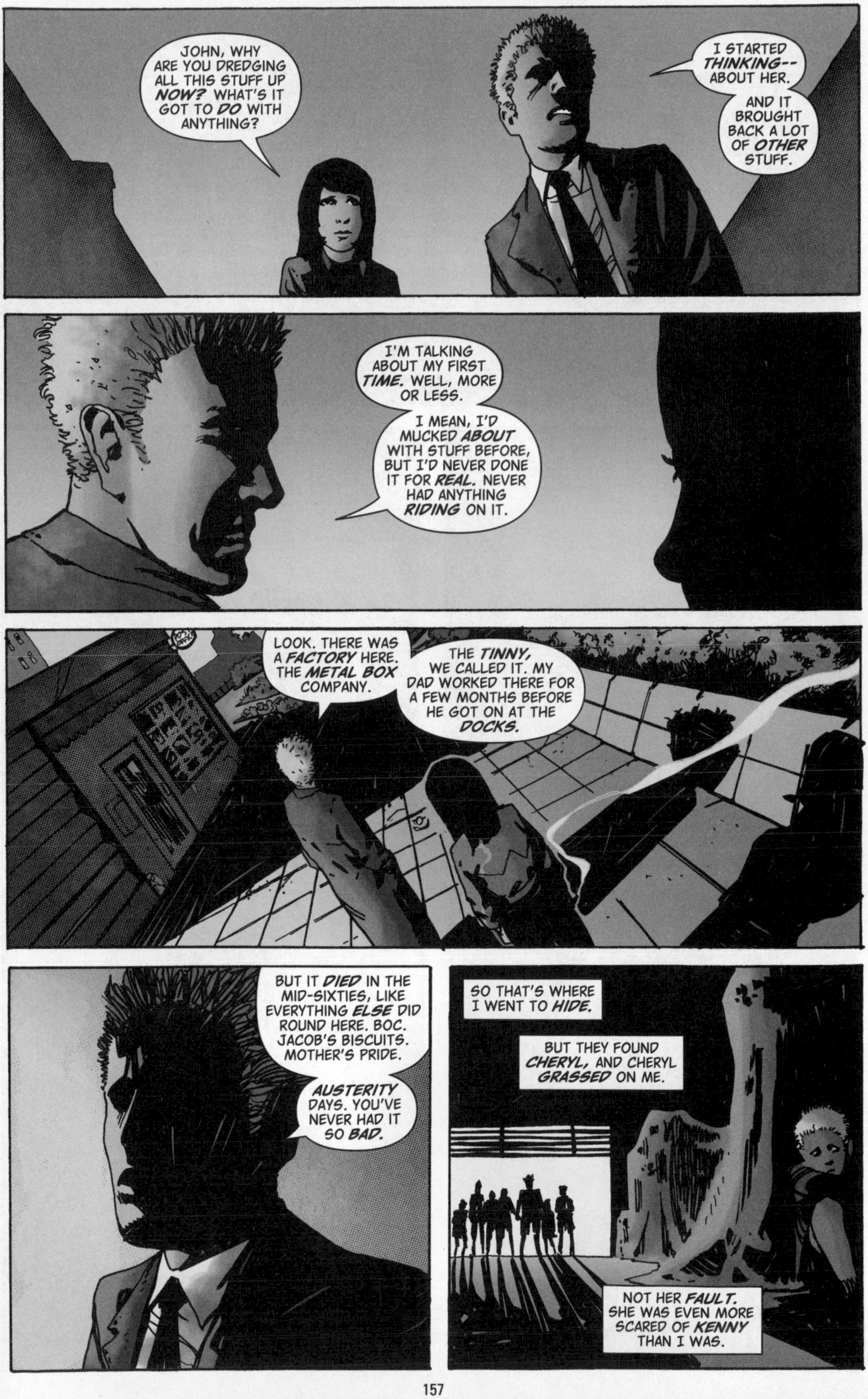
JOHN, WHY ARE YOU DREDGING ALL THIS STUFF UP NOW? WHAT'S IT GOT TO DO WITH ANYTHING?
I STARTED THINKING-- ABOUT HER.
AND IT BROUGHT BACK A LOT OF OTHER STUFF.
I'M TALKING ABOUT MY FIRST TIME. WELL, MORE OR LESS.
I MEAN, I'D MUCKED ABOUT WITH STUFF BEFORE, BUT I'D NEVER DONE IT FOR REAL. NEVER HAD ANYTHING RIDING ON IT.
LOOK. THERE WAS A FACTORY HERE. THE METAL BOX COMPANY.
THE TINNY, WE CALLED IT. MY DAD WORKED THERE FOR A FEW MONTHS BEFORE HE GOT ON AT THE DOCKS.
BUT IT DIED IN THE MID-SIXTIES, LIKE EVERYTHING ELSE DID ROUND HERE. BOC. JACOB'S BISCUITS. MOTHER'S PRIDE.
AUSTERITY DAYS. YOU'VE NEVER HAD IT SO BAD.
SO THAT'S WHERE I WENT TO HIDE.
BUT THEY FOUND CHERYL, AND CHERYL GRASSED ON ME.
NOT HER FAULT. SHE WAS EVEN MORE SCARED OF KENNY THAN I WAS.

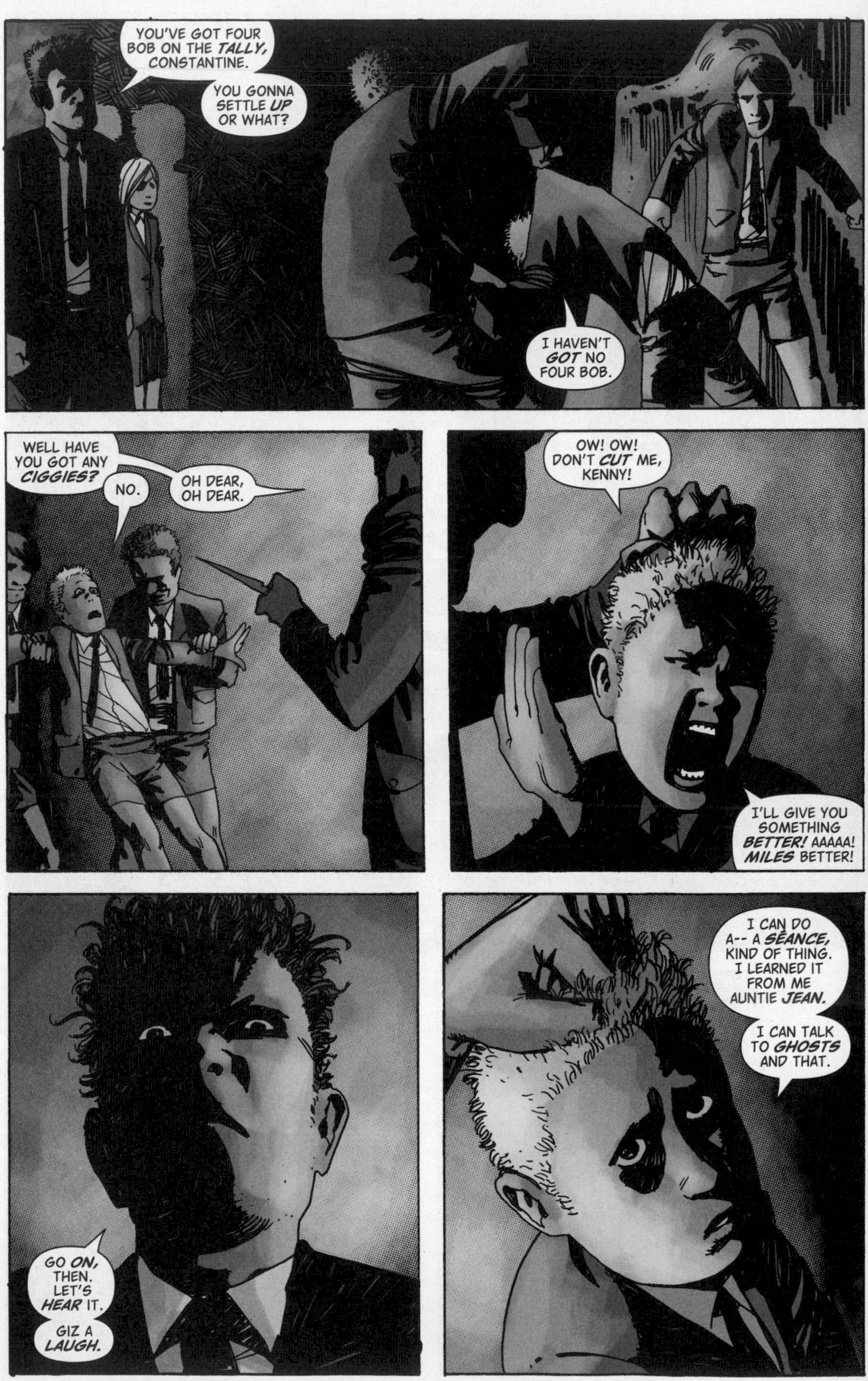
YOU'VE GOT FOUR BOB ON THE TALLY, CONSTANTINE.
YOU GONNA SETTLE UP OR WHAT?
I HAVEN'T GOT NO FOUR BOB.
WELL HAVE YOU GOT ANY CIGGIES?
NO.
OH DEAR, OH DEAR.
OW! OW! DON'T CUT ME, KENNY!
I'LL GIVE YOU SOMETHING BETTER! AAAAA! MILES BETTER!
GO ON, THEN. LET'S HEAR IT.
GIZ A LAUGH.
I CAN DO A-- A SÉANCE, KIND OF THING. I LEARNED IT FROM ME AUNTIE JEAN.
I CAN TALK TO GHOSTS AND THAT.

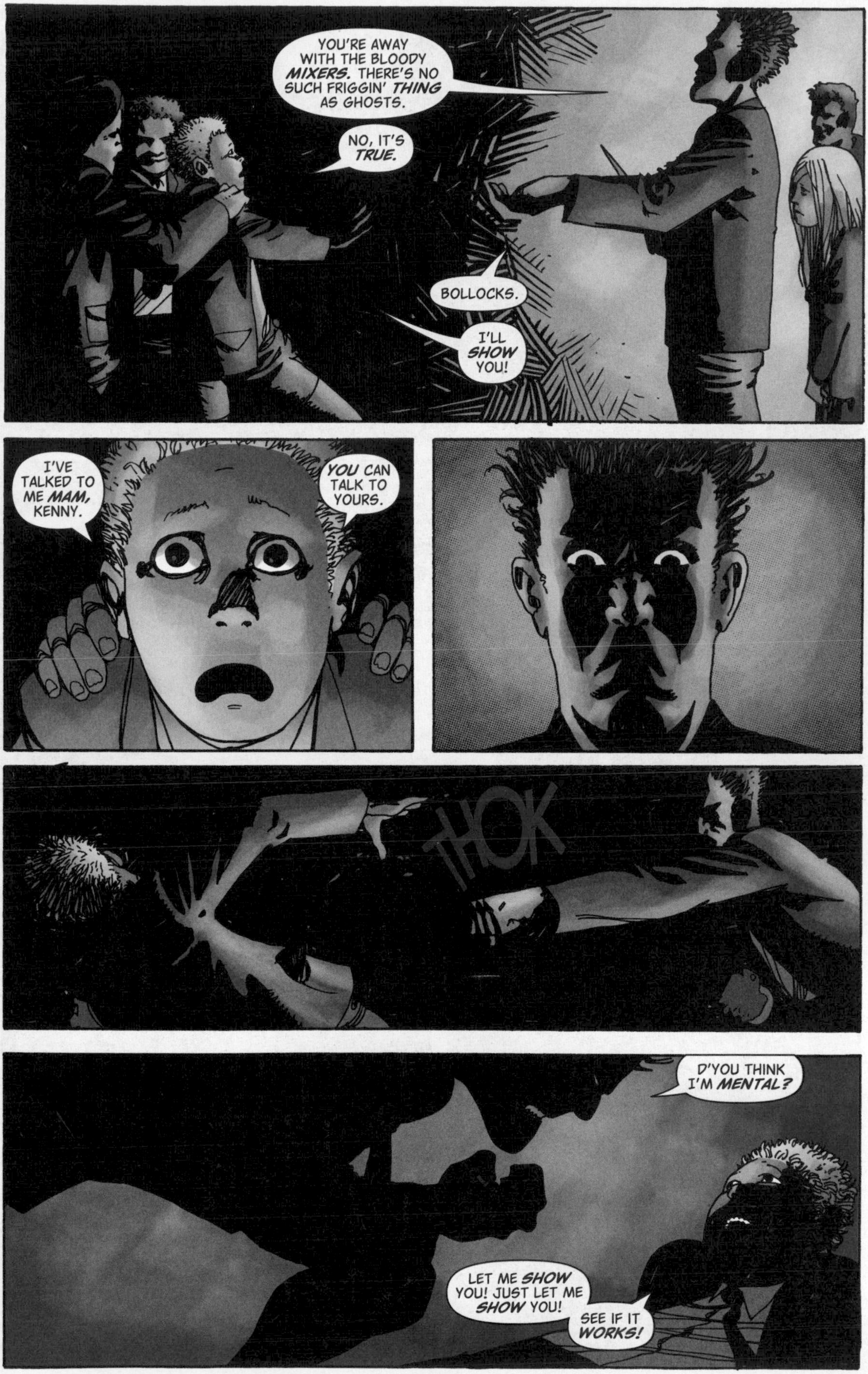
YOU'RE AWAY WITH THE BLOODY MIXERS. THERE'S NO SUCH FRIGGIN' THING AS GHOSTS.
NO, IT'S TRUE.
BOLLOCKS.
I'LL SHOW YOU!
I'VE TALKED TO ME MAM, KENNY.
YOU CAN TALK TO YOURS.
THOK
D'YOU THINK I'M MENTAL?
LET ME SHOW YOU! JUST LET ME SHOW YOU!
SEE IF IT WORKS!

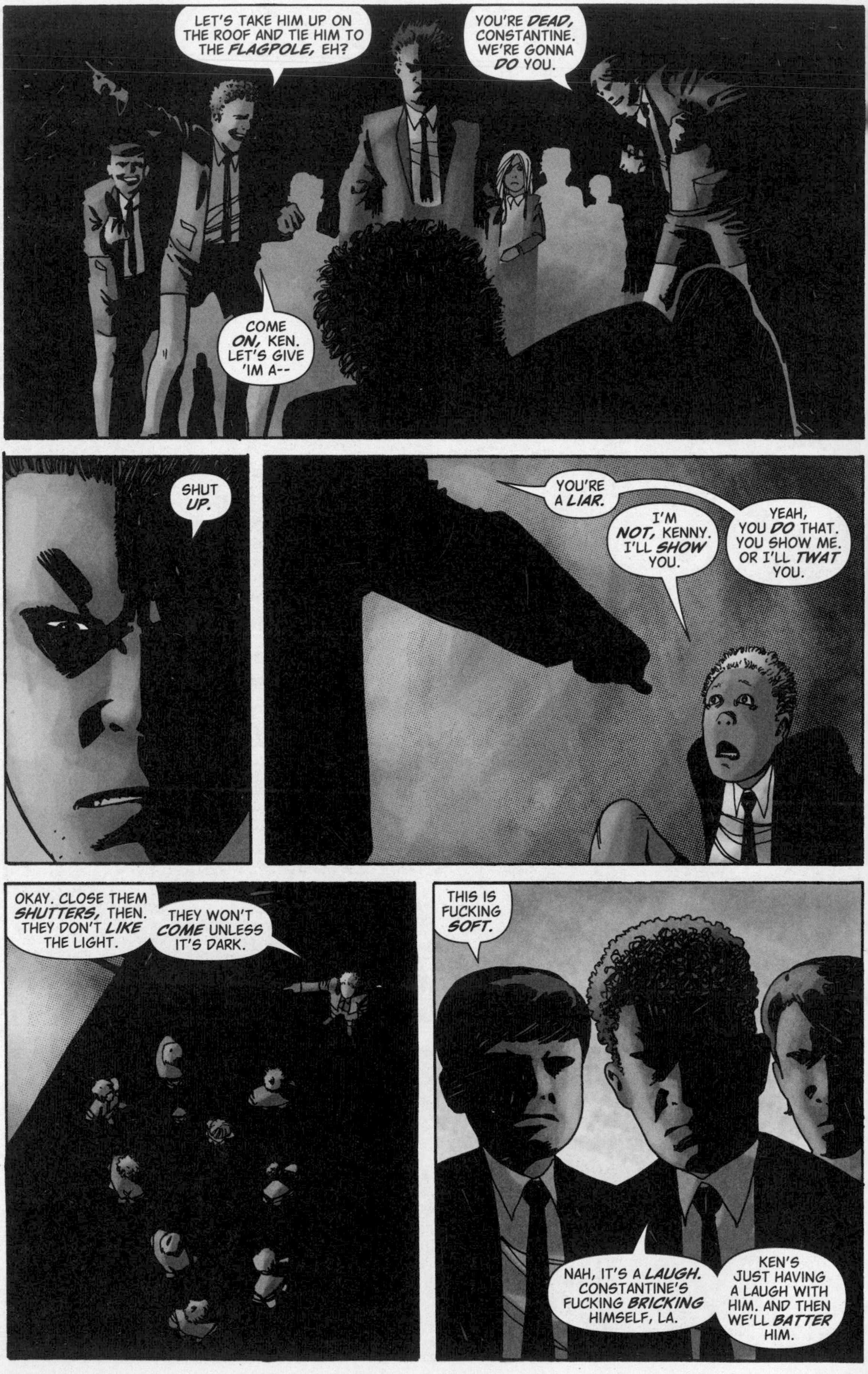
LET'S TAKE HIM UP ON THE ROOF AND TIE HIM TO THE FLAGPOLE, EH?
YOU'RE DEAD, CONSTANTINE. WE'RE GONNA DO YOU.
COME ON, KEN. LET'S GIVE 'IM A--
SHUT UP.
YOU'RE A LIAR.
I'M NOT, KENNY. I'LL SHOW YOU.
YEAH, YOU DO THAT. YOU SHOW ME. OR I'LL TWAT YOU.
OKAY. CLOSE THEM SHUTTERS, THEN. THEY DON'T LIKE THE LIGHT.
THEY WON'T COME UNLESS IT'S DARK.
THIS IS FUCKING SOFT.
NAH, IT'S A LAUGH. CONSTANTINE'S FUCKING BRICKING HIMSELF, LA.
KEN'S JUST HAVING A LAUGH WITH HIM. AND THEN WE'LL BATTER HIM.

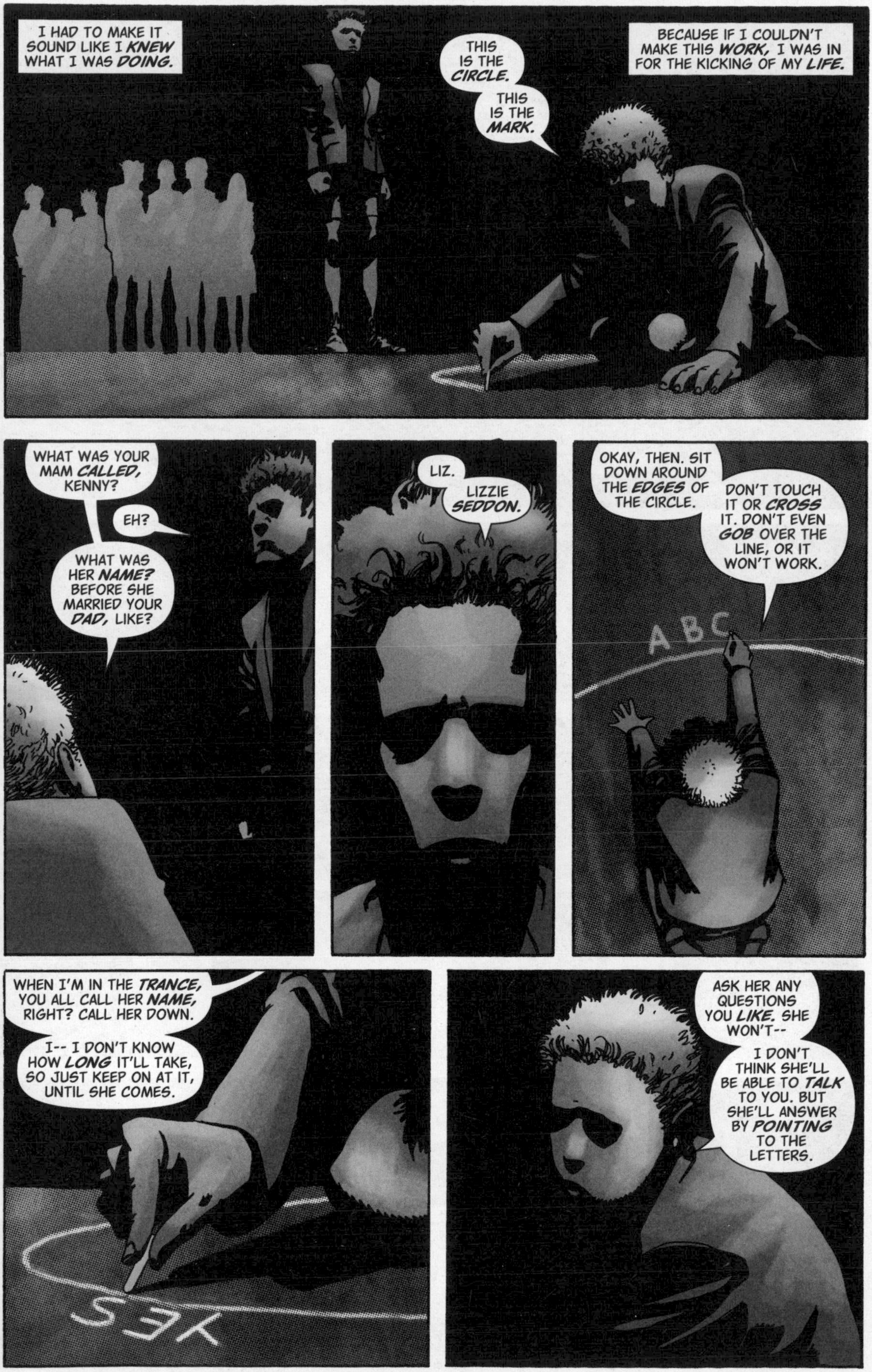
I HAD TO MAKE IT SOUND LIKE I KNEW WHAT I WAS DOING.
THIS IS THE CIRCLE.
THIS IS THE MARK.
BECAUSE IF I COULDN'T MAKE THIS WORK, I WAS IN FOR THE KICKING OF MY LIFE.
WHAT WAS YOUR MAM CALLED, KENNY?
EH?
WHAT WAS HER NAME? BEFORE SHE MARRIED YOUR DAD, LIKE?
LIZ.
LIZZIE SEDDON.
OKAY, THEN. SIT DOWN AROUND THE EDGES OF THE CIRCLE.
DON'T TOUCH IT OR CROSS IT. DON'T EVEN GOB OVER THE LINE, OR IT WON'T WORK.
A B C
WHEN I'M IN THE TRANCE, YOU ALL CALL HER NAME, RIGHT? CALL HER DOWN.
I-- I DON'T KNOW HOW LONG IT'LL TAKE, SO JUST KEEP ON AT IT, UNTIL SHE COMES.
YES
ASK HER ANY QUESTIONS YOU LIKE. SHE WON'T--
I DON'T THINK SHE'LL BE ABLE TO TALK TO YOU. BUT SHE'LL ANSWER BY POINTING TO THE LETTERS.

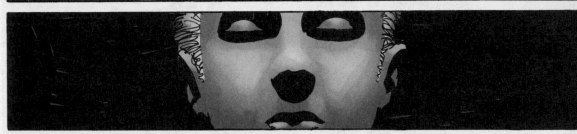

THIS IS *SPAZZEY*.

I *SAID* SHUT UP. LET HIM HAVE A *GO*.

GET *ON* WITH IT, CONSTANTINE.

LIZZIE.

SEDDON.

LIZZIE.

LIZZIE SEDDON.

LIZZIE SEDDON.

LIZZIE. COME LIZZIE.

COME DOWN LIZZIE. LIZZIE.

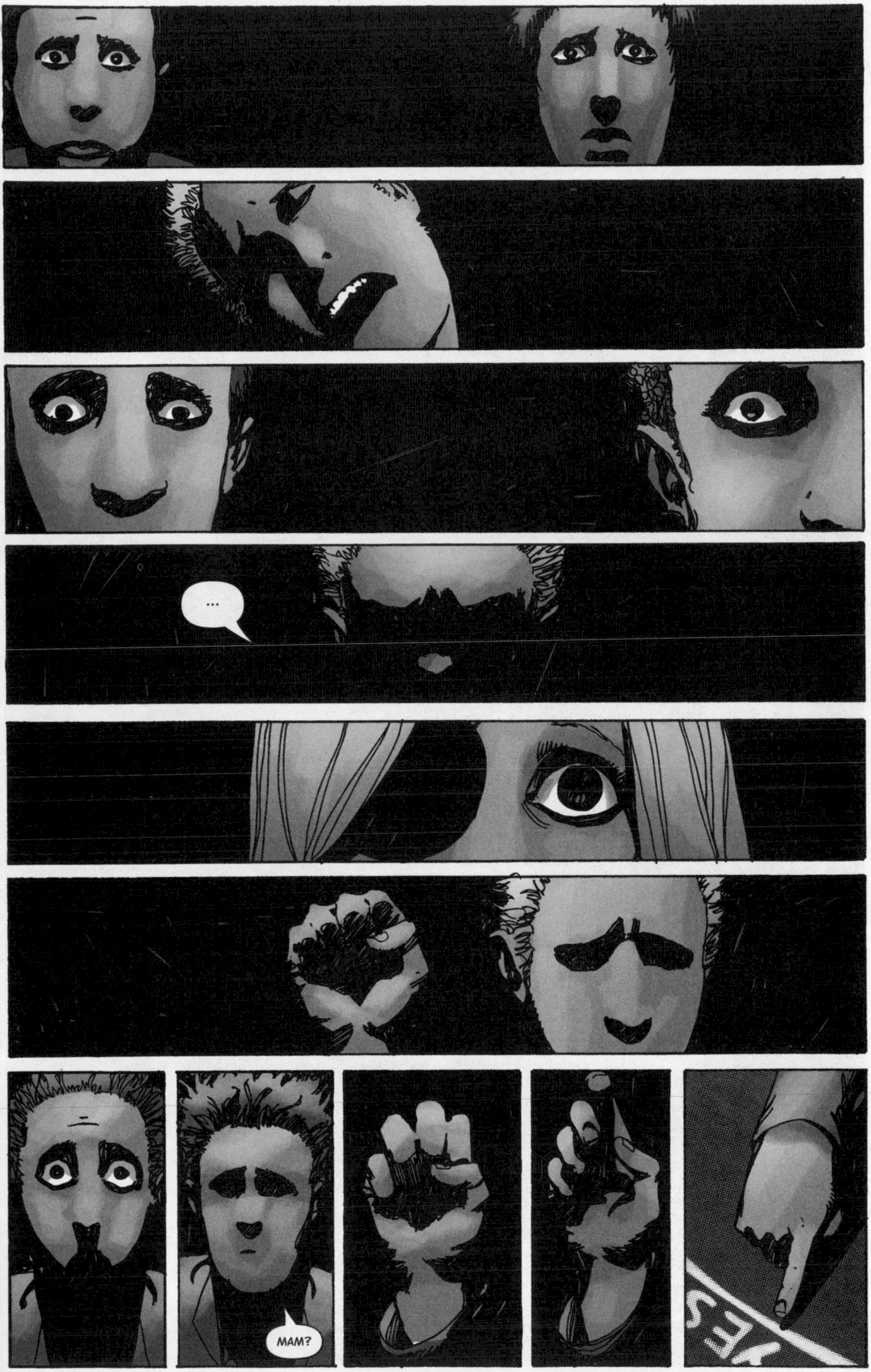
...
MAM?
YES

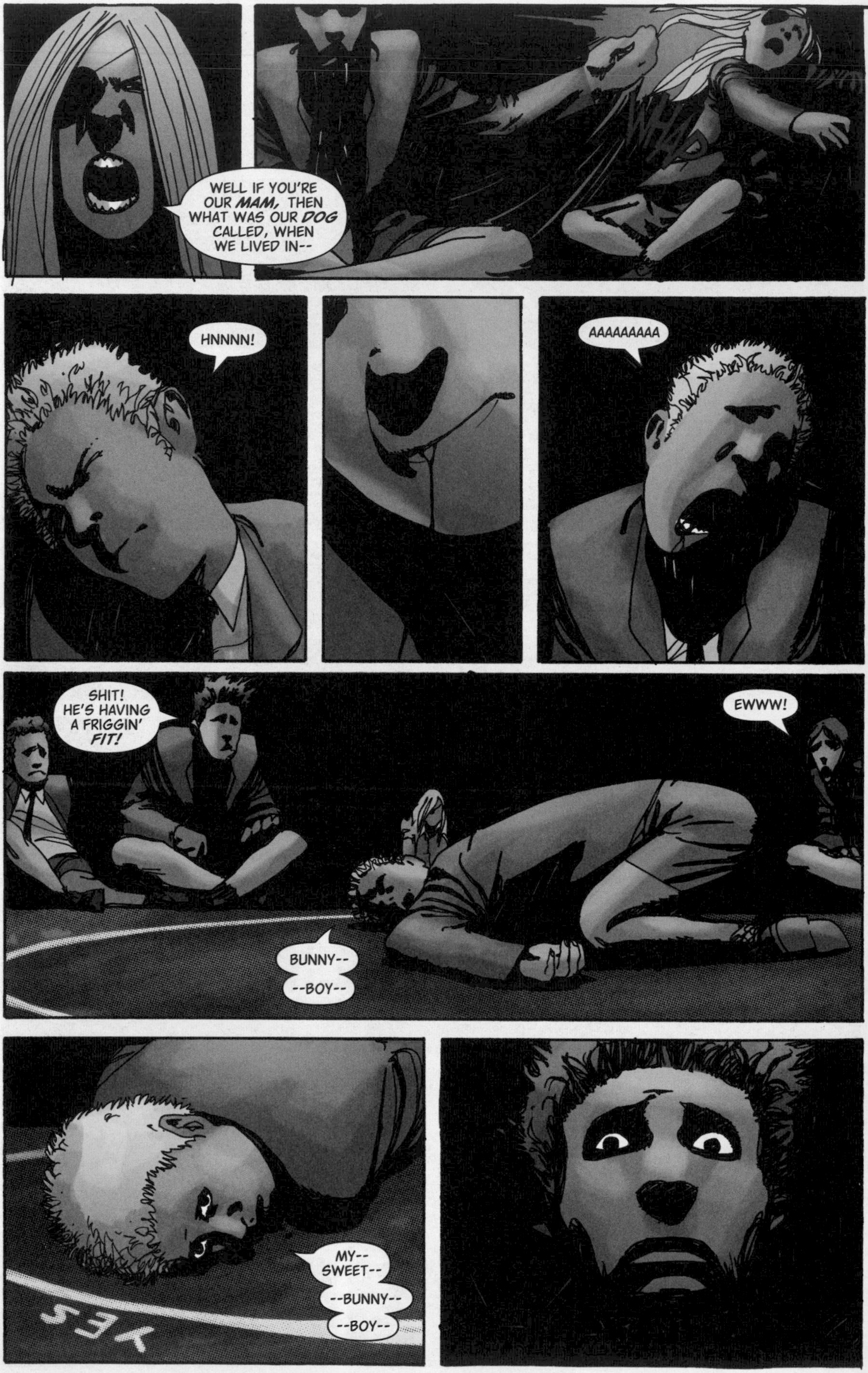
WELL IF YOU'RE OUR *MAM,* THEN WHAT WAS OUR *DOG* CALLED, WHEN WE LIVED IN--
WHAP
HNNNN!
AAAAAAAAA
SHIT! HE'S HAVING A FRIGGIN' *FIT!*
EWWW!
BUNNY--
--BOY--
MY-- SWEET--
--BUNNY--
--BOY--
YES

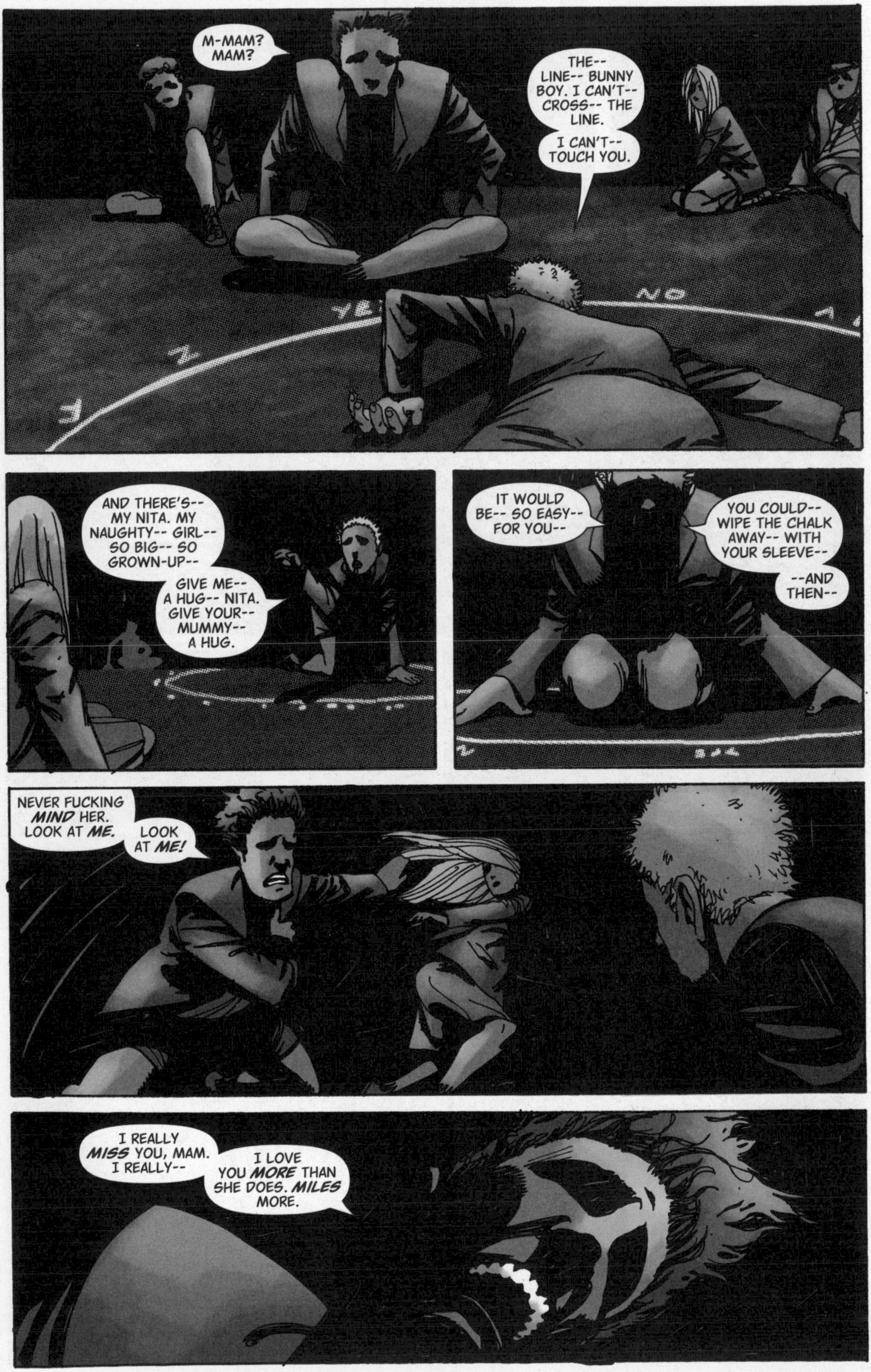

M-MAM? MAM?
THE-- LINE-- BUNNY BOY. I CAN'T-- CROSS-- THE LINE.
I CAN'T-- TOUCH YOU.
AND THERE'S-- MY NITA. MY NAUGHTY-- GIRL-- SO BIG-- SO GROWN-UP--
GIVE ME-- A HUG-- NITA. GIVE YOUR-- MUMMY-- A HUG.
IT WOULD BE-- SO EASY-- FOR YOU--
YOU COULD-- WIPE THE CHALK AWAY-- WITH YOUR SLEEVE--
--AND THEN--
NEVER FUCKING MIND HER. LOOK AT ME.
LOOK AT ME!
I REALLY MISS YOU, MAM. I REALLY--
I LOVE YOU MORE THAN SHE DOES. MILES MORE.

OH, BUNNY.
OH, BUNNY.

YOU
SHOULDN'T--

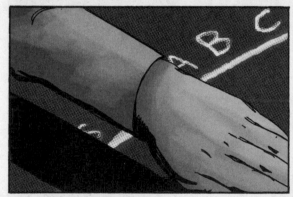

YOU SHOULDN'T
HAVE *DONE* IT,
BUNNY, THE CUSHION
IN MY FACE.

IT WAS
CRUEL.

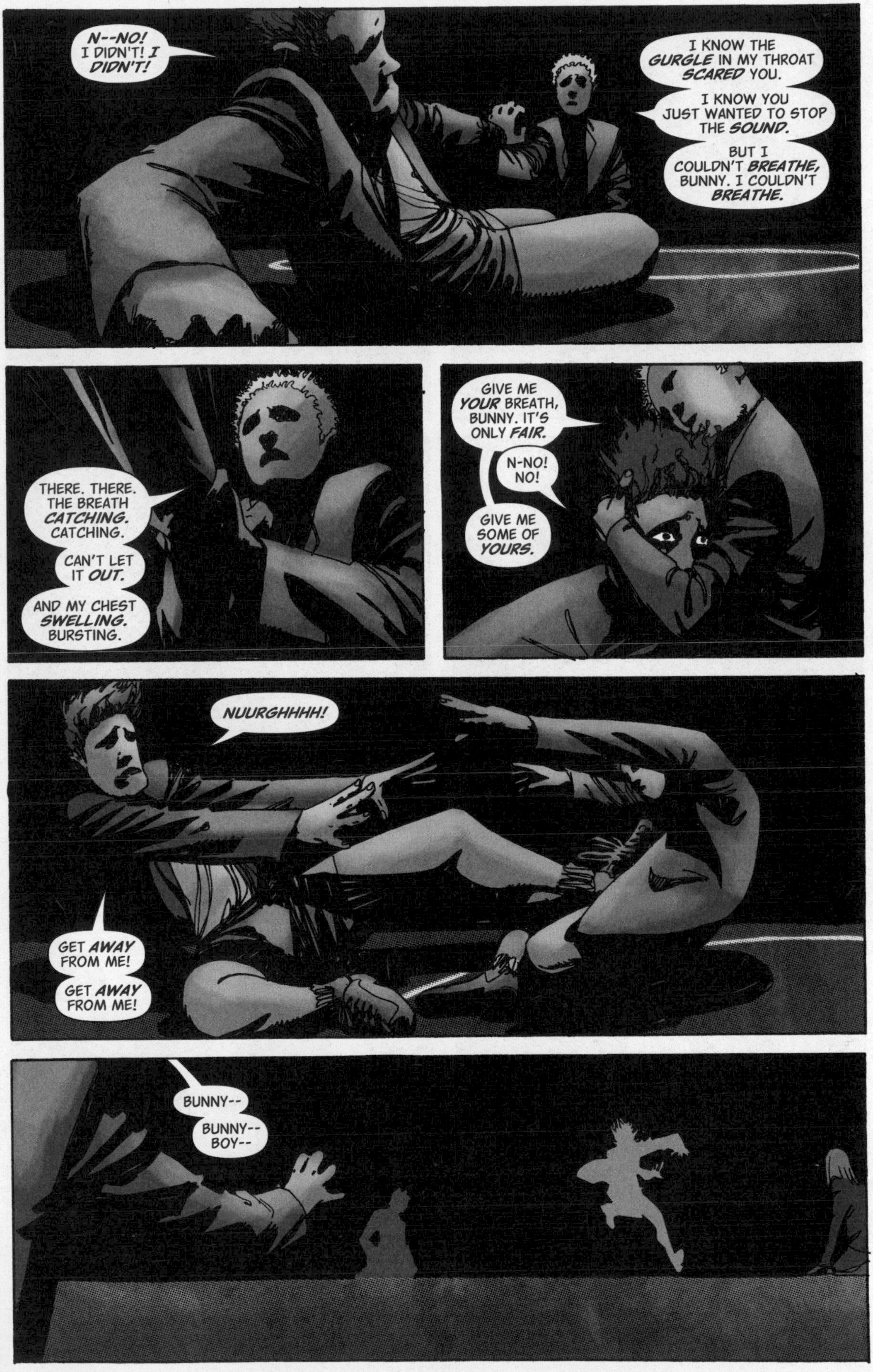
N--NO! I DIDN'T! I DIDN'T!
I KNOW THE GURGLE IN MY THROAT SCARED YOU.
I KNOW YOU JUST WANTED TO STOP THE SOUND.
BUT I COULDN'T BREATHE, BUNNY. I COULDN'T BREATHE.
THERE. THERE. THE BREATH CATCHING. CATCHING.
CAN'T LET IT OUT.
AND MY CHEST SWELLING. BURSTING.
GIVE ME YOUR BREATH, BUNNY. IT'S ONLY FAIR.
N-NO! NO!
GIVE ME SOME OF YOURS.
NUURGHHHH!
GET AWAY FROM ME!
GET AWAY FROM ME!
BUNNY--
BUNNY-- BOY--

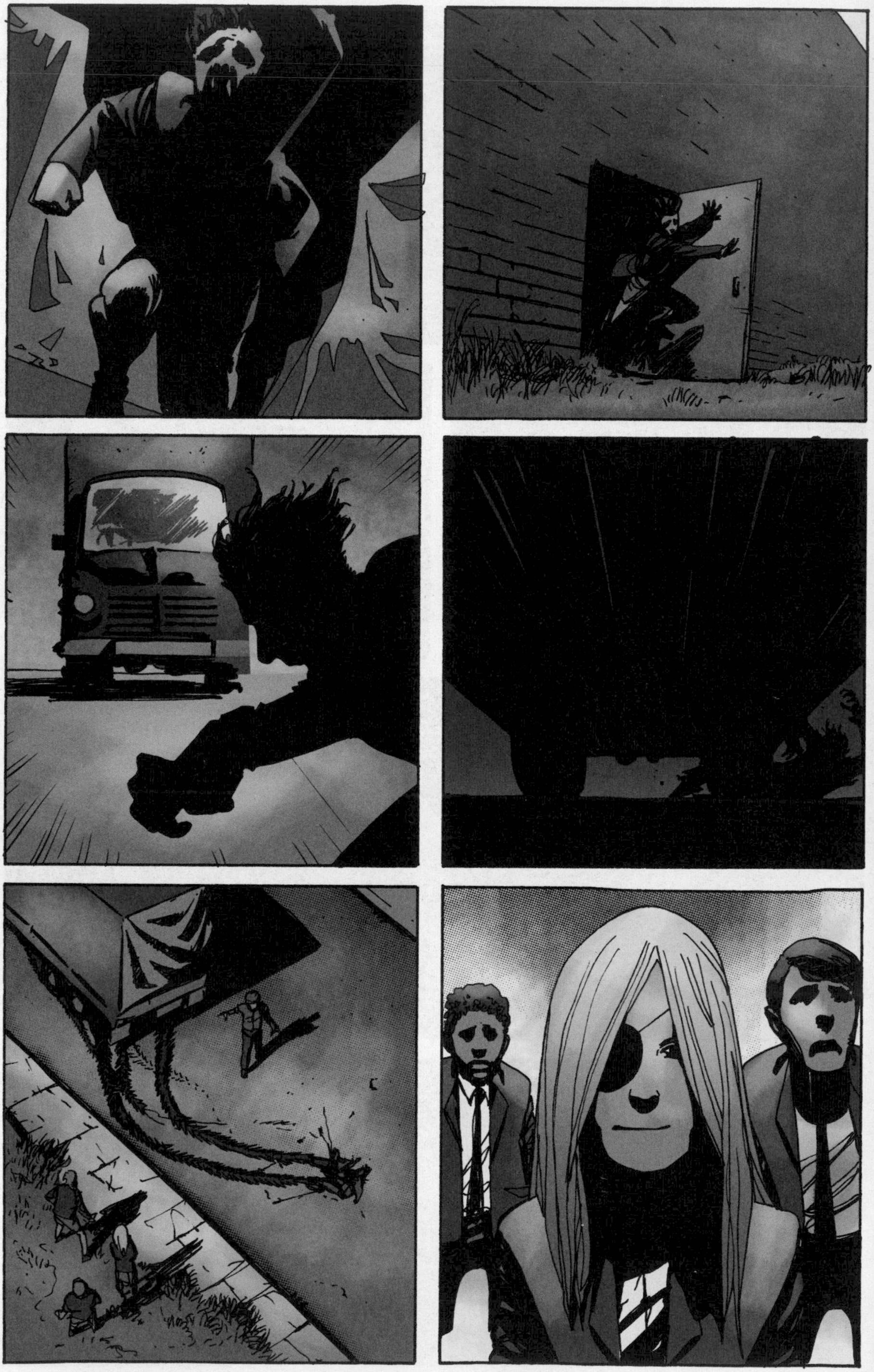

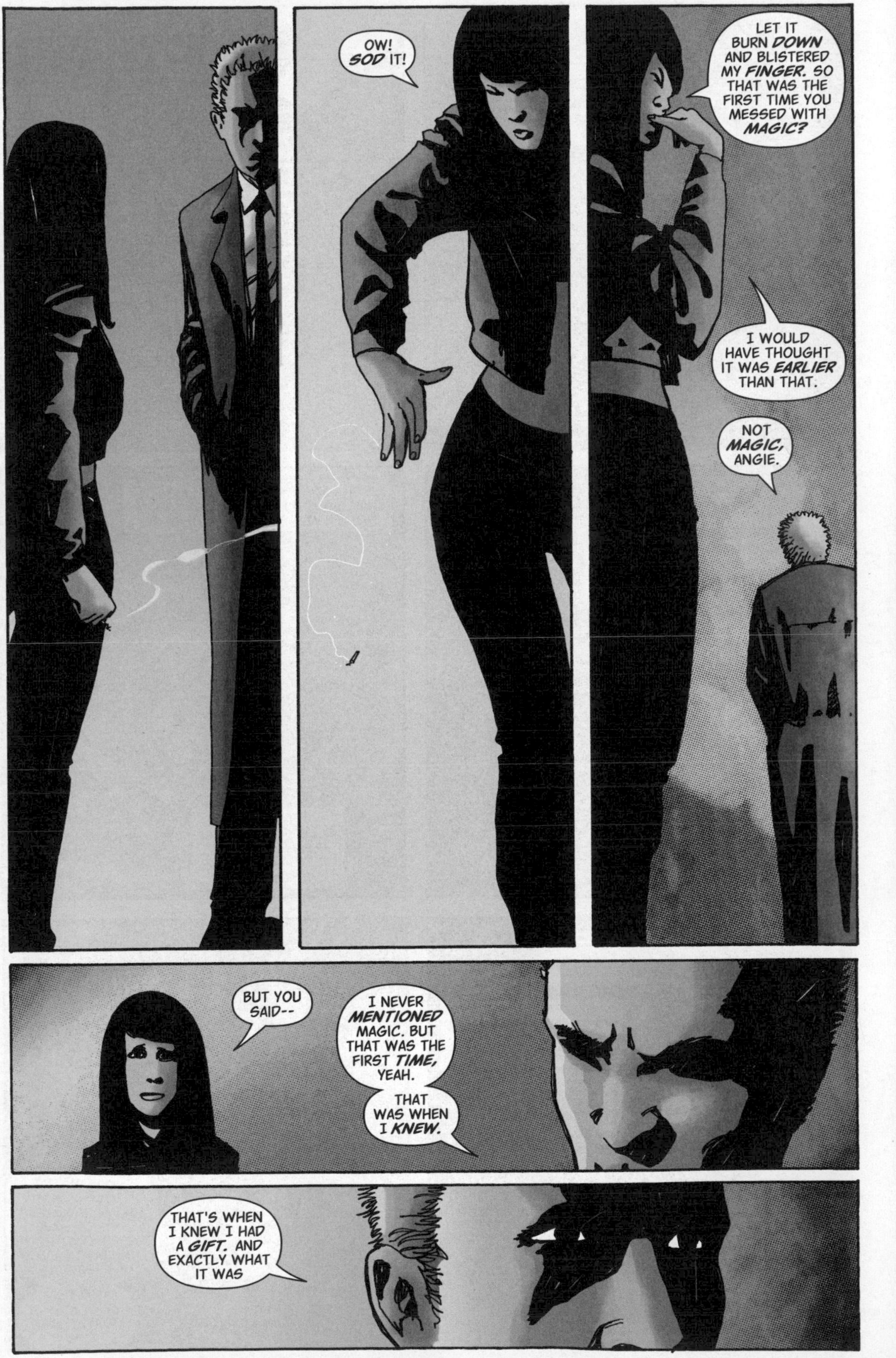
OW! SOD IT!
LET IT BURN DOWN AND BLISTERED MY FINGER. SO THAT WAS THE FIRST TIME YOU MESSED WITH MAGIC?
I WOULD HAVE THOUGHT IT WAS EARLIER THAN THAT.
NOT MAGIC, ANGIE.
BUT YOU SAID--
I NEVER MENTIONED MAGIC. BUT THAT WAS THE FIRST TIME, YEAH.
THAT WAS WHEN I KNEW.
THAT'S WHEN I KNEW I HAD A GIFT. AND EXACTLY WHAT IT WAS

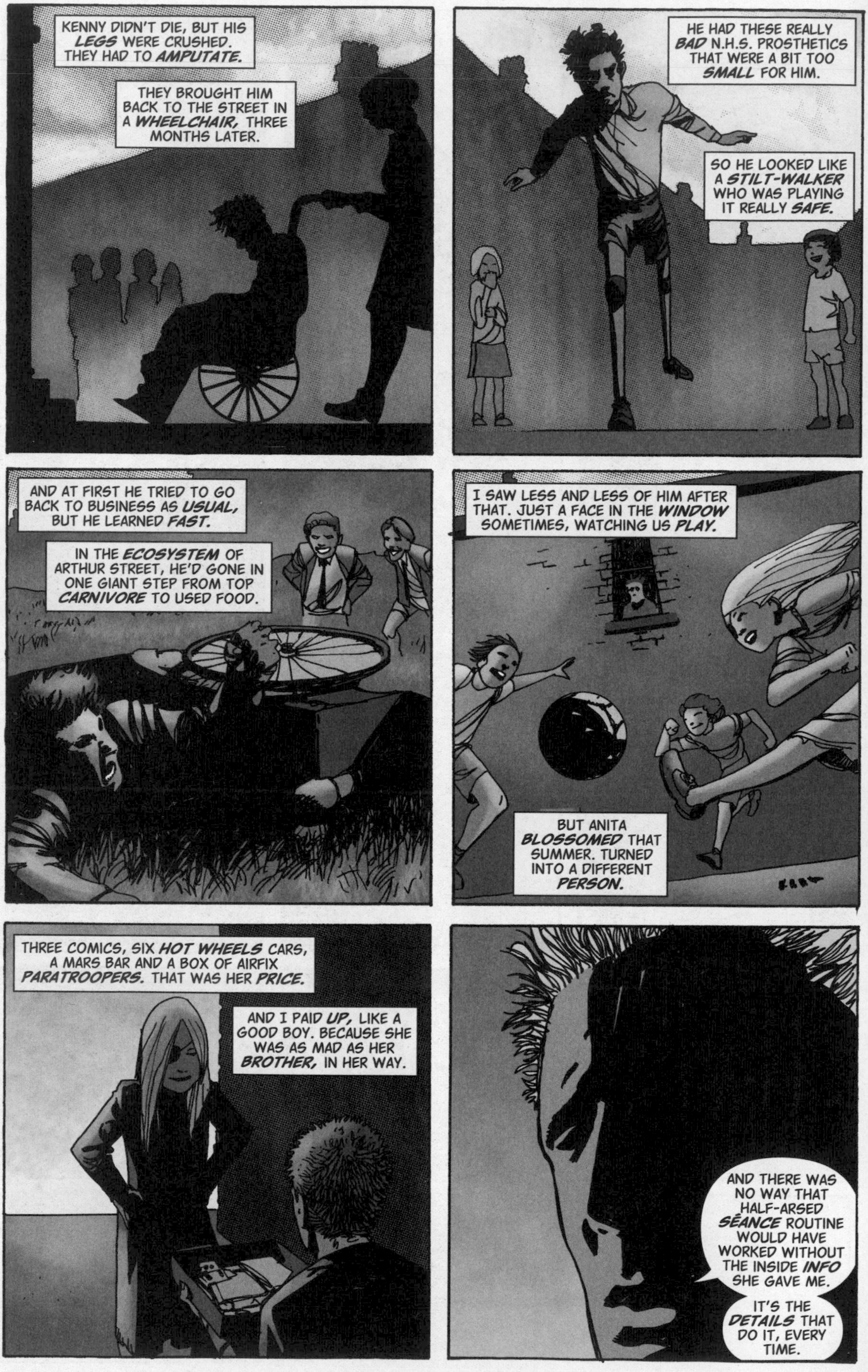
KENNY DIDN'T DIE, BUT HIS LEGS WERE CRUSHED. THEY HAD TO AMPUTATE.
THEY BROUGHT HIM BACK TO THE STREET IN A WHEELCHAIR, THREE MONTHS LATER.
HE HAD THESE REALLY BAD N.H.S. PROSTHETICS THAT WERE A BIT TOO SMALL FOR HIM.
SO HE LOOKED LIKE A STILT-WALKER WHO WAS PLAYING IT REALLY SAFE.
AND AT FIRST HE TRIED TO GO BACK TO BUSINESS AS USUAL, BUT HE LEARNED FAST.
IN THE ECOSYSTEM OF ARTHUR STREET, HE'D GONE IN ONE GIANT STEP FROM TOP CARNIVORE TO USED FOOD.
I SAW LESS AND LESS OF HIM AFTER THAT. JUST A FACE IN THE WINDOW SOMETIMES, WATCHING US PLAY.
BUT ANITA BLOSSOMED THAT SUMMER. TURNED INTO A DIFFERENT PERSON.
THREE COMICS, SIX HOT WHEELS CARS, A MARS BAR AND A BOX OF AIRFIX PARATROOPERS. THAT WAS HER PRICE.
AND I PAID UP, LIKE A GOOD BOY. BECAUSE SHE WAS AS MAD AS HER BROTHER, IN HER WAY.
AND THERE WAS NO WAY THAT HALF-ARSED SÉANCE ROUTINE WOULD HAVE WORKED WITHOUT THE INSIDE INFO SHE GAVE ME.
IT'S THE DETAILS THAT DO IT, EVERY TIME.

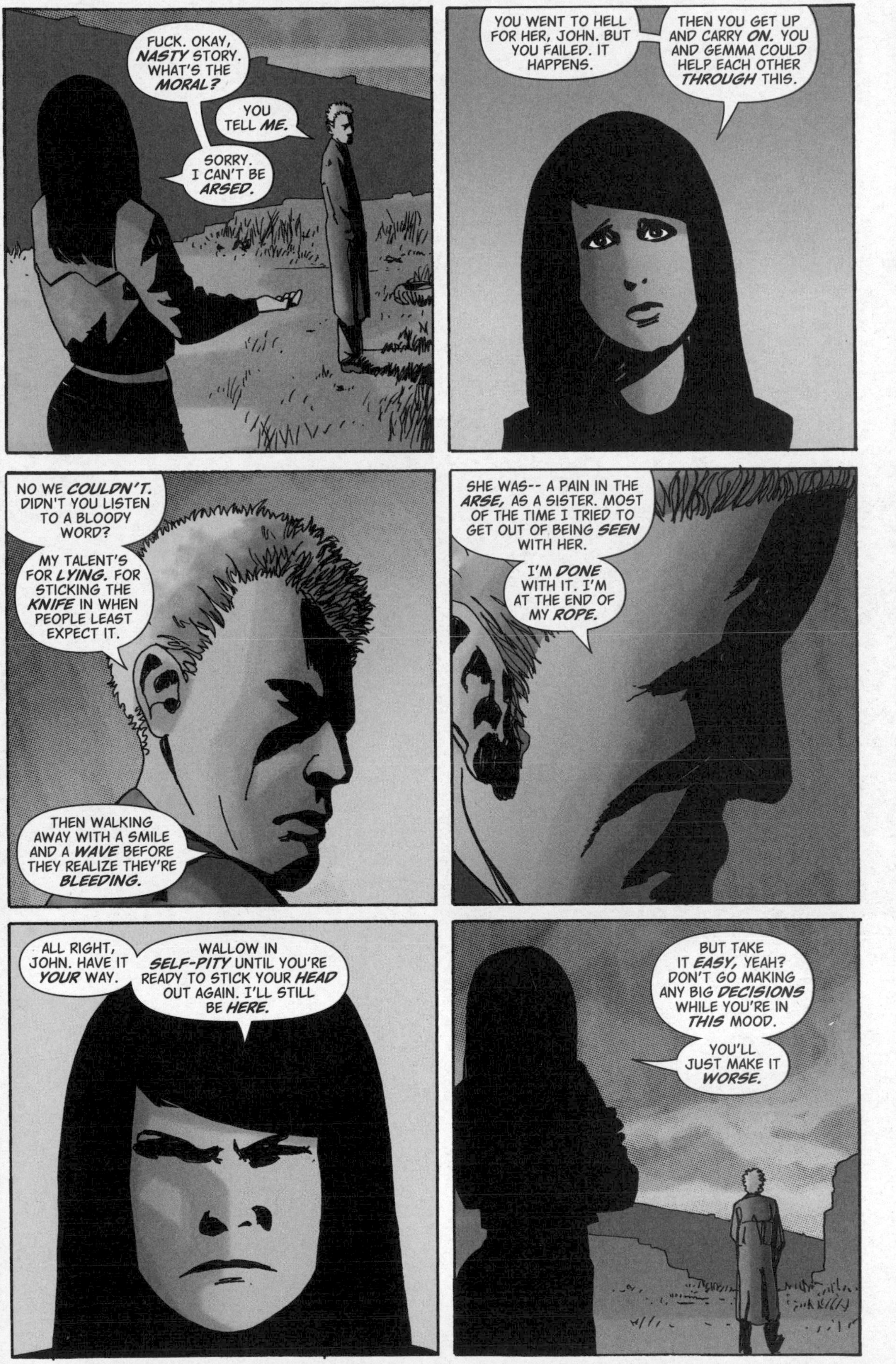

FUCK. OKAY, NASTY STORY. WHAT'S THE MORAL?
YOU TELL ME.
SORRY. I CAN'T BE ARSED.
YOU WENT TO HELL FOR HER, JOHN. BUT YOU FAILED. IT HAPPENS.
THEN YOU GET UP AND CARRY ON. YOU AND GEMMA COULD HELP EACH OTHER THROUGH THIS.
NO WE COULDN'T. DIDN'T YOU LISTEN TO A BLOODY WORD?
MY TALENT'S FOR LYING. FOR STICKING THE KNIFE IN WHEN PEOPLE LEAST EXPECT IT.
THEN WALKING AWAY WITH A SMILE AND A WAVE BEFORE THEY REALIZE THEY'RE BLEEDING.
SHE WAS-- A PAIN IN THE ARSE, AS A SISTER. MOST OF THE TIME I TRIED TO GET OUT OF BEING SEEN WITH HER.
I'M DONE WITH IT. I'M AT THE END OF MY ROPE.
ALL RIGHT, JOHN. HAVE IT YOUR WAY.
WALLOW IN SELF-PITY UNTIL YOU'RE READY TO STICK YOUR HEAD OUT AGAIN. I'LL STILL BE HERE.
BUT TAKE IT EASY, YEAH? DON'T GO MAKING ANY BIG DECISIONS WHILE YOU'RE IN THIS MOOD.
YOU'LL JUST MAKE IT WORSE.

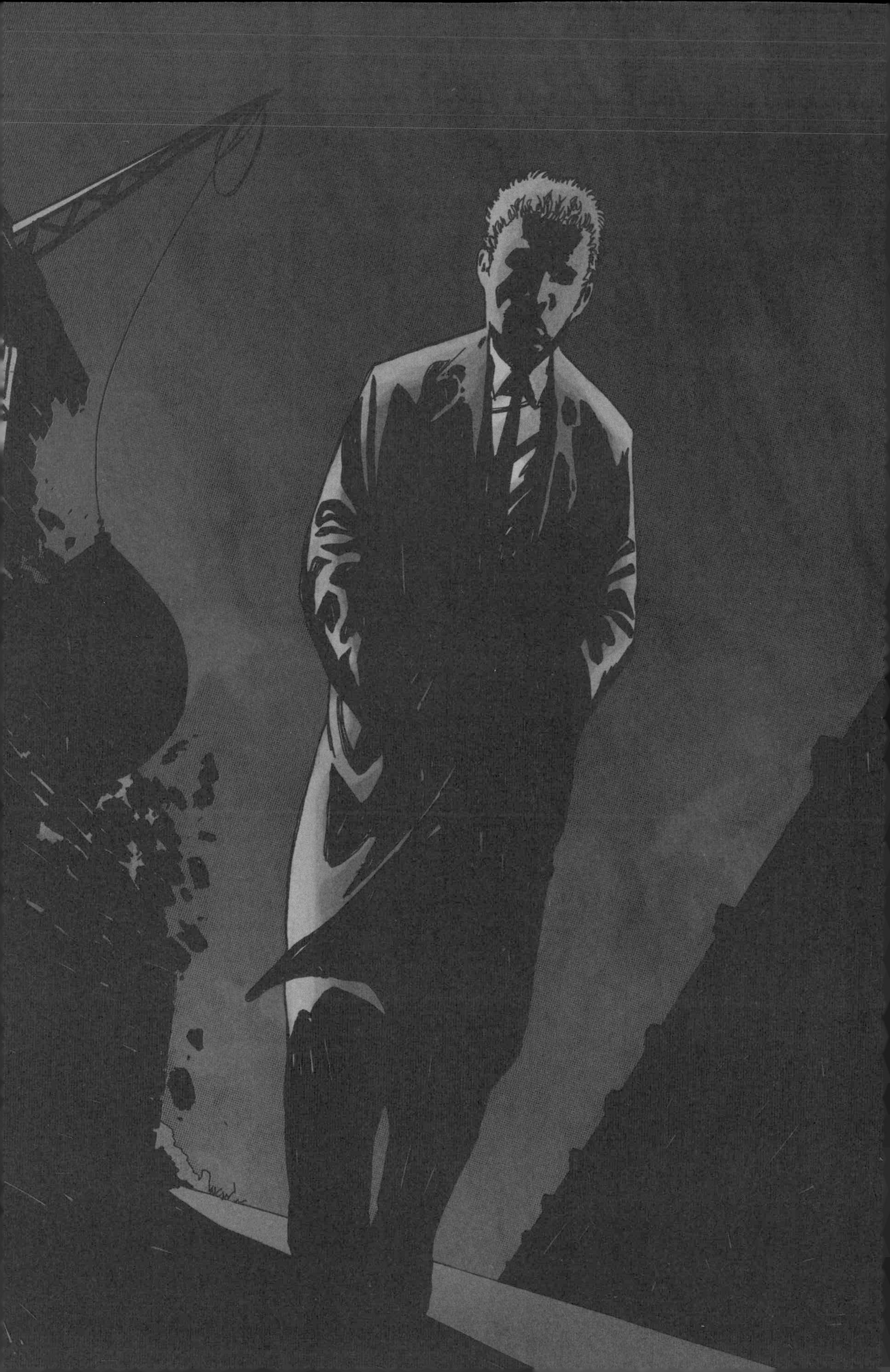

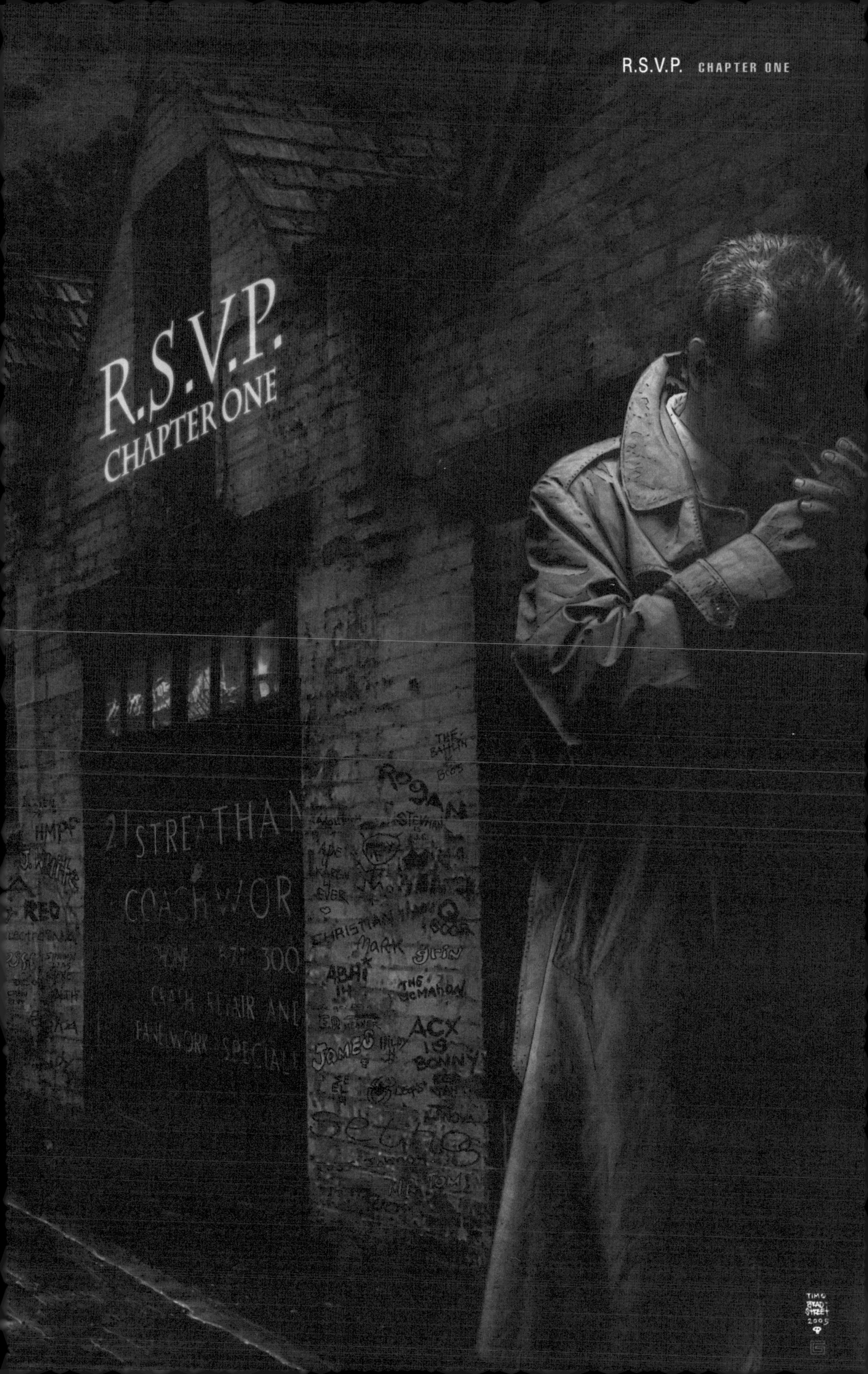
R.S.V.P.
CHAPTER ONE

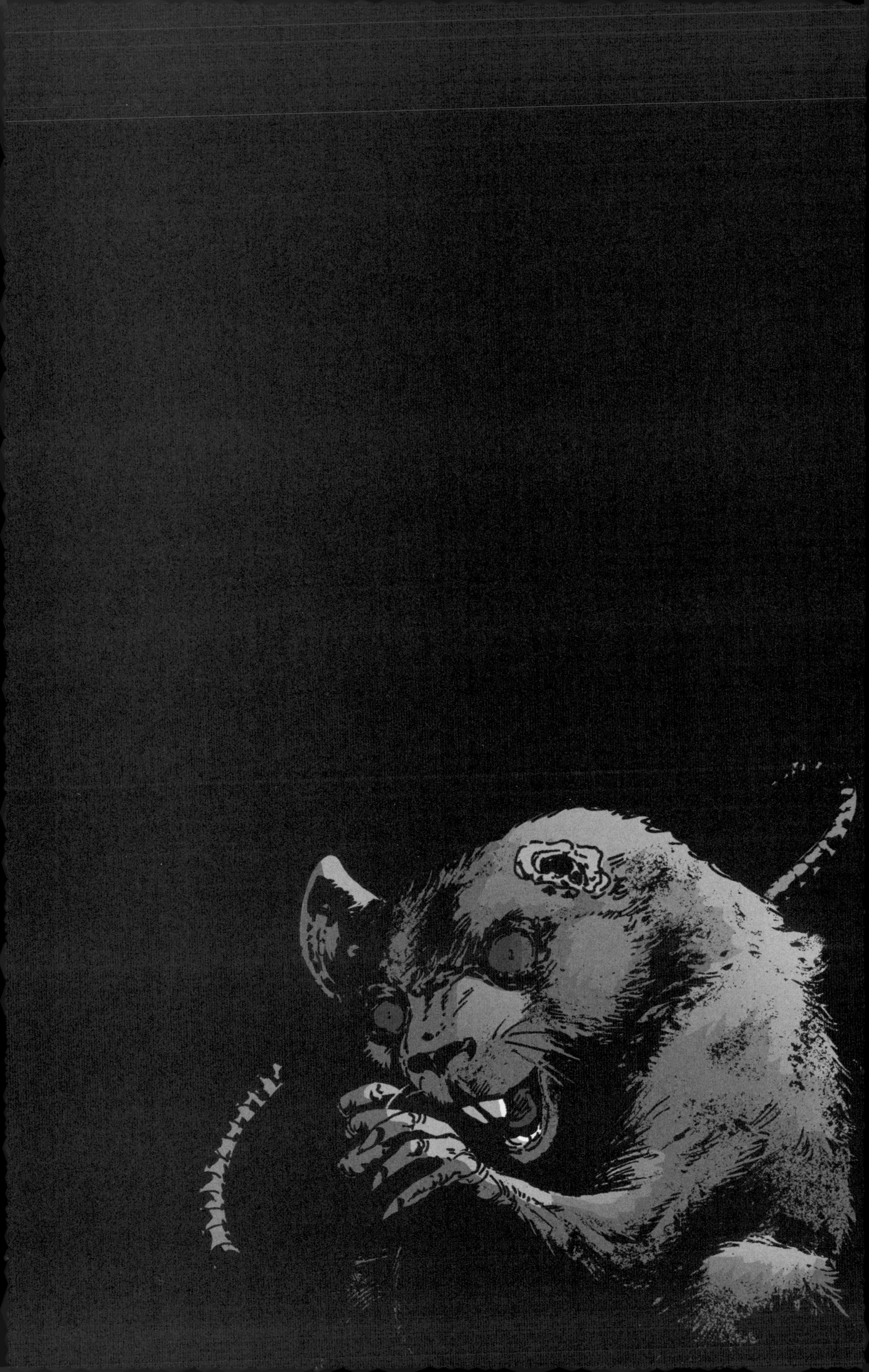

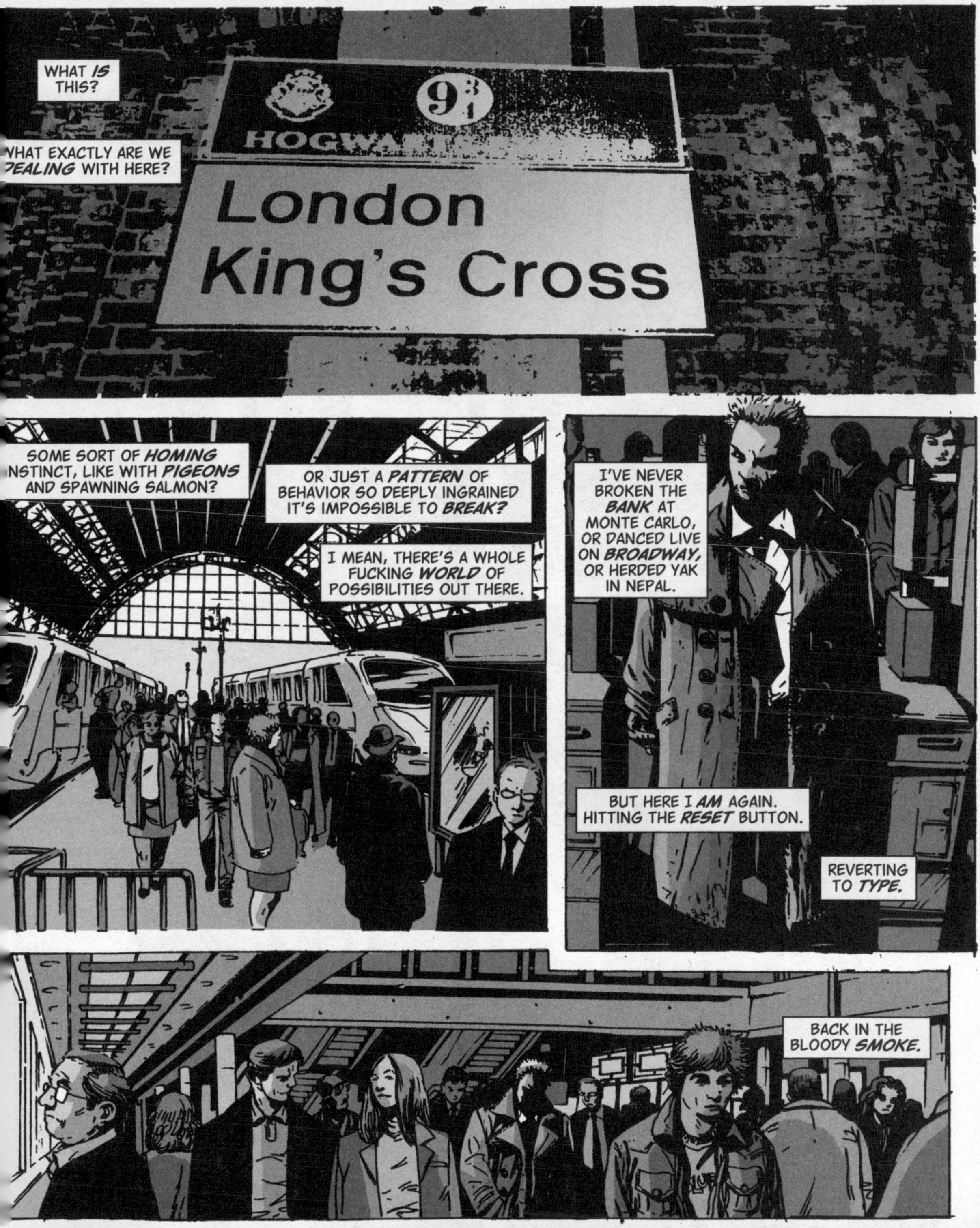
WHAT *IS* THIS?
WHAT EXACTLY ARE WE DEALING WITH HERE?
HOGWA
9¾
London King's Cross
SOME SORT OF *HOMING* INSTINCT, LIKE WITH *PIGEONS* AND SPAWNING SALMON?
OR JUST A *PATTERN* OF BEHAVIOR SO DEEPLY INGRAINED IT'S IMPOSSIBLE TO *BREAK?*
I MEAN, THERE'S A WHOLE FUCKING *WORLD* OF POSSIBILITIES OUT THERE.
I'VE NEVER BROKEN THE *BANK* AT MONTE CARLO, OR DANCED LIVE ON *BROADWAY,* OR HERDED YAK IN NEPAL.
BUT HERE I *AM* AGAIN. HITTING THE *RESET* BUTTON.
REVERTING TO *TYPE.*
BACK IN THE BLOODY *SMOKE.*

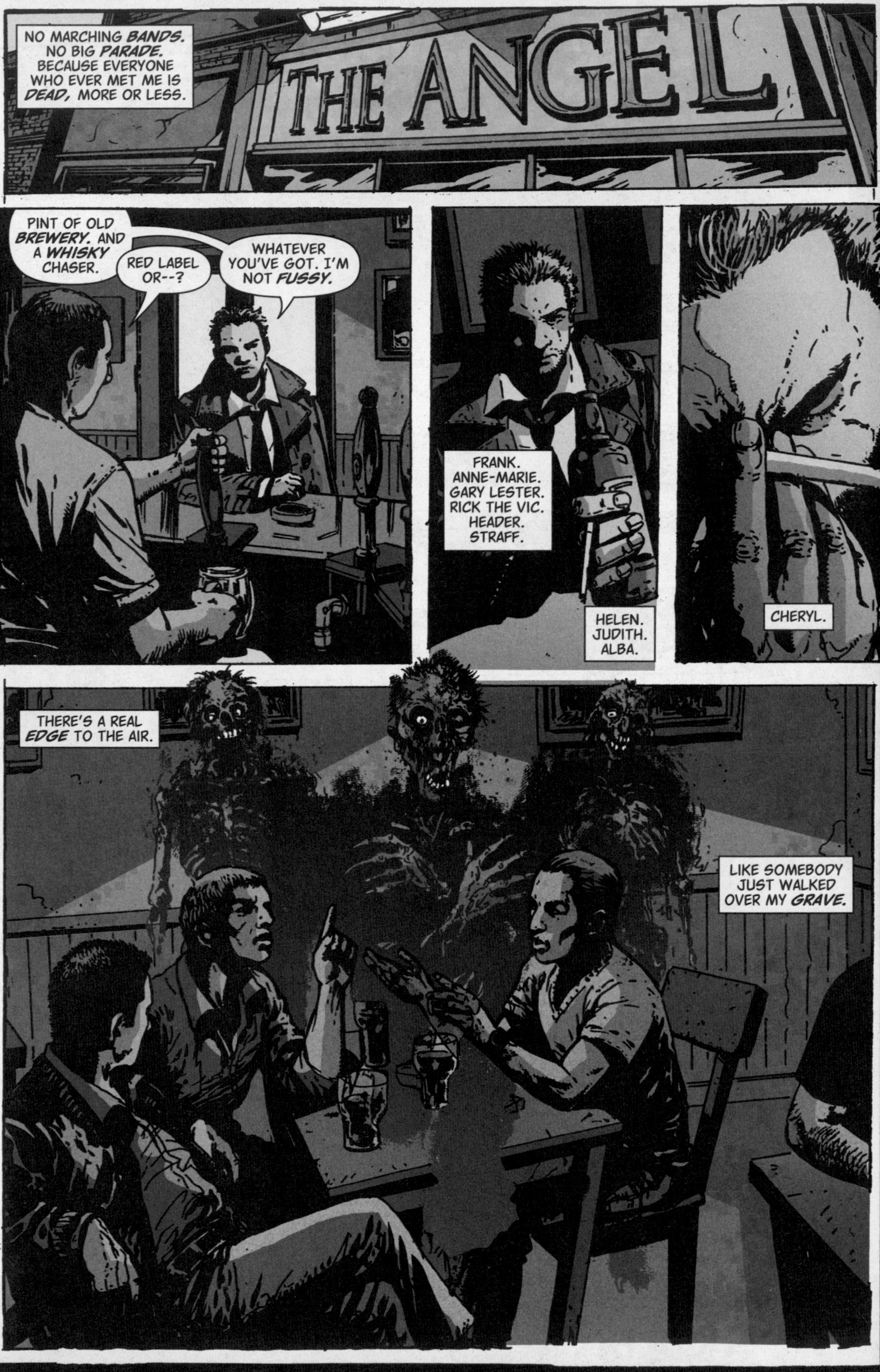
NO MARCHING BANDS. NO BIG PARADE. BECAUSE EVERYONE WHO EVER MET ME IS DEAD, MORE OR LESS.
THE ANGEL
PINT OF OLD BREWERY. AND A WHISKY CHASER.
RED LABEL OR--?
WHATEVER YOU'VE GOT. I'M NOT FUSSY.
FRANK. ANNE-MARIE. GARY LESTER. RICK THE VIC. HEADER. STRAFF.
HELEN. JUDITH. ALBA.
CHERYL.
THERE'S A REAL EDGE TO THE AIR.
LIKE SOMEBODY JUST WALKED OVER MY GRAVE.

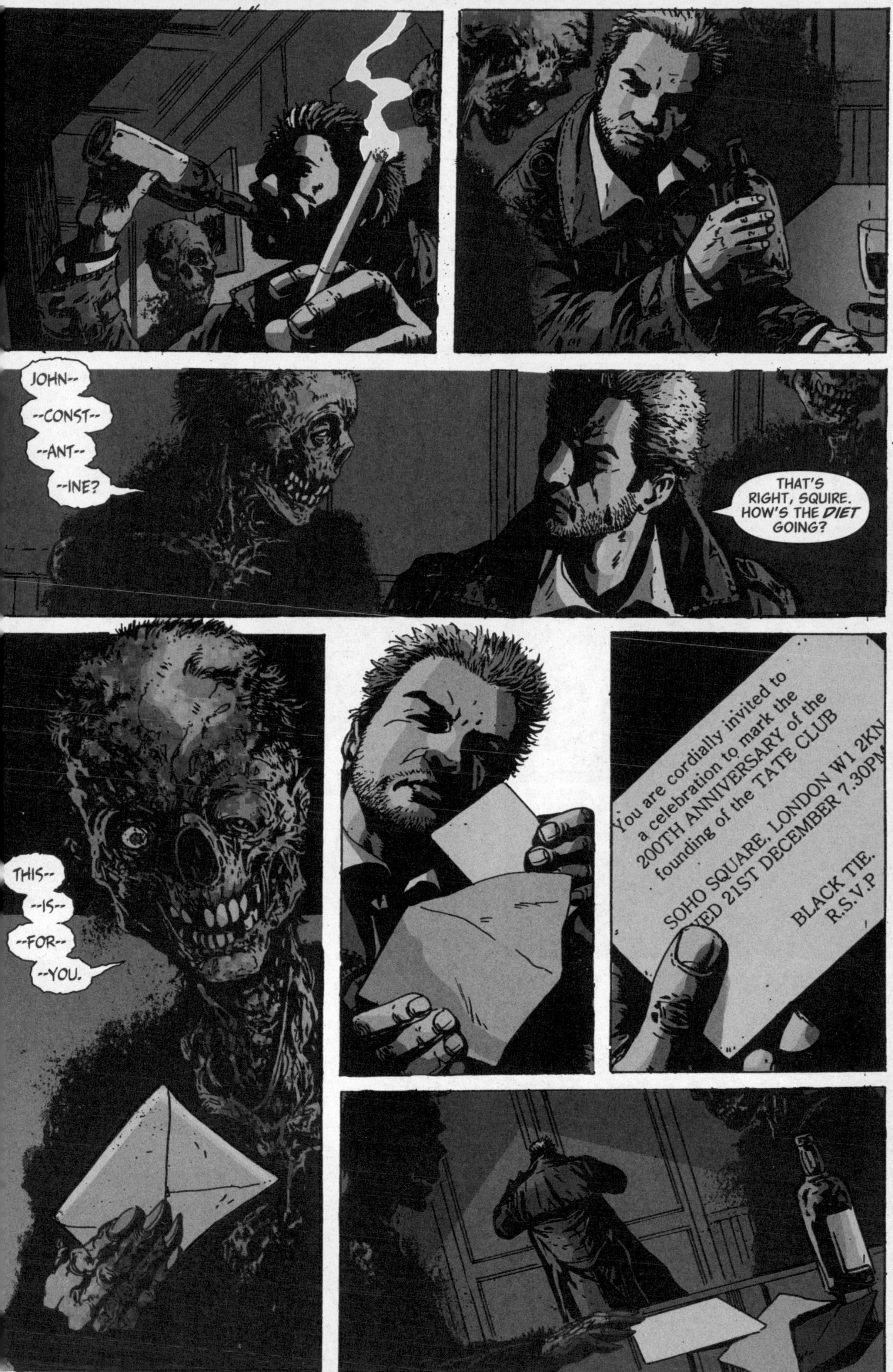
JOHN--
--CONST--
--ANT--
--INE?
THAT'S RIGHT, SQUIRE. HOW'S THE *DIET* GOING?
THIS--
--IS--
--FOR--
--YOU.
You are cordially invited to
a celebration to mark the
200TH ANNIVERSARY of the
founding of the TATE CLUB
SOHO SQUARE, LONDON W1 2KN
ED 21ST DECEMBER 7.30PM
BLACK TIE.
R.S.V.P

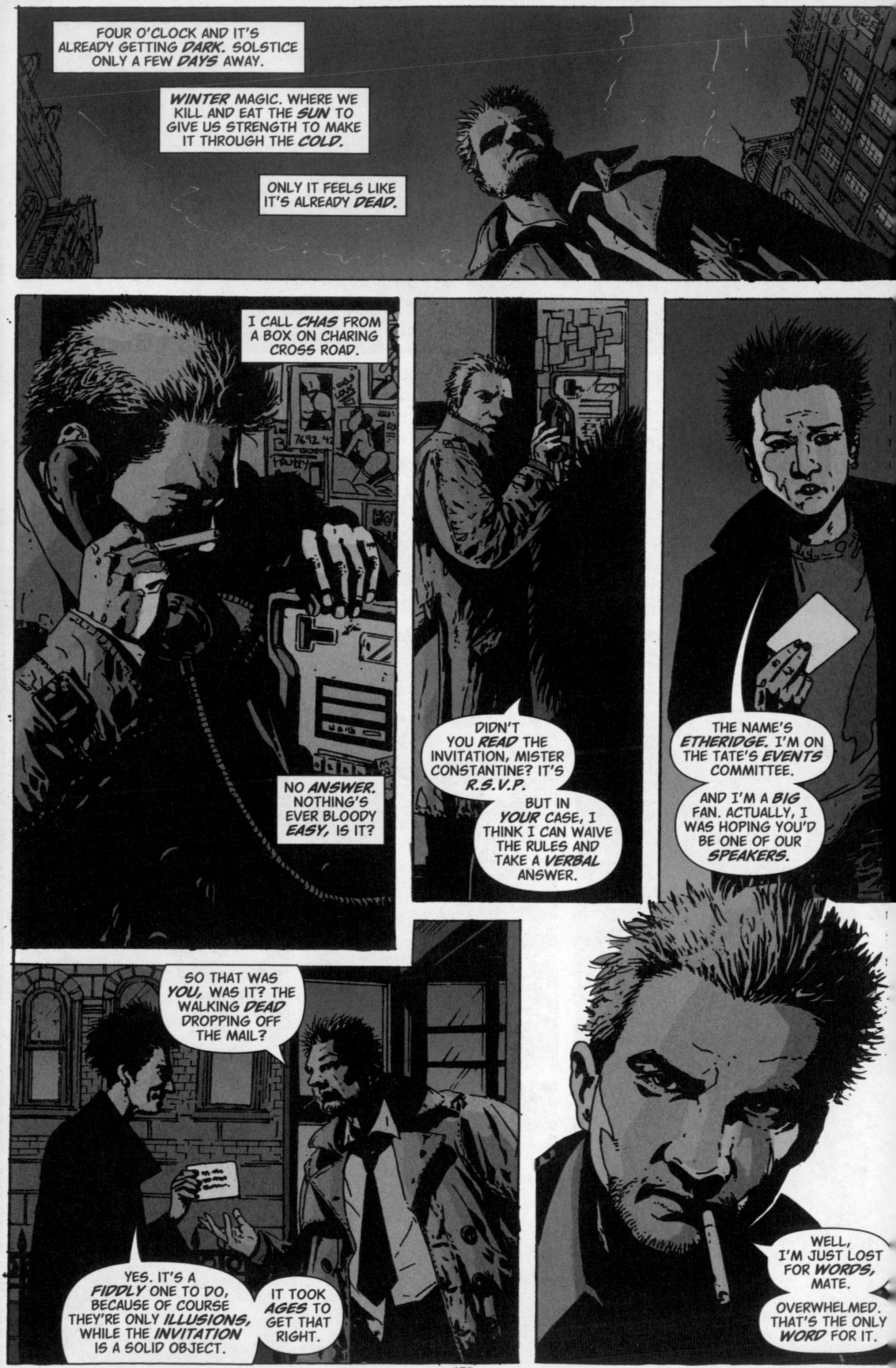
FOUR O'CLOCK AND IT'S ALREADY GETTING DARK. SOLSTICE ONLY A FEW DAYS AWAY.
WINTER MAGIC. WHERE WE KILL AND EAT THE SUN TO GIVE US STRENGTH TO MAKE IT THROUGH THE COLD.
ONLY IT FEELS LIKE IT'S ALREADY DEAD.
I CALL CHAS FROM A BOX ON CHARING CROSS ROAD.
NO ANSWER. NOTHING'S EVER BLOODY EASY, IS IT?
DIDN'T YOU READ THE INVITATION, MISTER CONSTANTINE? IT'S R.S.V.P.
BUT IN YOUR CASE, I THINK I CAN WAIVE THE RULES AND TAKE A VERBAL ANSWER.
THE NAME'S ETHERIDGE. I'M ON THE TATE'S EVENTS COMMITTEE.
AND I'M A BIG FAN. ACTUALLY, I WAS HOPING YOU'D BE ONE OF OUR SPEAKERS.
SO THAT WAS YOU, WAS IT? THE WALKING DEAD DROPPING OFF THE MAIL?
YES. IT'S A FIDDLY ONE TO DO, BECAUSE OF COURSE THEY'RE ONLY ILLUSIONS, WHILE THE INVITATION IS A SOLID OBJECT.
IT TOOK AGES TO GET THAT RIGHT.
WELL, I'M JUST LOST FOR WORDS, MATE.
OVERWHELMED. THAT'S THE ONLY WORD FOR IT.

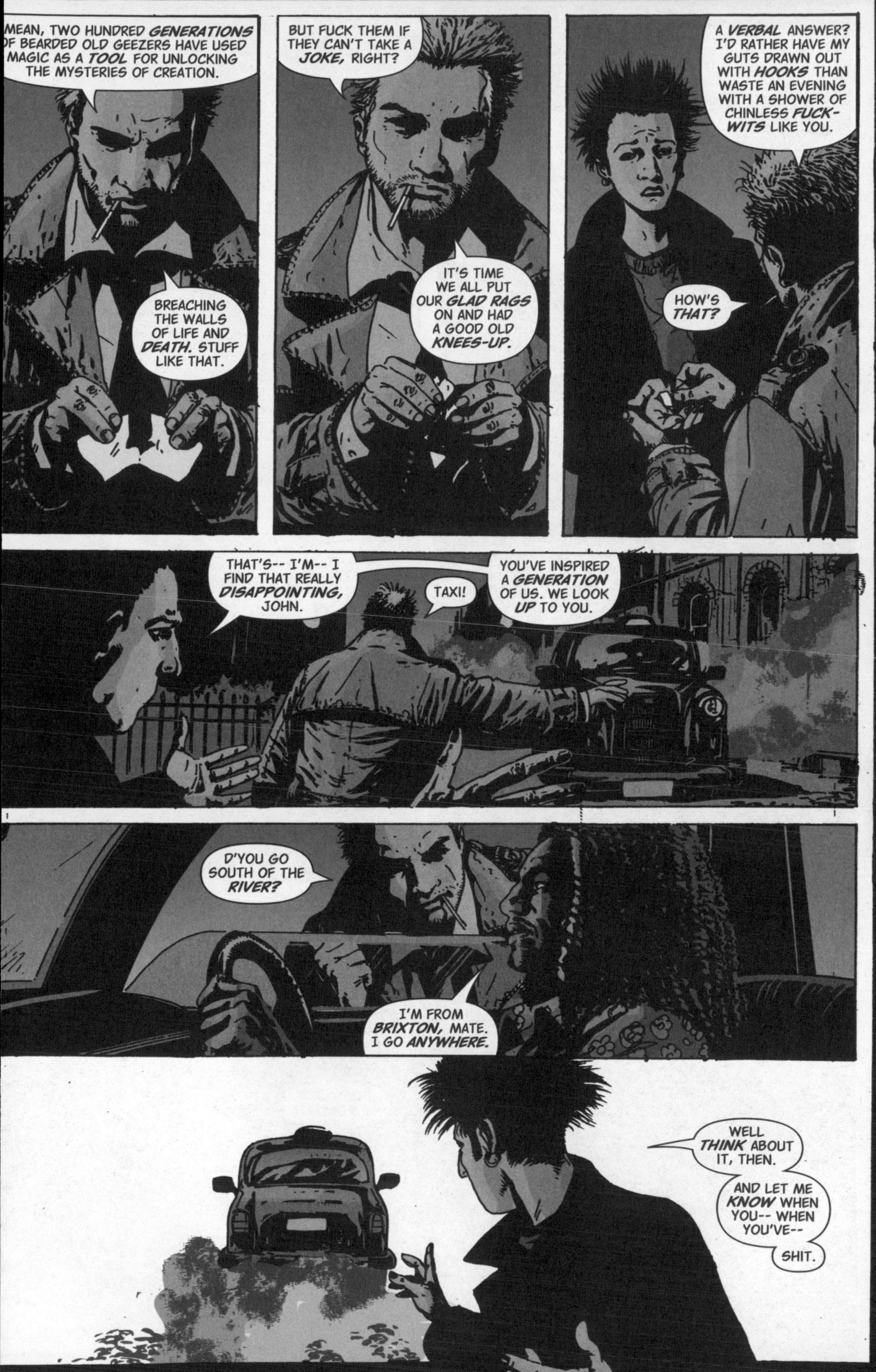
MEAN, TWO HUNDRED GENERATIONS OF BEARDED OLD GEEZERS HAVE USED MAGIC AS A TOOL FOR UNLOCKING THE MYSTERIES OF CREATION.
BREACHING THE WALLS OF LIFE AND DEATH. STUFF LIKE THAT.
BUT FUCK THEM IF THEY CAN'T TAKE A JOKE, RIGHT?
IT'S TIME WE ALL PUT OUR GLAD RAGS ON AND HAD A GOOD OLD KNEES-UP.
A VERBAL ANSWER? I'D RATHER HAVE MY GUTS DRAWN OUT WITH HOOKS THAN WASTE AN EVENING WITH A SHOWER OF CHINLESS FUCK-WITS LIKE YOU.
HOW'S THAT?
THAT'S-- I'M-- I FIND THAT REALLY DISAPPOINTING, JOHN.
YOU'VE INSPIRED A GENERATION OF US. WE LOOK UP TO YOU.
TAXI!
D'YOU GO SOUTH OF THE RIVER?
I'M FROM BRIXTON, MATE. I GO ANYWHERE.
WELL THINK ABOUT IT, THEN.
AND LET ME KNOW WHEN YOU-- WHEN YOU'VE--
SHIT.

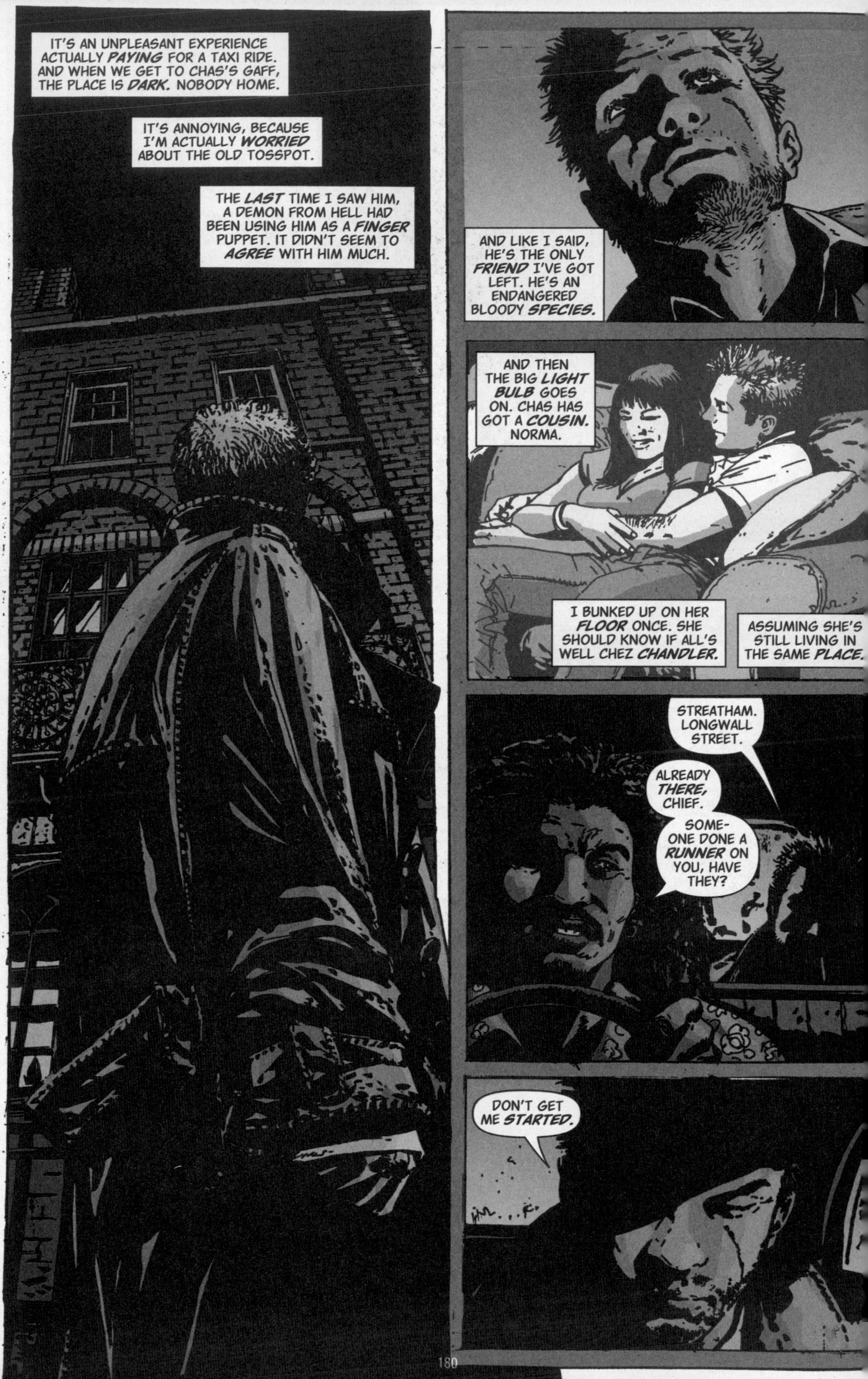
IT'S AN UNPLEASANT EXPERIENCE ACTUALLY PAYING FOR A TAXI RIDE. AND WHEN WE GET TO CHAS'S GAFF, THE PLACE IS DARK. NOBODY HOME.
IT'S ANNOYING, BECAUSE I'M ACTUALLY WORRIED ABOUT THE OLD TOSSPOT.
THE LAST TIME I SAW HIM, A DEMON FROM HELL HAD BEEN USING HIM AS A FINGER PUPPET. IT DIDN'T SEEM TO AGREE WITH HIM MUCH.
AND LIKE I SAID, HE'S THE ONLY FRIEND I'VE GOT LEFT. HE'S AN ENDANGERED BLOODY SPECIES.
AND THEN THE BIG LIGHT BULB GOES ON. CHAS HAS GOT A COUSIN. NORMA.
I BUNKED UP ON HER FLOOR ONCE. SHE SHOULD KNOW IF ALL'S WELL CHEZ CHANDLER.
ASSUMING SHE'S STILL LIVING IN THE SAME PLACE.
STREATHAM. LONGWALL STREET.
ALREADY THERE, CHIEF.
SOME-ONE DONE A RUNNER ON YOU, HAVE THEY?
DON'T GET ME STARTED.

WOOLWORTH'S ALL OUT OF FLUFFY *DICE*, WERE THEY?

WHAT? OH, ME *DANGLIES*, YOU MEAN.

DON'T *KNOCK* IT, MATE. THAT'S *INSURANCE*, THAT IS. LIKE THE AA.

THE *CRUCIFIX* WAS MY DAD'S. 'COS HE'S WATCHING ME FROM *HEAVEN* SORT OF THING.

AND THE NAIL AND THE FEATHER ARE FOR *MAITRE CARREFOUR*. MY MUM SHOWED ME HOW TO MAKE THAT.

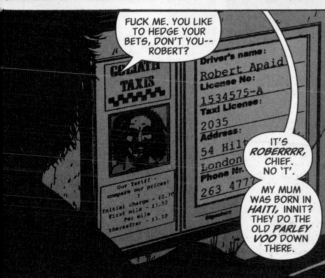

FUCK ME. YOU LIKE TO HEDGE YOUR BETS, DON'T YOU-- ROBERT?

GOLIATH TAXIS

Driver's name: Robert Apaid
License No: 1534575-A
Taxi License: 2035
Address: 54 Hilt... London
Phone Nr. 263 4777

Our tariff! - compare our prices! †
Initial charge - £2.70
First mile - £1.50
per mile thereafter - £1.10

Signature

IT'S *ROBERRRR*, CHIEF. NO 'T'.

MY MUM WAS BORN IN *HAITI*, INNIT? THEY DO THE OLD *PARLEY VOO* DOWN THERE.

IT'S ALL ABOUT *BELIEF*, YEAH? DOESN'T MATTER WHAT YOU BELIEVE *IN*, BUT THE INSTINCT'S THERE.

YOU DON'T BELIEVE IN NOTHING EXCEPT *YOURSELF*, YOU'RE NOT *HUMAN*.

I *COULD* TELL HIM THAT IT'S THE *BONEYARD BARON* WHO COMES TO A CROW FEATHER, NOT *MASTER CARE-FOR*.

AND THAT THE CRUCIFIX BEING *UPSIDE-DOWN* WILL GET SAMEDI'S JUICES FLOWING GOOD AND *PROPER*.

BUT I'M NOT IN THE *MOOD* RIGHT NOW.

YOU NEED TO START ASKING YOURSELF THE *BIG* QUESTIONS, CHIEF.

LIKE, WHAT AM I *DOING* HERE? WHAT HAPPENS AFTER I'M *DEAD*?

NO ONE'S *PAYING* ME TO SAVE THE WORLD FROM ITS FUCKING *SELF*.

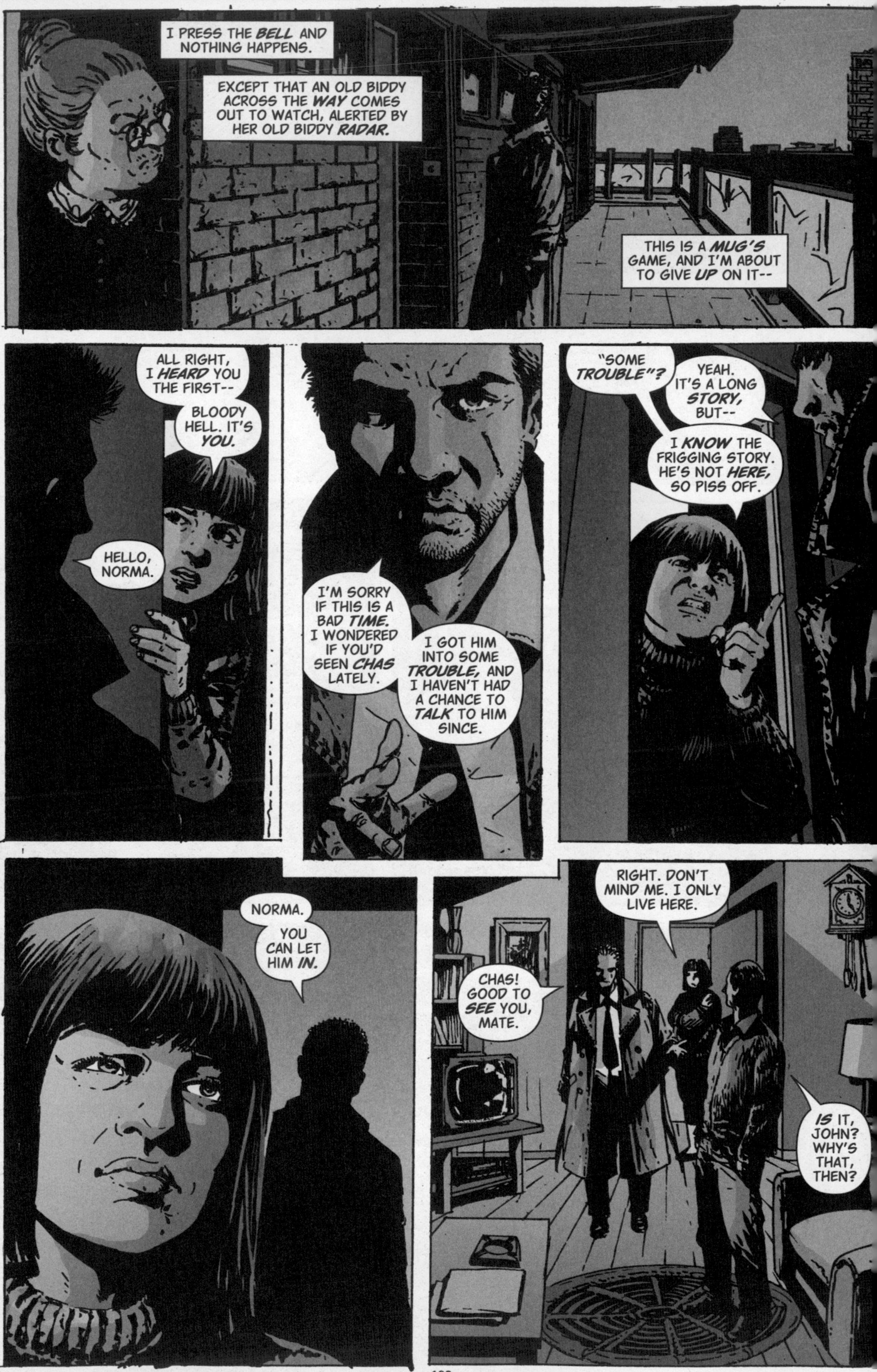

I PRESS THE BELL AND NOTHING HAPPENS.
EXCEPT THAT AN OLD BIDDY ACROSS THE WAY COMES OUT TO WATCH, ALERTED BY HER OLD BIDDY RADAR.
THIS IS A MUG'S GAME, AND I'M ABOUT TO GIVE UP ON IT--
ALL RIGHT, I HEARD YOU THE FIRST--
BLOODY HELL. IT'S YOU.
HELLO, NORMA.
I'M SORRY IF THIS IS A BAD TIME. I WONDERED IF YOU'D SEEN CHAS LATELY.
I GOT HIM INTO SOME TROUBLE, AND I HAVEN'T HAD A CHANCE TO TALK TO HIM SINCE.
"SOME TROUBLE"?
YEAH. IT'S A LONG STORY, BUT--
I KNOW THE FRIGGING STORY. HE'S NOT HERE, SO PISS OFF.
NORMA.
YOU CAN LET HIM IN.
RIGHT. DON'T MIND ME. I ONLY LIVE HERE.
CHAS! GOOD TO SEE YOU, MATE.
IS IT, JOHN? WHY'S THAT, THEN?

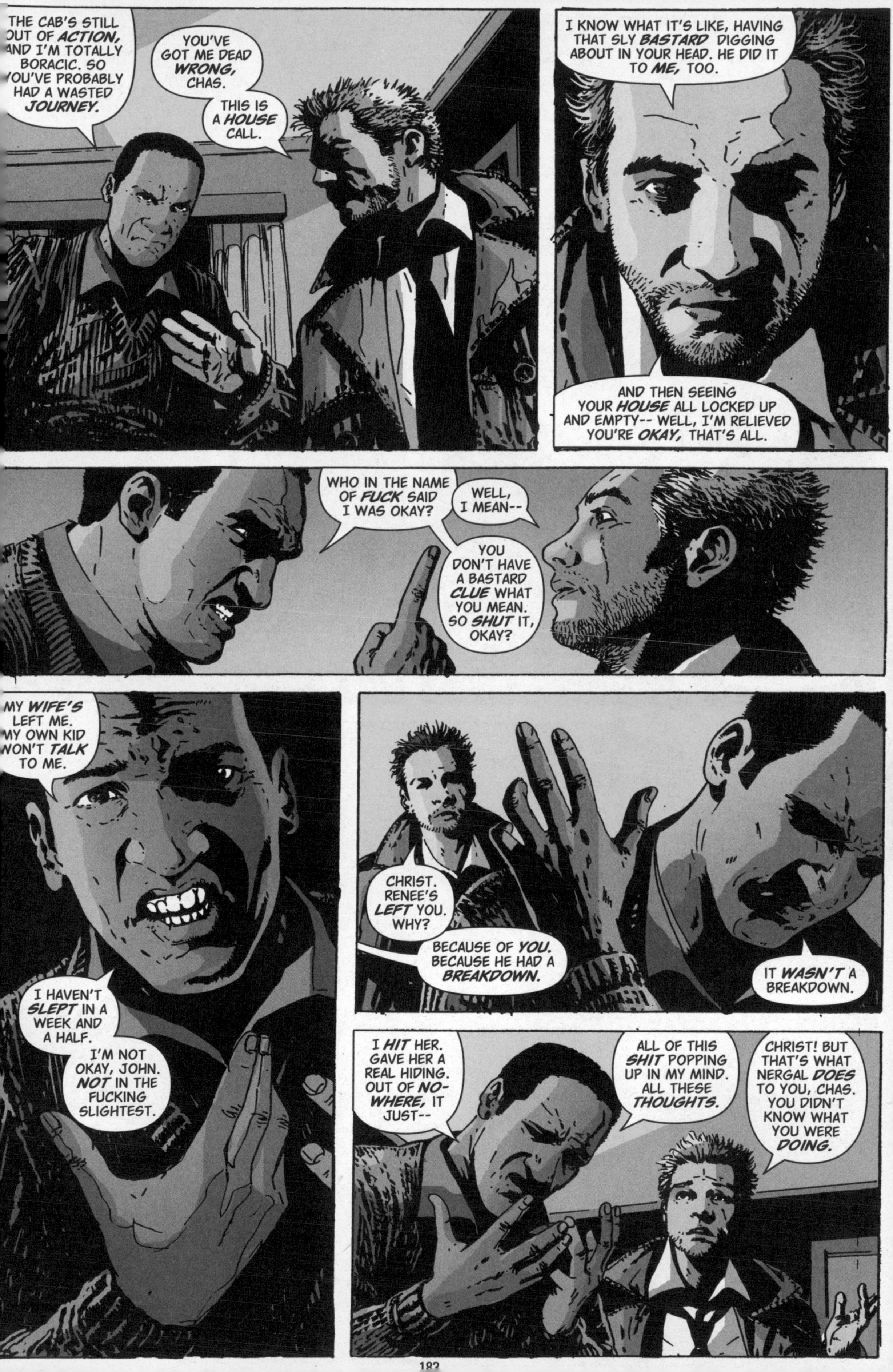

THE CAB'S STILL OUT OF ACTION, AND I'M TOTALLY BORACIC. SO YOU'VE PROBABLY HAD A WASTED JOURNEY.
YOU'VE GOT ME DEAD WRONG, CHAS.
THIS IS A HOUSE CALL.
I KNOW WHAT IT'S LIKE, HAVING THAT SLY BASTARD DIGGING ABOUT IN YOUR HEAD. HE DID IT TO ME, TOO.
AND THEN SEEING YOUR HOUSE ALL LOCKED UP AND EMPTY-- WELL, I'M RELIEVED YOU'RE OKAY, THAT'S ALL.
WHO IN THE NAME OF FUCK SAID I WAS OKAY?
WELL, I MEAN--
YOU DON'T HAVE A BASTARD CLUE WHAT YOU MEAN. SO SHUT IT, OKAY?
MY WIFE'S LEFT ME. MY OWN KID WON'T TALK TO ME.
I HAVEN'T SLEPT IN A WEEK AND A HALF.
I'M NOT OKAY, JOHN. NOT IN THE FUCKING SLIGHTEST.
CHRIST. RENEE'S LEFT YOU. WHY?
BECAUSE OF YOU. BECAUSE HE HAD A BREAKDOWN.
IT WASN'T A BREAKDOWN.
I HIT HER. GAVE HER A REAL HIDING. OUT OF NO-WHERE, IT JUST--
ALL OF THIS SHIT POPPING UP IN MY MIND. ALL THESE THOUGHTS.
CHRIST! BUT THAT'S WHAT NERGAL DOES TO YOU, CHAS. YOU DIDN'T KNOW WHAT YOU WERE DOING.

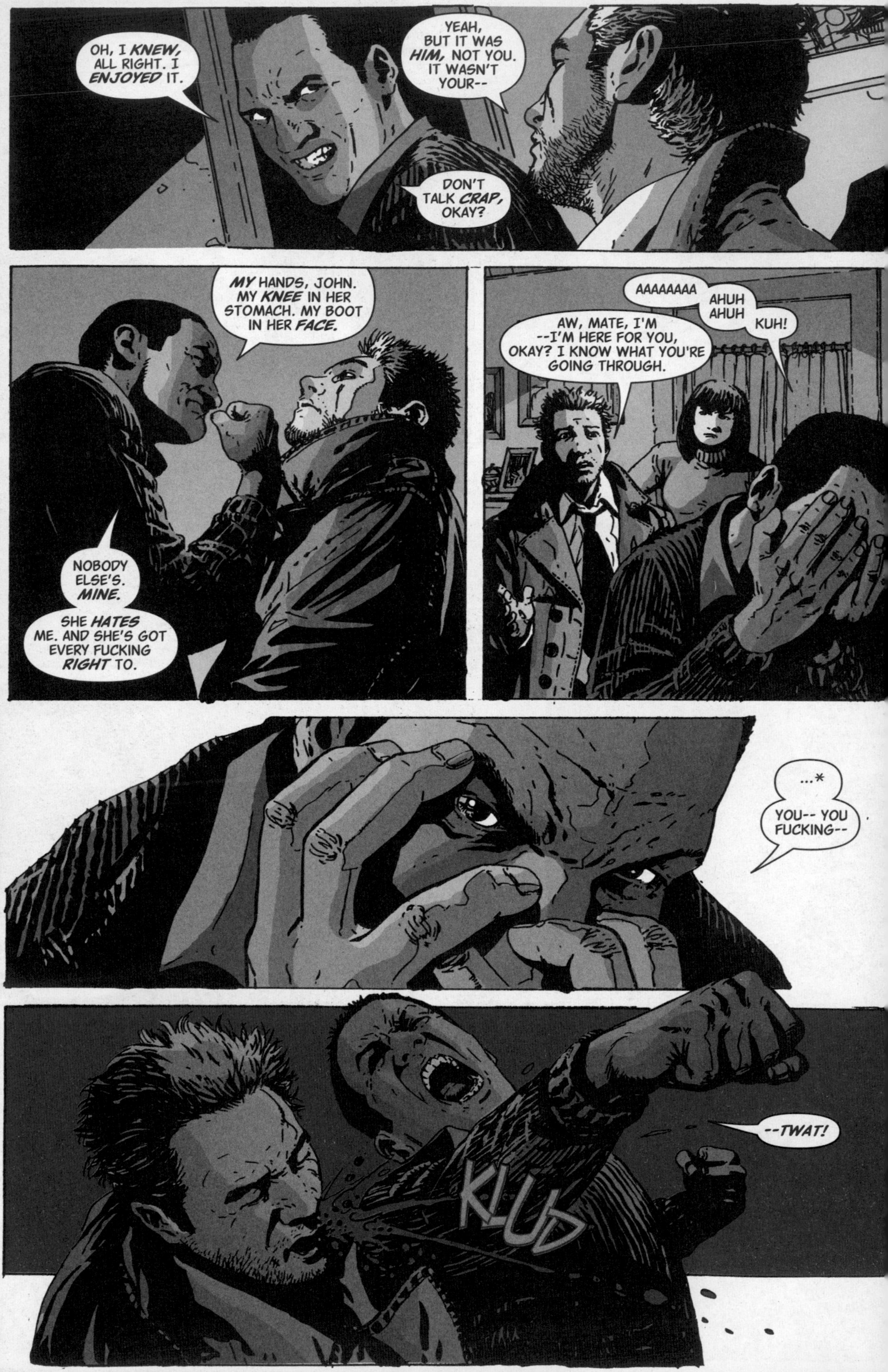
OH, I KNEW, ALL RIGHT. I ENJOYED IT.
YEAH, BUT IT WAS HIM, NOT YOU. IT WASN'T YOUR--
DON'T TALK CRAP, OKAY?
MY HANDS, JOHN. MY KNEE IN HER STOMACH. MY BOOT IN HER FACE.
NOBODY ELSE'S. MINE.
SHE HATES ME. AND SHE'S GOT EVERY FUCKING RIGHT TO.
AW, MATE, I'M --I'M HERE FOR YOU, OKAY? I KNOW WHAT YOU'RE GOING THROUGH.
AAAAAAAA
AHUH AHUH
KUH!
...*
YOU-- YOU FUCKING--
--TWAT!
KLUD

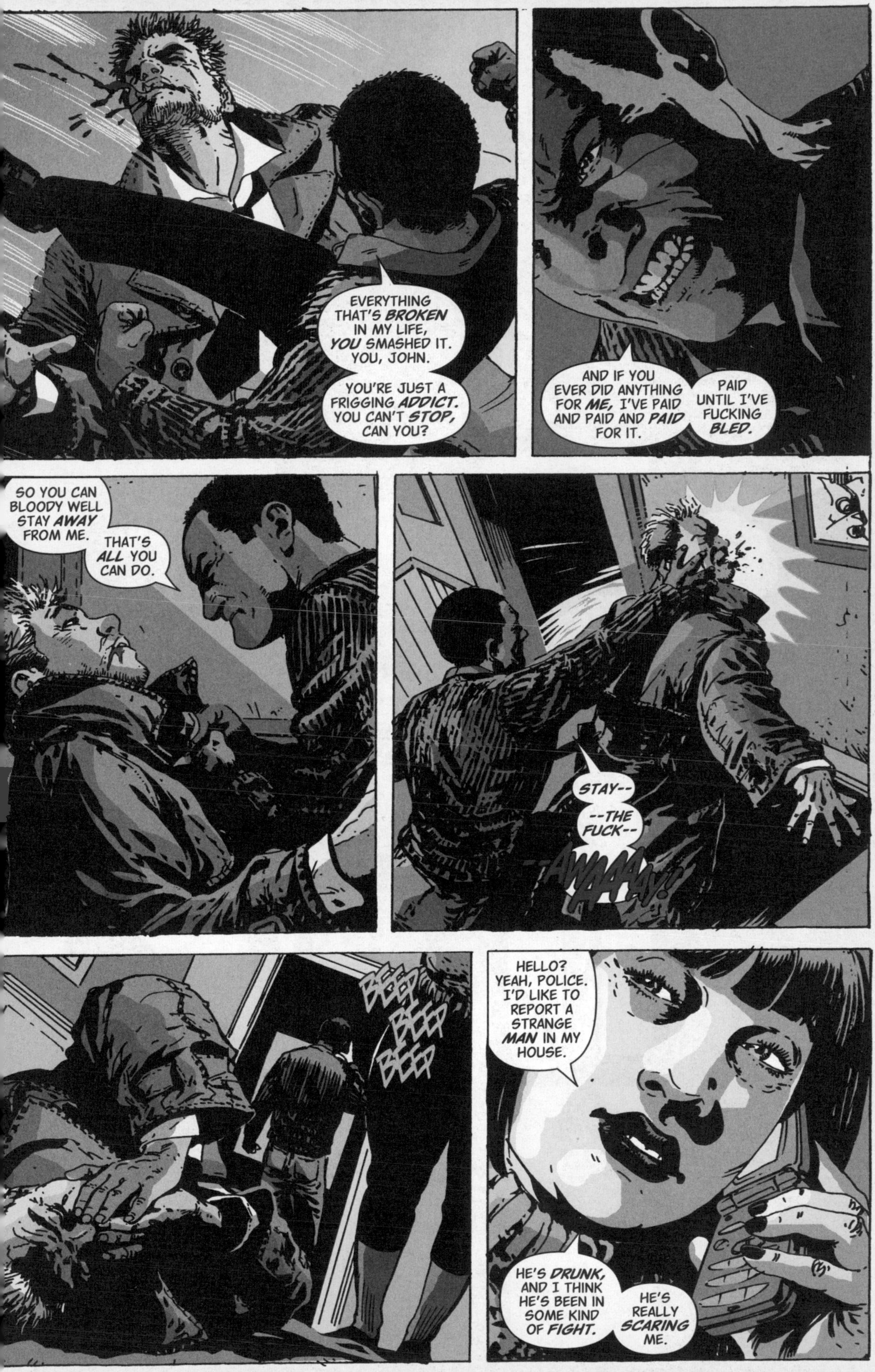
EVERYTHING THAT'S BROKEN IN MY LIFE, YOU SMASHED IT. YOU, JOHN.
YOU'RE JUST A FRIGGING ADDICT. YOU CAN'T STOP, CAN YOU?
AND IF YOU EVER DID ANYTHING FOR ME, I'VE PAID AND PAID AND PAID FOR IT.
PAID UNTIL I'VE FUCKING BLED.
SO YOU CAN BLOODY WELL STAY AWAY FROM ME.
THAT'S ALL YOU CAN DO.
STAY--
--THE FUCK--
AWAAAAAY!
BEEP BEEP BEEP
HELLO? YEAH, POLICE. I'D LIKE TO REPORT A STRANGE MAN IN MY HOUSE.
HE'S DRUNK, AND I THINK HE'S BEEN IN SOME KIND OF FIGHT.
HE'S REALLY SCARING ME.

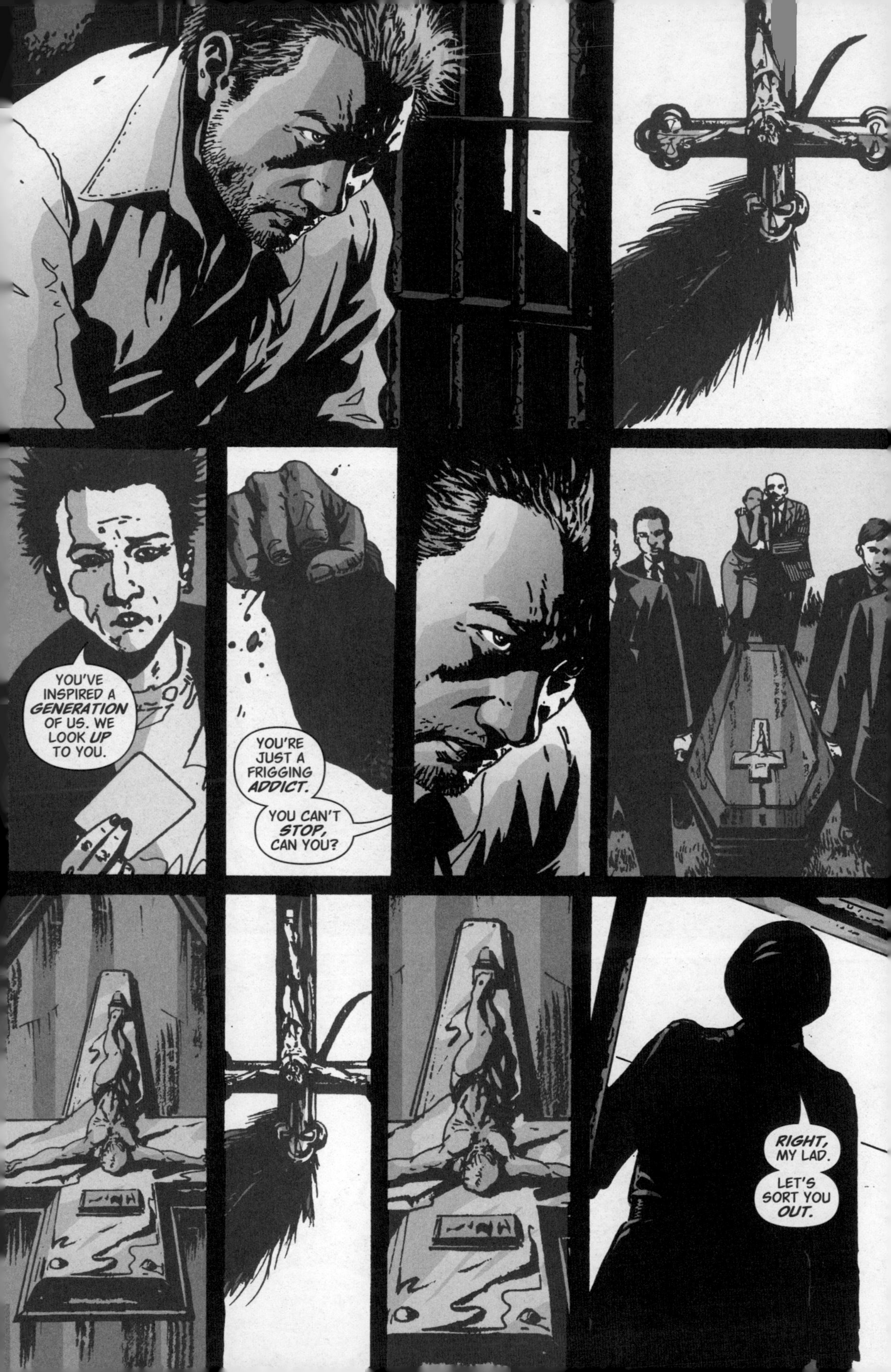
YOU'VE INSPIRED A GENERATION OF US. WE LOOK UP TO YOU.
YOU'RE JUST A FRIGGING ADDICT.
YOU CAN'T STOP, CAN YOU?
RIGHT, MY LAD.
LET'S SORT YOU OUT.

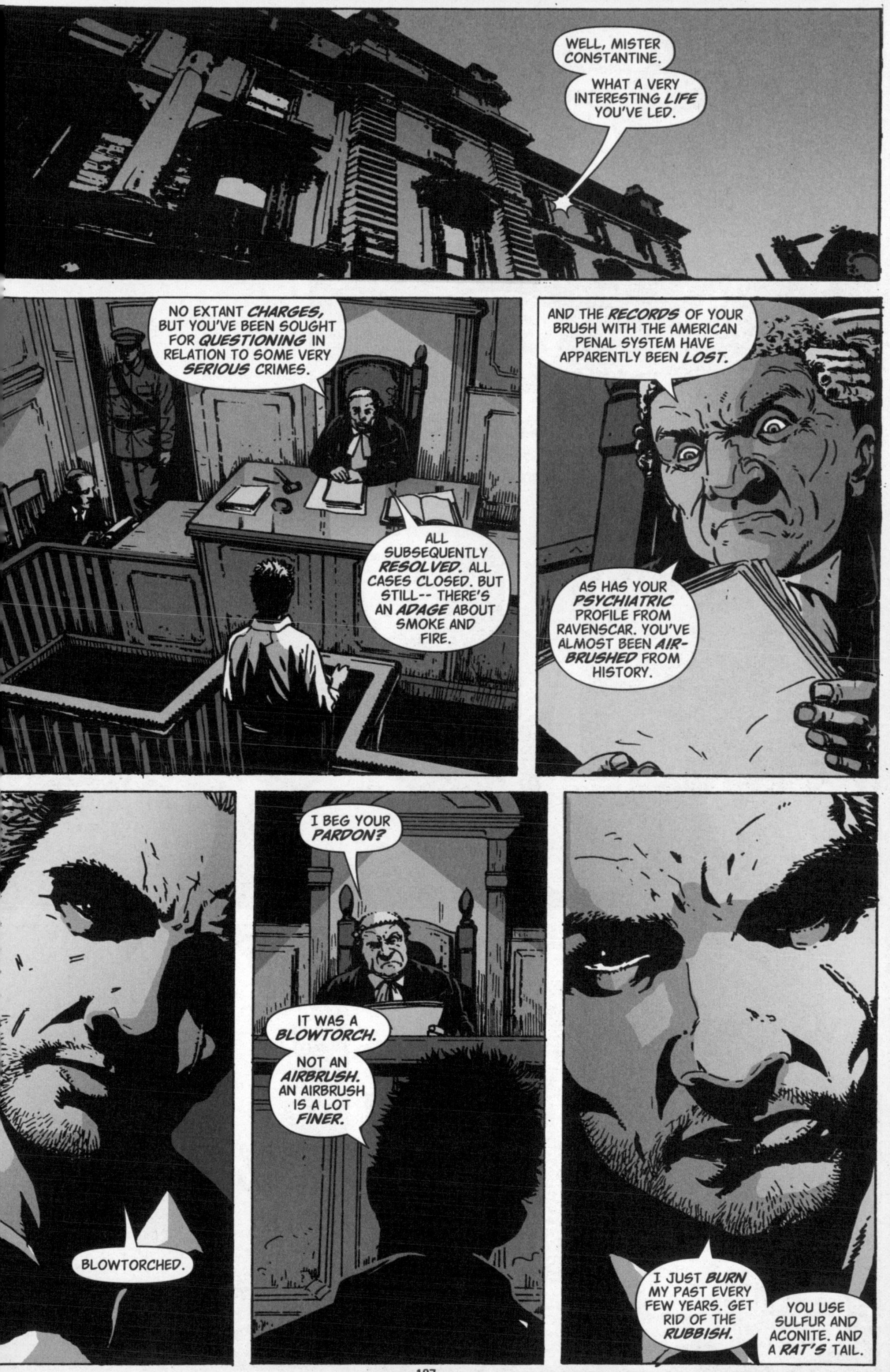
WELL, MISTER CONSTANTINE.
WHAT A VERY INTERESTING LIFE YOU'VE LED.
NO EXTANT CHARGES, BUT YOU'VE BEEN SOUGHT FOR QUESTIONING IN RELATION TO SOME VERY SERIOUS CRIMES.
ALL SUBSEQUENTLY RESOLVED. ALL CASES CLOSED. BUT STILL-- THERE'S AN ADAGE ABOUT SMOKE AND FIRE.
AND THE RECORDS OF YOUR BRUSH WITH THE AMERICAN PENAL SYSTEM HAVE APPARENTLY BEEN LOST.
AS HAS YOUR PSYCHIATRIC PROFILE FROM RAVENSCAR. YOU'VE ALMOST BEEN AIR-BRUSHED FROM HISTORY.
BLOWTORCHED.
I BEG YOUR PARDON?
IT WAS A BLOWTORCH.
NOT AN AIRBRUSH. AN AIRBRUSH IS A LOT FINER.
I JUST BURN MY PAST EVERY FEW YEARS. GET RID OF THE RUBBISH.
YOU USE SULFUR AND ACONITE. AND A RAT'S TAIL.

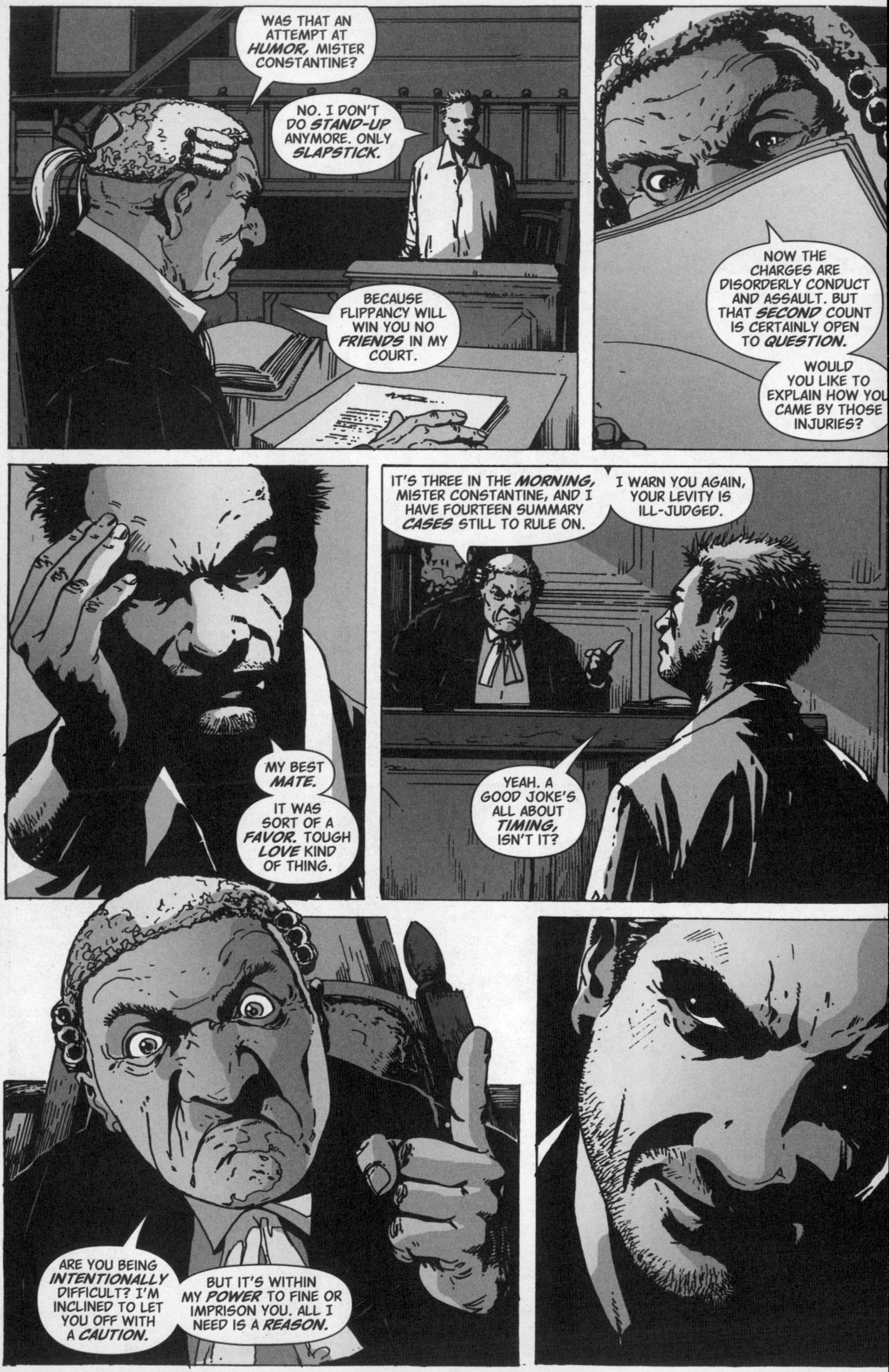
WAS THAT AN ATTEMPT AT HUMOR, MISTER CONSTANTINE?
NO. I DON'T DO STAND-UP ANYMORE. ONLY SLAPSTICK.
BECAUSE FLIPPANCY WILL WIN YOU NO FRIENDS IN MY COURT.
NOW THE CHARGES ARE DISORDERLY CONDUCT AND ASSAULT. BUT THAT SECOND COUNT IS CERTAINLY OPEN TO QUESTION.
WOULD YOU LIKE TO EXPLAIN HOW YOU CAME BY THOSE INJURIES?
MY BEST MATE.
IT WAS SORT OF A FAVOR. TOUGH LOVE KIND OF THING.
IT'S THREE IN THE MORNING, MISTER CONSTANTINE, AND I HAVE FOURTEEN SUMMARY CASES STILL TO RULE ON.
I WARN YOU AGAIN, YOUR LEVITY IS ILL-JUDGED.
YEAH. A GOOD JOKE'S ALL ABOUT TIMING, ISN'T IT?
ARE YOU BEING INTENTIONALLY DIFFICULT? I'M INCLINED TO LET YOU OFF WITH A CAUTION.
BUT IT'S WITHIN MY POWER TO FINE OR IMPRISON YOU. ALL I NEED IS A REASON.

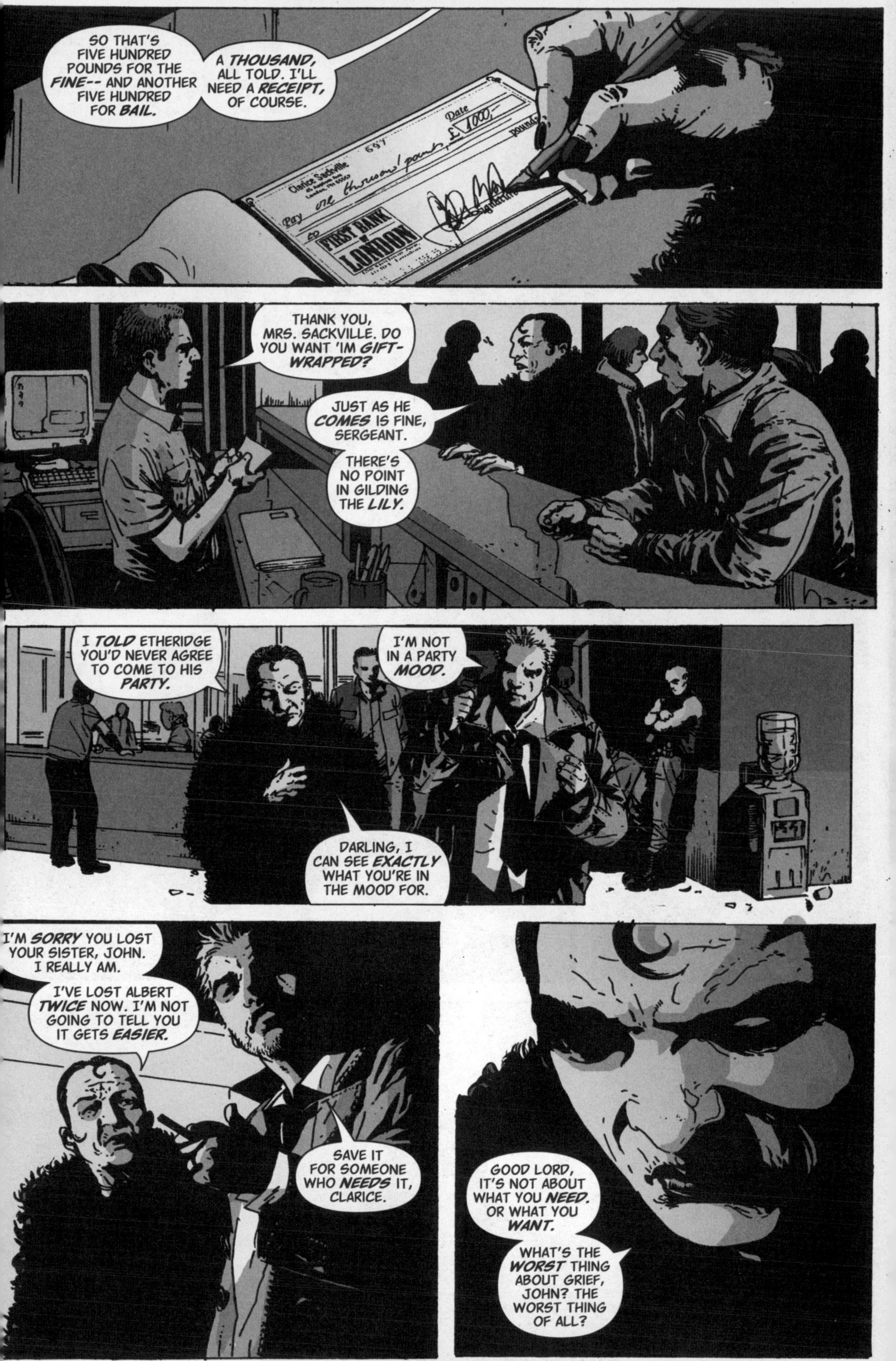

SO THAT'S FIVE HUNDRED POUNDS FOR THE FINE-- AND ANOTHER FIVE HUNDRED FOR BAIL.
A THOUSAND, ALL TOLD. I'LL NEED A RECEIPT, OF COURSE.
Clarice Sackville
FIRST BANK OF LONDON
THANK YOU, MRS. SACKVILLE. DO YOU WANT 'IM GIFT-WRAPPED?
JUST AS HE COMES IS FINE, SERGEANT.
THERE'S NO POINT IN GILDING THE LILY.
I TOLD ETHERIDGE YOU'D NEVER AGREE TO COME TO HIS PARTY.
I'M NOT IN A PARTY MOOD.
DARLING, I CAN SEE EXACTLY WHAT YOU'RE IN THE MOOD FOR.
I'M SORRY YOU LOST YOUR SISTER, JOHN. I REALLY AM.
I'VE LOST ALBERT TWICE NOW. I'M NOT GOING TO TELL YOU IT GETS EASIER.
SAVE IT FOR SOMEONE WHO NEEDS IT, CLARICE.
GOOD LORD, IT'S NOT ABOUT WHAT YOU NEED. OR WHAT YOU WANT.
WHAT'S THE WORST THING ABOUT GRIEF, JOHN? THE WORST THING OF ALL?

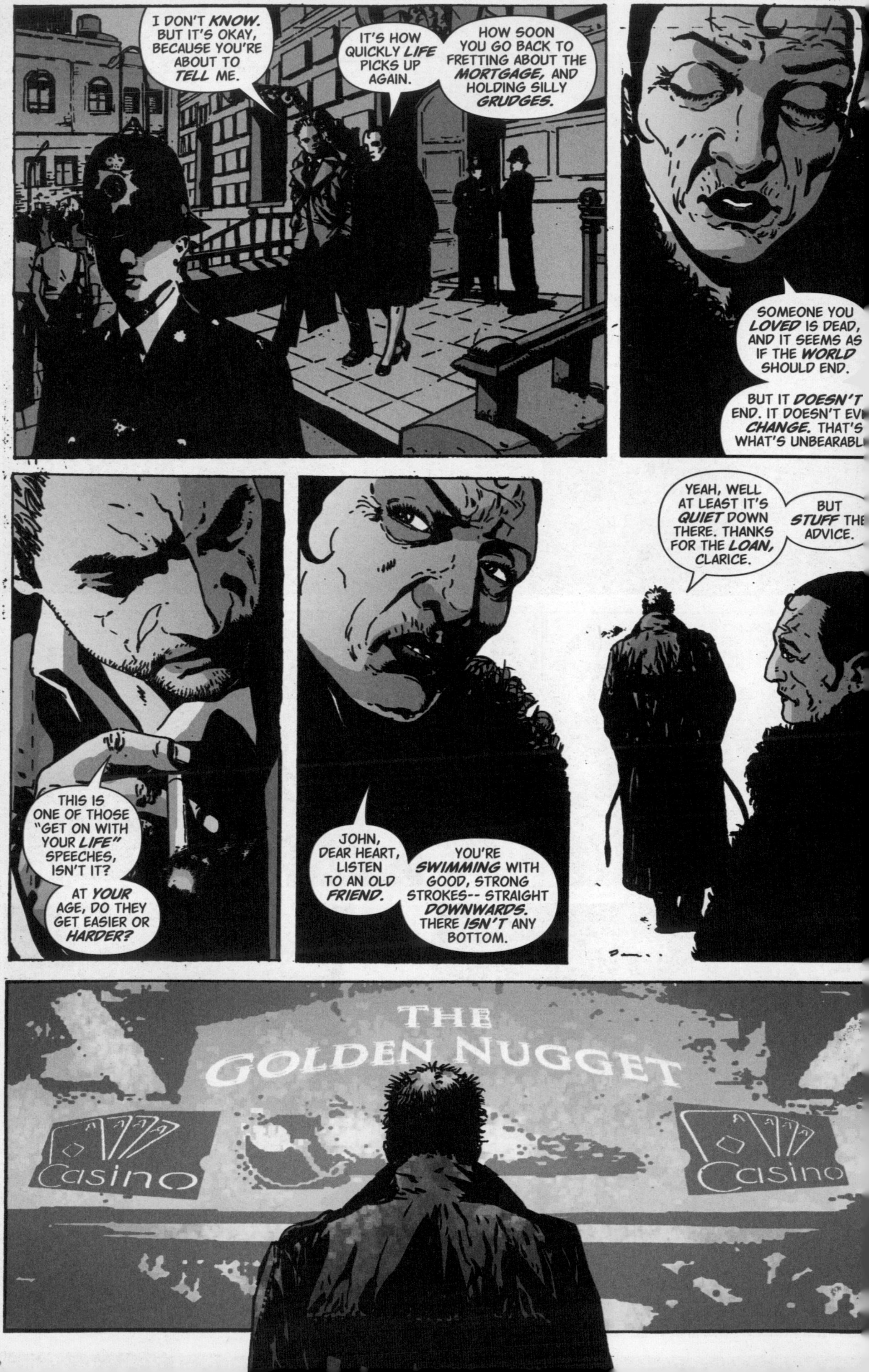
I DON'T KNOW. BUT IT'S OKAY, BECAUSE YOU'RE ABOUT TO TELL ME.
IT'S HOW QUICKLY LIFE PICKS UP AGAIN.
HOW SOON YOU GO BACK TO FRETTING ABOUT THE MORTGAGE, AND HOLDING SILLY GRUDGES.
SOMEONE YOU LOVED IS DEAD, AND IT SEEMS AS IF THE WORLD SHOULD END.
BUT IT DOESN'T END. IT DOESN'T EV CHANGE. THAT'S WHAT'S UNBEARABL
THIS IS ONE OF THOSE "GET ON WITH YOUR LIFE" SPEECHES, ISN'T IT?
AT YOUR AGE, DO THEY GET EASIER OR HARDER?
JOHN, DEAR HEART, LISTEN TO AN OLD FRIEND.
YOU'RE SWIMMING WITH GOOD, STRONG STROKES-- STRAIGHT DOWNWARDS. THERE ISN'T ANY BOTTOM.
YEAH, WELL AT LEAST IT'S QUIET DOWN THERE. THANKS FOR THE LOAN, CLARICE.
BUT STUFF TH ADVICE.
THE GOLDEN NUGGET
Casino
Casino

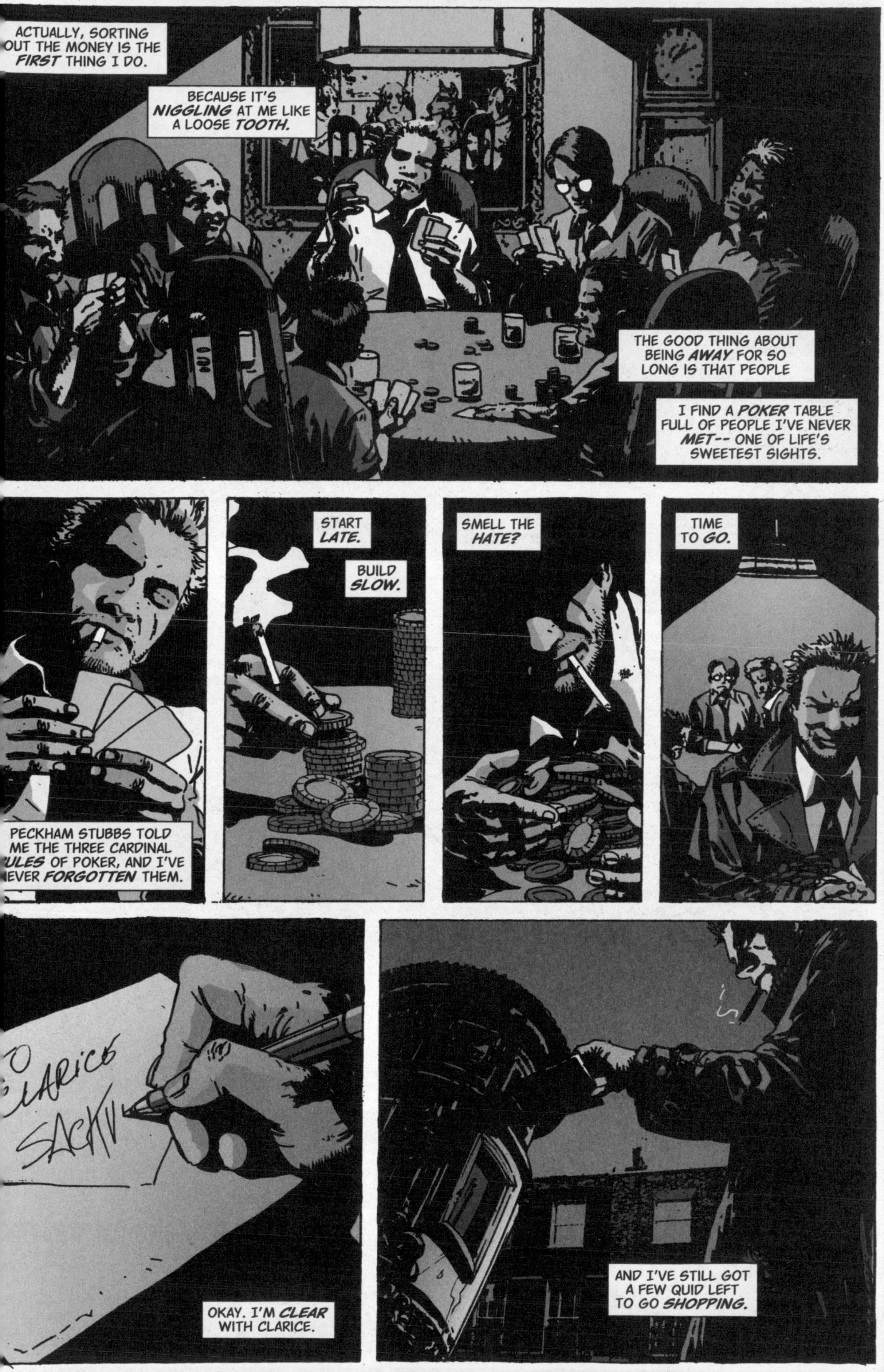
ACTUALLY, SORTING OUT THE MONEY IS THE *FIRST* THING I DO.
BECAUSE IT'S *NIGGLING* AT ME LIKE A LOOSE *TOOTH.*
THE GOOD THING ABOUT BEING *AWAY* FOR SO LONG IS THAT PEOPLE
I FIND A *POKER* TABLE FULL OF PEOPLE I'VE NEVER *MET*-- ONE OF LIFE'S SWEETEST SIGHTS.
PECKHAM STUBBS TOLD ME THE THREE CARDINAL ULES OF POKER, AND I'VE EVER *FORGOTTEN* THEM.
START *LATE.*
BUILD *SLOW.*
SMELL THE *HATE?*
TIME TO *GO.*
OKAY. I'M *CLEAR* WITH CLARICE.
AND I'VE STILL GOT A FEW QUID LEFT TO GO *SHOPPING.*

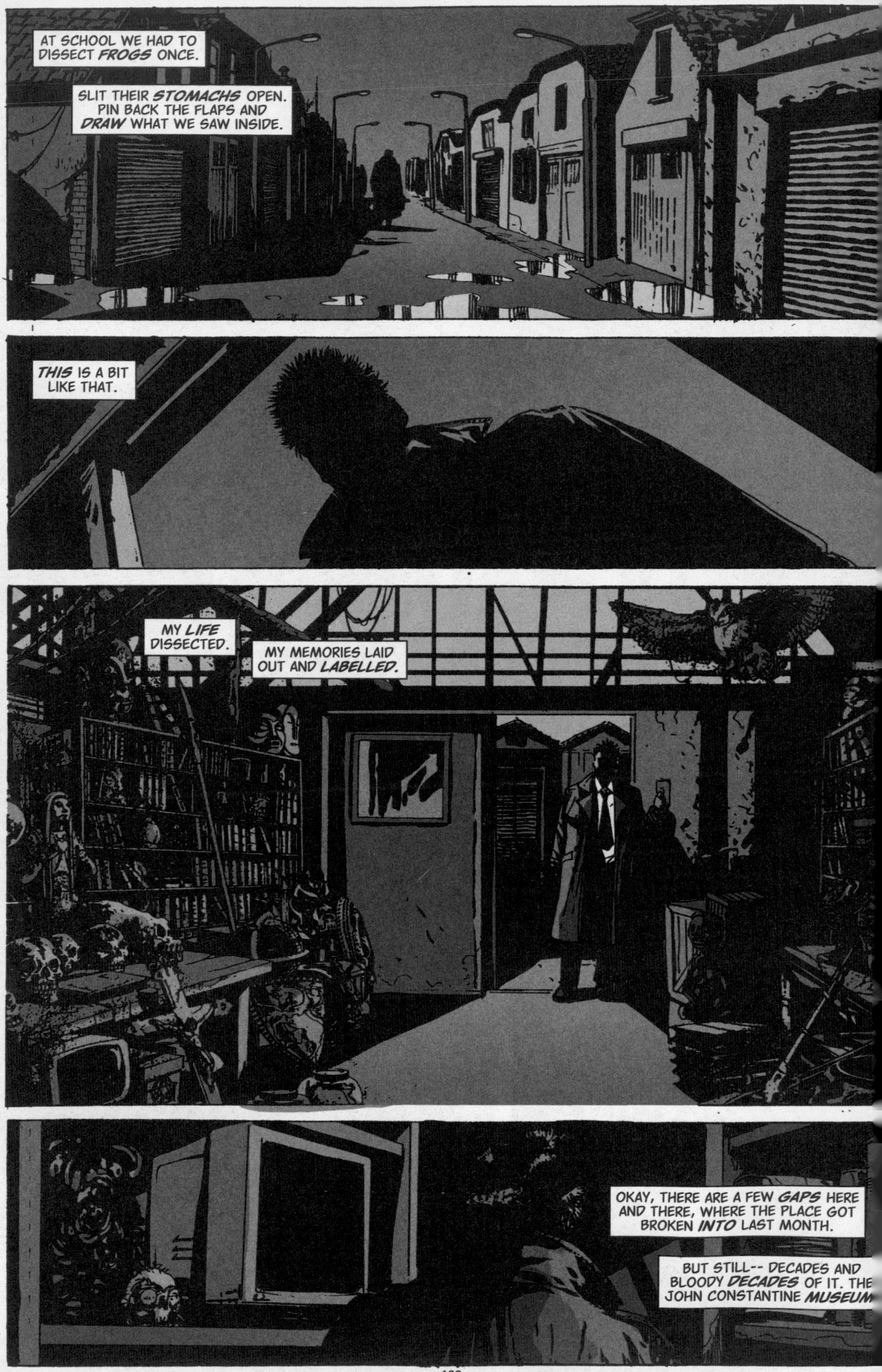
AT SCHOOL WE HAD TO DISSECT FROGS ONCE.
SLIT THEIR STOMACHS OPEN. PIN BACK THE FLAPS AND DRAW WHAT WE SAW INSIDE.
THIS IS A BIT LIKE THAT.
MY LIFE DISSECTED.
MY MEMORIES LAID OUT AND LABELLED.
OKAY, THERE ARE A FEW GAPS HERE AND THERE, WHERE THE PLACE GOT BROKEN INTO LAST MONTH.
BUT STILL-- DECADES AND BLOODY DECADES OF IT. THE JOHN CONSTANTINE MUSEUM

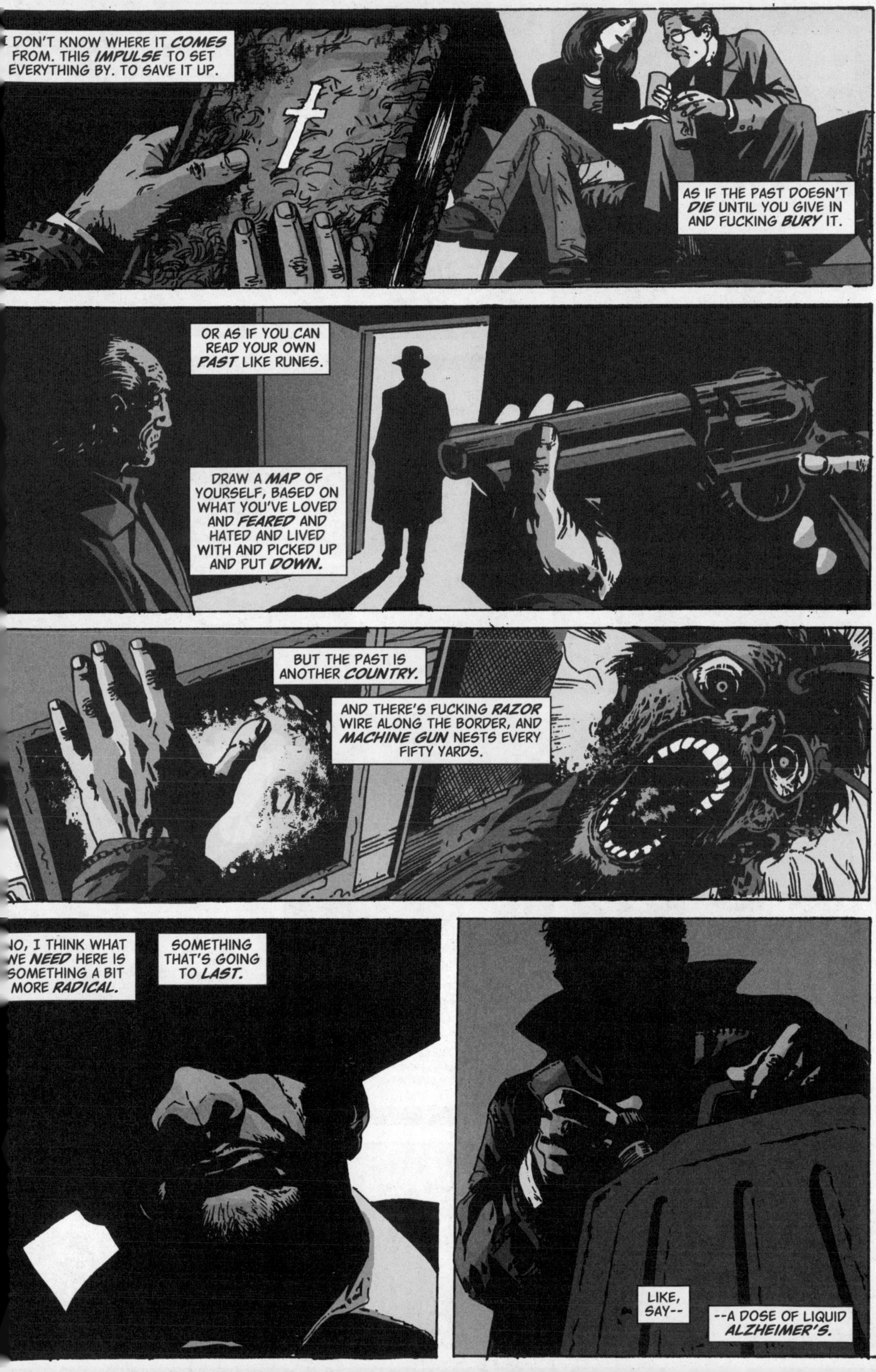
I DON'T KNOW WHERE IT COMES FROM. THIS IMPULSE TO SET EVERYTHING BY. TO SAVE IT UP.
AS IF THE PAST DOESN'T DIE UNTIL YOU GIVE IN AND FUCKING BURY IT.
OR AS IF YOU CAN READ YOUR OWN PAST LIKE RUNES.
DRAW A MAP OF YOURSELF, BASED ON WHAT YOU'VE LOVED AND FEARED AND HATED AND LIVED WITH AND PICKED UP AND PUT DOWN.
BUT THE PAST IS ANOTHER COUNTRY.
AND THERE'S FUCKING RAZOR WIRE ALONG THE BORDER, AND MACHINE GUN NESTS EVERY FIFTY YARDS.
NO, I THINK WHAT WE NEED HERE IS SOMETHING A BIT MORE RADICAL.
SOMETHING THAT'S GOING TO LAST.
LIKE, SAY--
--A DOSE OF LIQUID ALZHEIMER'S.

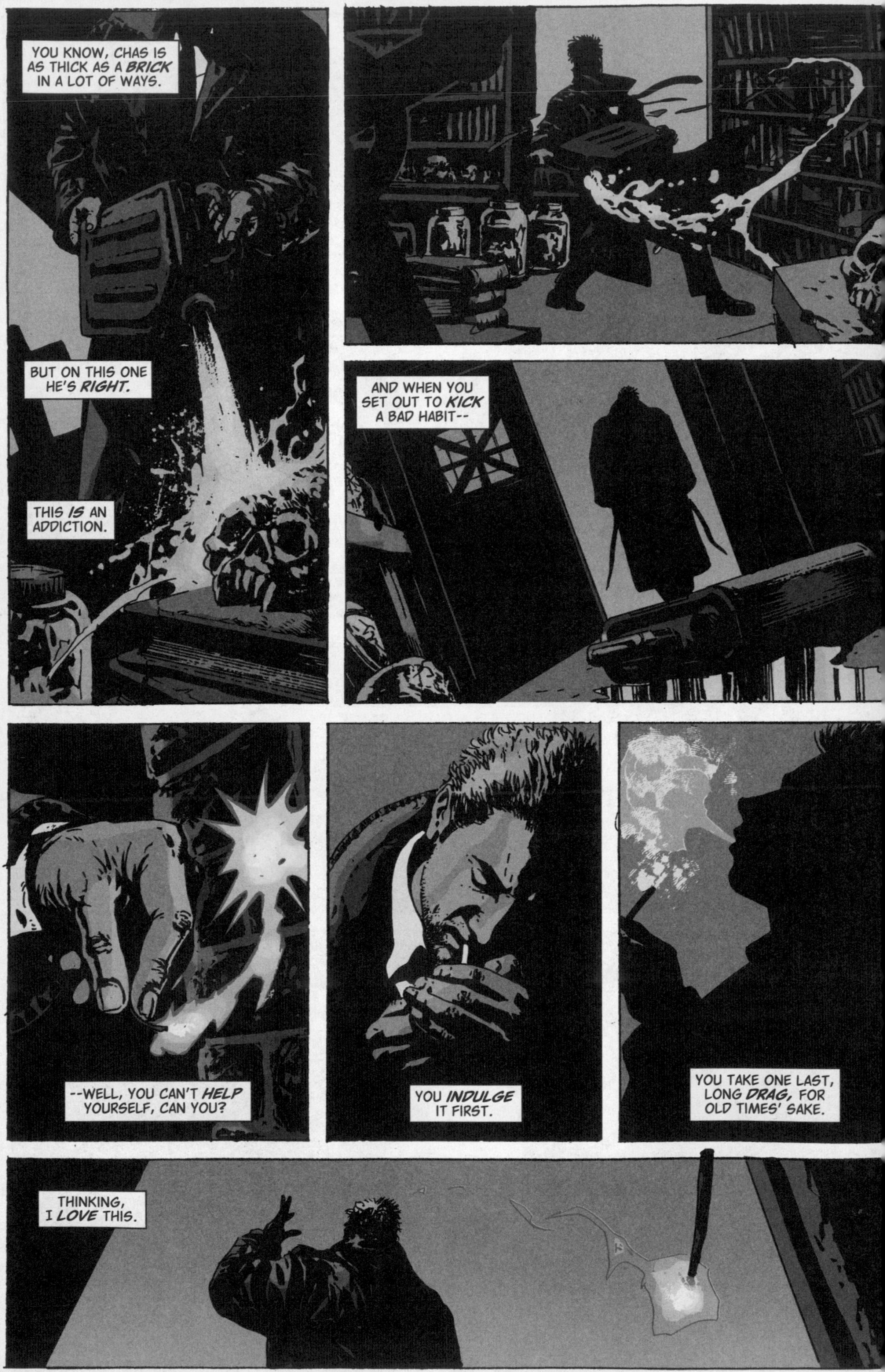

YOU KNOW, CHAS IS AS THICK AS A *BRICK* IN A LOT OF WAYS.
BUT ON THIS ONE HE'S *RIGHT.*
THIS *IS* AN ADDICTION.
AND WHEN YOU SET OUT TO *KICK* A BAD HABIT--
--WELL, YOU CAN'T *HELP* YOURSELF, CAN YOU?
YOU *INDULGE* IT FIRST.
YOU TAKE ONE LAST, LONG *DRAG,* FOR OLD TIMES' SAKE.
THINKING, I *LOVE* THIS.

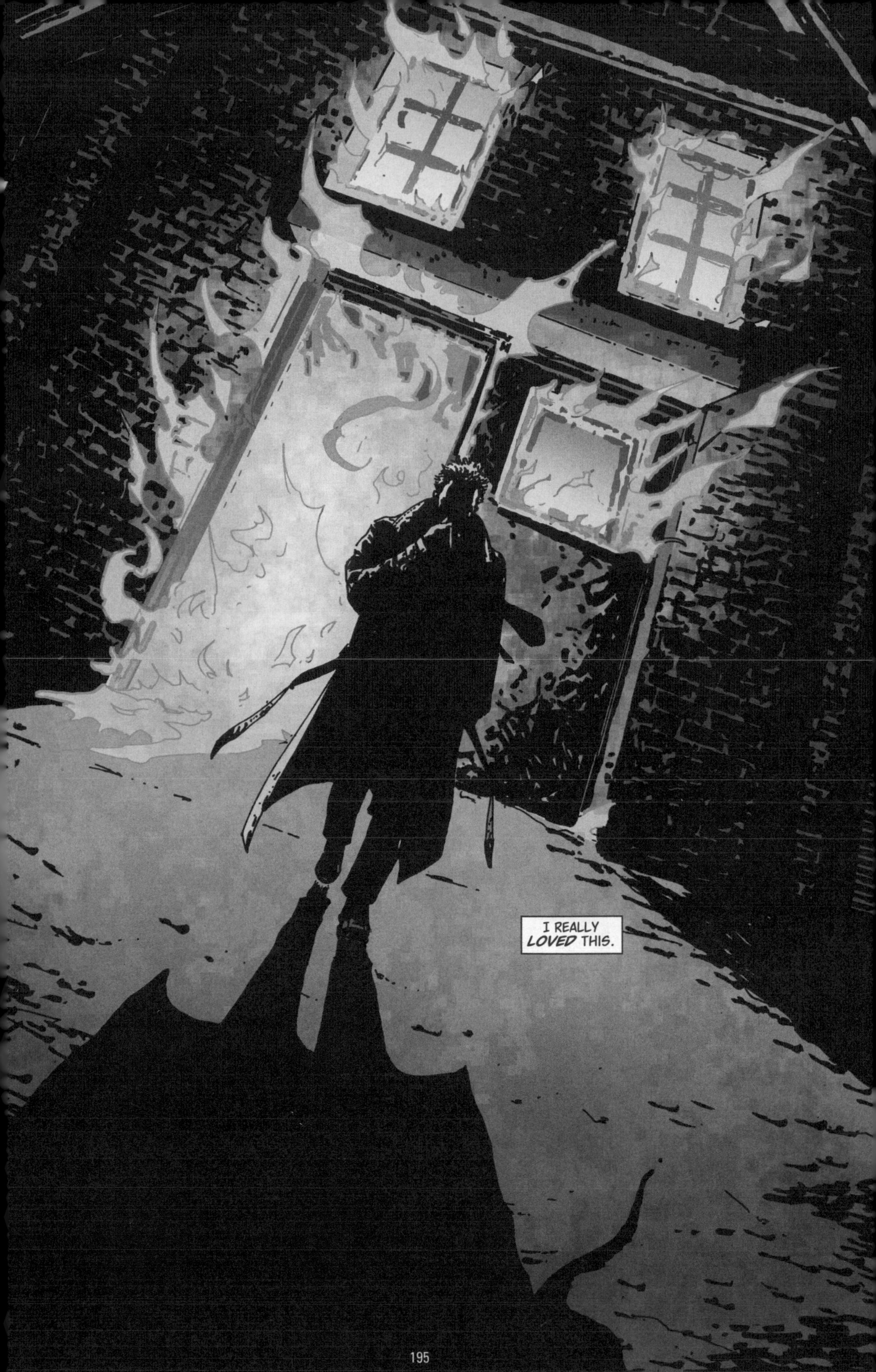
I REALLY LOVED THIS.

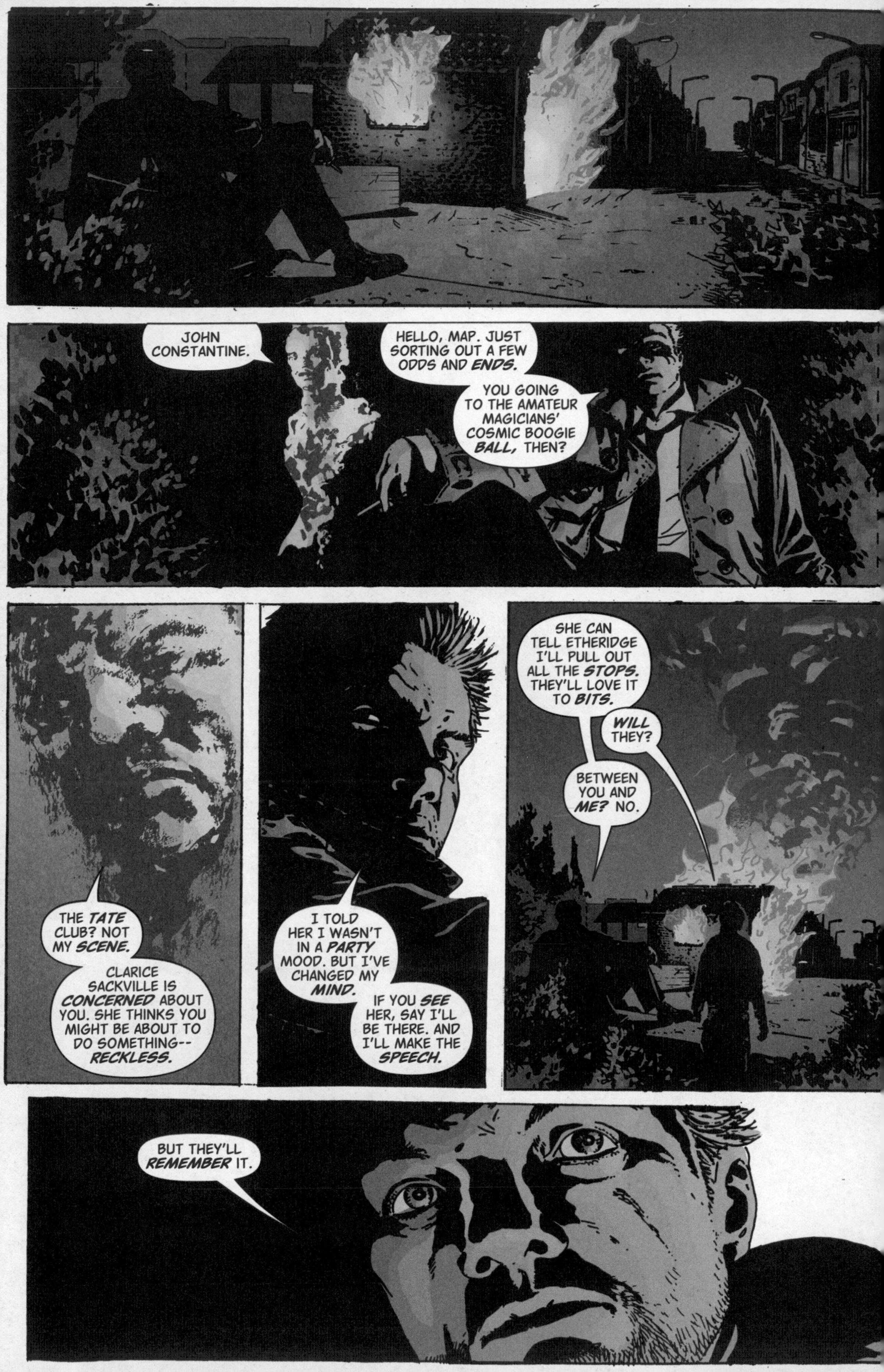
JOHN CONSTANTINE.
HELLO, MAP. JUST SORTING OUT A FEW ODDS AND ENDS.
YOU GOING TO THE AMATEUR MAGICIANS' COSMIC BOOGIE BALL, THEN?
THE TATE CLUB? NOT MY SCENE.
CLARICE SACKVILLE IS CONCERNED ABOUT YOU. SHE THINKS YOU MIGHT BE ABOUT TO DO SOMETHING-- RECKLESS.
I TOLD HER I WASN'T IN A PARTY MOOD. BUT I'VE CHANGED MY MIND.
IF YOU SEE HER, SAY I'LL BE THERE. AND I'LL MAKE THE SPEECH.
SHE CAN TELL ETHERIDGE I'LL PULL OUT ALL THE STOPS. THEY'LL LOVE IT TO BITS.
WILL THEY?
BETWEEN YOU AND ME? NO.
BUT THEY'LL REMEMBER IT.

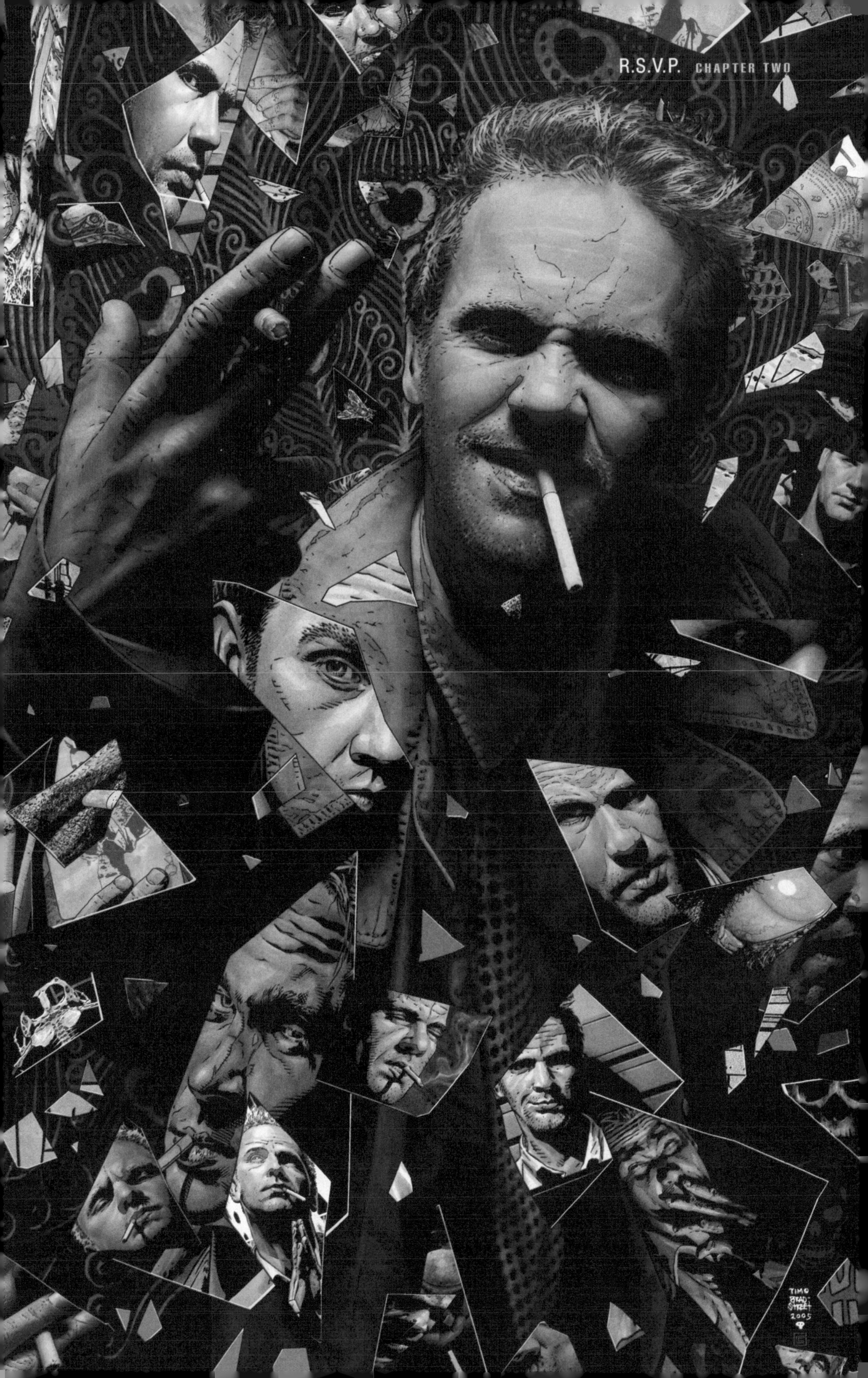
R.S.V.P. CHAPTER TWO
TIMO
2005

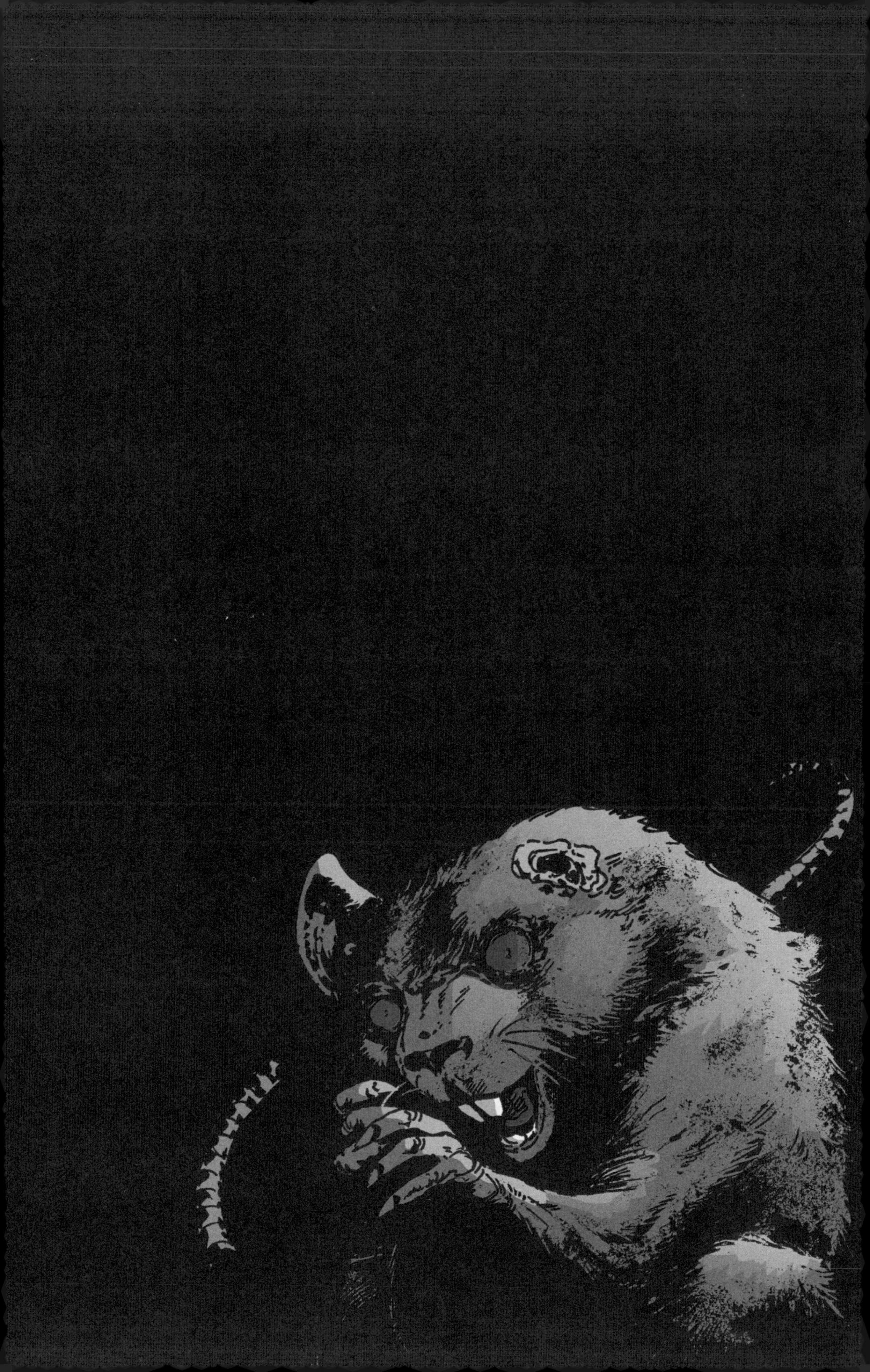

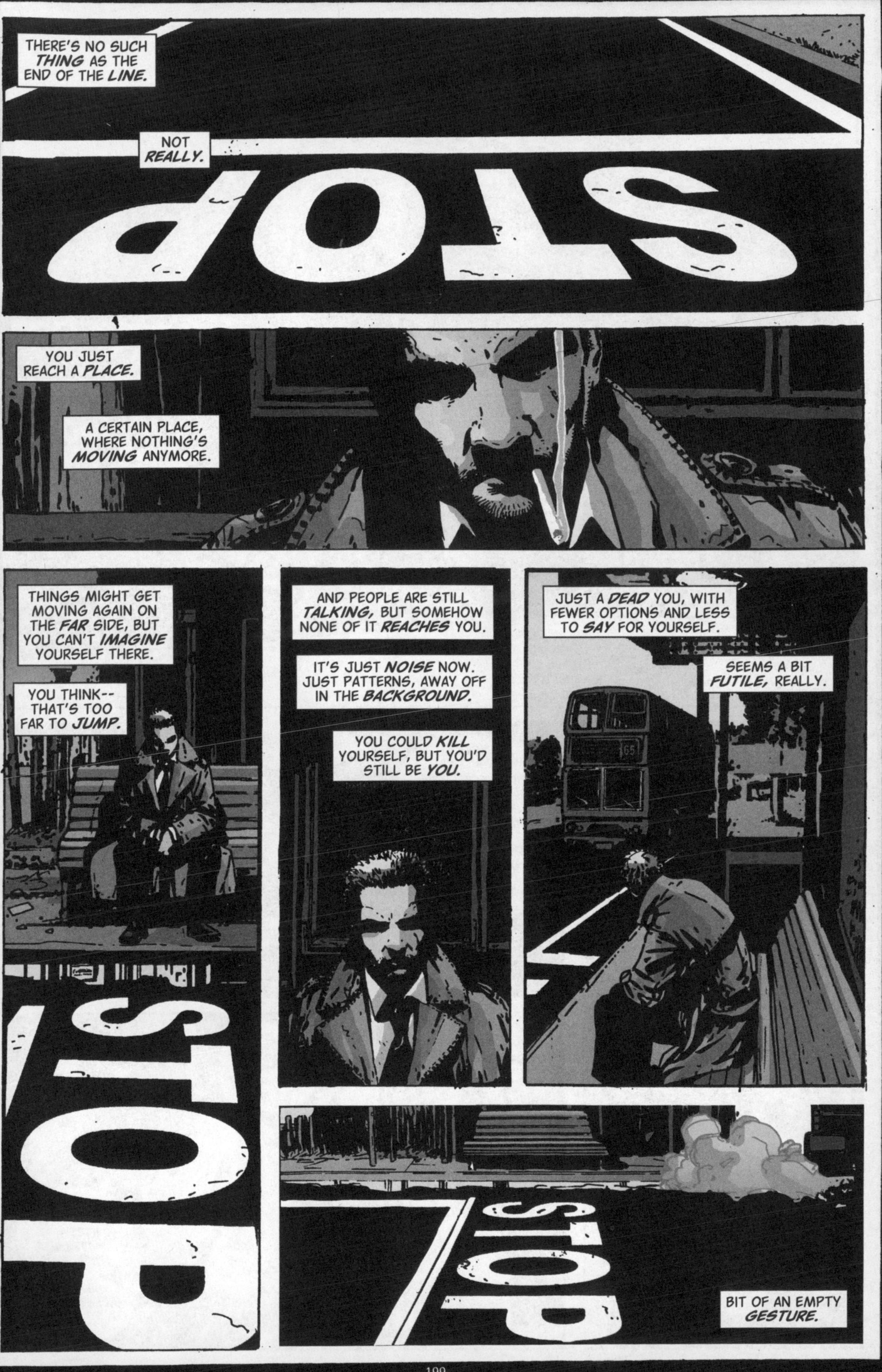
THERE'S NO SUCH THING AS THE END OF THE LINE.
NOT REALLY.
STOP
YOU JUST REACH A PLACE.
A CERTAIN PLACE, WHERE NOTHING'S MOVING ANYMORE.
THINGS MIGHT GET MOVING AGAIN ON THE FAR SIDE, BUT YOU CAN'T IMAGINE YOURSELF THERE.
YOU THINK-- THAT'S TOO FAR TO JUMP.
AND PEOPLE ARE STILL TALKING, BUT SOMEHOW NONE OF IT REACHES YOU.
IT'S JUST NOISE NOW. JUST PATTERNS, AWAY OFF IN THE BACKGROUND.
YOU COULD KILL YOURSELF, BUT YOU'D STILL BE YOU.
JUST A DEAD YOU, WITH FEWER OPTIONS AND LESS TO SAY FOR YOURSELF.
SEEMS A BIT FUTILE, REALLY.
65
STOP
STOP
BIT OF AN EMPTY GESTURE.

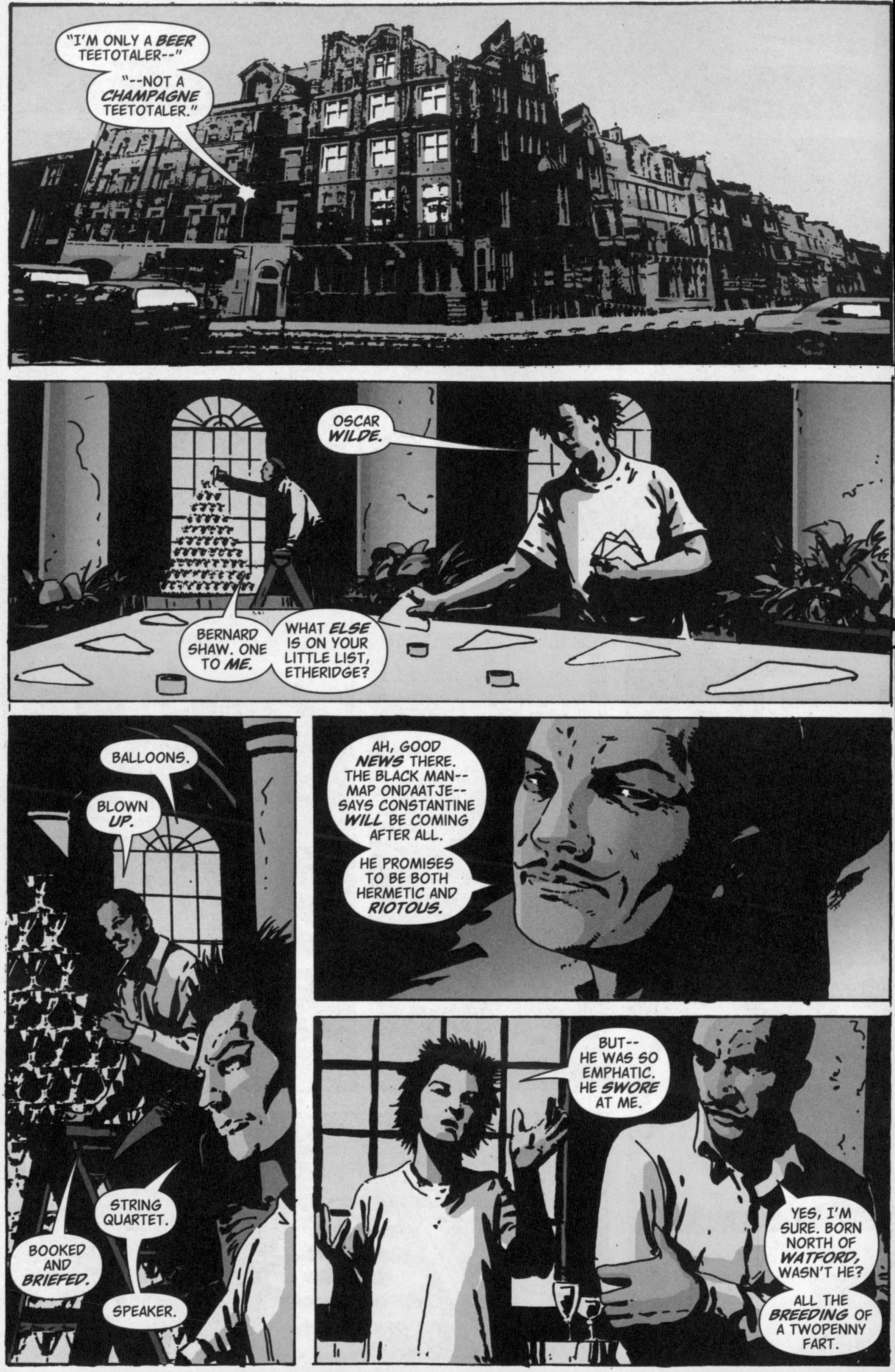
"I'M ONLY A BEER TEETOTALER--"
"--NOT A CHAMPAGNE TEETOTALER."
OSCAR WILDE.
BERNARD SHAW. ONE TO ME.
WHAT ELSE IS ON YOUR LITTLE LIST, ETHERIDGE?
BALLOONS.
BLOWN UP.
STRING QUARTET.
BOOKED AND BRIEFED.
SPEAKER.
AH, GOOD NEWS THERE. THE BLACK MAN-- MAP ONDAATJE-- SAYS CONSTANTINE WILL BE COMING AFTER ALL.
HE PROMISES TO BE BOTH HERMETIC AND RIOTOUS.
BUT-- HE WAS SO EMPHATIC. HE SWORE AT ME.
YES, I'M SURE. BORN NORTH OF WATFORD, WASN'T HE?
ALL THE BREEDING OF A TWOPENNY FART.

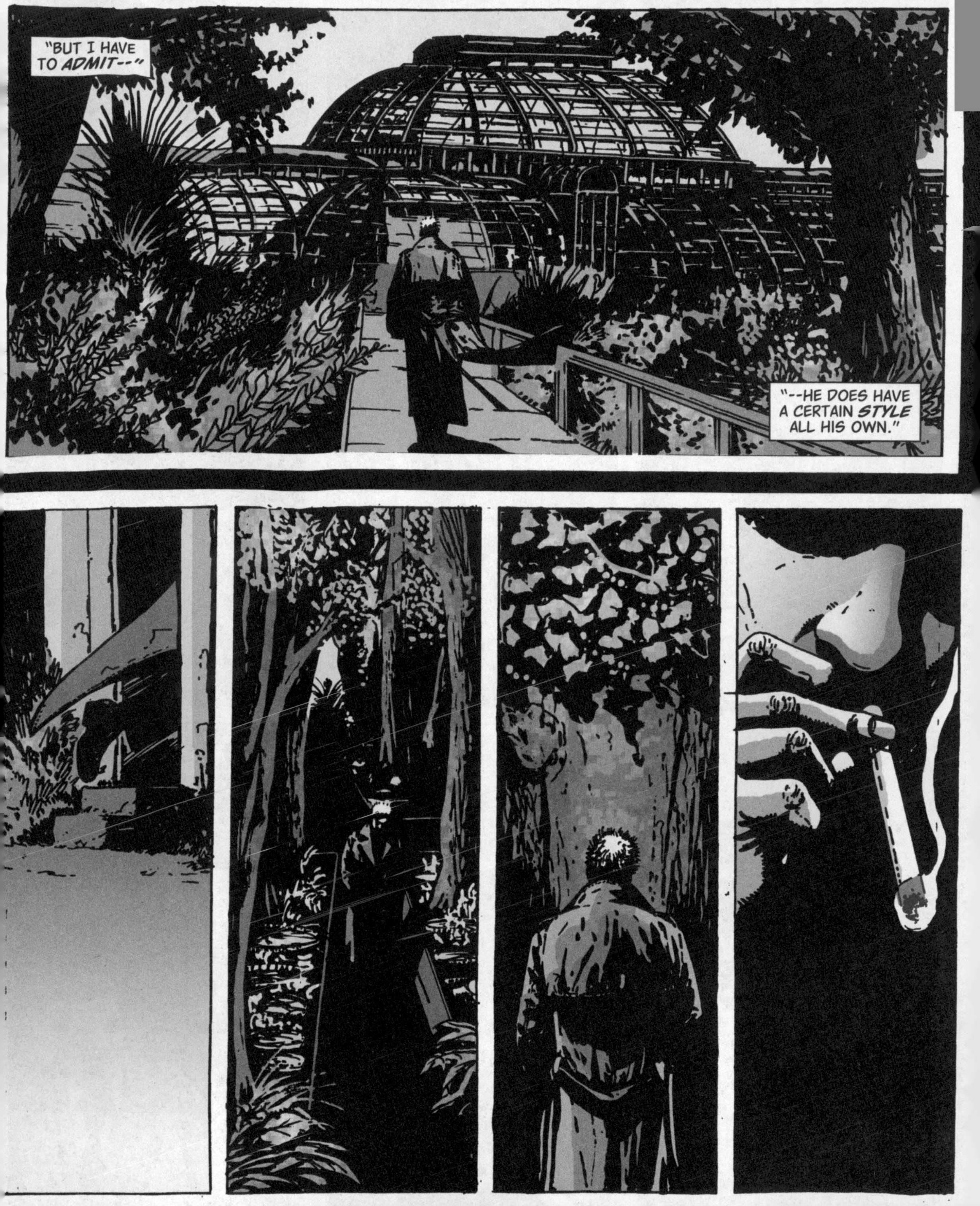
"BUT I HAVE TO ADMIT--"
"--HE DOES HAVE A CERTAIN STYLE ALL HIS OWN."

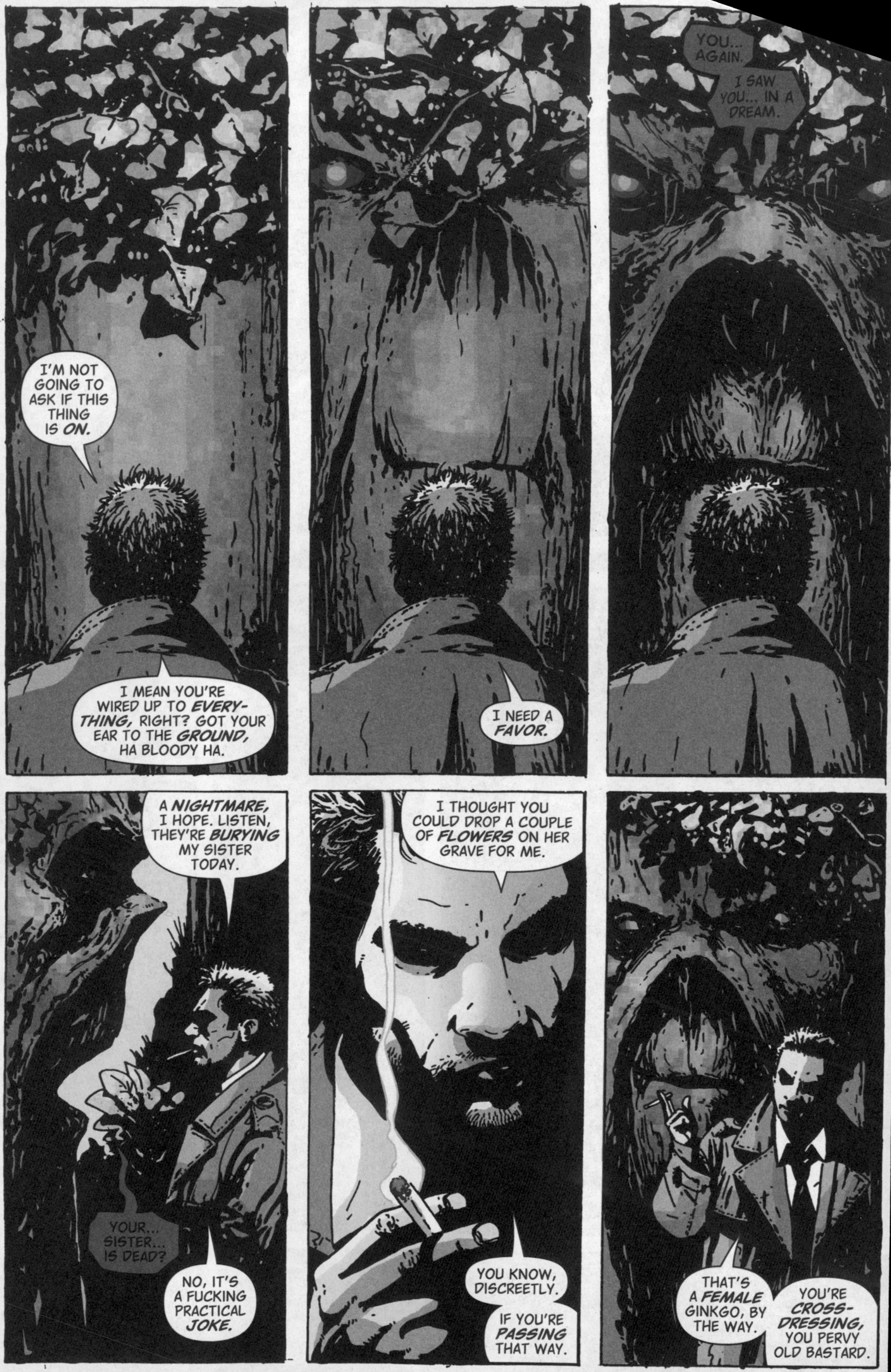
I'M NOT GOING TO ASK IF THIS THING IS ON.
I MEAN YOU'RE WIRED UP TO EVERY-THING, RIGHT? GOT YOUR EAR TO THE GROUND, HA BLOODY HA.
I NEED A FAVOR.
YOU... AGAIN.
I SAW YOU... IN A DREAM.
A NIGHTMARE, I HOPE. LISTEN, THEY'RE BURYING MY SISTER TODAY.
YOUR... SISTER... IS DEAD?
NO, IT'S A FUCKING PRACTICAL JOKE.
I THOUGHT YOU COULD DROP A COUPLE OF FLOWERS ON HER GRAVE FOR ME.
YOU KNOW, DISCREETLY.
IF YOU'RE PASSING THAT WAY.
THAT'S A FEMALE GINKGO, BY THE WAY.
YOU'RE CROSS-DRESSING, YOU PERVY OLD BASTARD.

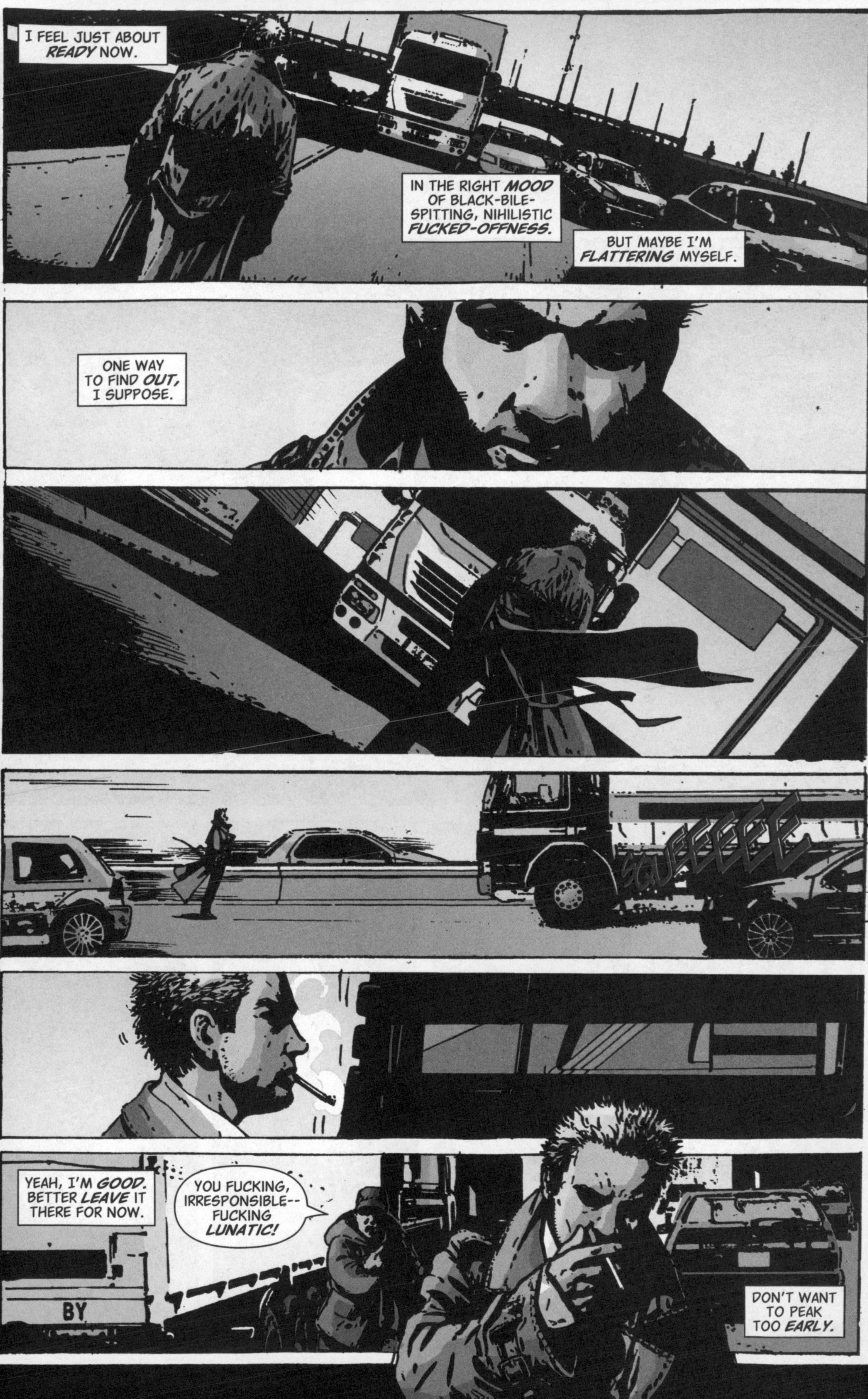
I FEEL JUST ABOUT *READY* NOW.
IN THE RIGHT *MOOD* OF BLACK-BILE-SPITTING, NIHILISTIC *FUCKED-OFFNESS.*
BUT MAYBE I'M *FLATTERING* MYSELF.
ONE WAY TO FIND *OUT,* I SUPPOSE.
SQUEEEEEE
YEAH, I'M *GOOD.* BETTER *LEAVE* IT THERE FOR NOW.
YOU FUCKING, IRRESPONSIBLE-- FUCKING *LUNATIC!*
DON'T WANT TO PEAK TOO *EARLY.*

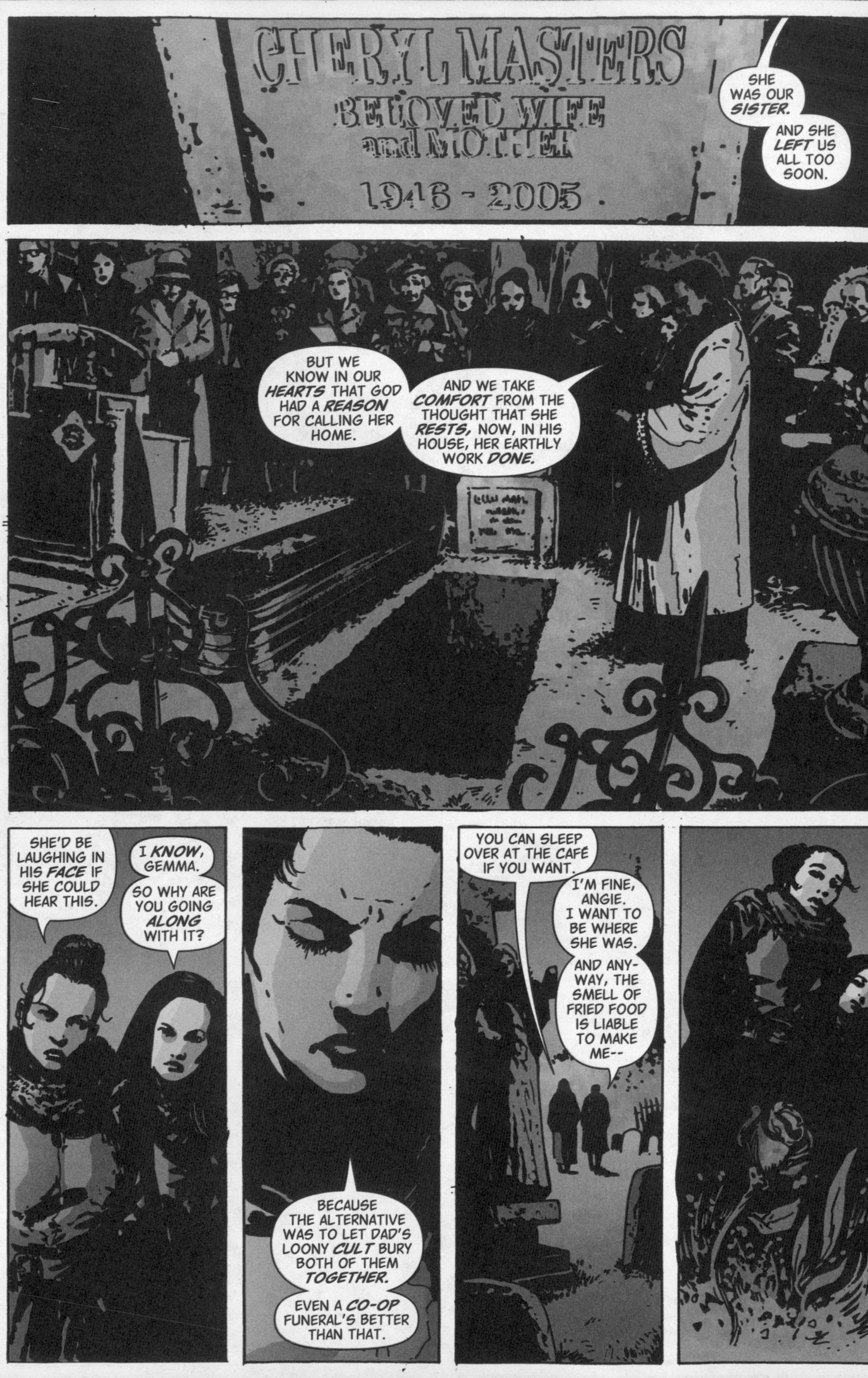
CHERYL MASTERS
BELOVED WIFE and MOTHER
1946 - 2005
SHE WAS OUR *SISTER.*
AND SHE *LEFT* US ALL TOO SOON.
BUT WE KNOW IN OUR *HEARTS* THAT GOD HAD A *REASON* FOR CALLING HER HOME.
AND WE TAKE *COMFORT* FROM THE THOUGHT THAT SHE *RESTS,* NOW, IN HIS HOUSE, HER EARTHLY WORK *DONE.*
SHE'D BE LAUGHING IN HIS *FACE* IF SHE COULD HEAR THIS.
I *KNOW,* GEMMA.
SO WHY ARE YOU GOING *ALONG* WITH IT?
BECAUSE THE ALTERNATIVE WAS TO LET DAD'S LOONY *CULT* BURY BOTH OF THEM *TOGETHER.*
EVEN A *CO-OP* FUNERAL'S BETTER THAN THAT.
YOU CAN SLEEP OVER AT THE CAFÉ IF YOU WANT.
I'M FINE, ANGIE. I WANT TO BE WHERE SHE WAS.
AND ANY-WAY, THE SMELL OF FRIED FOOD IS LIABLE TO MAKE ME--

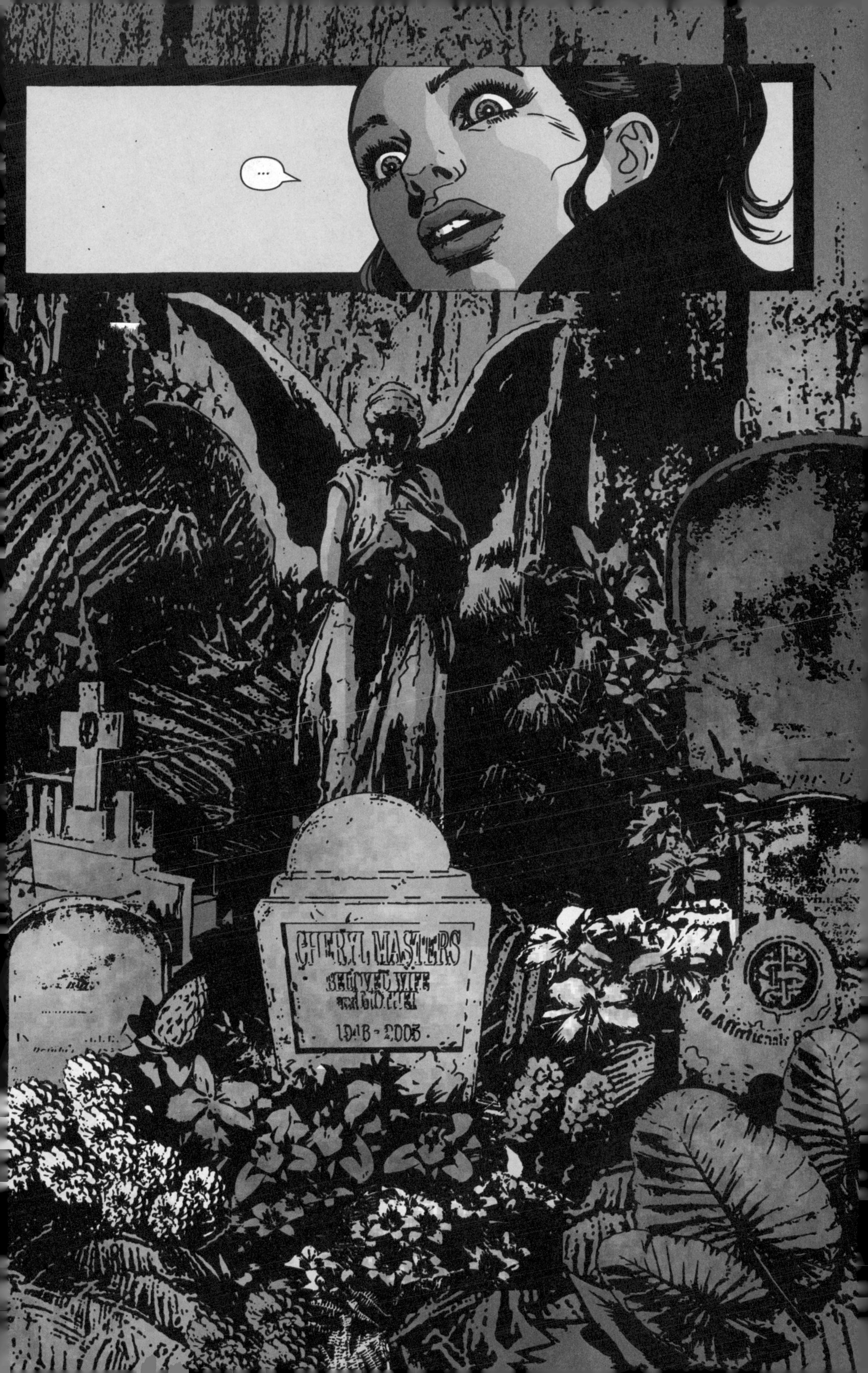
...
CHERYL MASTERS
BELOVED WIFE

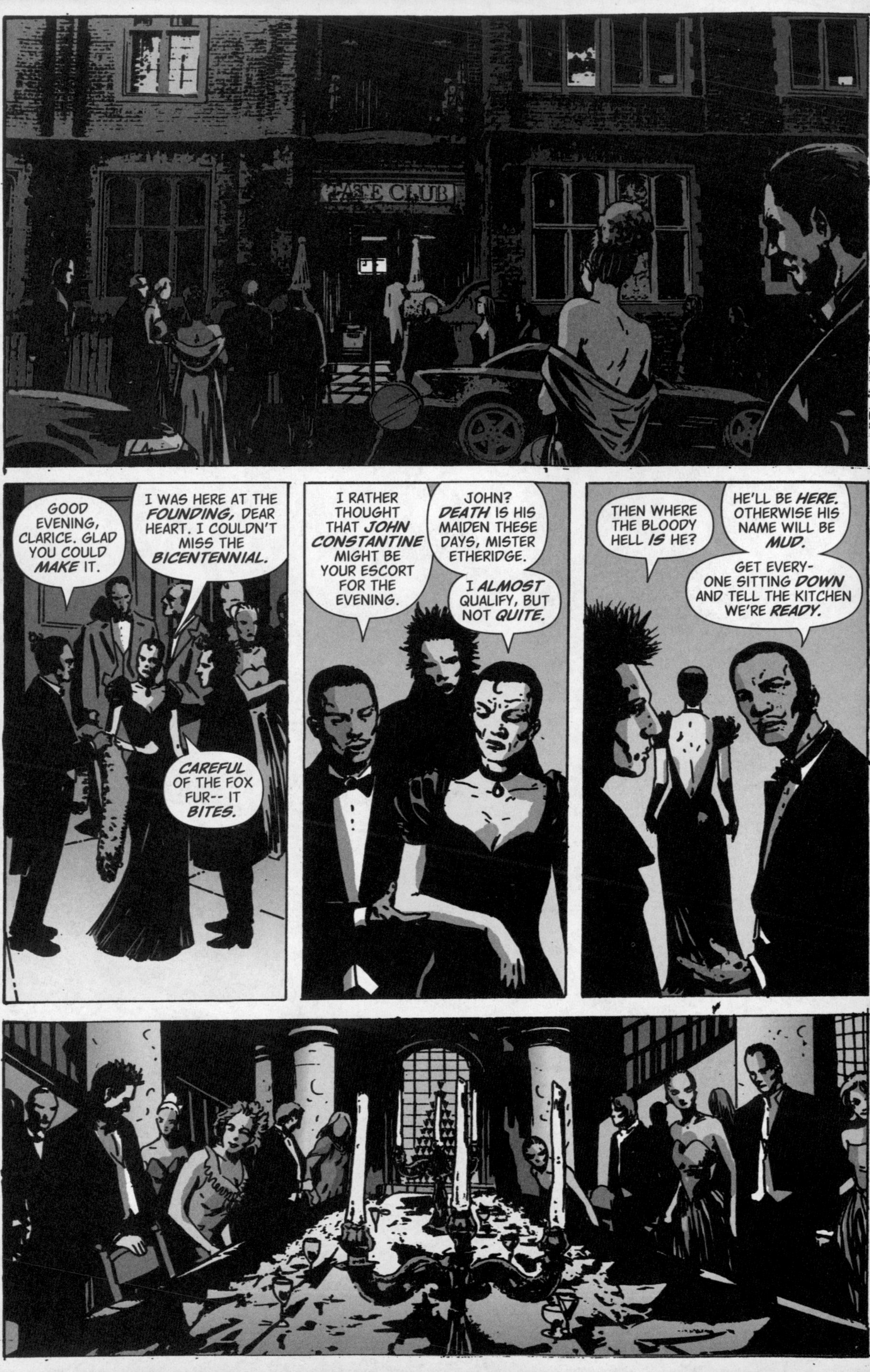

GATE CLUB
GOOD EVENING, CLARICE. GLAD YOU COULD MAKE IT.
I WAS HERE AT THE FOUNDING, DEAR HEART. I COULDN'T MISS THE BICENTENNIAL.
CAREFUL OF THE FOX FUR-- IT BITES.
I RATHER THOUGHT THAT JOHN CONSTANTINE MIGHT BE YOUR ESCORT FOR THE EVENING.
JOHN? DEATH IS HIS MAIDEN THESE DAYS, MISTER ETHERIDGE.
I ALMOST QUALIFY, BUT NOT QUITE.
THEN WHERE THE BLOODY HELL IS HE?
HE'LL BE HERE. OTHERWISE HIS NAME WILL BE MUD.
GET EVERY-ONE SITTING DOWN AND TELL THE KITCHEN WE'RE READY.

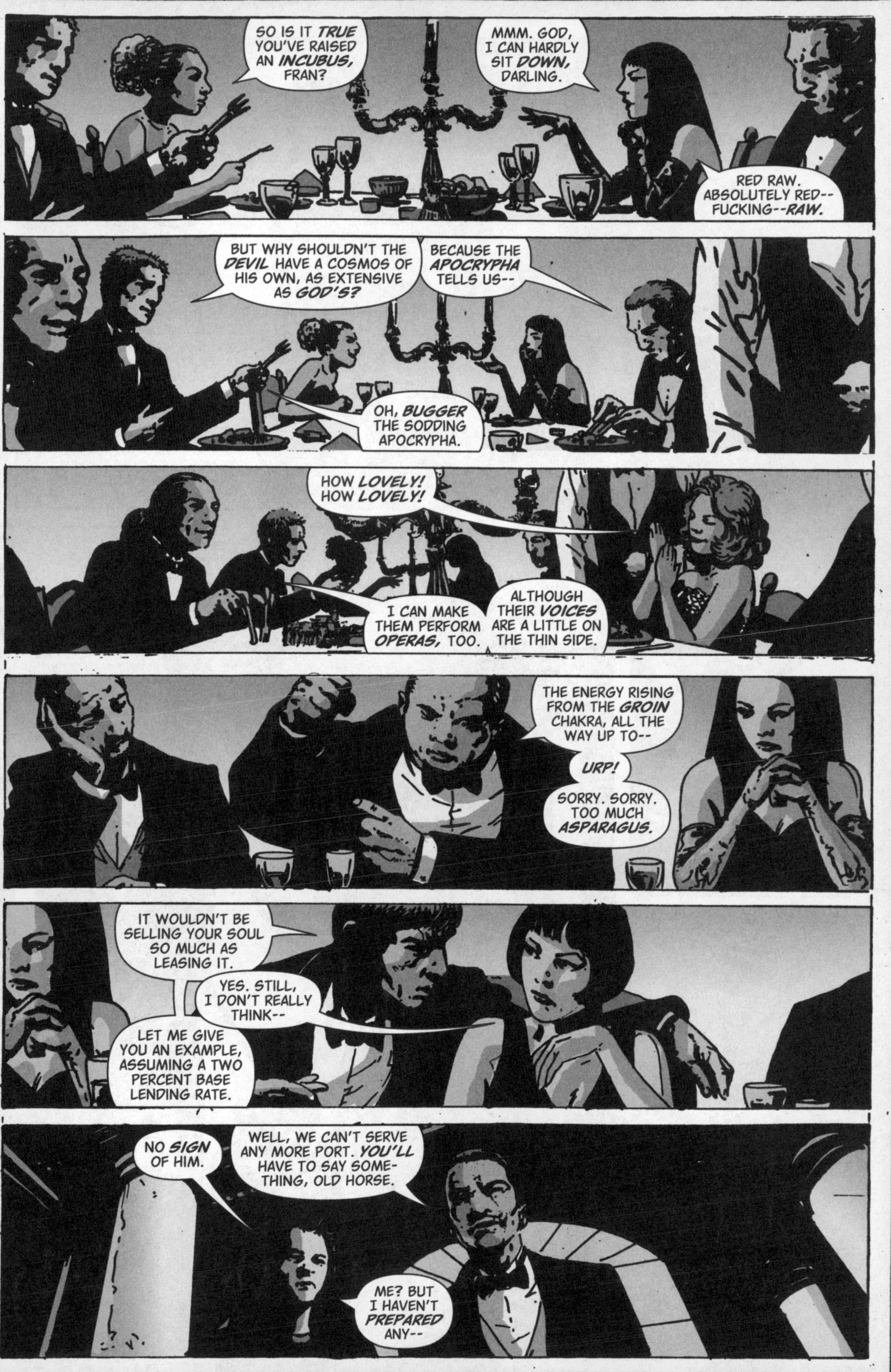
SO IS IT TRUE YOU'VE RAISED AN INCUBUS, FRAN?
MMM. GOD, I CAN HARDLY SIT DOWN, DARLING.
RED RAW. ABSOLUTELY RED--FUCKING--RAW.
BUT WHY SHOULDN'T THE DEVIL HAVE A COSMOS OF HIS OWN, AS EXTENSIVE AS GOD'S?
BECAUSE THE APOCRYPHA TELLS US--
OH, BUGGER THE SODDING APOCRYPHA.
HOW LOVELY! HOW LOVELY!
I CAN MAKE THEM PERFORM OPERAS, TOO.
ALTHOUGH THEIR VOICES ARE A LITTLE ON THE THIN SIDE.
THE ENERGY RISING FROM THE GROIN CHAKRA, ALL THE WAY UP TO--
URP!
SORRY. SORRY. TOO MUCH ASPARAGUS.
IT WOULDN'T BE SELLING YOUR SOUL SO MUCH AS LEASING IT.
YES. STILL, I DON'T REALLY THINK--
LET ME GIVE YOU AN EXAMPLE, ASSUMING A TWO PERCENT BASE LENDING RATE.
NO SIGN OF HIM.
WELL, WE CAN'T SERVE ANY MORE PORT. YOU'LL HAVE TO SAY SOME-THING, OLD HORSE.
ME? BUT I HAVEN'T PREPARED ANY--

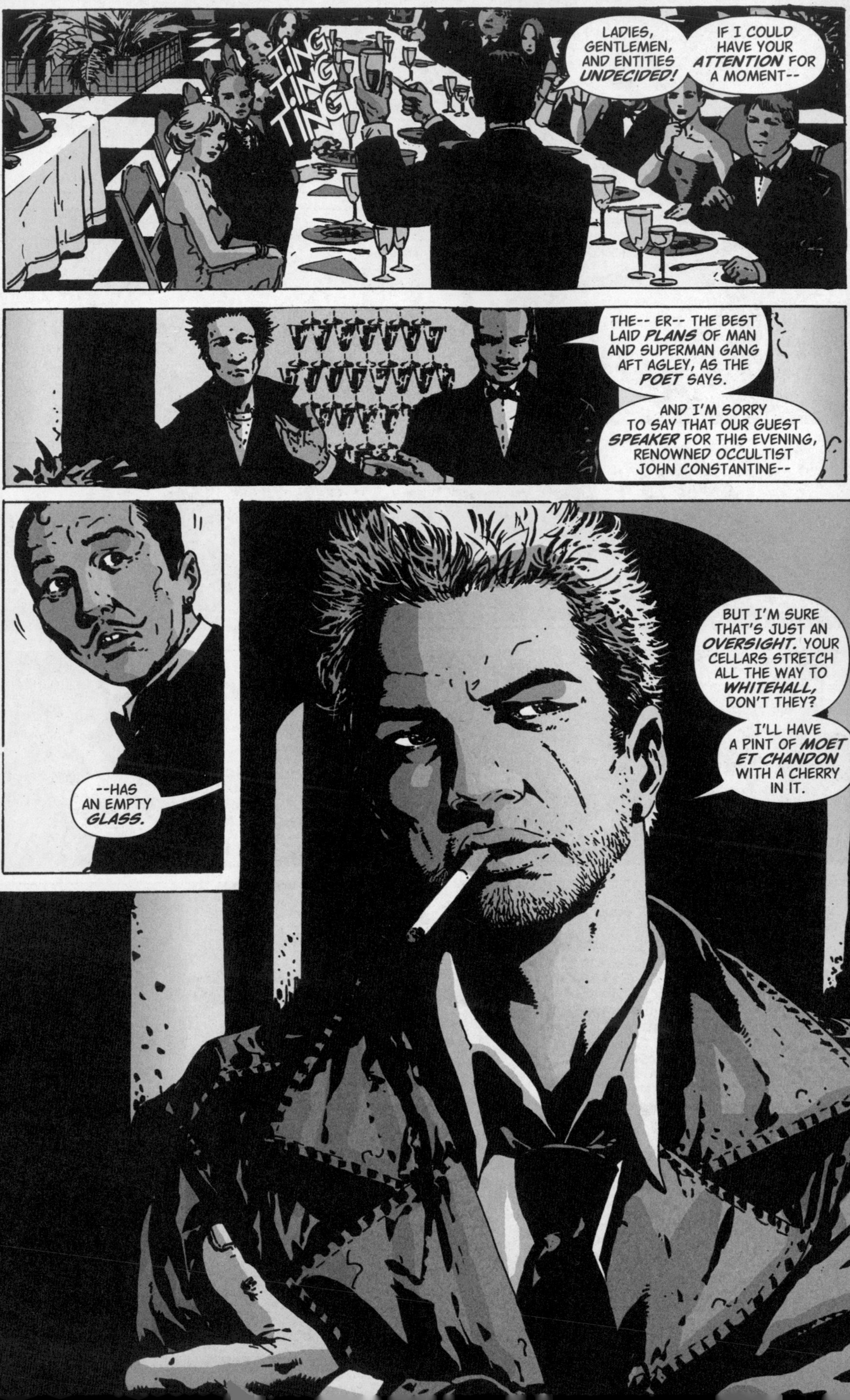

TING! TING! TING!
LADIES, GENTLEMEN, AND ENTITIES UNDECIDED!
IF I COULD HAVE YOUR ATTENTION FOR A MOMENT--
THE-- ER-- THE BEST LAID PLANS OF MAN AND SUPERMAN GANG AFT AGLEY, AS THE POET SAYS.
AND I'M SORRY TO SAY THAT OUR GUEST SPEAKER FOR THIS EVENING, RENOWNED OCCULTIST JOHN CONSTANTINE--
--HAS AN EMPTY GLASS.
BUT I'M SURE THAT'S JUST AN OVERSIGHT. YOUR CELLARS STRETCH ALL THE WAY TO WHITEHALL, DON'T THEY?
I'LL HAVE A PINT OF MOET ET CHANDON WITH A CHERRY IN IT.

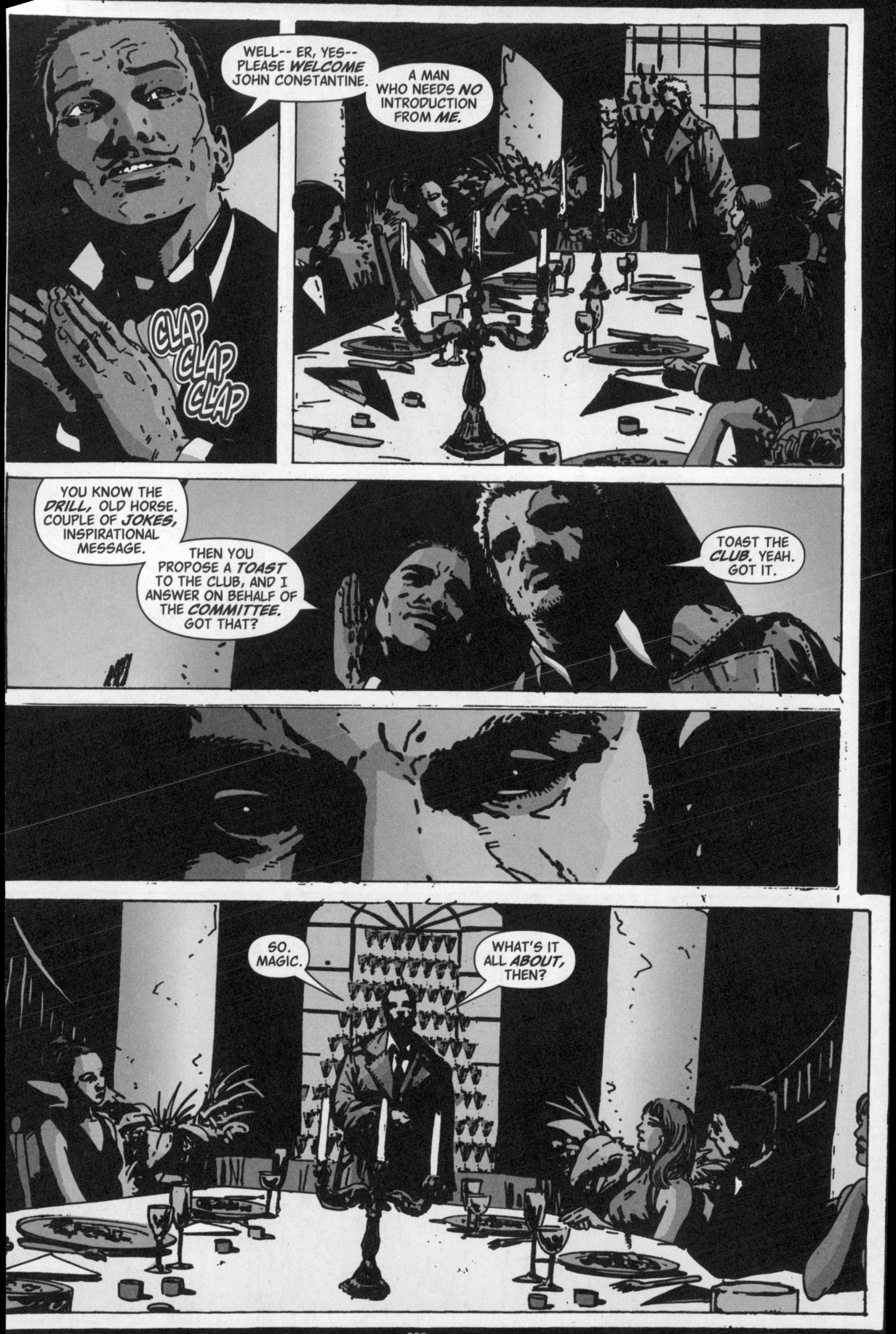
WELL-- ER, YES-- PLEASE WELCOME JOHN CONSTANTINE.
A MAN WHO NEEDS NO INTRODUCTION FROM ME.
CLAP CLAP CLAP
YOU KNOW THE DRILL, OLD HORSE. COUPLE OF JOKES, INSPIRATIONAL MESSAGE.
THEN YOU PROPOSE A TOAST TO THE CLUB, AND I ANSWER ON BEHALF OF THE COMMITTEE. GOT THAT?
TOAST THE CLUB. YEAH. GOT IT.
SO. MAGIC.
WHAT'S IT ALL ABOUT, THEN?

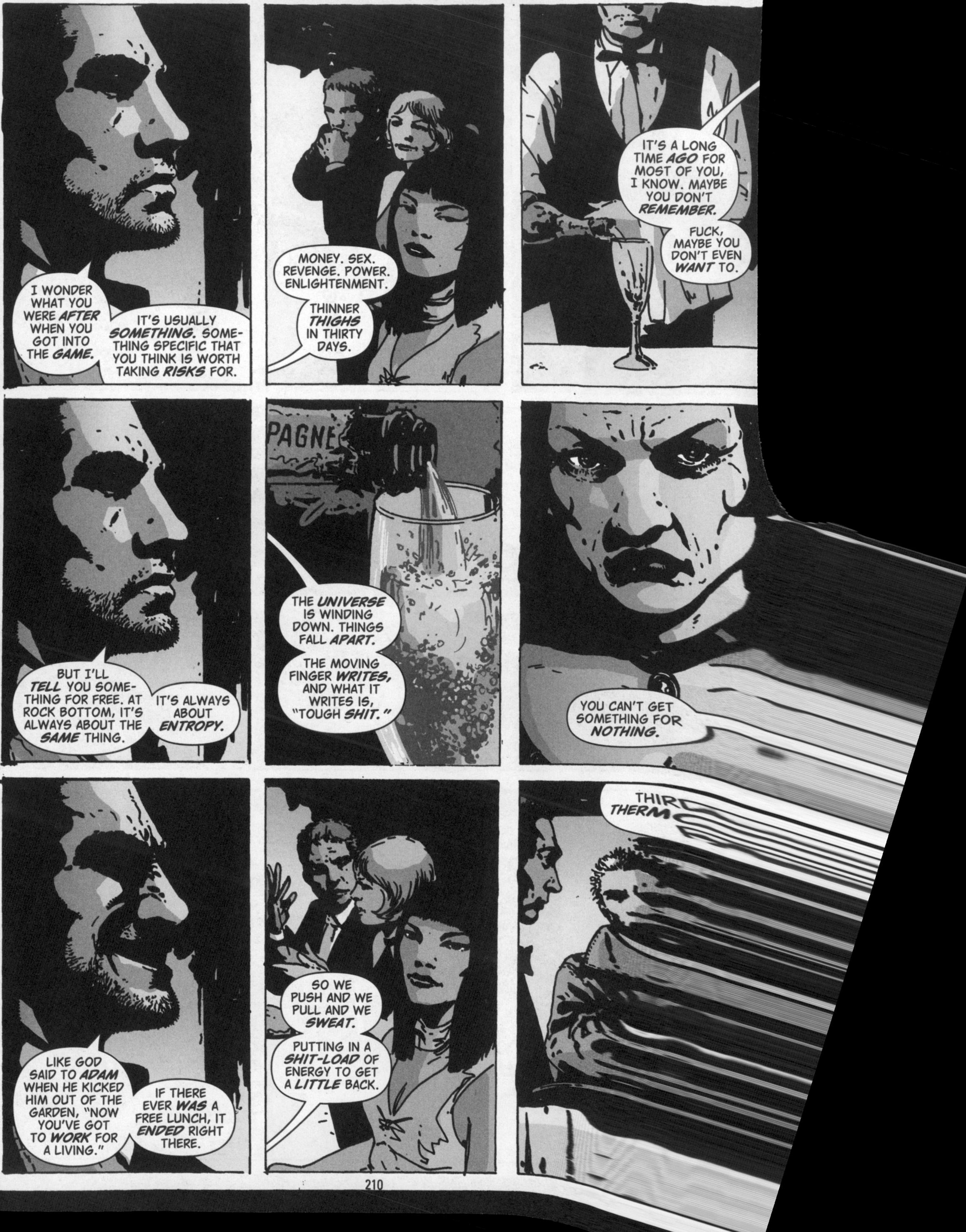
I WONDER WHAT YOU WERE AFTER WHEN YOU GOT INTO THE GAME.
IT'S USUALLY SOMETHING. SOMETHING SPECIFIC THAT YOU THINK IS WORTH TAKING RISKS FOR.
MONEY. SEX. REVENGE. POWER. ENLIGHTENMENT.
THINNER THIGHS IN THIRTY DAYS.
IT'S A LONG TIME AGO FOR MOST OF YOU, I KNOW. MAYBE YOU DON'T REMEMBER.
FUCK, MAYBE YOU DON'T EVEN WANT TO.
BUT I'LL TELL YOU SOMETHING FOR FREE. AT ROCK BOTTOM, IT'S ALWAYS ABOUT THE SAME THING.
IT'S ALWAYS ABOUT ENTROPY.
PAGNE
THE UNIVERSE IS WINDING DOWN. THINGS FALL APART.
THE MOVING FINGER WRITES, AND WHAT IT WRITES IS, "TOUGH SHIT."
YOU CAN'T GET SOMETHING FOR NOTHING.
LIKE GOD SAID TO ADAM WHEN HE KICKED HIM OUT OF THE GARDEN, "NOW YOU'VE GOT TO WORK FOR A LIVING."
IF THERE EVER WAS A FREE LUNCH, IT ENDED RIGHT THERE.
SO WE PUSH AND WE PULL AND WE SWEAT.
PUTTING IN A SHIT-LOAD OF ENERGY TO GET A LITTLE BACK.

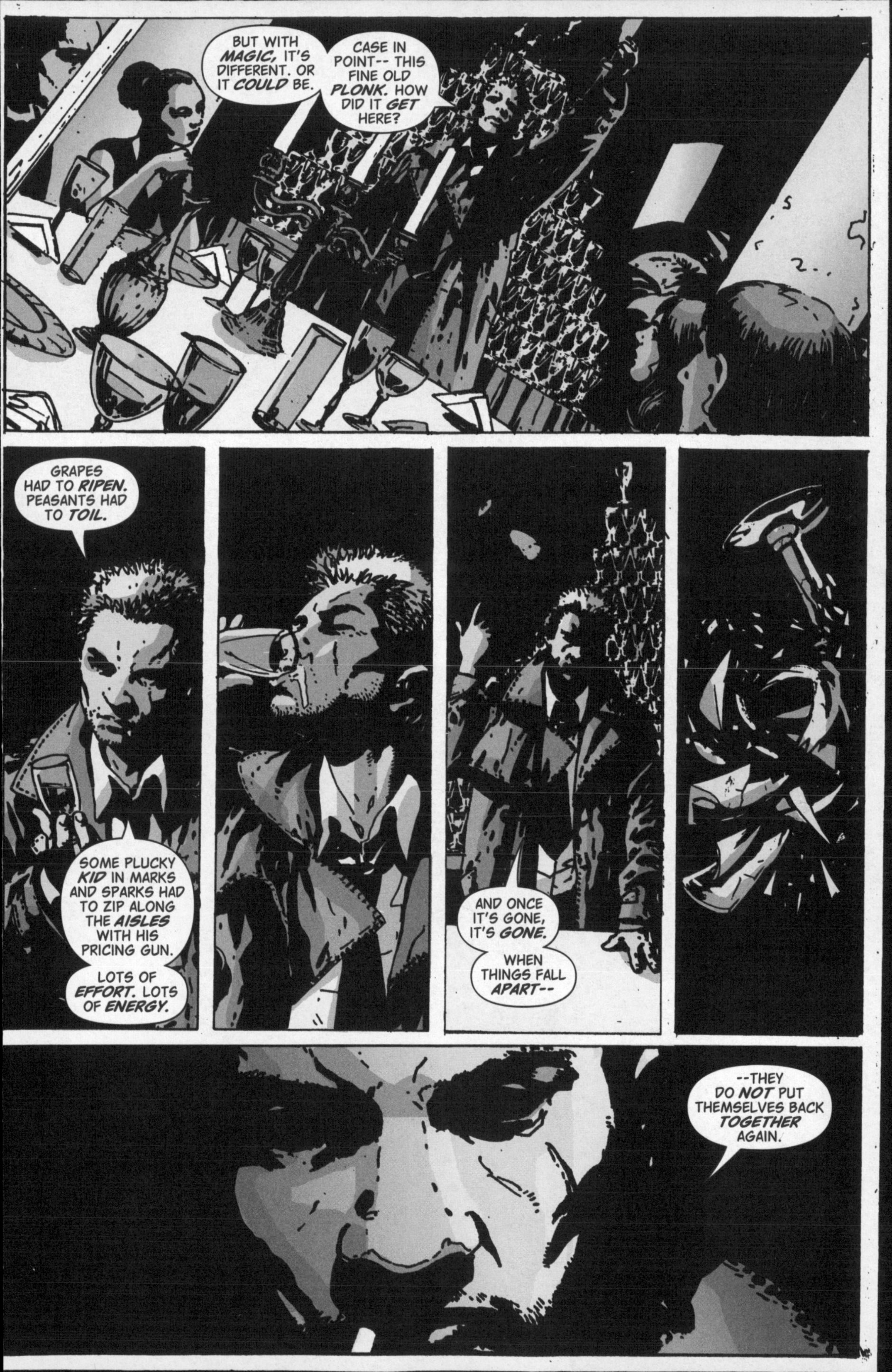
BUT WITH MAGIC, IT'S DIFFERENT. OR IT COULD BE.
CASE IN POINT-- THIS FINE OLD PLONK. HOW DID IT GET HERE?
GRAPES HAD TO RIPEN. PEASANTS HAD TO TOIL.
SOME PLUCKY KID IN MARKS AND SPARKS HAD TO ZIP ALONG THE AISLES WITH HIS PRICING GUN.
LOTS OF EFFORT. LOTS OF ENERGY.
AND ONCE IT'S GONE, IT'S GONE.
WHEN THINGS FALL APART--
--THEY DO NOT PUT THEMSELVES BACK TOGETHER AGAIN.

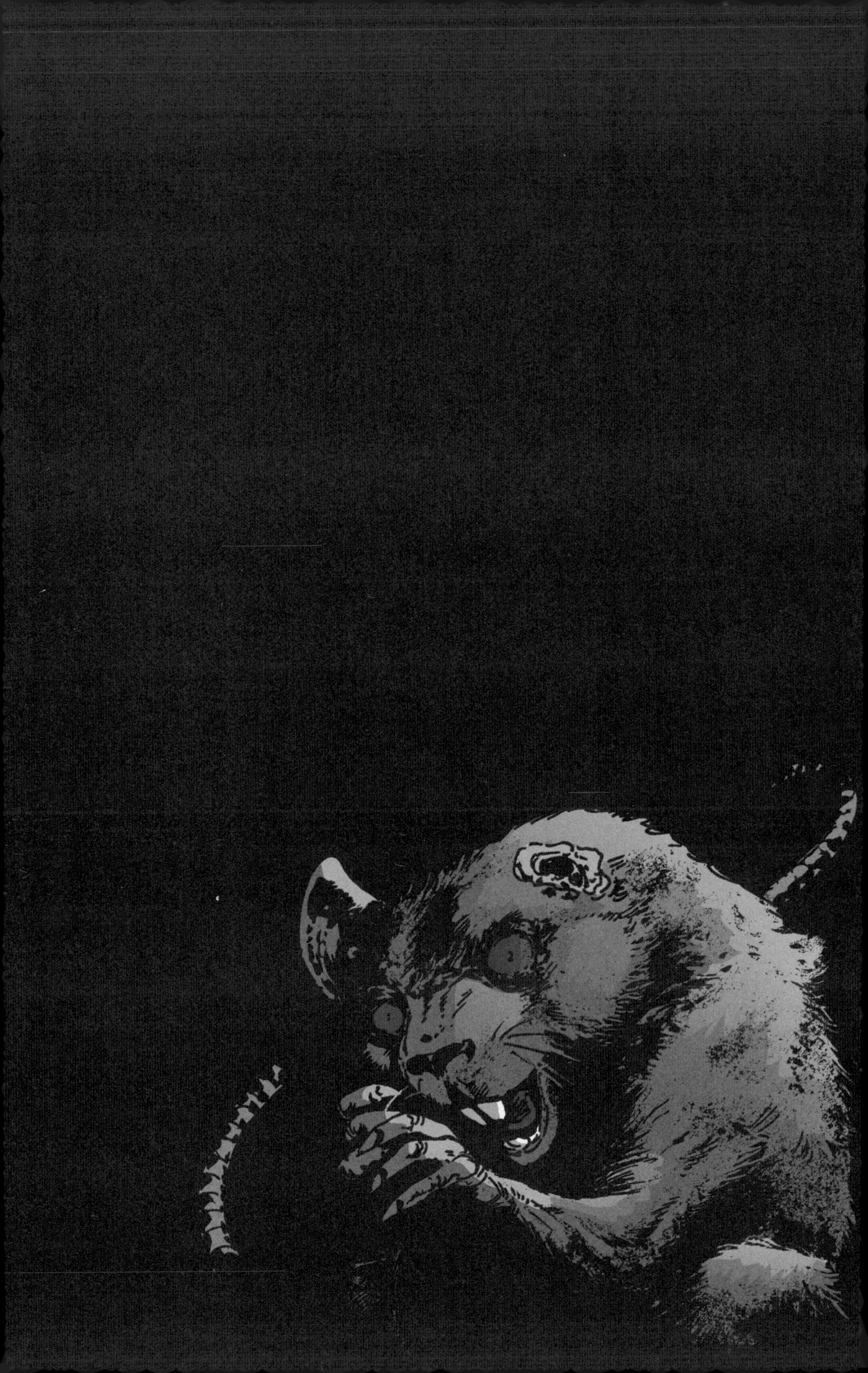

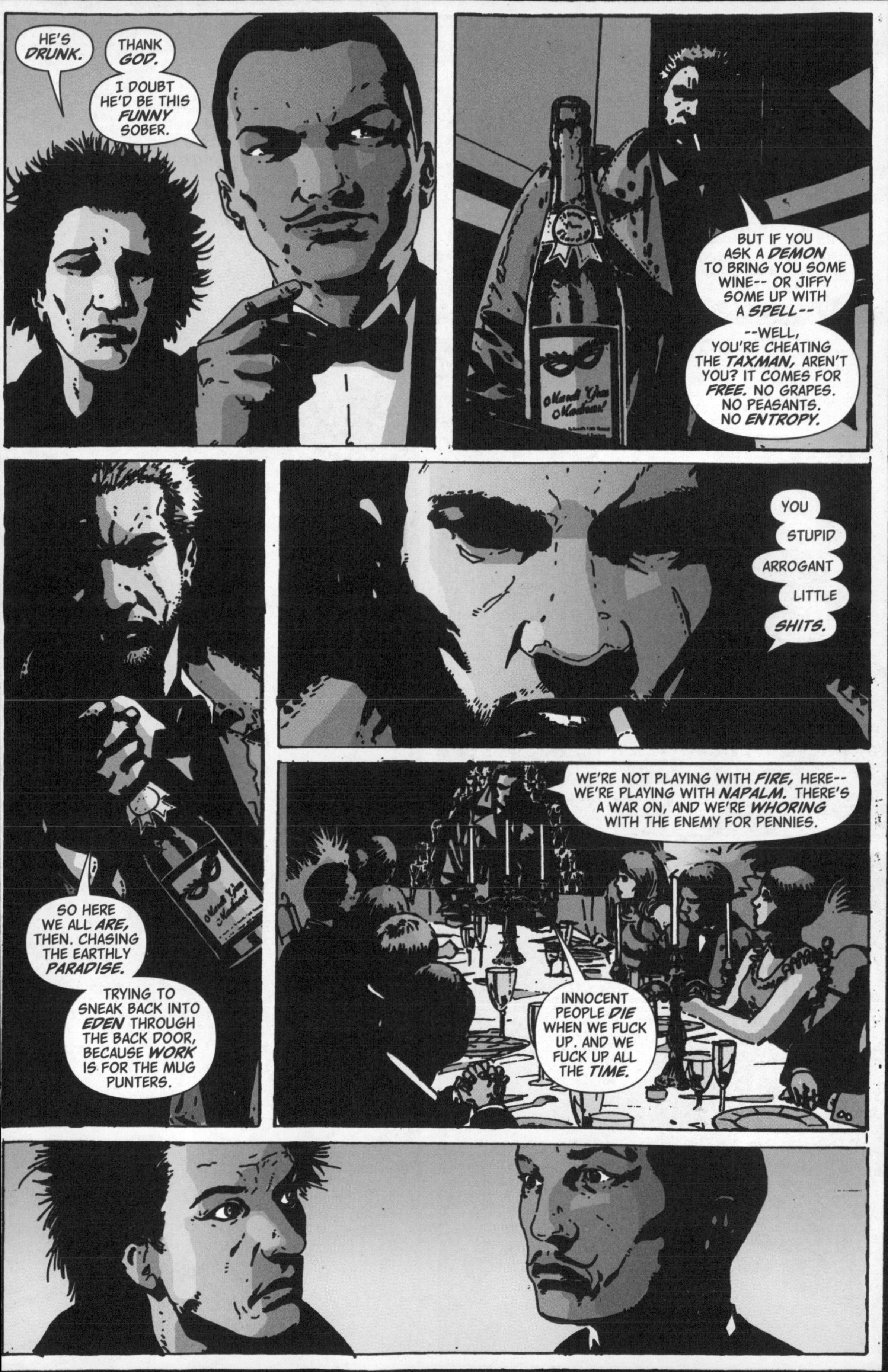
HE'S DRUNK.
THANK GOD.
I DOUBT HE'D BE THIS FUNNY SOBER.
BUT IF YOU ASK A DEMON TO BRING YOU SOME WINE-- OR JIFFY SOME UP WITH A SPELL--
--WELL, YOU'RE CHEATING THE TAXMAN, AREN'T YOU? IT COMES FOR FREE. NO GRAPES. NO PEASANTS. NO ENTROPY.
SO HERE WE ALL ARE, THEN. CHASING THE EARTHLY PARADISE.
TRYING TO SNEAK BACK INTO EDEN THROUGH THE BACK DOOR, BECAUSE WORK IS FOR THE MUG PUNTERS.
YOU
STUPID
ARROGANT
LITTLE
SHITS.
WE'RE NOT PLAYING WITH FIRE, HERE-- WE'RE PLAYING WITH NAPALM. THERE'S A WAR ON, AND WE'RE WHORING WITH THE ENEMY FOR PENNIES.
INNOCENT PEOPLE DIE WHEN WE FUCK UP. AND WE FUCK UP ALL THE TIME.

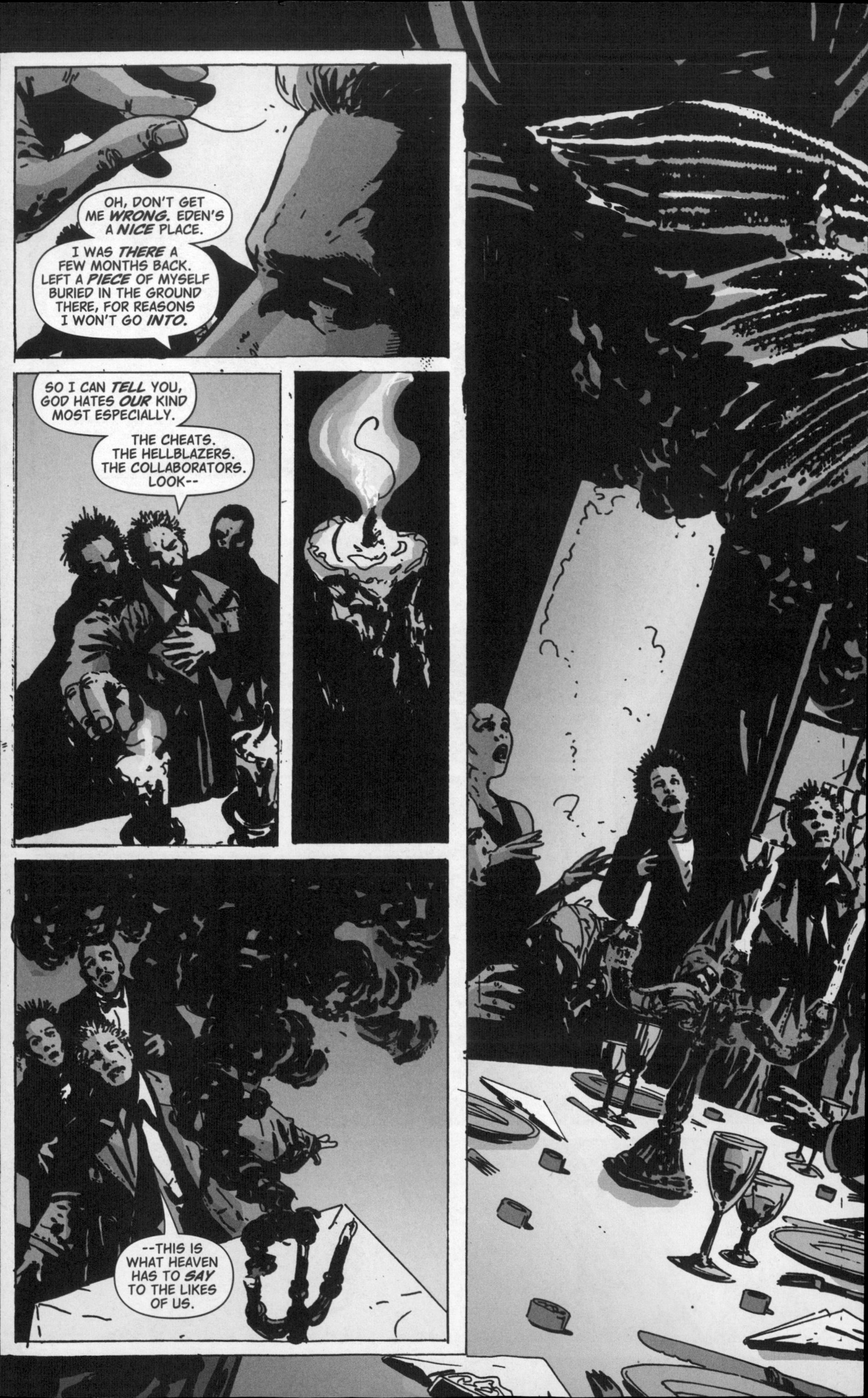

OH, DON'T GET ME WRONG. EDEN'S A NICE PLACE.
I WAS THERE A FEW MONTHS BACK. LEFT A PIECE OF MYSELF BURIED IN THE GROUND THERE, FOR REASONS I WON'T GO INTO.
SO I CAN TELL YOU, GOD HATES OUR KIND MOST ESPECIALLY.
THE CHEATS. THE HELLBLAZERS. THE COLLABORATORS. LOOK--
--THIS IS WHAT HEAVEN HAS TO SAY TO THE LIKES OF US.

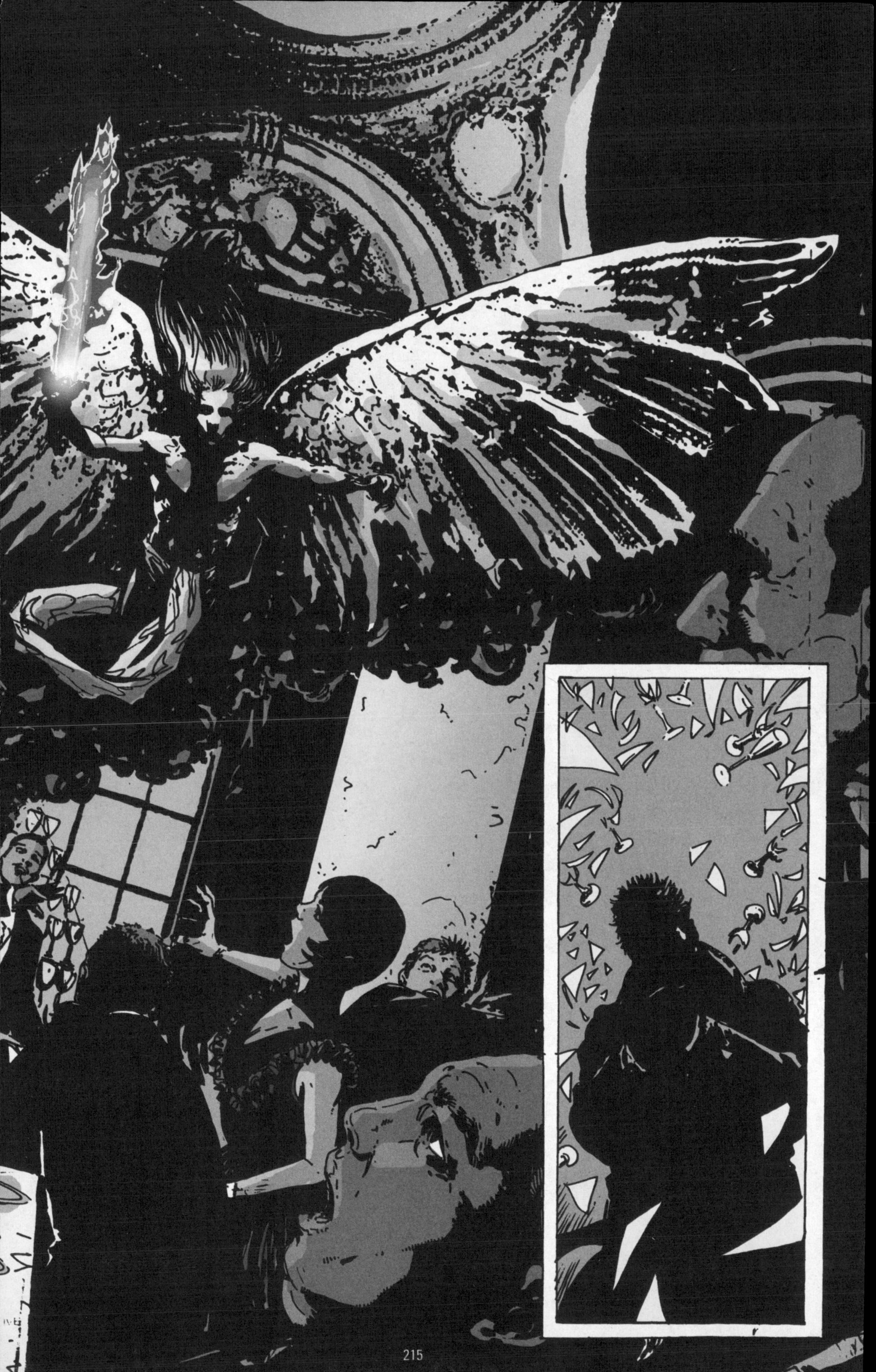

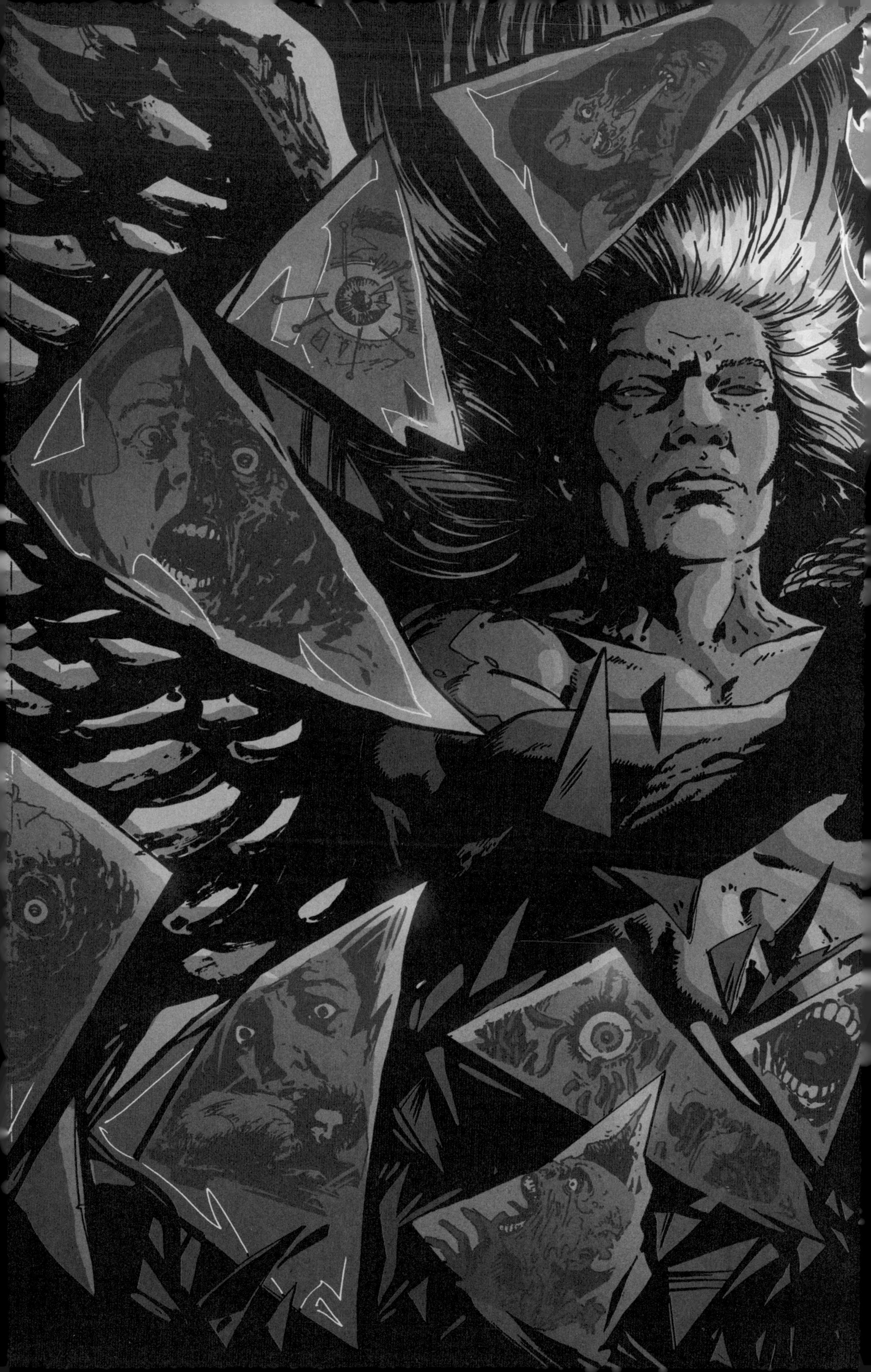

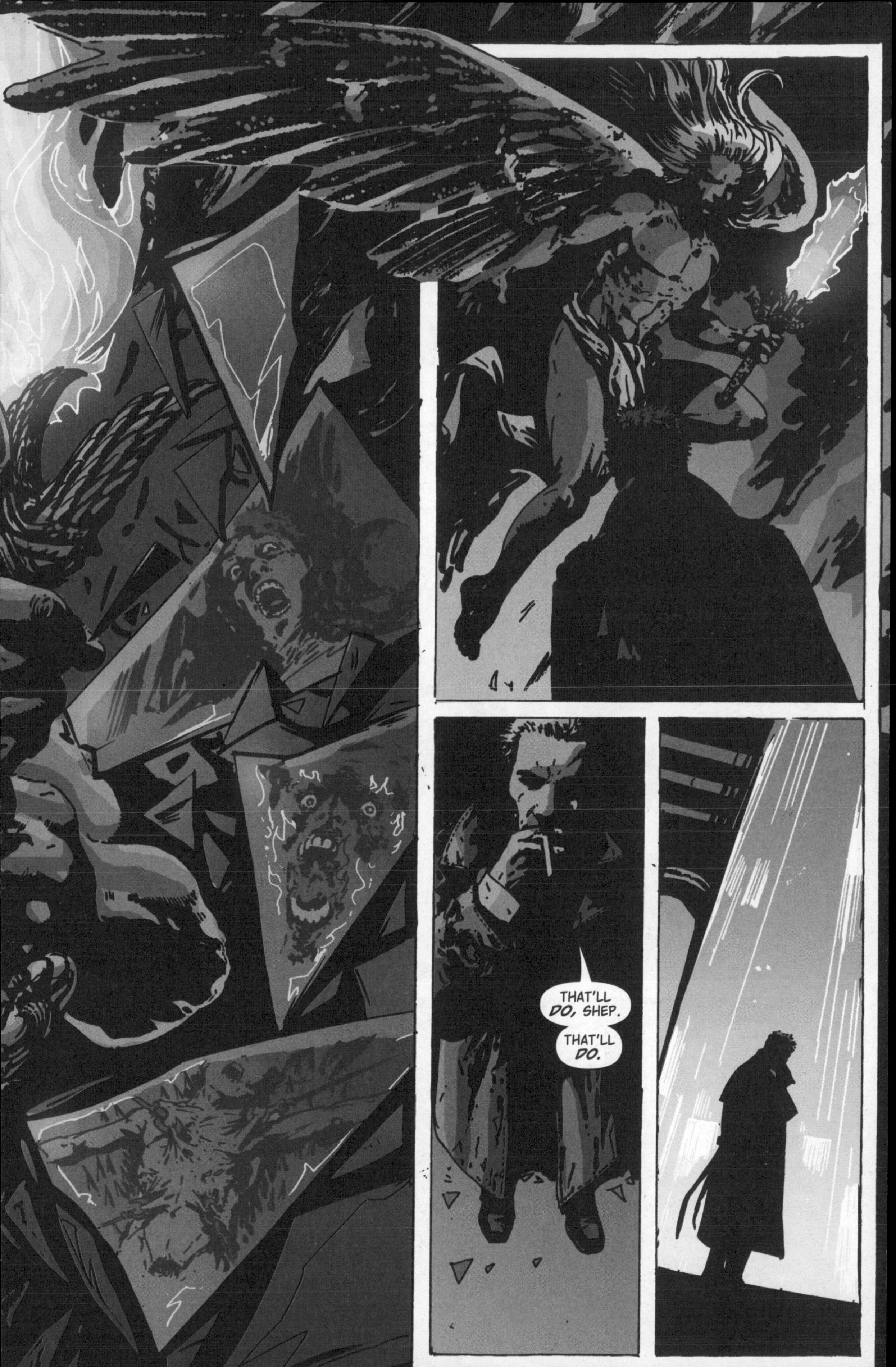
THAT'LL *DO*, SHEP.
THAT'LL *DO*.

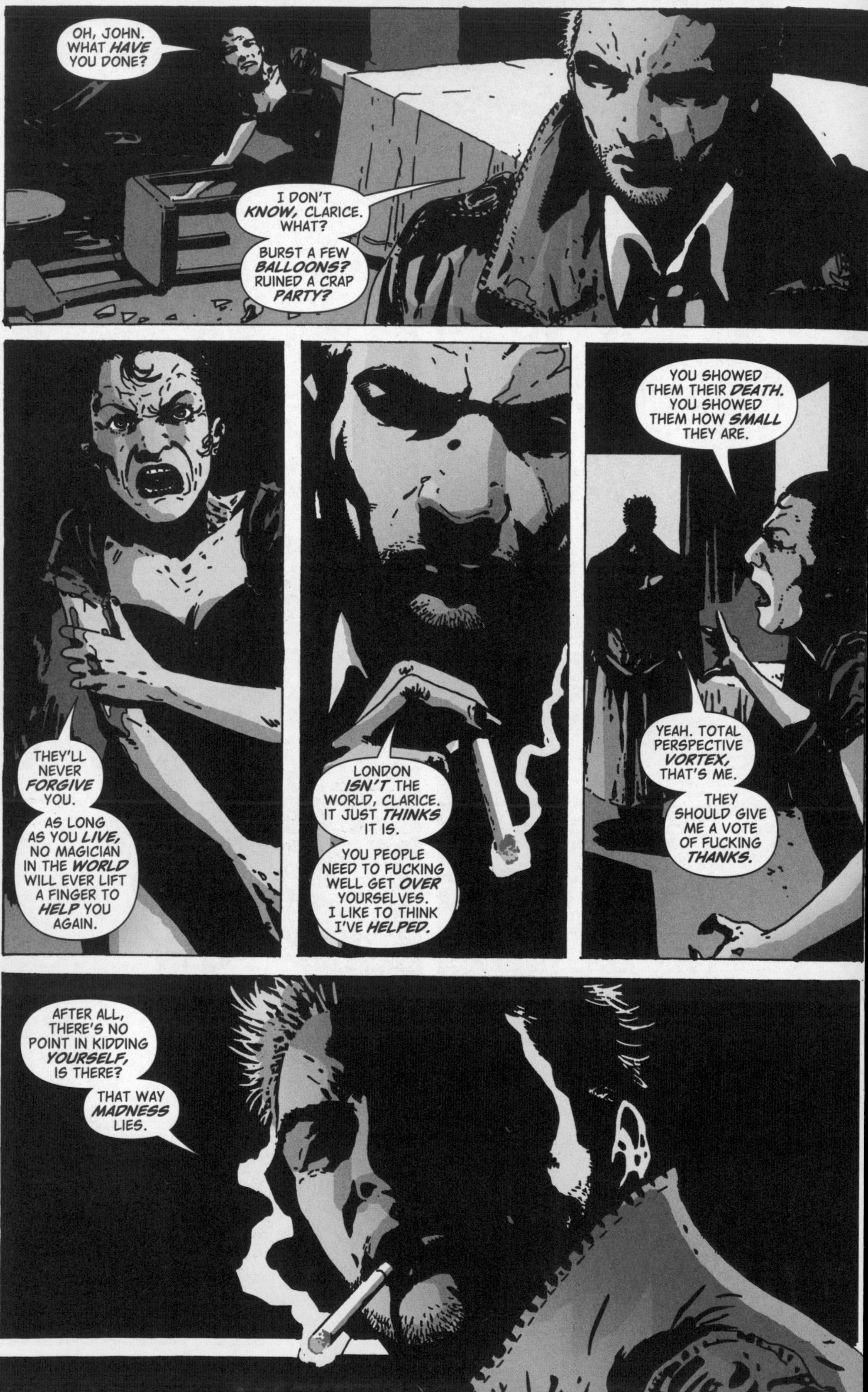

OH, JOHN. WHAT HAVE YOU DONE?
I DON'T KNOW, CLARICE. WHAT?
BURST A FEW BALLOONS? RUINED A CRAP PARTY?
THEY'LL NEVER FORGIVE YOU.
AS LONG AS YOU LIVE, NO MAGICIAN IN THE WORLD WILL EVER LIFT A FINGER TO HELP YOU AGAIN.
LONDON ISN'T THE WORLD, CLARICE. IT JUST THINKS IT IS.
YOU PEOPLE NEED TO FUCKING WELL GET OVER YOURSELVES. I LIKE TO THINK I'VE HELPED.
YOU SHOWED THEM THEIR DEATH. YOU SHOWED THEM HOW SMALL THEY ARE.
YEAH. TOTAL PERSPECTIVE VORTEX, THAT'S ME.
THEY SHOULD GIVE ME A VOTE OF FUCKING THANKS.
AFTER ALL, THERE'S NO POINT IN KIDDING YOURSELF, IS THERE?
THAT WAY MADNESS LIES.

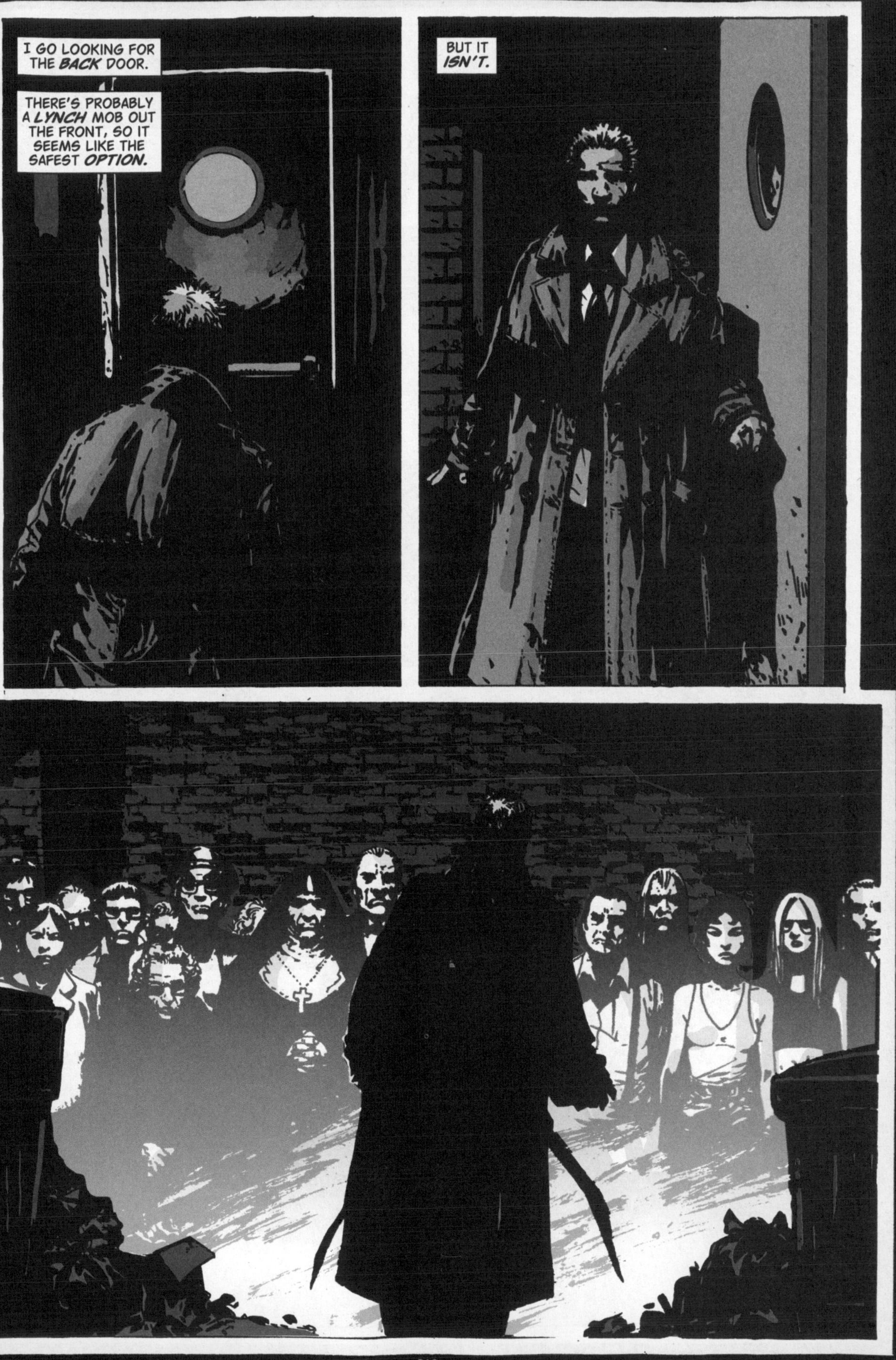
I GO LOOKING FOR THE *BACK* DOOR.
THERE'S PROBABLY A *LYNCH* MOB OUT THE FRONT, SO IT SEEMS LIKE THE SAFEST *OPTION*.
BUT IT *ISN'T*.

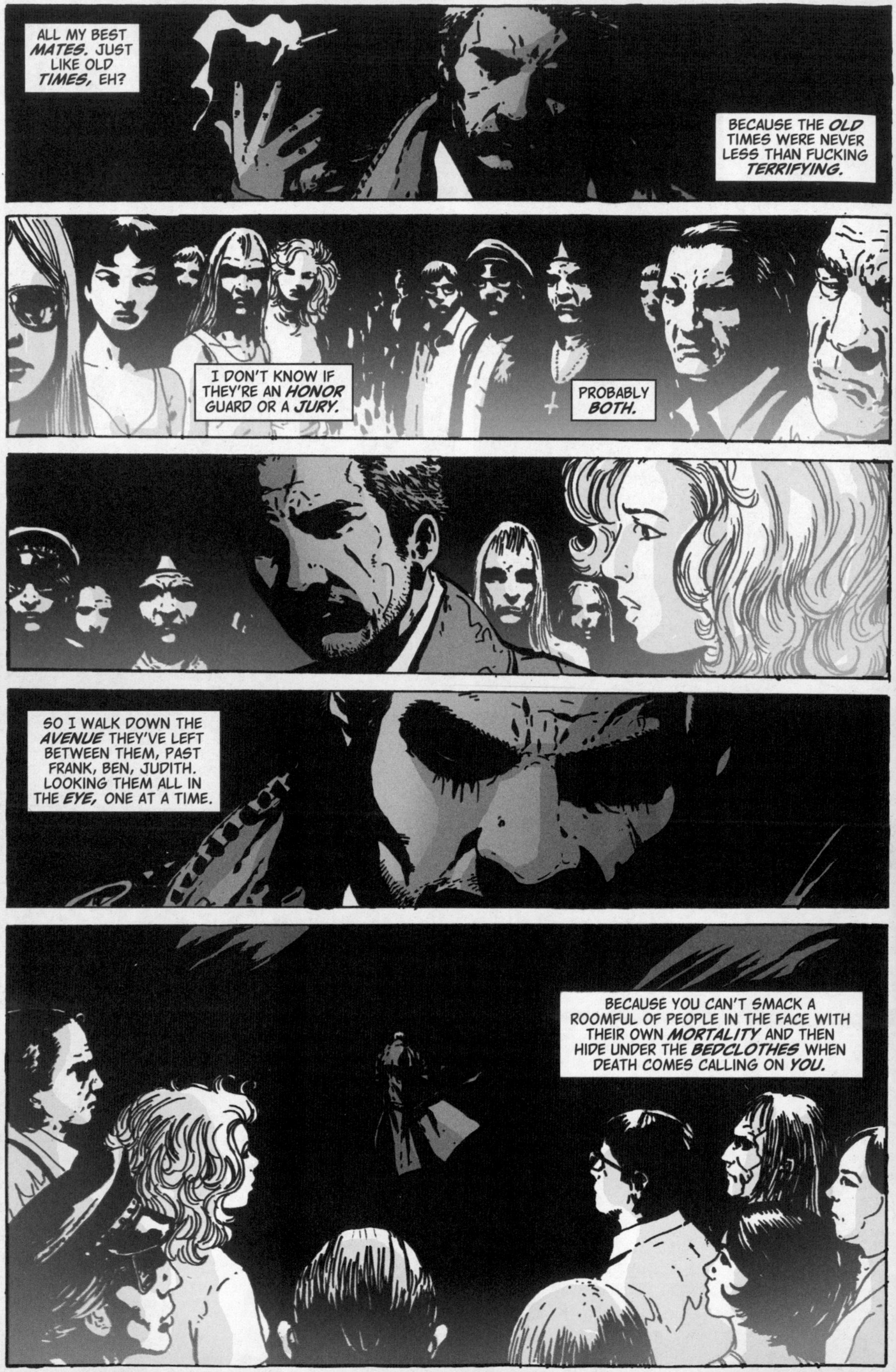
ALL MY BEST MATES. JUST LIKE OLD TIMES, EH?
BECAUSE THE OLD TIMES WERE NEVER LESS THAN FUCKING TERRIFYING.
I DON'T KNOW IF THEY'RE AN HONOR GUARD OR A JURY.
PROBABLY BOTH.
SO I WALK DOWN THE AVENUE THEY'VE LEFT BETWEEN THEM, PAST FRANK, BEN, JUDITH. LOOKING THEM ALL IN THE EYE, ONE AT A TIME.
BECAUSE YOU CAN'T SMACK A ROOMFUL OF PEOPLE IN THE FACE WITH THEIR OWN MORTALITY AND THEN HIDE UNDER THE BEDCLOTHES WHEN DEATH COMES CALLING ON YOU.

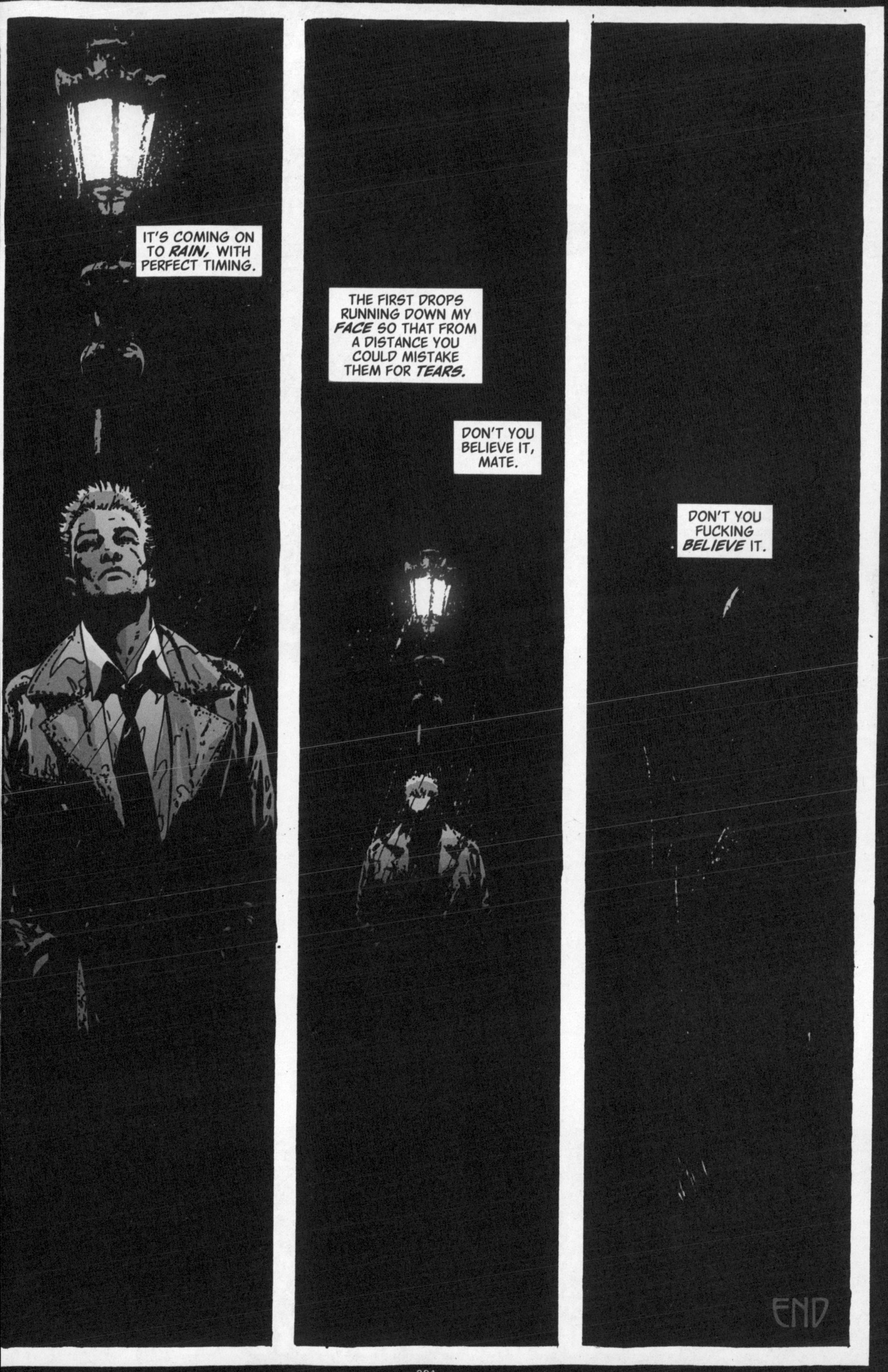
IT'S COMING ON TO RAIN, WITH PERFECT TIMING.
THE FIRST DROPS RUNNING DOWN MY FACE SO THAT FROM A DISTANCE YOU COULD MISTAKE THEM FOR TEARS.
DON'T YOU BELIEVE IT, MATE.
DON'T YOU FUCKING BELIEVE IT.
END

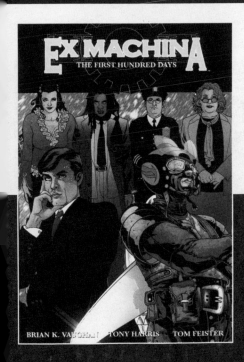

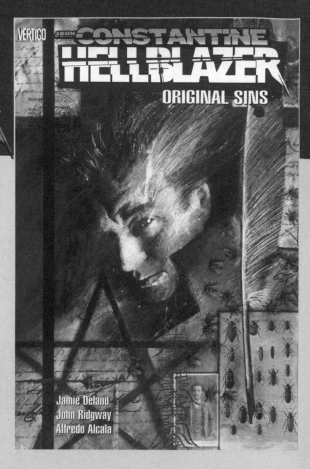

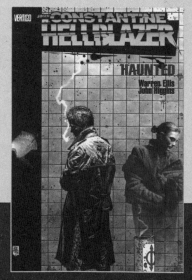